# INTRODUCTION TO
# PARALLEL ALGORITHMS

# WILEY SERIES ON PARALLEL AND DISTRIBUTED COMPUTING

EDITOR:

**ALBERT Y. ZOMAYA**

# INTRODUCTION TO PARALLEL ALGORITHMS

C. Xavier
S. S. Iyengar

A WILEY-INTERSCIENCE PUBLICATION

**JOHN WILEY & SONS, INC.**

New York • Chichester • Weinheim • Brisbane • Singapore • Toronto

Copyright © 1998 by John Wiley & Sons, Inc. All rights reserved.

Published simultaneously in Canada.

*Library of Congress Cataloging-in-Publication Data:*

Xavier, C.
    Introduction to parallel algorithms / C. Xavier and S. S. Iyengar.
        p.      cm.
    "A Wiley-Interscience publication."
    Includes bibliographical references and index.
    ISBN 0-471-25182-8 (cloth : alk. paper)
    1. Parallel processing (Electronic computers)    2. Computer
algorithms.    I. Iyengar, S. S. (Sundararaja S.)    II. Title.
QA76.58.X38    1998
005.2'75—dc21                                                                97-41015
                                                                                   CIP

10  9  8  7  6  5  4  3  2  1

# CONTENTS

xii  PREFACE

# ■■■■■ PREFACE

In recent years there has been increasing interest in the study, design, and analysis of parallel algorithms. This is partly because of the availability of new technology machines, which makes processing economically feasible, and mainly due to the increasing complexity of today's information processing requirements. This book presents the concept of parallel algorithms in four stages: Part 1 presents the foundation concepts in the design of parallel algorithms. Here the concepts of pipelining, multiprocessing, time sharing, and shared memory models are introduced. Because data structures are a vital part of parallel algorithms, a separate chapter is devoted to them. Special emphasis is given on the graph models because of their importance in information processing. Important paradigms used in the design of parallel algorithms are explained with numerous illustrations.

Part 2 deals with the parallel algorithms used in graph theoretic problems. A diverse class of graph problems are studied and parallel algorithm are developed for them. A separate chapter is devoted to chordal graphs. Here the recognition algorithm and algorithms for some optimization problems are developed for chordal graphs. Part 3 deals with array manipulation algorithms. The important algorithms for sorting, searching, and merging problems are presented in two chapters.

Part 4 presents the parallel algorithms for numerical and computational methods. Parallel algorithms for algebraic equations are treated in one chapter. The algorithms for differentiation, integration, and differential equations, including partial differential equations, are developed in detail. Parallel methods for interpolation and extrapolation are also presented.

The salient features of this book include

- Step-by-step methods for developing parallel algorithms with elaborate illustrations;
- Detailed analysis and implementation of parallel algorithms;
- Every concept is illustrated by a large number of examples;
- Every chapter concludes with a detailed bibliography.

This book is the result of collaboration with equal contributions by the authors; they thus share equal responsibility for the material contained in it.

The authors gratefully acknowledge the comments and helpful suggestions for the improvement of the quality of the book.

C. XAVIER
S. S. IYENGAR

# ACKNOWLEDGMENTS

The material in this book reflects the results published from our research papers on data structures and parallel algorithms, which were published in the following journals: *IEEE Transactions on Computers, Journal of Computer Science and Informatics, Journal of Theoretical Computer Science, Information Processing Letters*, and *Advances in Computers*.

This work is made possible by the support of our collaborators, who include Abha Moitra, R. L. Kashyap, N. S. V. Rao, Dekl and N. Chandra Sekharan. We also wish to thank Brooks and N. S. V. Rao, for carefully reviewing the preliminary versions of the manuscript. The comments and suggestions given by Sartaj Sahni, Bella Bose, S. Q. Zheng, and X. E. Sun have improved the quality of this book substantially, and so we extend our sincere gratitude to them. Rev. Fr. Francis Peter S. J., Rev. Fr. Albert Muthumalai, S. J., Rev. Fr. Antony A. Pappuraj S. J., Rev. Fr. Sebastin S. J., Rev. Fr. Francis Jeyapathy S. J., Dr. G. Arumugam, and Dr. S. Ambrose have greatly supported C. Xavier during the preparation of the manuscript. He thanks them very much for their generosity.

Mrs. Agnes Xavier and Mrs. Manorama Iyengar have supported the authors and made it possible for them to devote the required time to the preparation of the manuscript. They deserve our gratitude. The authors thank Almighty God for planning this work and getting it done through them.

C. XAVIER
S. S. IYENGAR

## C. XAVIER

Dr. C. Xavier earned his M.Sc. and M.Phil. degrees in Mathematics, and his Ph.D. degree in Computer Science. His Ph.D. thesis was on Parallel Algorithms. He is currently teaching in the Department of Computer Science, St. Xavier's College (Autonomous), Tirunelveli, India. He has published research papers on Parallel Algorithms in international journals and conference proceedings. He has written more than ten textbooks in computer science. Two of his books—*FORTRAN 77* and *Numerical Methods* and *Introduction to Computers* and BASIC *Programming*—have been published by New Age International Publishing Company, India (formerly Wiley Eastern Ltd.) New Age International Publishing Company is also publishing another book, *C Language and Numerical Methods* shortly. Dr. Xavier is a senior life member of the Computer Society of India. He is the principal investigator for several projects funded by the University Grants Commission (UGC), and Department of Science and Technology Government of India. He was the chief editor for the *Proceedings of the National Seminar on Mathematical Modeling and Computer Simulations of Real Life Situations*, held at Tirunelveli, India, in August of 1996. He was a co-convener for that seminar.

## S. SITHARAMA IYENGAR

Dr. S. S. Iyengar is the chairman of the Computer Science Department, and Professor of Computer Science Department at Louisiana State University. He has been involved with research in high-performance algorithms and data structures since receiving his Ph.D. degree (in 1974), his M.S. degree from the Indian Institute of Science (1970), and has directed over 27 Ph.D. dissertations at LSU. He has served as a principal investigator on research projects supported by the Office of Naval Research, the National Aeronautics and Space Administration (NASA), the National Science Foundation, California Institute of Technology's Jet Propulsion Laboratory, the Department of Navy–NORDA, the Department of Energy, LEQFS–Board of Regents, and the U.S. Army Office. His publications include several books (Prentice-Hall Inc., CRC Press, Inc., IEEE Computer Society Press, etc.) and over 250 research papers in areas of high-performance parallel and distributed algorithms and data structures for image processing and pattern recognition, autonomous navigation, and distributed sensor networks. He was a visiting professor at the Jet Propulsion Laboratory, Oak Ridge National Laboratory, and the Indian Institute of Science.

Dr. Iyengar is a series editor for *Neuro Computing of Complex Systems*, and an editor for the *Journal of Computer Science and Information*. He has served as guest editor for the *IEEE Transactions on Knowledge and Data Engineering, IEEE Transactions and SMC, IEEE Transactions on Software Engineerng, Journal of Theoretical Computer Science, Journal of Computer and Electrical Engineerng*, and the *Journal of the Franklin Institute*.

He is also a fellow of the IEEE, and is a Distinguished Visitor of the IEEE Computer Society (1995–1998). In addition, he has served as an ACM National Lecturer since 1985, and is a member of the New York Academy of Sciences. He has been the Program Chairman for many national/international conferences. He has been on the prestigious NIH-NLM Review Committee, in the area of Medical Informatics.

In 1997 Dr. Iyengar is the winner of the prestigous IEEE Technical Achievement Award for Outstanding Contributions to Data Structures and Algorithms in Image Processing and Sensor Fusion Problems.

Dr. Iyengar was awarded the LSU Distinguished Faculty Award for Excellence in Reserch, and the LSU Tiger Athletic Foundation Teaching Award in 1996. He has been a consultant to several industrial and government organizations. (JPL, NASA etc.)

# PART 1

# FOUNDATIONS OF PARALLEL COMPUTING

# Introduction

## 0.1 INTRODUCTION TO COMPUTERS

Parallel computing is a central and important problem in many computationally intensive applications, such as image processing, robotics, and so forth. Given a problem, the parallel computing is the process of splitting the problem into several subproblems, solving the subproblems simultaneously, and combining the solutions of subproblems to get the solution to the original problem. This book attempts to give course material on the design of parallel algorithms for various classes of problems.

When the architecture for a computer was first proposed by Von Neumann, he visualized the machine as a fast calculating device. He suggested a five unit system for the computer:

1. Input Unit;
2. Output Unit;
3. Memory;
4. Arithmetic Logic Unit; and
5. Control Unit.

The architecture is represented by a block diagram in Figure 0.1. The control unit controls the entire system. The control lines in the diagram are shown in broken lines, in order to differentiate them from the data lines. The input unit takes care of the work of getting input to the computer. Punched cards, punched paper tapes, magnetic tapes, magnetic disks, and keyboards are some of the input devices that have been used throughout computing history. The output unit takes care of the output. Printers and plotters are some popular output devices. Over the past forty years or so, dramatic increases in computing speeds were achieved, largely due to the use of inherently fast electronic components. The memory and arithmetic logic units were designed by semiconductor devices first.

Development in the electronics industry supported the computer designers to construct faster computers. When the electronics industry came out with the transistor, the computer industry manufactured machines with transistors.

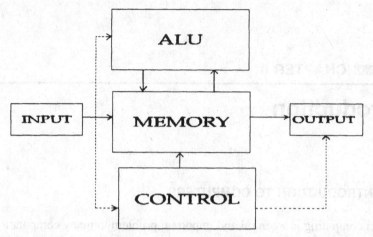

**Figure 0.1** Block diagram of a computer of Von Neumann's architecture.

In the late 1960s, the concept of *circuit integration* became a reality in the electronics industry. It was possible to build a small one-centimeter chip, with the capability of hundreds of transistors. This enabled construction of faster computers with more memory capacity, but smaller in size. Computers built in the above three stages are called *first-*, *second-* and *third-generation computers*, respectively.

In the early 1970s, the circuit integration technology made great strides, with the introduction of techniques to produce *Very Large Scale Integrated Circuits* (*VLSI*). The *microprocessor*, invented by Ted Hoff of the Intel Company Laboratory, in 1971, was a major breakthrough in VLSI technology. The computers designed using microprocessors are called *microcomputers*. The microcomputers and other computers that use VLSI circuit design are called *fourth-generation computers*. Table 0.1 contains the details of some early microprocessors.

In 1974, Ed Roberts, of MIT, built a microcomputer which he called *Altair*. It was the first *personal computer* (PC). Then Apple Macintosh and IBM PCs entered the market. They were very fast and efficient in handling data. Then Intel 486 DX2 had a remarkable speed of 66 MHz. The *Pentium* is a 64-bit processor, and it claims to deliver twice the performance of an Intel 486 DX2 processor in mathematical intensive applications, because of its redesigned floating-point unit. Recently, Pentium processors with 133 MHz speed have also been released. *Pentium Pro* is an even more advanced microprocessor from Intel. Another company, Alpha, has brought out 400 MHz microprocessors. A Japanese team of scientists thought that, for satisfying the computing needs of future society in the field of *artificial intelligence*, the capabilities of computers with the present architecture would be inadequate. In 1979, the Japanese government appointed a committee headed by Tohru Moto Oka, to envisage the computing needs of society in the 1990s. The committee consisted of three subcommittees. The 10-member first committee, headed by Hajime Karatsu, studied the type of computer needed in

**TABLE 0.1   Some Early Microprocessors**

| Micro Processor | Year of Issue | No. of Components in a Chip | Speed | Significance |
|---|---|---|---|---|
| Intel 4004 | 1971 | 2,250 | Adds two 4-bit numbers in 11 milliseconds | First micro processor. |
| Intel 8080 | 1974 | 4,500 | Adds two 8-bit numbers in 2.5 microseconds | First micro-processors used to build a general purpose computer |
| Mostech Metal Oxide Semiconductor 6502 | 1975 | 4,300 | Adds two 8-bit numbers in 1 microsecond | Used in home computers |
| Motorola 68000 | 1979 | 70,000 | Multiplies two 16-bit numbers in 3.2 microseconds | Circuits inbuilt for direct multiplication |
| HP Super Chip | 1981 | 450,000 | Multiplies two 32-bit numbers in 1.8 microseconds | First 32 bit processor |

the future. The 12-member second subcommittee, headed by Hideo Aiso, studied the architecture of the computer needed. The 13-member subcommittee, headed by Hazuhiro Fuchi, worked on the fundamental concepts of the future computer. These three subcommittees submitted their proposals, and Chairman Oka formulated the final proposal for the future computer, which came to be known as the *Fifth-Generation Computer*. The Japanese government agreed to implement the *fifth-generation computers* project, and convened the First World Conference of Fifth Generation Computers in October of 1981. In the conference, the fifth-generation computer proposals were discussed in detail, and the participants, consisting of the scientists from all over the world, accepted the proposal. When these fifth-generation computers come to the market, present computers will not become useless. For solving problems in most of the computing fields, the older computers will still be useful. The fifth-generation computers will not be effective for ordinary applications. However, they will be used for Information Management, Natural Language Processing, Speech, Character and Image Recognition, and other artificial intelligence applications. The architecture of fifth-generation computers will be entirely different from that of present-day computers of Von Neuman architecture. The Japanese government has established the Institute for New Generation Computer Technology (ICOT) for constructing the fifth-generation computers.

The data and instructions in fifth-generation computers are stored in computer's memory. Whenever processing has to take place, data are retrieved from the memory. If we consider any of our day-to-day activities, a similar procedure is followed by almost all of us.

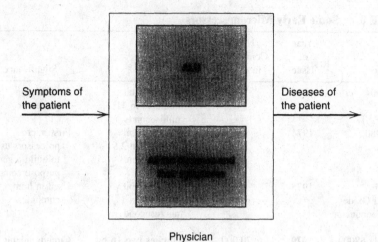

Symptoms of
the patient

Diseases of
the patient

Physician

**Figure 0.2** Medical diagnosis.

For example, consider a physician attending a patient (see Fig. 0.2). The physician gathers the symptoms (data) from the patient. The physician already knows about all the diseases and their symptoms. These are already available in his memory. Now the physician compares the patient's symptoms with the registered data in his memory and diagnoses the disease.

In the absence of a physician, can we use a computer? In other words, can a computer replace a physician? Scientists have taken this as a challenge, and are trying to equip a computer to meet this challenge. These types of applications need a lot of processing work to be done in a fraction of a second. These problems pertain to the area of Artificial Intelligence. Computer systems to solve Artificial Intelligence problems are called *expert systems*. The following are some more areas in the field of Artificial Intelligence.

- Natural Language Processing (NLP);
- Image Recognition and Processing;
- Pattern Recognition;
- Character Recognition;
- Speech Recognition;
- Weather Forecasting;
- Medical Diagnosis; and
- Intelligent Machines.

*Natural Language Processing.* Consider the sentences produced in languages like English, French, German, and so forth. People understand them and act accordingly. Depending upon the context, the same sentence may have different meanings. For example, consider the sentence,

**Joseph called his friend a taxi.**

Did Joseph call a taxi for his friend, or did he use the nickname 'taxi' to call his friend? The meaning of the sentence depends upon the context. The same sentence can mean different things, and different sentences may mean the same thing. Human beings can understand them by recognizing the context. Making a computer store a context-free grammar of language and making it apply the grammar for purposes of comprehension and translation is called *Natural Language Processing* (*NLP*).

*Image Recognition and Processing.* Satellites launched by different countries continuously keep sending photographs of earth taken from outer space. By analyzing the images in the photographs, weather changes, forests and agricultural areas and the like, can be recognized. Another interesting application of image processing is recognition of persons from their photographs. After scanning the photograph of a person, computers can create pictures of the same person, with various modifications to his/her features, such as hairstyle, beard, or moustache. This application is of immense use to police departments in tracking down criminals. An image is usually represented by a matrix of pixels. Each pixel is represented by its color, intensity, brightness, and other data. In certain applications, a picture is considered as 14,400 pixels per inch and converted into digital data. The image operations are performed on every pixel in the image. This makes most of these operations computationally intensive. In real-time processing of images, the total response time has to be kept to a minimum. Hence, it is mandatory to speed up the pixel operation.

*Pattern/Character Recognition.* On seeing a chair, we recognize that it is chair. How? It has four legs. A cow also has four legs. But a cow is not a chair. Even if one leg of a chair is broken, we could recognize the object as a chair. There is an intuitive way in which we have learned to recognize a chair. Similarly, a computer can be taught to recognize a chair at sight, and it involves the use of *learning theory*. This field of application in computer science is called *pattern recognition*. The alphabet letter *A* is written in different styles by different persons, and people are able to recognize the character.

A computer's ability to understand hand-written script is called *character recognition*. In Japan, when a computer capable of character recognition was first introduced to sort mail in a post office, it worked only with 90 percent accuracy. When Tokyo was misspelled as *Tokey*, the computer could not tolerate the error in the spelling, but it considered *Tokey* as another city not contained in the list of cities programmed into it. In such circumstances, the computer needed a certain amount of error tolerance. In order to achieve a desirable error tolerancé capacity, the processing speed of the machine must be increased. Various modifications to postal sorting machines have been carried out since then, and such machines are used now in various countries.

In character recognition, intensive computations are involved. A hand-written character is scanned by a camera as an image of very high resolution, such as 14,400 pixels per inch (see Fig. 0.3). The color, intensity of light, and

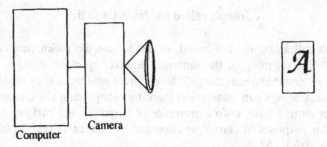

**Figure 0.3** Character recognition.

other parameters convert the image into its digital representation. This digital representation is compared with the standard digital representation of the character, say $A$. From this comparison, the probability that the observed character is $A$ is evaluated, using complex computational procedures. The same process is done for computing the probability that the observed character is $B, C, \ldots$, and so forth. These probabilities are compared, and the character is recognized as the one having maximum probability.

From the above discussion, it is evident that intensive computations are needed to evaluate the probabilities.

$$\{P(a)/a = A, B, C, \ldots\},$$

where $P(a)$ denotes the probability that the observed character is $a$. For this type of application, ordinary computers are not sufficient.

**Speech Recognition.** Speech recognition is the capacity to understand the speech of a person. People can understand different speech patterns with ease. But programming a computer for speech recognition is a very difficult task, because no two persons speak alike. So scientists have not had much success in this field. Machines have been designed, which have limited capability to understand the speech of particular persons, but not of all people.

**Weather Forecasting.** Weather forecasting is made by obtaining a large amount of data, such as temperature, pressure, humidity, and so forth, and performing complicated numerical calculations on these data to predict weather status. These complicated calculations require a very fast computer. Weather forecasting calculations must give the results immediately. The atmospheric sphere is divided into various small regions, and the moisture, pressure, and other conditions, are measured in fixed time intervals. This is also compared with photographs taken by satellites. Based on this input, the computers forecast the weather for the next 24 or 48 hours. If the observation is taken at one instant, the forecast for the next 24 hours will be useful, only if the calculations are done, results obtained, and communicated to the public before the lapse of 24 hours. The reliability of the forecast increases when the quantity of data processed is more, that is, when the region is divided into smaller subregions and more data are collected and processed. However, when more data are processed, it takes more than 24 hours for the ordinary computer to forecast the weather. So, in order to get highly reliable forecast quickly, present computers are not of much use.

**Medical Diagnosis.** This is the computer application that was discussed earlier. A computer capable of medical diagnosis takes the symptoms of the patient and diagnoses the diseases.

**Intelligent Machines.** A robot is a special-purpose autonomous computer, capable of doing a particular job, such as assembling a car, working as a receptionist, and so forth. Robots need a variety of capabilities mentioned above. The software written for robots is therefore very complicated, and involves the highest imaginable speed of calculations. Autonomous Mobile Robots (AMRs) are artificially intelligent operating systems, which have capabilities for autonomous decision-making and action. AMRs are able to govern themselves in accomplishing given objectives, while at the same time managing their resources and maintaining their integrity. These capabilities result from their ability to interact effectively with dynamic environments, on the basis of sensed and computed information. Research in the design of AMRs involve the following tasks:

1. *Rapid multi-model sensing and integration.* The capability to rapidly sense external events via multiple, diverse sensors and to meaningfully integrate the information gained.

2. *Real-time response.* The capability to make decisions and take appropriate action to achieve the goals, without undue delay.

3. *Real-time interruptability.* The capability to interrupt normal operation and respond in a timely manner, to external events occurring in its domain, and then to resume the interrupted task after responding.

4. *Fault tolerance.* The capability to rely on the other functional units to continue operations, in the event of an internal failure, is called *fault tolerance*.

The above works involve highly complex and rapidly fast processing, for which our present computers are not useful.

The practical importance of AMR research has steadily increased as developments in technology have brought such systems closer to reality. Already, industrial robots are employed in applications that involve monotonous and tedious tasks, as well as in applications in hazardous environments, such as nuclear reactors. Next-generation robots are being planned for applications such as deep-sea mining and salvage operations, servicing/assembly tasks in space, and maintenance activities in toxic environments, such as chemical plants.

The applications of high-performance fifth-generation computing also include *aircraft testing, development of new drugs, oil exploration, modeling fusion, reactors, real-time economic planning, cryptoanalysis, astronomy, biomedical analysis, seismology, aerodynamics, atomic, nuclear, and plasma physics.*

## 0.2   PARALLEL COMPUTERS

In the previous section we have seen that present computers are not useful for certain vital applications. In this section we introduce the concept of parallel computers, which may be useful for vital applications. A simple model of a computer is given in Fig. 0.4. The input/output operations are not considered here, for simplicity. The processor has access to the memory. The values stored in the memory are read by the processor, and after processing them, the results are stored in the memory. Due to the very advanced inventions in VLSI technology, high-performance processor chips, with more than $10^6$ gates, are available now. They have a very thin line width of less than 0.5 microns (1 microns = $10^{-6}$ meter), and have a storage density of 1000 KB per cm. A recent microprocessor introduced by Alpha is said to have 400 MHz clock speed. With these chips, we have reached the so-called highest possible speed, and scientists doubt very much whether a faster device could ever be constructed. Unfortunately, these fastest processors cannot satisfy our computing needs in the areas such as weather prediction, oceanography, astrophysics, aerodynamics, image processing, and remote sensing, which we have discussed in the previous section.

In an ordinary computer there is only one processor. In order to improve the speed further, we would like to have more processors in a computer. Such a computer is called a *parallel computer*. Computers with one processor are called *sequential computers*. The parallelism can be explained using the character recognition application introduced in the previous section (refer to Figure 0.3). When a sequential computer is used, the probabilities P(A), P(B), ... are calculated one after the other, by a single processor. Instead, we can use several processors to calculate each of these probabilities simultaneously. This is illustrated in Fig. 0.5.

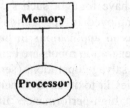

**Figure 0.4**   Model of a sequential computer.

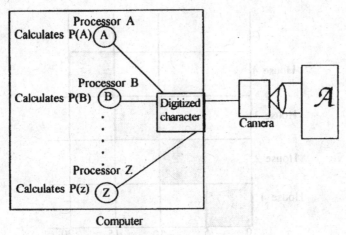

**Figure 0.5**    Parallelism for character recognition.

## 0.3   PARALLEL PROCESSING CONCEPTS

In order to solve a problem using a parallel computer, one must decompose the problem into small subproblems, which can be solved in parallel. Then these results must be efficiently combined to get the final result of the main problem. It is not easy to decompose every large problem into subproblems, because there may be *data dependency* between the subproblems. Because of the data dependency, the processors may have to communicate among each other. The important point to be stressed here is the time taken for communication, usually the time for a communication between two processors, is very high when compared with the processing time. Due to this factor, the communication scheme should be very well planned, to get a good parallel algorithm.

The *decomposability* and the *data dependency* are now illustrated by a simple real-life example. Consider a building contractor who has the manpower and other resources to carry out the construction of a house in a period of five months.

Let us assume that the contractor cannot carry out the construction of more than one house simultaneously. If such a contractor is assigned the work of constructing 100 houses by a housing board, he constructs these houses, one after the other, and it will take 500 months to complete the work. Figure 0.6 illustrates the process for four houses only. If the housing board wants to speed up the process, it can employ 100 different constructors to carry out the construction of the 100 houses simultaneously. In this case, the construction of all the 100 houses will be completed in five months. If 100 contractors are not available and only 10 are available, the work could be completed in 50 months. Figure 0.7 illustrates the completion of six houses by two contractors in 15 months. This is an example in which the work is easily decomposable. Here, each house is an independent one, and so we could easily decompose the main work.

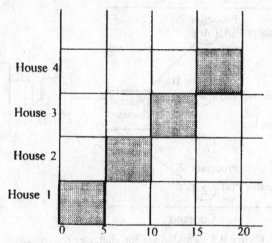

**Figure 0.6**   Sequential house construction.

Now consider the work of constructing one house. Let us divide the work into five different steps.

Step 1. Building the basement;

Step 2. Building the superstructure;

Step 3. Completing woodwork, such as fitting windows, doors, etc.;

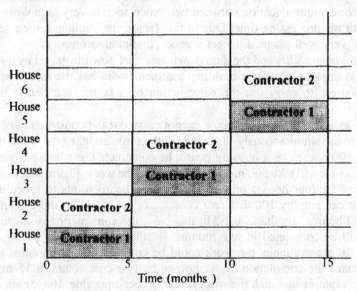

**Figure 0.7**   Parallelism in house construction.

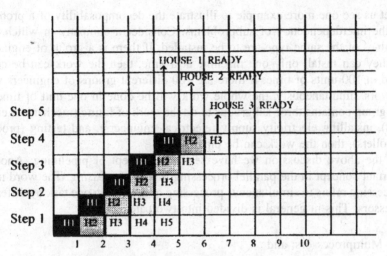

**Figure 0.8**  Pipelining in house construction.

Step 4. Installing electrical systems; and

Step 5. Painting and finishing.

Notice that all these five steps cannot be carried out simultaneously, since each step can begin only if the previous steps are complete. We say that these are *inherently sequential*. In this case, dividing the work into subworks is a difficult one. However, if a contractor has five different groups of people to carry out these five steps, he or she can complete the work more efficiently. Let us assume that each group can do one step in one month. When the first step is over for the first house, the second group will start the second step of the first house. At the same time, the first group will start the work of Step 1 of the second house. It is shown in Fig. 0.8.

This procedure of parallelizing is called *pipelining*. In the above example of pipelining, during the fifth month all the groups are working on different houses.

Group 1 is doing Step 1 for House 5.

Group 2 is doing Step 2 for House 4.

Group 3 is doing Step 3 for House 3.

Group 4 is doing Step 4 for House 2.

Group 5 is doing Step 5 for House 1.

At the end of the fifth month, the first house is complete. From the fifth month, one house is completed each subsequent month. In this case, the contractor is capable of giving delivery of completed houses at the rate of one house every month.

Let us see one more example to illustrate the decomposability of a problem and the interdependency of subproblems. Consider a company in which 100 machines of the same type are to be installed. If there is a group of engineers and they can install only one machine at a time, then the work can be completed in 100 units of time. If there are 100 different groups of engineers who can work simultaneously, the whole work will be done in one unit of time. If each group contains three subgroups to do the work of fitting (mechanical engineers), installing electricity supply (electrical engineers), and testing (process controllers), then the work can be pipelined.

In the above discussion we have seen the concept of pipelining. Another important concept in the parallel processing is *multiprocessing*. The word multiprocessing refers to simultaneous processing of more than one task by different processors. This in general is divided into two categories.

1. Multiprocessors; and
2. Multicomputers.

In a multiprocessor system, many processors work simultaneously and there is a common shared memory. In a multicomputer, there is a group of processors, in which each of the processors has sufficient amount of local memory. The communication between the processors is through messages. This is also called *distributed processing*. There is neither a common memory nor a common clock.

## 0.4 HIGH-PERFORMANCE COMPUTERS

Spurred by the advances in technologies, the past four-and-a-half decades have seen a plethora of hardware designs, which have helped the computer industry to experience generations of unprecedented growth and development, physically marked by a rapid change of computer building blocks from relays and vacuum tubes (1940s–1950s) to the present ultra-scaled integrated circuits (ICs).

As a result of these technological advances and improved designs, computers have undergone a remarkable metamorphosis from the slow uniprocessors of the 1950s to today's high-performance machines, which include supercomputers, whose peak performance rates are thousands of orders of magnitude over those of earlier computers. The requirements of engineers and scientists for ever more powerful digital computers have been the main driving force in the development of digital computers. The attainment of high computing speeds has been one of the most challenging requirements. The computer industry's response to these challenges has been tremendous, and the result is the remarkable evolution in computers in just four short decades, as exemplified by an existence of commercial and experimental high-performance computing systems produced in these decades. The quest for even more powerful systems for sundry scientific applications, such as those mentioned above, continues unabated into the twenty-first century.

The technology transformation has been accelerated by revolutionary design, which often occurred in tandem with improved technology. The most common design technique has been to incorporate some parallel features into the modern computer. Since the 1960s, literally hundreds of highly parallel structures have been proposed, and many have been built and put into operation by the 1970s.

The Illiac IV was operational at NASA's Ames Research Center in 1972—the first Texas Instruments Inc. Advanced Scientific Computer (TI-ASC) was used in Europe in 1972; the first Control Data Corp. Star-100 was delivered to the Lawrence Livermore National Laboratory in 1974; the first Cray Research Inc.'s Cray-1 was put into service at Los Alamos National Laboratory in 1976.

The machines mentioned above not only were the pioneers in innovative designs, which have endowed these machines with an unprecedented power, but were also the forerunners of even more powerful computing systems yet to come. Therefore, while their fames were still undimmed, they soon gave way to other generations of more powerful computers, which culminate in today's supercomputing systems. Thus, by the 1980s, a substantial number of high-speed processors of the 1960s and 1970s either ceased to be operational or played a less significant computing role. In the same decades, the advance of the processing speeds and the improvement in the cost/performance ratio continued unabated. The overall results were the introduction of new and more radical architectural design philosophies, such as evidenced in the Reduced Instruction Set Computers (RISC), a widespread commercialization of multiprocessing, and the launching of the initial releases of massively parallel processors. Thus Illiac-IV ceased operation in 1981; TI-ASC is no longer in production since 1980; since 1976, the Star-100 has evolved into the CDC Cyber 203 (no longer in production), and also into the Cyber 205, which signaled the CDC's entry in the supercomputing field; The Cray-1 (pipelined uniprocessor) has evolved into Cray-1S, which has considerably more memory capacity than the original Cray-1. The following are also some more high-performance computers:

- Cray XMP4 (4-processor, 128 MWord supercomputer, with a peak performance rate of 840 MFLOPS);
- Cray-2 (256 Mword, 4-processor reconfigurable supercomputer, with 2 GFLOPS peakperformance); and
- Cray-3 (16-processor, 2 GWord supercomputer, with 16 GFLOPS peak performance rate).

Other super-performance computers produced in the 1980s include Eta-10, Fujitsu VP-200, Hitachi S-810, and IBM 3090/400/VF. Thus, by the 1980s, the high-speed processors of the 1960s to 1970s have evolved in the supercomputers of the 1980s through the 1990s.

Other computers of some historical interest, although their primary purpose was not for numerical computation, include Goodyear Corporation's STARAN and the C.mmp system at Carnegie-Mellon University. Also of some historical interest, although it was not commercialized, is Burroughs Corporation's Scientific Processor (CSP).

**Advent of Array Processor.** The Illiac-4 had only 64 processors. Other computers consisting of a large number of processors, include Denelcor HEP and the International Computers Ltd. Data Array Processor (ICL DAP), the Finite Element Machine at NASA's Langley Research Center; MIDAS at the Lawrence Berkeley Laboratory; Cosmic Cube at the California Institute of Technology, TRAC at the University of Texas, CM* at Carnegie-Mellon University, ZMOB at the University of Maryland, Pringle at the University of Washington and Purdue University, and the Massively Parallel Processor (MPP) at NASA's Goddard Space Flight Center. Only a few (e.g., MPP, ICL DAP) are designed primarily for numerical computation, while the others are for research purposes.

## 0.5 ORGANIZATION AND SCOPE OF THE BOOK

This book presents the concept of parallel algorithms in four stages. Part 1 of the book presents the foundation concepts in the design of parallel algorithms. The concept of pipelining, multiprocessing, time sharing, and shared-memory models are introduced. As data structures form a vital part of parallel algorithms, a separate chapter presents the various data structures. A special emphasis is given on the graph models, since it is a prominent data structure in information processing. Important paradigms used in the design of parallel algorithms are explained with a number of illustrations.

Part 2 of the book deals with the parallel algorithms for graph algorithms. A diverse class of graph problems have been studied and parallel algorithms developed. A separate chapter is devoted for the class of chordal graphs. The recognition algorithm and algorithms for some optimization problems have been developed for chordal graphs.

Part 3 deals with the array manipulations. Many important algorithms for sorting and searching and merging problems have been given in two chapters.

Part 4 presents the parallel algorithms for Numerical and Computational methods. Parallel algorithms for algebraic equations have been given in one chapter. The algorithms for differentiation, integration, and differential equations, including partial differential equations, have been developed in two chapters.

## BIBLIOGRAPHY

Aho, A., Hopcroft, J., and Ullman, J. (1974). *The Design and Analysis of Computer Algorithms*, Addison-Wesley, Reading, MA.

Akl, S. G. (1989) *The Design and Analysis of Parallel Algorithms*, Prentice-Hall, Englewood Cliffs, NJ.

Cook, S. A. (1981) Towards Complexity Theory of Synchronous Parallel Computation, *L'enseignment Mathematique XXVII*, pp. 99–124.

Cook, S. A. (1983) Overview of Computational Complexity, *Commun. ACM*, **26**(6), 400–409.

Duncan, R. (1990) A Survey of Parallel Computer Architectures, Private Communication.

Golub, G. and Ortega, J. M. (1993) *Scientific Computing: An Introduction with Parallel Computing*, Academic Press, Boston and New York.

Haynes, L. et al., (1982) A Survey of Highly Parallel Computers, *Computer*, **15**(1), 9–24.

Hockney, R. and Jesshope, C. (1983) *Parallel Computers*, Adam Hilger, Bristol and Philadelphia.

Hockney, R. W. (1987) Classification and Evaluation of Parallel Computer Systems, Springer-Verlag Lecture Notes in Computer Science, No. 295, pp. 13–25.

Hwang, K. and Briggs, F. A. (1984) Computer Architecture and Parallel Processing, McGraw-Hill, New York.

Hwang, K. and Degroot, F. (1989) Parallel Processing for Super Computers and Artificial Intelligence, McGraw-Hill, New York.

Kuck, D. J. (1971) A Survey of Parallel Machine Organisation and Programming. *ACM Comput. Survey*, **9**, 29–59.

Moto-oka, T., ed. (1982) *Fifth Generation Computer Systems*, North-Holland, New York.

Wold, E. H. and Despain, A. M. (1984) Pipeline and Parallel-Pipeline FFT Processors for VLSI Implementations, *IEEE Transactions on Computers*, **C-33**, 414–426.

# ■■■■■■ CHAPTER 1

# Elements of Parallel Computing

The need for parallel computers has been introduced in the previous chapter. This chapter focuses on the basic concepts needed for parallel computers. The taxonomy of parallel computers and the various parallel computing models are elaborately discussed in this chapter.

## 1.1 LEVELS OF PARALLELISM

Parallelism can be achieved at different levels. For example, if ten jobs are given, which are different in nature and pairwise independent, then these ten jobs can be given to ten different machines. This is a high-level parallelism, because the jobs are implemented in parallel. This is usually called *job level parallelism* or *program level parallelism*. In order to increase the efficiency of the program further, we can go in for the next level of parallelism. Each job can be divided into smaller subtasks. These subtasks can be executed in parallel, and the results consolidated to get the final result. For each subtask, there will be a subprogram, and these subprograms may be executed in parallel. This is usually called *subprogram level parallelism*. In any program (or subprogram) there are several statements. These statements may be done in parallel. This possibility is called *statement level parallelism*. In a statement, several operations are carried out. We can think of parallelizing these operations, and this is called *operation level parallelism*. Usually, any operation consists of several micro-operations. For example, consider the operation of adding the contents of two variables $A$ and $B$ and storing the result in $C$. This operation consists of the following micro-operations.

1. Load the accumulator with the content of $A$.
2. Add the content of $B$ with the content of the accumulator.
3. Store the content of the accumulator in the variable $C$.

If micro-operations are done in parallel, this will be called *micro-operation level parallelism* (see Figure 1.1). The program level parallelism and subprogram level parallelism are very clear and need no further explanation. In order

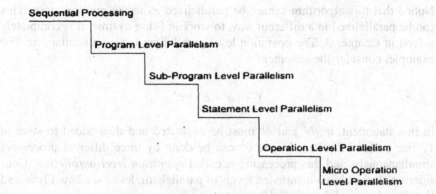

**Figure 1.1** Levels of parallelism.

to explain the statement level parallelism, consider the sample algorithm given below:

$$\text{For } i = 1 \text{ to } n \text{ do}$$
$$x_i \leftarrow x_i + 1.$$

In the above algorithm, each $x_i$ is incremented. This statement is repeated $n$ times sequentially and so $0(n)$ time is needed. This can be parallelized. This can be done by $n$ processors simultaneously in $0(1)$ time. In such a case, we write the parallel algorithm as follows:

For $i = 1$ to $n$ do in parallel

$x_i \leftarrow x_i + 1$

End parallel

The above algorithm tells that $n$ processing elements must be involved and they may be $P_1, P_2, \ldots P_n$. The processing element $P_i$ does the work $x_i \leftarrow x_i + 1$. All the processors work simultaneously and the work is completed in $0(1)$ time. This type of parallelism is called *statement level parallelism*.

Now consider the algorithm given below:

$$S \leftarrow = 0;$$
$$\text{For } i = 1 \text{ to } n \text{ do}$$
$$S \leftarrow S + x_i$$

This algorithm finds the sum

$$S = x_1 + x_2 + \ldots + x_n$$

Notice that this algorithm cannot be parallelized as in the previous case. This can be parallelized in a different way, to work in $O(\log n)$ time. It is completely solved in Chapter 3. The operation level parallelism is also a similar one. For example, consider the statement

$$Y \leftarrow a^i + b^j + c^k$$

In this statement, $a^i$, $b^j$ and $c^k$ must be evaluated and then added to store in $Y$. The evaluation of $a^i$, $b^j$ and $c^k$ can be done by three different processors simultaneously, and this processing is called *operation level parallelism*. Considering all the above-mentioned levels of parallelism, let us see how Flynn and Handler classified the parallel machines.

## 1.2   TAXONOMY OF PARALLEL COMPUTERS

The last three decades of the twentieth century have witnessed the introduction of a variety of new computer architectures for parallel processing, which complement and extend the major approaches to parallel computing. The recent proliferation of parallel processing technologies has included several new hardware architectures. Now the field faces a substantial obstacle—to comprehend what kind of parallel architectures exist, and how their relationship to one another defines an orderly schema. We first examine Flynn's taxonomy, which is the oldest one, but the most popular attempt to classify the parallel architectures. We then discuss Handler's (Erlangen) classification, which is a more recent classification method proposed to redress the inadequacy of Flynn's scheme and some more classification.

### 1.2.1   Flynn's Classification

Any system is based upon two important elements:

1. Instruction; and
2. Data.

The data elements are manipulated according to the instructions. Depending upon the number of instructions executed and data elements manipulated simultaneously, Flynn makes the following classification. The simplest of these is our usual sequential computer, where one instruction manipulates only one data set at a time. Flynn calls them *Single Instruction Single Data* (SISD) systems. Figure 1.2 illustrates the SISD model.

The *Single Instruction Multiple Data* (SIMD) system is a system in which the same instruction is carried out for different sets of data in parallel. Here the number of data sets is the number of processors working simultaneously. Figure

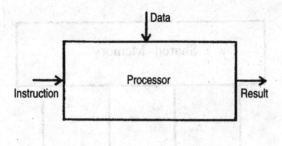

**Figure 1.2** SISD model.

1.3 illustrates a SIMD model. For example, consider the work of incrementing each entry of an array.

$$\text{For } i = 1 \text{ to } n \text{ do}$$
$$x_i \leftarrow x_i + 1;$$

This can be parallelized straight. We can assign $n$ processors, $P_1, P_2, \ldots P_n$. If they are according to the SIMD architecture, the common instruction "increment the data" can be given to all the processors. Each processor $P_i$ will have

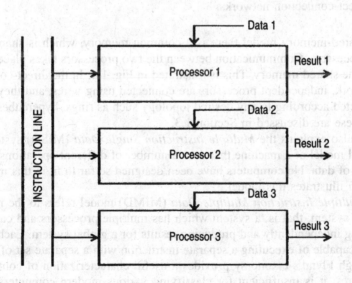

**Figure 1.3** SIMD model.

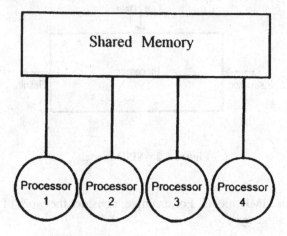

**Figure 1.4**    Shared-memory model.

the data $x_i$ and increment it. Notice that the data for different processor are different, whereas the instruction is the same. In the SIMD model there are two types of architectures:

1. Shared-memory model; and
2. Direct-connection networks.

In the shared-memory model there is a common memory, which is shared by all the processors. Communication between the two processors takes place only through the shared memory. This is illustrated in Fig. 1.4. In the direct-connection network, independent processors are connected using wires, and they may be connected according to any desired topology such as rings, hypercubes, and so on. These are discussed in Section 1.3.

Flynn also explains the *Multiple Instruction Single Data* (MISD) system, a theoretical model of a machine that does a number of different operations for a single set of data. No computers have been designed so far to fit in this model. Figure 1.5 illustrates this model.

The *Multiple Instruction Multiple Data* (MIMD) model refers to the multiprocessor system, that is, a system which has multiple processors and capable of working independently and producing results for a global system. Each processor is capable of executing a separate instruction with a separate set of data.

Although Flynn's taxonomy provides a useful characterization of computer architectures, it is insufficient for classifying various modern computers. For example, pipelined vector processors merit inclusion as parallel architectures, since they exhibit substantial concurrent arithmetic execution and can manipulate hundreds of vector elements in parallel. However, they cannot be regarded

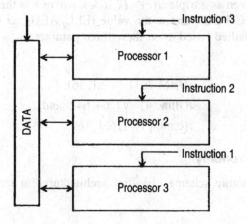

**Figure 1.5**   MISD model.

as any of the Flynn's classification, because of the difficulty to accommodate them into the taxonomy, as these computers lack processors that execute the same instruction in SIMD lockstep, and fail to possess the autonomy of the MIMD category. Because of the deficiency of Flynn's taxonomy, attempts have been made to extend Flynn's taxonomy to accommodate modern parallel computers. There are two more taxonomies that are distinctively different from the Flynn's, mainly because they are based upon criteria different from those of Flynn's taxonomy. But these taxonomies generally lack the simplicity inherent in Flynn's, and consequently are not as widely used as Flynn's. Below we give a brief summary of the distinctive features of these two taxonomies, in the subsequent sections. These are the Erlangen taxonomy, which was developed at the Friederich Alexander University of Erlangen-Numberg by Handler, and the Giloi taxonomy, proposed by Giloi.

### 1.2.2   Erlangen Taxonomy (Handler's Taxonomy)

The Erlangen system of classification, unlike the Flynn's, is based on distinction of the three levels of hardware:

1. Program control unit (PCU);
2. Arithmetic logic unit (ALU); and
3. Elementary logic circuit (ELC).

In general, a given computer consists of one or more PCUs; each PCU controls one or more ALUs; an ALU, in turn, consists of as many ELCs as there are bits in the ALU data path. The number, $w = (ELC/ALU)$ is, of course, the machine's word length. In this classification system, a minimal description of a computer $c$ is given as a triple: $t(c) = (k, d, w)$, where $k$ is the number of PCUs, $d$ the value (ELC/PCU), and $w$ the value (ELC/ALU), as given before. Any computer is classified based upon these three parameters.

*Example:*

$$t(\text{IBM } 701) = (1, 1, 36);$$
$$t(\text{Illiac } 4) = (1, 64, 64); \text{ and}$$
$$t(\text{c.mmp}) = (16, 1, 16).$$

### 1.2.3 Giloi Taxonomy

The Giloi taxonomic scheme classifies architectures in terms of the formal grammar,

$$G = \langle V_N, V_T, P, S \rangle,$$

where $V_N$ is the set of nonterminal symbols denoting certain complex or higher architectural features; $V_T$, the set of terminal symbols, denotes elementary, undefined or "axiomatic" architectural characteristics; $P$, the production set, denotes the composition of each complex architectural feature in terms of other (elementary or complex) features; and $S$ denotes the starting symbol of the computer architecture. Based upon these concepts, Giloi's scheme can completely classify any architecture by a parse tree.

Besides the Erlangen and Giloi taxonomies, which are based on classification criteria distinctively different from those of Flynn's, there are reported in the literature other taxonomies, which are mere extensions of Flynn's scheme to include the modern architectures. The most notable of these taxonomies are Hwang-Brigg's and Duncan's.

### 1.2.4 Hwang-Brigg's Taxonomy

Hwang-Brigg's taxonomy is obtained from Flynn's taxonomy with the following four modifications:

1. Elimination of the MISD taxon.
2. Refinement of the original SISD taxon into two taxa—processors with single functional units SISD-S, those with multiple functional units (SISD-M).
3. Refinement of the original SIMD taxon into two taxa—machines with word-slice processing (SIMD-W), those with bit-slice processing SIMD-B.
4. Refinement of the original MIMD taxon into two taxa—machines with loosely coupled processors (MIMD-L), and those with tightly-coupled processors (MIMD-T).

Hwang-Brigg's modification enhances the predictive power of the original scheme to the extent that the SISD-M taxon will, in general, have higher performance than those in the SISD-S taxon. However, no such general inference can be made for the SIMD-B and SIMD-W taxa. We classify below a few machines using Hwang-Brigg's taxonomic scheme.

*Example.* Using the maximum degree of potential parallelism, the following machines can be placed, in ascending order of performance:

STARAN : (SIMD-B)
Illiac4 : (SIMD-W)
PEPE : (SIMD-W)
MPP (Aerospace) : (SIMD-B)

Therefore, bit-slice machines perform both better and worse than word-slice machines.

## 1.2.5 Duncan's Taxonomy

Duncan proposed some modification to Flynn's taxonomy to include pipelined vector processors and other architectures that intuitively seem to merit inclusion as parallel architectures, but cannot be graciously accommodated by the original Flynn's scheme. This was achieved simply by broadening the criteria of classification, with some subcategories not found in Flynn's scheme, to reflect permutations of architectural characteristics and to cover lower level features of parallelism. Figure 1.6 shows a taxonomy based upon the Ducan's modification. These are three major classes.

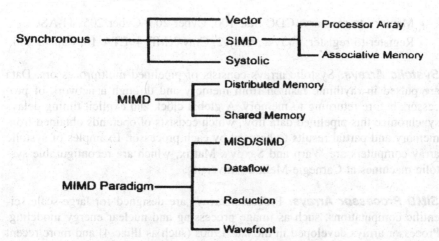

**Figure 1.6** Duncan's modification of Flynn's Taxonomy.

1. Synchronous;
2. MIMD; and
3. MIMD Paradigm.

**Synchronous Architectures.** Synchronous architectures coordinate concurrent operations in lockstep through global clocks, central control units, or vector unit controllers. This class includes three subclasses. They are

1. Vector Processors;
2. Systolic Arrays; and
3. SIMD Architectures.

SIMD architectures are further classified as processor arrays and associative memory processors.

**Vector Processors.** Vector processors are characterized by multiple, pipelined functional units, which provide parallel vector processing on vector operands. There are two types of vector processors, namely, register-to-register vector processors and memory-to-memory vector processors. In register-to-register vector processors, operands and the results of vector operation are held in special high-speed register, while in memory-to-memory vector processor, these data are held in special memory buffer. Efficient performance of vector processor is obtained when vector lengths are large. Recent vector processing supercomputers (such as Cray-XMP/4 and ETA-10) unite four to ten processors through a large shared memory. Since such architectures can support task-level parallelism, they could be termed MIMD architectures, although vector processing capabilities are the fundamental aspect of their design. Examples of vector processors are:

- Memory-to-memory: CDC Star 100, Cyber 203, Cyber 205, TI-ASC
- Register-to-register; Cray-1, Cray-2, Cray-XMP/4, ETA-10, Fujitsu-200.

**Systolic Arrays.** Systolic arrays consists of pipelined multiprocessors. Data are pulsed in rhythmic fashion from memory and through a network of processors before returning to memory. A global clock and explicit timing delays synchronize this pipelined data flow, which consists of operands obtained from memory and partial results to be used by each processor. Examples of systolic array computers are Warp and Saxpy's Matrix, which are reconfigurable systolic machines at Carnegie-Mellon University.

**SIMD Processor Arrays.** Processor arrays are designed for large-scale scientific computations, such as image processing and nuclear energy modeling. Processor arrays developed in the late 1960s (such as Illiac-4) and more recent ones such as Burroughs Scientific Processor (BSP), utilize processors which accommodate word-sized operands. These operands are usually floating-point (or complex) values, typically ranging from 32 to 64 bits in length. One variant of processor arrays involves large numbers of one-bit processors arranged in grid (such as 64 × 64). These processor arrays are known as *Massively Parallel Processors* (MPP). Loral's MPP, ICL DAP, FPS 164/MAX, Goodyear's MasPar Models of MPP, Thinking Machine Corporation's Connection Machine, and SX-2 SCS-40 are some examples of massively parallel processors.

**Associative Memory Processors.** Associative memory processors are built around associative memories, and constitute a distinctive type of SIMD architecture which uses special comparison logic to access stored data in parallel, according to its contents. Research in constructing associative memories began in the late 1950s, with the obvious goal of being able to search memories in parallel for data that matched some specified criteria. Most current associative memory processors use bit-serial organization, which involves concurrent operations on a single bit-slice (bit-column) of all the words in associative memory. Examples of the associative memory computers are Bell Laboratories' Parallel Element Processing Ensemble (PEPE), and Loral's Associative Processor (Aspro).

**MIMD Architectures.** MIMD architectures employ multiple processors that can execute independent instruction streams using local data. Thus MIMD computers support parallel execution that require processors to operate in a largely autonomous manner. Although software processes executing on MIMD architectures are synchronized by passing messages through an interconnecting network or by accessing data in shared-memory units, MIMD architectures are asynchronous computers, characterized by decentralized hardware control. Hence, MIMD architectures are also popularly known as *multiprocessors* and are divided into two subcategories.

1. Shared-memory (tightly-coupled); and
2. Distributed-memory (loosely coupled).

**Shared-Memory Multiprocessors (Tightly-Coupled).** Tightly-coupled MIMD architectures use shared memory among its processors. The interconnected architecture falls essentially into one of two classes: bus-biconnected and directly connected. In bus-connected architecture, the processors, parallel memories, network interfaces, and device controllers are tied to the same connection bus, whereas in directly connected architectures, the processors are connected directly to the high-end mainframes. Examples of tightly coupled multiprocessors are: Univac 1100/94, Cray-XMP, Alliant/8, and IBM 3090/400 multiprocessor.

**Distributed-Memory Multiprocessors (Loosely Coupled).** Loosely coupled MIMD architectures have distributed local memories attached to multiple processor nodes. The popular interconnect topologies include the hypercube, ring, butterfly switch, hypertrees, and hypernets (refer to Section 1.3). Message passing is the major communication method among the processor. Most multiprocessors are designed to be scalable in performance. Examples of loosely coupled multiprocessors: DADO2, Non-Von of Columbia University, Cosmic Cube, Ametec Series 2010, Intel Personal Supercomputer, Ncube/10, Lawrence Snyder's Configurable Highly Parallel Computer (CHIP), and Howard Siegel's Partitionable SIMD/MIMD System (Pasm).

**MIMD-Based Architectural Paradigms.** MIMD/SIMD hybrids, dataflow architectures, reduction machines, and wavefront array processor all pose difficulty for an orderly classification into Flynn's taxa. For example, each of these architectural types is predicted on the MIMD principles of asynchronous execution and concurrent manipulation of multiple instruction and data streams. However, each of these architectures is also based on a distinctive organizing principle as fundamental to its overall design as MIMD characteristics. These architectures, therefore, are described under the category "MIMD-based paradigms" to highlight their distinctive foundations, as well as the MIMD characteristics they have in common.

MIMD/SIMD Architectures have selected portions of a MIMD architecture that are controlled in a SIMD function. The implementation mechanisms employed for reconfiguring architectures and controlling SIMD execution are quite diverse. A popular implementation utilizes a tree-structured, message-passing computer as the base architecture. Examples of MIMD/SIMD machines are DADO, Non-Van, Pasm, and Texas Reconfigurable Array Computer (TRAC).

*Data-flow Architectures* have a fundamental feature, which is an execution paradigm in which instructions are enabled for execution as soon as all of their operands become available. Thus, the sequence of executed instructions is based on data dependencies, allowing dataflow architectures to exploit concurrency at the task, routine, and instruction levels. The major incentive for the dataflow architectures is to explore new computational models and languages that can be effectively exploited to achieve large-scale parallelism. Some of the best known dataflow computers are the manchester DataFlow Computer, MIT Tagged Token DataFlow architecture, and LAU System.

**Reduction (or Demand-Driven) Machines.** These machines implement an execution paradigm, in which an instruction is enabled for execution when its results are required as operands for another instruction already enabled for execution. Reduction machines execute programs that consist of nested expressions. Expressions are recursively defined as literals or function applications on arguments that may be literals of expressions. Practical challenges for implementing reduction architectures include synchronizing demands for instruction's results, and maintaining copies of expression evolution results. Examples of reduction machines include Newcastle Reduction Machine, North Carolina Cellular Tree Machine, and Utah Applicative Multiprocessing System.

*Wavefront Array Processors* combine systolic data pipelining with an asynchronous dataflow execution paradigm. S-Y. Kung developed wavefront array concepts in the early 1980s. This stimulated the design of systolic array research, producing efficient, cost-effective architectures for special-purpose systems that balance intensive computations with high I/O bandwidth. Wavefront and systolic architectures are both characterized by modular processors and regular, local interconnection networks. However, wavefront arrays replace the global clock and explicit time delays used for synchronizing systolic data pipelining with an asynchronous handshaking mechanism for coordinating interprocessor data movement. The handshaking mechanism allows computational wavefronts to pass smoothly through the arrays without intersecting, as the array's processors act as a wave-propagating medium. Kung argued that wavefronts enjoy several advantages over systolic arrays, including greater scalability, simpler programming, and greater fault tolerance. Examples of wavefront array processors are those constructed at Johns Hopkins University and at Stanford Telecommunications, and Royal Signals and Radar Establishment (United Kingdom).

## 1.3 MODELS FOR PARALLEL COMPUTATION

Any parallel algorithm is designed with an assumption of an architecture of a parallel computer. This is called a *parallel computing model*. A number of very different models of machines have been assumed for designing parallel algorithms by various researchers. This section introduces some important models.

### 1.3.1 Binary Tree Model

The processing of the whole problem is represented in the form of a binary tree, in which every non-leaf node has two children. (A formal definition of the binary tree is given in Chapter 2). Every non-leaf node represents an operation. All the operations at one level are done in parallel. The binary tree model is sometimes called the *directed acyclic graph (DAG) model*

For example, suppose we are interested in finding the sum of eight numbers. A binary tree of minimum height must be drawn with these eight data as the eight leaves. The internal nodes represent the addition of the values corresponding to its two children. Figure 1.7 illustrates the process. Assume that there are four processors available. These processors could now be scheduled for the operations represented by the internal nodes. Scheduling is a function SCH, which assigns for each internal node an ordered pair $(p, t)$, where $p$ represents the processor number and $t$ represents the time at which this operation takes place. The internal nodes have been denoted by the serial numbers 1, 2, 3, 4, 5, 6, and 7 in Fig. 1.7.

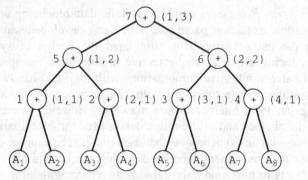

**Figure 1.7**   Scheduling of summation algorithm.

The following is a schedule function:

| SCHEDULE | MEANING |
|----------|---------|
| SCH(1) = (1, 1) | Processor 1 does at time 1. |
| SCH(2) = (2, 1) | Processor 2 does at time 1. |
| SCH(3) = (3, 1) | Processor 3 does at time 1. |
| SCH(4) = (4, 1) | Processor 4 does at time 1. |
| SCH(5) = (1, 2) | Processor 1 does at time 2. |
| SCH(6) = (2, 2) | Processor 2 does at time 2. |
| SCH(7) = (1, 3) | Processor 1 does at time 3. |

Here the task of adding eight numbers has been carried out by 4 processors in 3 units of time. A complete binary tree with $n$ nodes is of height log $n$, and so the work of adding $n$ numbers could be done by $n/2$ processors in log $n$ time units.

This means that, at time interval from $t = 0$ to $t = 1$, the following works are done simultaneously:

Processor 1 adds $A_1$ and $A_2$.

Processor 2 adds $A_3$ and $A_4$.

Processor 3 adds $A_5$ and $A_6$.

Processor 4 adds $A_7$ and $A_8$.

Now the values $(A_1 + A_2)$, $(A_3 + A_4)$, $(A_5 + A_6)$, and $(A_7 + A_8)$ are known. During the time interval $t = 1$ to $t = 2$, the following works are done simultaneously:

Processor 1 adds $(A_1 + A_2)$ and $(A_3 + A_4)$.

Processor 2 adds $(A_5 + A_6)$ and $(A_7 + A_8)$.

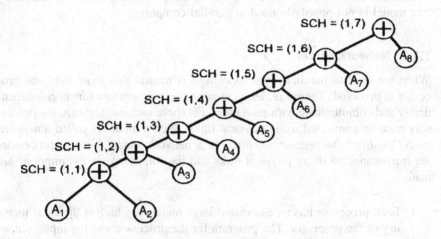

**Figure 1.8**   Binary tree model for sequential computing.

Now the values $A_1+A_2+A_3+A_4$ and $A_5+A_6+A_7+A_8$ are known. During the time interval $t = 2$ to $t = 3$, the work of adding $(A_1+A_2+A_3+A_4)$ and $(A_5+A_6+A_7+A_8)$ is done by processor 1. The work is done as per the expression,

$$\{(A_1 + A_2) + (A_3 + A_4)\} + \{(A_5 + A_6) + (A_7 + A_8)\}$$

Suppose there is only one processor available. In this case, the computing procedure can be represented by the skewed tree shown in Fig. 1.8. The schedule function values are also shown near each internal node. The time taken in this case is 7. For $n$ numbers to be added, the time taken is $n - 1$.

When there are only three processors available, the binary tree model to add eight numbers is shown in Fig. 1.9. Here the time taken is 4 units.

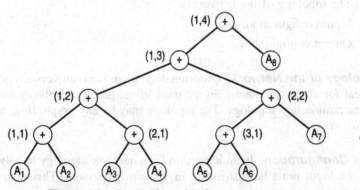

**Figure 1.9**   Summation with three processors.

Because of the tedious work in defining the scheduling function, the binary tree model is not popularly used in parallel computing.

### 1.3.2  Network Model

When we want to parallelize the system, it is natural that more than one processor is involved. Therefore, let us assume these processors function independently and communicate with each other. For these communications, the processors must be connected using physical links. Such a model is called a *network model* or *direct-connection machine*. In a network model, several processors are interconnected using physical links and the following six assumptions are made:

1. Each processor has an associated large memory, which is the local memory of the processor. The program for the processor and the input, output values are stored in this memory.
2. There is no common memory that can be accessed by all the processors.
3. The processors are connected directly with physical link and the interconnection topology is called the *network topology*. The network topology is a graph having processors as vertices and the interconnection as edges. The links may be *unidirectional* or *bidirectional*.
4. If two processors are adjacent, data can be moved from one processor to the other directly.
5. In one clock cycle, a unit operation takes place in any processor.
6. A processor can communicate a data to any of its adjacent processor in unit time.

When an algorithm is to be designed for a network model system the following must be first specified:

1. The topology of the network;
2. Input configuration; and
3. Output configuration.

***Topology of the Network.*** Unfortunately, there is no universal topology that is ideal for all the problems. So we must investigate the problem and propose the interconnection topology. The topology may be any graph, ring, tree, cube, and so on.

***Input Configuration.*** In an algorithm for a network topology to solve a problem, the input must be distributed in various processors. This distribution is called *input configuration*.

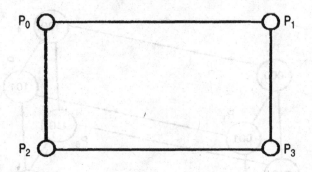

**Figure 1.10**   2-cube.

***Output Configuration.*** The distribution of output in various processors is called the *output configuration*.

Now let us study certain network topologies that have been used to solve some interesting problems. We begin with the most popular topology—hypercube.

### 1.3.3   Hypercubes (*k*-cubes)

Let us define the *k*-cube in a recursive way first. A 0-cube is a single processor. A 1-cube is a network of two processors connected to each other. A 2-cube is a network of four processors joined in the form of a square with the processors at the four vertices. A 2-cube is constructed with two 1-cubes, namely, $P_0 - P_1$ and $P_2 - P_3$ which are then connected as $P_0$ to $P_2$ and $P_1$ to $P_3$. Figure 1.10 shows a 2-cube. A 3-cube is a pair of 2-cubes,

$$P_0 P_1 P_2 P_3 \qquad \text{and} \qquad P_4 P_5 P_6 P_7,$$

such that connections are also established between

$$P_0 \text{ to } P_4$$
$$P_1 \text{ to } P_5$$
$$P_2 \text{ to } P_6$$
$$P_3 \text{ to } P_7.$$

Figure 1.11 depicts a 3-cube (ignore the label in the node for the time being). In general, a *k*-cube is defined to be a pair of $(k - 1)$-cubes, such that the connection is established between the corresponding nodes. A *k*-cube is also called a *hypercube of dimension k*.

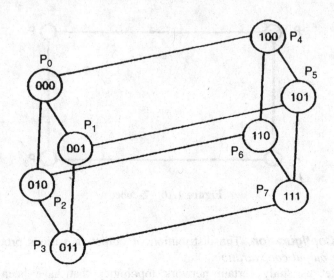

**Figure 1.11** 3-cube.

The above definition of $k$-cube is a recursive one. A $k$-cube contains $2^k$-nodes, which are labeled by the $k$-bit binary numbers. Two nodes are connected by an edge if and only if their binary labels differ exactly in one bit. For example, a 3-cube contains 8 nodes, which are labeled by the 3-bit binary numbers 000, 001, 010, 011, 100, 101, 110, 111. The node 000 is connected to the nodes 100, 010, and 001. In general, any node $(b_1 b_2 \ldots b_k)$ is joined by an edge to the following $k$ nodes:

$$b_1 b_2 b_3 \ldots b_k$$
$$b_1 b_2 b_3 \ldots b_k$$
$$\ldots$$
$$b_1 b_2 b_3 \ldots b_k.$$

For example, in a 3-cube, 000 is joined to 100, 010, and 001. 001 is joined to 101, 011, and 000. 010 is joined to 110, 000, and 011. 011 is joined to 111, 001, and 010. 100 is joined to 000, 110, and 101. 101 is joined to 001, 111, and 100. 110 is joined to 010, 100, and 111. 111 is joined to 011, 101, and 110. This is depicted in Fig. 1.11. From the definition of $k$-cubes, we observe the following properties:

**Property 1**  A $k$-cube is a $k$-regular graph with $2^k$ nodes. A $k$-regular graph is a graph in which each node has degree $k$.

**Property 2**  The distance between two nodes $a = (a_1 a_2 \ldots a_k)$ and $b =$

$(b_1b_2 \ldots b_k)$ is the number of bits in which $a$ and $b$ differ. For example, in a 5-cube, the distance between (11100) and (11011) is 3. This is because they differ in 3 bits. (11100) is adjacent to (11000), which is adjacent to (11010), and it is adjacent to (11011).

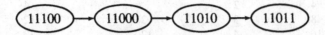

Since a datum can be moved from one node to an adjacent node in unit time, the time taken to move a datum from node (111000) to (11011) is 3 units.

In a six-dimensional cube, suppose we want to move a datum from $P_{27}$ to $P_{43}$. We have $(27)_{10} = (011011)_2$ and $(43)_{10} = (101011)_2$.

These two labels differ in 2 bits. So, in 2 units of time, we can move a datum between $P_{27}$ and $P_{43}$ of a 6-cube. The route can be determined by matching the bits of the binary numbers.

$$
\begin{array}{ccc}
P_{27} & P_{59} & P_{43} \\
(011011) & (111011) & (101011).
\end{array}
$$

**Property 3**   In a hypercube with $n$ nodes (where $n = 2^k$), data can be moved from any node to any other node in at most $\log_2 n$ time. This is because of property 2 and the fact that $n = 2^k$, which implies that $\log_2 n = k$. In this book, $\log_2 n$ is denoted simply as $\log n$, because we deal with the logarithms only to the base 2.

**Property 4**   Let $e(k)$ be the number of edges in a $k$-cube. By the recursive construction of $k$-cube, we have the recursive equation,

$$e(k) = 2e(k-1) + 2^{k-1}.$$

Substituting recursively for $e(k-1)$, we get

$$
\begin{aligned}
e(k) &= 2(2e(k-2) + 2^{k-2}) + 2^{k-1} \\
&= 2^2 e(k-2) + 2.2^{k-1} \\
&= 2^3 e(k-3) + 3.2^{k-1} \\
&= 2^{k-1} e(1) + (k-1)2^{k-1} \\
&= 2^{k-1} + (k-1)2^{k-1}, \text{because } e(1) = 1 \\
&= k2^{k-1}
\end{aligned}
$$

If $n = 2^k$ is the number of nodes in the $k$-cube, we get

**TABLE 1.1 Comparison of k-cube and a Complete Graph.**

| Number of Vertices n | log n | Number of Edges in a Complete Graph n(n − 1)/2 | Number of Edges in a k-cube (n/2) log n |
|---|---|---|---|
| 2 | 1 | 1 | 1 |
| 4 | 2 | 6 | 4 |
| 8 | 3 | 28 | 12 |
| 16 | 4 | 120 | 32 |
| 32 | 5 | 496 | 80 |
| 64 | 6 | 2016 | 192 |
| 128 | 7 | 8128 | 448 |
| 1024 | 10 | 523776 | 5120 |

$$e(k) = k2^{k-1} = (\log n)n/2$$

This gives the number of edges in a $k$-cube.

When $n$ nodes are connected as a complete graph, we have $n(n-1)/2$ edges. In a complete graph, since any two nodes are adjacent, data can be moved from one node to any other node in unit time. But this is achieved only using $n(n - 1)/2$ edges, which is a very costly affair, since each edge is a physical link. However, if they are connected as a $k$-cube, we need only $(n/2)$ log $n$ edges and we can communicate a data from any vertex to any other vertex in log $n$ time. Table 1.1 shows the values of $n(n-1)/2$ and $(n/2)$ log $n$ for various $n$ values.

Table 1.1 also shows how a $k$-cube topology is economically advantageous when compared with a complete graph. Now let us explain how an algorithm can be designed for a $k$-cube topology in the direct connection network. We are going to design an algorithm to choose the smallest entry of an array with $n$ entries.

Let the array be denoted by

$$a_0 a_1 a_2 \ldots a_{n-1}.$$

The following is the simple sequential algorithm:

```
BEGIN
    small = a₀
    For i = 1 to n − 1 do
        If small > aᵢ then
            small = aᵢ
        endif
    edfor
END
```

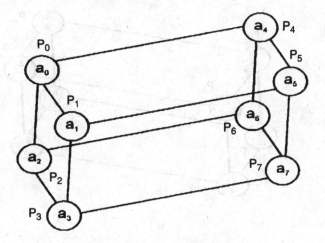

**Figure 1.12** Input configuration.

This sequential algorithm takes $O(n)$ time. Using a $k$-cube connected network of processor, we are going to design an algorithm that works in $O(\log n)$ time. We begin with the input configuration.

**Input Configuration.** We assign the $n$ numbers to the $n$ processors. For convenience, let us assume that $n = 2^k$. Initially $a_i$ is in the local memory of processor $P_i (0 \le i \le n - 1)$. This is shown in Fig. 1.12.

**Output Configuration.** We want the result (smallest entry of the array) to be stored in $P_0$.

**Processing.** Now we are going to effectively apply the definition of the $k$-cube that it is a pair of two $(k - 1)$-cubes, such that $P_i$ is connected to $P_{i+2}$. Now we are going to transfer the content of $P_{i+2}$ to $P_i (0 \le i < 2^{k-1})$. Now the processor $P_0$ contains $a_0$ as well as $a_2$. Similarly any $P_i$ contains $a_i$ as well as $a_{i+2}$. Now each processor $P_i$ compares $a_i$ and $a_{i+2}$ and finds the smaller and stores it in $a_i$. After this process, the smallest number is in the array

$$a_0 a_1 a_2 \ldots a_{(n/2) - 1}$$

The procedure is repeated on the $(k - 1)$-cube, consisting of the processors $P_0 P_1 \ldots P_{(n/2) - 1}$, so that the smallest number is stored to one of the elements of the array.

Repeating the procedure $k$ times, the smallest number reaches the node $P_0$. Considering the array of 8 numbers 15, 10, 20, 9, 8, 7, 21, 5, the procedure is illustrated in Fig. 1.13(a) through 1.13(g).

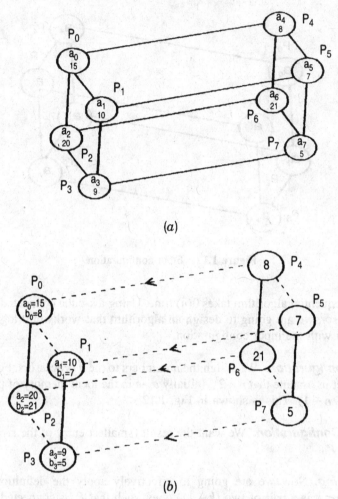

(a)

(b)

**Figure 1.13(a)** Initial position of numbers. **(b)** Numbers $a_{i+4}$ are received from $P_{i+4}(0 \leq i \leq 3)$ by $P_i$ and stored as $b_i$.

The above algorithm can be formally described as follows:

## Algorithm *k*-CUBE-Min

**Input:** Each processor $P_i$ contains a value $a_i$ in its local memory ($0 \leq i \leq n - 1$). Assume that $n = 2^k$.

**Output:** The minimum of the array $a_0, a_1, \ldots, a_{n-1}$ is stored in the variable $a_0$.

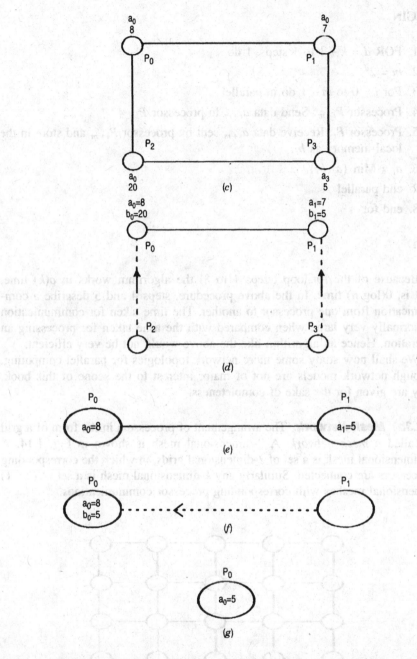

**Figure 1.13(c)** For each processor pi ($0 \leq i \leq 3$), the operation ai Min $\{a_1, b_1\}$ is done. The figure shows $a_0$, $a_1$, $a_2$, $a_3$ values after the operation. **(d)** Processor $p_i (0 \leq i \leq 1)$ receives $a_{i+2}$ from processor $p_{i+2}$. **(e)** The content of the processors after the operation $a_i = \text{Min}\{a_i, b_i\}$ for $i = 0, 1$. **(f)** Processor $P_1$ sends $a_1$ to $P_0$. **(g)** $a_0 = \text{Min}\{a_0, b_0\}$.

BEGIN

1. FOR $d = k - 1$ to 1 step $-1$ do
2. $m \doteq 2^d$
3. For $i = 0$ to $m - 1$ do in parallel
4. Processor $P_{i+m}$: Send data $a_{i+m}$ to processor $P_i$
5. Processor $P_i$: Receive data $a_{i+m}$ sent by processor $P_{i+m}$ and store in the local memory as $b_i$.
6. $a_i = \text{Min } \{a_i, b_i\}$
7. end parallel
8. end for

END

Because of the for-loop (steps 1 to 8) the algorithm works in $o(k)$ time, that is, $0(\log n)$ time. In the above procedure, steps 4 and 5 describe a communication from one processor to another. The time taken for communication is normally very large when compared with the time taken for processing an operation. Hence an algorithm like the above would not be very efficient.

We shall now study some more network topologies for parallel computing. Though network models are not of major interest to the scope of this book, they are given for the sake of completeness.

*1.3.3b* **Mesh Network.** The arrangement of processors in the form of a grid is called *a mesh network*. A 2-dimensional mesh is shown in Fig. 1.14. A 3-dimensional mesh is a set of 2-dimensional grids, in which the corresponding processors are connected. Similarly any $k$-dimensional mesh is a set of $(k - 1)$ dimensional meshes with corresponding processor communications.

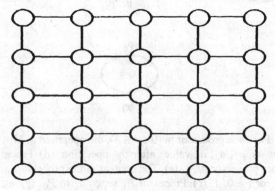

**Figure 1.14**   A two-dimensional mesh.

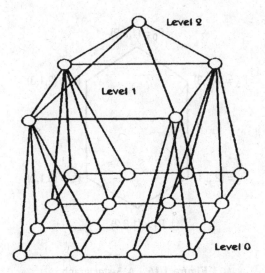

**Figure 1.15**  A pyramid network of size 16.

**1.3.3c  Pyramid Network.** A pyramid network is constructed similar to a rooted tree. The root contains one processor. At the next level there are four processors in the form of a 2-dimensional mesh and all the four are children of the root. For each of the four nodes at level 1 there are four children at level 2. All the nodes at the level 2 are connected in the form of a mesh. Similarly, the pyramid can be constructed up to any desired height. A pyramid of height 2 is shown in Fig. 1.15.

**1.3.3d  Star Graphs.** The $k$-cube has already been defined as the set of $2^k$ nodes labeled by the numbers 0 to $2^{k-1}$ in binary form, such that there is an edge between any two vertices if and only if their labels differ only by one bit. A 3-cube is given in Fig. 1.11 with the above-mentioned labeling. The above definition has motivated the researchers to define a star graph as follows: Let $k$ be a positive integer. Consider the permutation with $k$ symbols. There are $k$ permutations with $k$ symbols. $k$ vertices are defined corresponding to the $k$ permutations and two vertices are adjacent, if and only if their corresponding permutations differ only in the leftmost and in any one other position. The graph thus obtained is called a $k$-star graph. For example, consider the case when $k = 3$. In this case there are six permutations:

$$P_0 = (1, 2, 3) \qquad P_1 = (1, 3, 2) \qquad P_2 = (2, 1, 3)$$
$$P_3 = (2, 3, 1) \qquad P_4 = (3, 1, 2) \qquad P_5 = (3, 2, 1).$$

Writing elaborately,

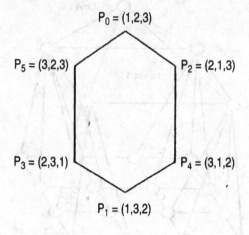

**Figure 1.16**    A 3-star graph.

$$P_0 = 1, 2, 3$$
$$1, 2, 3$$

That is, $P_0(1) = 1$, $P_0(2) = 2$ and $P_0(3) = 3$.

$$P_1 = 1, 2, 3$$
$$1, 3, 2$$

That is, $P_1(1) = 1$, $P_1(2) = 3$ and $P_1(3) = 2$.

The 3-star graph is shown in Fig. 1.16. A star graph can also be defined by the recursive construction rule as follows: In order to construct a $k$-star graph, consider $k$ copies of $(k - 1)$-star graphs. In any $(k - 1)$-star graph, each vertex is labeled by a permutation of $k - 1$ symbols. We denote these $k$ copies of the $(k - 1)$-star graphs by $S_1, S_2, \ldots S_k$. Now we label the vertices of $S_i(1 \leq i \leq k)$ by the permutations of the symbols 1 to $k$ except $i$. That is, each vertex of $S_1$ is labeled with a permutations of the symbols 2, 3, 4, ... $k$. The vertices of $S_2$ are labeled with permutation of the symbols 1, 3, 4, ... $k$. Similarly, the other graphs must also be labeled. We now add the symbol $i$ in graph $S_i$ at the rightmost position of the permutation for each vertex of the permutation of $S_i$ and create new edges as follows: Two vertices $A$ and $B$ are connected if and only if one permutation can be obtained from the other by exchanging the first and the last symbols. Day and Tripathi (1991) have studied the topological properties of $k$-cubes and $k$-star graphs. The following table gives the basic parameters of the two topologies.

| Property | $k$-cube | $k$-star |
|----------|----------|----------|
| No. of Vertices | $2k$ | $k$ |
| degree | $k$ | $k-1$ |
| diameter | $k$ | $3/2(k-1)$ |

Day and Tripathi (1992) present another interconnection topology called *arrangement graphs*, which is a generalization of star graph topology. They show that the arrangement graphs are more flexible than star graphs in terms of choosing the major design parameters such as degree, diameter, and number of nodes. Any star graph is also an arrangement graph. Day and Tripathi (1993) propose an assignment of directions to the edges of the $k$-star graphs and derive several interesting properties of the $k$-star graphs.

## 1.4 PRAM MODEL

In the direct connection network we studied that the processors are connected directly using physical links. In the PRAM (Parallel Random Access Machine) model, all the processors are connected in parallel to a global large memory. This memory is shared by all the processors, depicted in Fig. 1.17. This is also called a *shared-memory model*. All the processors are assumed to work synchronously on a common clock. Every processor is capable of accessing (reading/writing) the entire memory. The communication between processors takes place only through the shared memory. That is, a datum from processor $P_i$ is communicated to processor $P_j$ in the following steps:

1. Processor $P_i$ writes the data in the global memory.
2. Processor $P_j$ reads the data from the global memory.

This is illustrated in Fig. 1.18. The PRAM models discussed throughout this book works in SIMD type, as per Flynn's classification. However, SISD and MIMD machines with a common memory cannot be ruled out. In our PRAM model there are four different types, depending upon the capability of more than one processor to read from/write to a memory location.

1. Exclusive Read Exclusive Write PRAM (EREW).
2. Concurrent Read Exclusive Write PRAM (CREW).
3. Exclusive Read Concurrent Write PRAM (ERCW).
4. Concurrent Read Concurrent Write PRAM (CRCW).

An Exclusive Read Exclusive Write PRAM permits only one processor at one instant to read from/write to a memory location. Simultaneous reading or

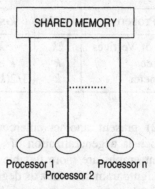

**Figure 1.17** PRAM model.

simultaneous writing by more than one processor in a memory location is not permitted here. The CREW PRAM permits concurrent reading of a location by more than one processor, but does not permit concurrent writing. The ERCW model permits concurrent writing alone. The CRCW PRAM is the most powerful model, which permits concurrent reading, as well as concurrent writing,

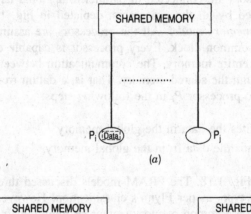

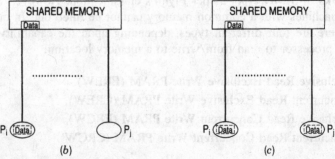

**Figure 1.18(a)** Processor $P_i$. **(b)** Processor $P_i$ writes the data in the global memory. **(c)** Processor $P_j$ reads the data.

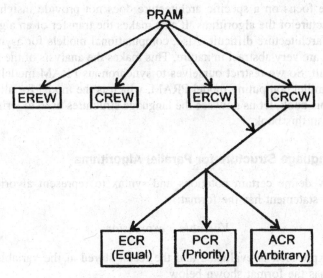

**Figure 1.19**  Models of PRAM.

in a memory location. When one or more processors tries to read the content of a memory location concurrently, we assume that all those processor succeed in reading. However, when more than one processor try to write to the same location concurrently, the conflict has to be properly resolved. Three different methods of resolving this conflict have been suggested.

1. Equality Conflict Resolution (ECR);
2. Priority Conflict Resolution (PCR); and
3. Arbitrary Conflict Resolution (ACR).

In the case of ECR, we assume that the processors succeed in writing, only if all the processors try to write the same value to the location. In PCR we assume that each processor has its priority number. When more than one processors try to write to the same location simultaneously, the processor with highest priority succeeds. In ACR we assume that, among the processors trying to write simultaneously, some arbitrary processor succeeds.

There are Multiple Instruction Multiple Data (MIMD) machines, in which each processor has its own clock and the processors work asynchronously. Each processor is a separate computer with its own local memory and also has access to the global memory. Each processor is called a *processing element*. If the processing elements are attached through a central switching mechanism to reach the global memory, the communication among the processors does not take much time and is not complex. Such a MIMD system is said to be a *tightly coupled* MIMD model. Otherwise it is said to be *loosely coupled*.

The parallel architectures mentioned so far have some inherent drawbacks, namely, the focus on a specific architecture does not provide insight into the logical structure of the algorithms. It also makes the transfer of an algorithm to a different architecture difficult. Also, computational models for asynchronous parallelism are very abstract in nature. This makes the analysis of the algorithm very difficult. So we restrict ourselves to synchronous PRAM models. Having seen the parallel computing model PRAM, which is the model for all the algorithms in this book, let us now see the language structures used to write parallel algorithms in this book.

### 1.4.1 Language Structure for Parallel Algorithms

Let us now define certain notations and syntax to represent algorithms. An assignment statement has the format:

$$Variable = expression.$$

Here the expression is evaluated and the result stored at the variable. The IF statement has the format shown below:

$$If\ cond\ then$$
$$s_1$$
$$s_2$$
$$\vdots$$
$$Else$$
$$s_1'$$
$$s_2'$$
$$\vdots$$
$$Endif$$

In this syntax *cond* is a valid logical condition. If the condition is true, then $s_1, s_2, \ldots$ are executed and otherwise $s_1', s_2' \ldots$ are executed.

The For loop has the form shown below:

$$For\ variable = s\ to\ e\ step\ h$$
$$s_1$$
$$s_2$$
$$\ldots$$
$$end\ for$$

Here the statements $s_1, s_2 \ldots$ are repeated with the value of variable set to $s, s + h, s + 2h, \ldots$ until $s + kh > e$. We also use the while loop, which has the format shown below:

$$\textit{While cond do}$$
$$s_1$$
$$s_2$$
$$\dots$$
$$\textit{end while}$$

The statements $s_1$, $s_2$ ... are repeated as long as the condition *cond* is true. Parallelism is represented by the ***For-in-Parallel*** statement. This statement is written in two different structures:

## Structure 1

$$\textit{For variable} = 1 \textit{ to n do in parallel}$$
$$s_1$$
$$s_2$$
$$\dots$$
$$\textit{End parallel}$$

The same instructions $s_1$, $s_2$, ... are all carried out by each of the $n$ processors simultaneously. The running variable in the For statement denotes the processor index.

## Structure 2

$$\textit{For } x \in S \textit{ do in parallel}$$
$$s_1$$
$$s_2$$
$$\dots$$
$$\textit{End parallel}$$

Here also the statements $s_1$, $s_2$, ... are all executed by each of the processors simultaneously. Here the number of processors working simultaneously is the number of elements in $S$.

Suppose $x$, $y$, $z$ are three variables in the global memory and we write

$$x = y + z$$

in the parallel algorithm. This work is carried out by a processor as follows:

1. Read the content of the variable $y$ and call it $v_1$ ($v_1$ is a variable in the processor's local memory).
2. Read the content of the variable $z$ and call it $v_2$ ($v_2$ is a variable in the processor's local memory).

3. $v_3 = v_1 + v_2$ ($v_3$ is a variable in the processor's local memory).

4. Write the value $v_3$ in the global variable $x$.

With this background, let us now develop some simple parallel algorithms to illustrate the Concurrent Read and the Concurrent Write operations.

## 1.5 SOME SIMPLE ALGORITHMS

Consider the problem of finding the boolean AND value of $n$ values stored in an array $A(1:n)$. We want to evaluate.

$$\text{RESULT} = A(1)^\wedge A(2)^\wedge A(3)^\wedge \ldots ^\wedge A(n)$$

A sequential $O(n)$ time algorithm is given below:

> BEGIN
>> RESULT = .TRUE.
>> For $i = 1$ to $n$ do
>>> RESULT = RESULT$^\wedge A(i)$
>> End For
> END.

Let us assume a ERCW PRAM model with arbitrary conflict resolution (ACR) $A(1:n)$ is an array of boolean values and we want to evaluate

> RESULT = .FALSE. If any one of the values $A(i)$ is FALSE.
> = .TRUE. otherwise

Let us have RESULT as a global variable having TRUE value initially. We want to engage $n$ processors and the processor $P_i$ will read $A(i)$ from the global memory and check if $A(i)$ is .FALSE. If $A(i)$ = FALSE., the processor $P_i$ immediately writes .FALSE in the global variable RESULT. Since $n$ processors are working in parallel, the work is completed in unit time. If more than one $A(i)$ values are FALSE, then more than one processors try to write the value FALSE in the global variable RESULT concurrently. This is resolved by the arbitrary conflict resolution (ACR). If all the $A(i)$ have. TRUE value, then no processor tries to write in RESULT and so its initial value. TRUE. is preserved.

We formally present now the parallel algorithm to run on a ERCW PRAM with ACR.

**Algorithm Boolean-AND**
**Input:** The Boolean Array $A(1:n)$
**Output:** The Boolean value RESULT

```
        BEGIN
            RESULT = TRUE
                For i = 1 to n do in parallel If A(i) = .FALSE.
        then            RESULT = .FALSE. endif
        END
```

In the above algorithm $0(n)$ processor are working to complete the work in $0(1)$ time. Notice that if the concurrent write is resolved by any one of the three types (ECR, PCR or ACR), we get the correct result in the above algorithm.

Consider the following algorithm for the same problem, which works correctly on ERCW–ECR model.

**Algorithm Boolean-AND-1**
**Input:** The Boolean array $A(1:n)$
**Output:** The Boolean value RESULT.

```
            BEGIN
                RESULT = .FALSE.
                    For i = 1 to n do in parallel
                RESULT = A(i)
                    End Parallel
            END
```

Here each of the $n$ processors tries to write the value of $A(i)$ to the value RESULT. If the conflict resolution model is ERCW-ACR type, we will not get the correct result. The above algorithm will correctly give the RESULT only if the PRAM models is of ECRW-ECR type. Now we design an algorithm for the same problem to work in EREW PRAM.

The elementary AND operation is a binary operation. So, a processor can perform the AND operation of only two quantities at a time. When $n$ is the size of the data, employ $n/2$ processors. The $n$ data are divided among the $n/2$ processors 2 each. The AND operation is performed by the $n/2$ processors simultaneously. Now the $n/2$ results are to be used as data and the above procedure must be repeated. We get $n/4$ results. Repeating in this manner, we get the final result in $0(\log n)$ time. For example, if there are 8 numbers $A(1:8)$, the first step does the following operation:

Processor $P_1 : A(1) \leftarrow A(1)^\wedge A(2)$    Processor $P_2 : A(2) \leftarrow A(3)^\wedge A(4)$
Processor $P_3 : A(3) \leftarrow A(5)^\wedge A(6)$    Processor $P_4 : A(4) \leftarrow A(7)^\wedge A(8)$

In general, processor $P_i$ does the work $A(i) \leftarrow A(2i - 1)^\wedge A(2i)$. Now our final results can be achieved by evaluating $A(1)^\wedge A(2)^\wedge A(3)^\wedge A(4)$. This is also evaluated in the same way. Two processors are employed. Processor $P_1$ evaluate $A(1)^\wedge A(2)$ and stores in $A(1)$. Processor $P_2$ evaluates $A(3)^\wedge A(4)$ and stores in $A(2)$. We can now get the final result by evaluating $A(1)^\wedge A(2)$. This is formally presented in the following algorithm:

**Algorithm Boolean-AND-2**
**Input:** The Boolean values $A(1:n)$
**Output:** RESULT

$$p = \text{number of processors used.}$$
$$\text{BEGIN}$$
$$p = n/2$$
$$\text{While } p > 0 \text{ do}$$
$$\text{For } i = 1 \text{ to } p \text{ do in parallel}$$
$$A(i) = A(2i - 1)^\wedge A(2i)$$
$$\text{End Parallel}$$
$$p = \lceil p/2 \rceil$$
$$\text{End while}$$
$$\text{RESULT}$$
$$\text{END}$$

The working of this algorithm when $n = 8$ is illustrated in Fig. 1.20. The while loop in the algorithm is repeated $\log n$ times and, hence, the time complexity of this algorithm is $0(\log n)$. We need $n/2$ processors in EREW PRAM.

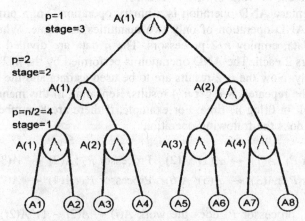

**Figure 1.20**   Boolean-AND-2 for $n = 8$.

## 1.6  PERFORMANCE OF PARALLEL ALGORITHMS

The performance of a parallel algorithm is assessed primarily by the following three factors:

1. Computing time (Time Complexity);
2. Number of processors required (Processor Complexity); and
3. Model of the machine required.

For example, the performance of the algorithms we studied in Section 1.5 are shown in table below:

| Algorithm | Time Complexity | Processor Complexity | PRAM Model |
|---|---|---|---|
| Boolean-AND | $O(1)$ | $O(n)$ | ERCW |
| Boolean-AND-1 | $O(1)$ | $O(n)$ | ERCW-ECR |
| Boolean-AND-2 | $O(\log_2 n)$ | $O(n)$ | EREW |

The complexity bounds are expressed in terms of usual notations as defined below:

1. $T(n) = O(f(n))$ if there are positive numbers $c$ and $n_0$, such that $T(n) < cf(n)$ for all $n > n_0$.
2. $T(n) = \Omega(f(n))$ if there are positive constants $c$ and $n_0$, such that $T(n) > cf(n)$ for all $n > n_0$.
3. $T(n) = \theta(f(n))$ if there exist positive constants $c_1$, $c_2$, $n_0$ and $n_1$, such that $T(n) < c_1 f(n)$ for all $n > n_0$ $T(n) > c_2 f(n)$ for all $n > n_1$.

That is, $T(n) = \theta f(n)$ if $T(n) = O(n)$ and $T(n) = \Omega(n)$. Two more quantities studied to analyze the performance of a parallel algorithm are its *speedup* and *efficiency*.

**Speedup and Efficiency.**  Consider a problem for which the best known sequential algorithm has the time complexity $T_s$. We have a parallel algorithm for the same problem that has time complexity $T_p$ and processor complexity $P$. We define

$$\text{Speedup} = T_s/T_p$$

$$\text{Efficiency} = T_s/PT_p.$$

The speedup is at most equal to the number of processors, and we always attempt to develop parallel algorithms with the speedup nearly equal to the number of processors. In reality, we can achieve this much of speedup only for a limited number of problems. The efficiency is at most 1. The efficiency provides an indication of the effective utilization of all the processors.

Performance measurements in the parallel domain have been made more complex by our desire to know "how much faster are we running our application on a parallel computer?" That is, what benefit are we deriving from the use of parallelism? This is measured in terms of speedup.

*Speedup = serial execution time/parallel execution time.*

There are various methods of defining serial and parallel execution times. This diversity results in five different definitions of speedup. They are relative speedup, real speedup, absolute speedup, asymptotic real speedup, and asymptotic relative speed up. Sahni and Thanvantri have studied these performance metrices in detail. For a broader treatment on these see Sahni [1997] and Thanvantri.

***Relative Speedup.*** The serial time is defined here as the execution time of the parallel program when run on a single processor of that parallel computers. So the relative speedup obtained by the parallel algorithm $A$ when solving problem instance $p$ of size $n$ using $p$ processor is:

$$\text{Relative Speedup } (n, p) = \frac{\text{Time to solve } P \text{ using algorithm } A \text{ with 1 processor}}{\text{Time to solve } P \text{ using algorithm } A \text{ with } p \text{ processors}}$$

The relative speedup of a parallel system is not a fixed number. Rather, it depends on the problem size $n$, as well as on the number of processors. Relative speedup is a function of $n$ and $p$. Fixing $n$, we can draw the relative speedup curve taking $p$ in one axis and the relative speedup in the other axis. This can be used to analyze the performance of the algorithm when number of processors increases. Similarly, we can fix $p$ and then draw the curve with $n$ in one axis and the relative speedup in another axis. This will enable us to study the behavior of the algorithm when the size of the problem increases. Using these two curves, we can find the point where the relative speedup is maximum. This is called the *maximum relative speedup*. Average relative speedup, minimum relative speedup, and expected relative speedup are also defined similarly.

***Real Speedup.*** In this measure, the parallel execution time is compared with the time needed by the fastest serial algorithm/program for the application. The fastest algorithm's execution time on a single processor of the parallel computer is used. Since for many applications, we may not know the fastest algorithm, and for some applications no one algorithm might be fastest for all instances, the run time of the sequential algorithm that is used in "practice" is used instead of the run time of the fastest algorithm. The resulting speedup is called the *real speedup*.

$$\text{Real Speedup } (n,p) = \frac{\text{Time to solve using the best serial algorithm}}{\text{Time to solve using } p \text{ processors}}$$

We may define maximum real speedup, minimum real speedup, average real speedup, expected real speedup, and so forth, in the same way as we did for relative speedup.

**Absolute Speedup.** In yet another definition of speedup, the parallel execution time is compared with that of the fastest sequential algorithm run on the fastest serial computer. As in the case of real speedup, in reality, the comparison is done using the serial algorithm that would be used in "practice".

$$\text{Absolute Speedup } (n,p) = \frac{\substack{\text{Time to solve using the best serial program} \\ \text{using the fastest processor}}}{\substack{\text{Time to solve using algorithm} \\ A \text{ and } P \text{ processors}}}$$

The definition of absolute speedup may be extended to maximum absolute speedup, minimum absolute speedup, average absolute speedup, and so on.

**Asymptotic Real Speedup.** Let $S(n)$ be the asymptotic complexity of the best serial algorithm for the problem and let $P(n)$ be the asymptotic complexity of the parallel algorithm $A$ under the assumption that the parallel computer has available to it as many processor as it can gainfully use. The asymptotic real speedup is defined as

$$\text{Asymptotic Real Speedup}(n) = S(n)/P(n)$$

For problems such as sorting, where the asymptotic complexity isn't uniquely characterized by the instance size $n$, we use the worst-case complexity.

**Asymptotic Relative Speedup.** This differs from asymptotic real speedup, in that for the serial complexity, we use the asymptotic time complexity of the parallel algorithm when run on a single processor.

**Cost Normalized Speedup.** Often, in addition to knowing how much faster the parallel system runs, we want to get a measure of the cost at which this improved performance has been accomplished. So, we define a cost normalized speedup (CNS):

$$\text{CNS } (n,p) = \frac{\text{speedup } (n,p)}{(\text{cost of parallel system})/(\text{cost of serial system})}$$

To obtain the cost normalized speedup, we need to know the costs of the parallel and serial systems in addition to the speedup. The cost of the parallel system should include the hardware and software cost. Should it also include the maintenance cost, operating cost, cost of the support personnel, and the like? Because of differences in discounts, the hardware cost varies from installation to installation. The same computer bought a year ago may cost substantially less today. Should we use last year's cost (i.e., its cost to us) or today's (i.e., its replacement cost) or next year's projected cost (i.e., its cost to future purchasers of the system)? Furthermore, the parallel hardware may see a different number of users than the serial hardware, and we may wish to amortize the hardware cost over the users. The software cost may be difficult to determine, unless the software was bought off the shelf (an unlikely scenario in parallel computing, but a possibility in serial computing). Even with software, we have the issue of using total cost over amortized cost—today's cost over tomorrow's cost, amortizing the maintenance cost, factoring in the learning cost, and so forth. The serial system cost depends on the version of speedup in use. So, once we know which version of speedup is in use, the serial system is well defined. However, actually determining the serial system cost to use might be quite difficult. The reasons for this are the same as those for a parallel system. Even though cost normalized speedup appears to be an attractive measure, the difficulties associated with determining the cost to attribute to the parallel and serial systems have prevented this measure from becoming a commonly reported one.

**Efficiency.** Efficiency is a performance metric closely related to speedup. As we have already seen, it is the ratio of speedup and the number of processors $p$. Depending on the variety of speedup used, one gets a different variety of efficiency. Efficiency, like speedup, should not be used as a performance metric independent of run time. The reasons for this are the same as for not using speedup as a metric independent of run time.

Alternate formulations of efficiency can be found in the literature. For example, some authors define efficiency as the ratio of work accomplished ($wa$) by a parallel algorithm and the work expended ($we$) by the algorithm. We define the work accomplished by the parallel algorithm to be the work that would have been done by the "best" serial algorithm. We define the work expended to be the product of the parallel execution time, the speed($s$) of an individual parallel processor, and the number ($p$) of processors. Assuming all processors have the same speed, we have

$$we = (\text{parallel time}) * s * p$$

$$wa = (\text{best sequential time}) * s$$

$$\frac{wa}{we} = \frac{\text{best sequential time}}{p * \text{parallel time}}.$$

This efficiency equals real speedup divided by $p$. So, $wa/we$ equals the real efficiency. Similarly, if *wa* is defined as the work done by the parallel algorithm when executed on a single processor, then *wa/we* equals the relative efficiency (i.e., relative speedup divided by *p*).

Another alternate, but equivalent, formulation of efficiency is provided by defining the wasted work, *ww* to be *we* − *wa*. Then efficiency may be written as

$$\text{efficiency} = \frac{wa}{we} = \frac{wa}{ww + wa} = \frac{1}{1 + ww/wa}$$

***Scalability.*** In the case of many parallel systems (i.e., parallel algorithm–parallel computer combinations), speedup declines when the problem size is fixed and the number of processors is increased and that speedup increases when the number of processor is fixed and the problem size increases. The term *scalability* of a parallel system is used to refer to the change in performance of the parallel system as the problem size and computer size increase. Intuitively, a parallel system is scalable if its performance continue to improve as we scale (i.e., increase) the size of the system (i.e., problem size as well as machine size increase). For details on fundamentals of scalability see Sun.

## 1.7  SUMMARY

In this chapter the concept of parallelism has been introduced. This has been explained with sufficient number of examples that are easy and appropriate. Three different models have been introduced. As the main thrust of this book is not the study of the binary tree or network models, they have not been dealt with elaborately. The PRAM model has been explained with necessary illustrations. Most of the algorithms in this book are for PRAM models. Exclusive and concurrent Read/Write capabilities of the PRAM models have been introduced. For the concurrent write models, in order to resolve the conflict when more than one processor tries to write at the same location, three different methods, ECR, PCR, and ACR have been suggested. The factors that determine the performance of parallel algorithms have been discussed. The notion of speedup and efficiency have been explained. While introducing all these fundamentals, some parallel algorithms have been developed for illustrations.

## BIBLIOGRAPHY

Aho, A., Hopcroft, J., and Ullman, J. (1974) The Design and Analysis of Computer Algorithms, Addison-Wesley, Reading, MA.

Akl, S. G. (1989) The Design and Analysis of Parallel Algorithms, Prentice-Hall, Englewood Cliffs, NJ.

Chaudhuri, P. (1991) Parallel Algorithms, Design and Analysis, Prentice-Hall, Englewood Cliffs, NJ.

Cook, S. A. (1981) Towards Complexity Theory of Synchronous Parallel Computation, L'enseignement Mathematique, **XXVII,** 99–124.

Cole, R. and Zajicek, O. (1989) The APRAM: Incorporating Asynchrony into the PRAM Model, *Proceedings ACM SPA*, 169–178.

Cook, S. A. (1983) Overview of Computational Complexity *Comm. ACM*, **26**(6), 400–409.

Day, K., and Tripathy, A. (1992) Arrangement Graphs: A Class of Generalized Star Graphs, *Information Processing Letters* **42,** 235–241.

Gupta, A. and Kumar, V. (1993) Scalability of Parallel Algorithms for Matrix Multiplication, *Proc. International Conf. on Parallel Processing*, **III,** 115–119.

Hall, D. and Driscoll, M. (1995) Hardware for Fast Global Operations on Multicomputers, *Proc. 9th Intl. Parl. Proc. Symposium*, 673–679.

Helmbold, D. and McDowell, C. (1989) Modeling Speedup($n$) Greater than $n$, *Proc. 1989 International Conf. on Parallel Processing*, **III,** 219–225.

Hwang, K. and Briggs, F. A. (1984) Computer Architecture and Parallel Processing, McGraw-Hill, New York.

Joseph, J. (1992) An Introduction to Parallel Algorithms, Addison-Wesley, Reading, MA.

Kuck, D. J. (1976) Parallel Processing of Ordinary Programs, *Advances in Computers*, **15,** 119–179.

Kuck, D. J. (1977) A Survey of Parallel Machine Organisation and Programming, *ACM Comput. Survey*, **9,** 29–59.

Kung, H. T. (1980) The Structure of Parallel Algorithms, *Advances in Computers*, **19,** 65–112.

Kumar, V., Grama, A., Gupta, A. and Karypis, G. (1994) *Introduction to Parallel Computing*, Benjamin/Cummings, California.

Leighton, T. (1992) Introduction to Parallel Algorithms and Architectures, Morgan Kaufman, California.

Mead, C. A. and Conway, L. A. (1980) *Introduction to VLSI Systems*, Addison-Wesley Reading, MA.

Miller, R. and Stout, Q. F. (1992) *Parallel Algorithms for Regular Architectures*, MIT Press, Cambridge, MA.

Sahni, S. and Thanvantri, V. (1996) "Performance Metrices: Keeping the Focus on Runtime," IEEE-PDT, 1996 (Spring) 43–46.

Stone, H. (1987) *High Performance Computer Architecture*, Addison-Wesley, Reading, MA.

Valiant, L. G. (1982) Parallel Computations, *Proc. 7th IBM Symp. Math. Foundations of Comput. Sci.*

Yoo, Y. B. (1983) Parallel processing for some network optimization problems, Ph.D. dissertation, Washington State University, Pullman, WA.

X. H. Sun and D. Rover, "Scalability of Parallel Algorithm-Machine Combinations," IEEE TPDS, Vol. 5, pp. 599–613, June, 1994.

## EXERCISES

**1.1.** Draw the DAG for the following computations, assuming that the most five processing elements are available to work in parallel.

$$\text{a) } u = \sum_{i=1}^{10} x_i^2$$

$$\text{b) mean} = \frac{1}{10} \sum_{i=1}^{10} x_i$$

**1.2.** Consider the problem of finding the value of the polynomial

$$y = a_{10}x^{10} + a_9x^9 + \cdots + a_3x^3 + a_2x^2 + a^1x + a_0.$$

Assuming that ten processors are available to work in parallel, draw the binary tree model of the computation.

**1.3.** A value $x$ is initially available at one node of a hybercube. Write an algorithm to send this value $x$ to all the other nodes of the hybercube. This problem is called the *message broadcasting problem*.

**1.4.** In a hypercube of dimension $k$, $2^k$ data are available, one in each node. We want to rearrange the data in such a way that the smallest number $s$ in the processor $P_0$, the next smallest in $P_1$, the next in $P_2$, and so on. The highest number must be finally in $p_{n-1}$, where $n = 2^k$. Develop a parallel algorithm for this problem.

**1.5.** Consider array $A(0:n-1)$ of numbers. For a number $x$, rank $(x:A)$ is the number of elements in $A$ which are less than or equal to $x$. Suppose an array $A(0:n-1)$ of numbers are available in the hybercube, such that $A_i$ is in Processor $Pi(0 < i < n)$. The processor $P_0$ also contains a key $X$. Develop an $O(\log n)$ time algorithm that finds rank $(X:A)$ and stores in $P_0$. Assume $n = 2^k$.

**1.6.** Each processor $P_i$ of a hybercube contains a value $a_i$. Develop an $O(\log n)$ time algorithm to find the mean of the array $a_0, a_1, \ldots a_{n-1}$.

**1.7.** What is a ring network? What is its diameter?

**1.8.** What are chordal ring networks? Explain why it is more advantageous than ordinary networks?

**1.9.** What are Barrel Shifter network? Draw a Barrel Shifter network with 15 nodes.

**1.10.** Let $A$ be an upper triangular matrix of order $n \times n$. The back substitution method to solve the equations $AX = B$ begins with finding of the value $x_n$ from the last equation $a_{nn}x_n = b_n$. Then it is substituted to the previous equation to get the value of $x_{n-1}$, and so on. Draw a DAG and give a scheduling when we have $p \leq n$ processors, choosing some specific $p$ and $n$ values.

**1.11.** Develop an $O(n)$ time algorithm to compute the product of two $n \times n$ matrices on a hypercube with $n^2$ processors.

**1.12.** Explain the cube connected cycles network.

**1.13.** What is a star network? What is its main advantage?

**1.14.** Given a sequence of $n = 2^k$ elements of an array stored on a $k$-cube such that the $i^{th}$ element $a_i$ is in the processor $P_i$. Develop an algorithm to determine the number of elements which are less than a specific number $X$, which is also known to all processors.

**1.15.** Solve problem 1.13 on a linear array.

**1.16.** Solve problem 1.14 on a ring network.

**1.17.** Solve problem 1.14 on a Chordal ring network.

## CHAPTER 2

# Data Structures for Parallel Computing

An algorithm is nothing but manipulation of data in a suitably chosen data structure. The underlying data structure is a vital entity in the design and analysis of parallel algorithms. A deep understanding of the structural properties of certain data structures will yield very efficient algorithms for several important classes of problems. Due to the great importance for the data structure, this entire chapter deals with various data structures used in the design and analysis of parallel algorithms. For completeness, all the data structures are discussed. Those who are already familiar with the data structures may skip these topics.

## 2.1 ARRAYS AND LISTS

An *array* usually represents a collection of homogeneous data items. An array is also a list. For example, the marks of ten students are usually represented in the form of an array as follows:

| Student | 1 | 2 | 3 | 4 | 5 | 6 | 7 | 8 | 9 | 10 |
|---------|---|---|---|---|---|---|---|---|---|----|
| Mark | 85 | 90 | 60 | 52 | 71 | 80 | 65 | 53 | 42 | 96 |

In the design and analysis of algorithms, we frequently come across two special types of arrays:

1. Stack; and
2. Queue.

A stack is a one-dimensional data array in which the addition, as well as deletion take place from one end. Suppose a stack contains five data items. Then a designated variable top = 5 denotes that there are five items in the stack and the fifth item is the topmost entity. If anything new has to be added to the stack, it can be added as the sixth item and the top will now become 6.

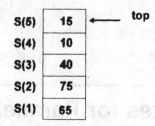

**Figure 2.1** A Stack with five entities.

From a stack with five entities (see Fig. 2.1) if we want to delete one entity, we can remove only the topmost entity. The simple procedure for adding a new entity to a stack is shown below:

**Procedure STACK-ADD(S(1:n), Top,item)**
      BEGIN
         IF top = n then
         call STACK-FULL
         ELSE
         top ← top+1
         S(top) ← item;
         Endif
      END

In the above procedure it is assumed that the maximum capacity of the stack is $n$. If the stack is already full we cannot insert a new item in the stack. So, if top = $n$ we call a procedure STACK-FULL, which (we assume that) will take care of further processing. In a similar way we can write a procedure for deleting one item from the stacks. If top = 0, we assume that the stack is already empty. In this case we cannot delete anything from the stack.

**Procedure STACK-DEL(S(1:n), top, item)**
      BEGIN
         IF top = 0 then
      call STACK-EMPTY
      else
         item S(top)
         top ← top − 1
         Endif
      END

The data structure STACK has numerous applications in the algorithms—both sequential and parallel. The Prefix, Postfix, and Infix representation of arithmetic expression, recursive procedure, scheduling, and polynomial evaluation are some important areas of application of the STACK data structure.

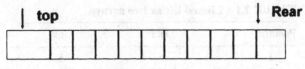

**Figure 2.2** A queue.

The *queue* (see Fig. 2.2) is an array in which the additions take place through one end called *rear* and deletions take place through the other end called *front*. In order to make the queue a convenient data structure for designing algorithms, it is represented in the form of a circular array. We assume that the queue is empty if and only if rear = front. It is easy to design procedures for insertion and deletions in a queue, and so it is left to the reader as an exercise.

## 2.2 LINKED LISTS

The abstract data type called a *list* is a sequential collection of data items, called *atoms*, along with operations to work with the collection. If $a_1, a_2, \ldots, a_n$ are the atoms in a list, then we write the lists as $(a_1, a_2, \ldots, a_n)$. A list differs from a set in that

1. There is an order to the items; and
2. An item may appear more than once, if this is desirable in a given application.

The common operations that one can perform on a list are

1. FIND(item)—check if the item is in the list and in that case tell its position in the list;
2. INSERT(item)—insert an item in the list (usually in a particular location); and
3. DELETE(item)—delete first (or possibly all) occurrences of the item.

The flexibility in the operation definitions is there to accommodate different environments. If there is a way of comparing items $a_i$ and $a_j$, to say that $a_i < a_j$, or $a_i > a_j$, or $a_i = a_j$, then we may define sorted lists. An ascending sorted list is one where $a_i \leq a_{i+1}$ for all $i$.

If a list is implemented by keeping the list atoms in an array, then we have a linear list. A typical linear list representation is in the form of an array $A(0:N)$, where $A(0)$ holds the number of items in the list. Such a representation requires limiting the number of entries to $N$ and is clearly wasteful in the sense that $A(A(0) + 1), \ldots, A(N)$ are unused. To keep a collection of several linear lists is awkward. Say, for example, the lists $(A, B, C, D)$, $(M, N, O)$, and $(W, X, Y, Z)$ are to be kept and the lists are allowed to grow to hold as many as ten entries each. The lists may be thought of in a two-dimensional array $A(0:3, 0:10)$.

**TABLE 2.1  Linked list as two arrays.**

| Position | Data | Link |
|---|---|---|
| 1 | A | 5 |
| 2 | X | 11 |
| 3 | M | 8 |
| 4 | W | 2 |
| 5 | B | 9 |
| 6 | O | 0 |
| 7 | D | 0 |
| 8 | N | 6 |
| 9 | C | 7 |
| 10 | Z | 0 |
| 11 | Y | 10 |

| Name | Pointer |
|---|---|
| One | 1 |
| Two | 3 |
| Three | 4 |

Table 2.1 describes the data structure of the above lists. Now consider holding all three lists in one array with an array of pointers into the array, shown below.

| Name | Size | | | | |
|---|---|---|---|---|---|
| List 1 | 4 | A | B | C | D |
| List 2 | 3 | M | N | O | ... |
| List 3 | 4 | W | X | Y | Z | ... |

| Name | Pointer |
|---|---|
| One | 1 |
| Two | 5 |
| Three | 8 |

The array of pointers is called an *index*. This has the advantage of removing the upper bound on the list length; the only requirement is that the lists do not have a total length greater than the array size. Each list occupies only the space it needs and new lists may be easily added at the end (see Figure 2.3). The problem here is, however, in inserting an item into the lists. The room to insert E in list one to make (A, B, C, D, E) can only be obtained by moving

**Data**

| 1 | 2 | 3 | 4 | 5 | 6 | 7 | 8 | 9 | 10 | 11 | | |
|---|---|---|---|---|---|---|---|---|----|----|--|--|
| A | B | C | D | M | N | O | W | X | Y  | Z  | | |

**Figure 2.3** Continuous list.

other data to the right, as shown Fig. 2.4. Note that even the index must be changed.

| Name | Pointer |
|-------|---------|
| One   | 1       |
| Two   | 6       |
| Three | 9       |

Another problem is that of deleting lists. It is awkward to keep track of free space within this large array. Thus an effective implementation for the maintenance of several lists is not to be found using linear lists.

*Examples of Linked Lists.* An alternative data structure to linear lists which allows for a greater amount of flexibility is the *linked list*. List elements are called *nodes*. A node consists of data and a link to another node in the list. The beginning of the list is indicated by a pointer. If there is a variable holding a pointer to the beginning of a list, it is called the name of the list. A linked list structure for our previous example is given in Table 2.1.

The pointer value 0 written means any value that cannot be used as a link. If we extract the first, second, and third lists, we could draw it as shown in Fig. 2.5. The name of the list structure is ONE.

In particular, the lists can grow to arbitrary length. We may be able to keep several list simultaneously in one area of storage and the only space restriction is that their total storage utilization is less than or equal to the area available.

There is an obvious disadvantage to linked lists in terms of searching. If a linear list is kept in sorted order, then it may be searched with a binary search. Consider the linear list $T$ shown in Fig. 2.6(a) and the equivalent representation in linked lists shown in Fig. 2.6(b).

| A | B | C | D | E | M | N | O | W | X | Y | Z |
|---|---|---|---|---|---|---|---|---|---|---|----|
| 1 | 2 | 3 | 4 | 5 | 6 | 7 | 8 | 9 | 10 | 11 | 12 |

**Figure 2.4** List after inserting E in the first list.

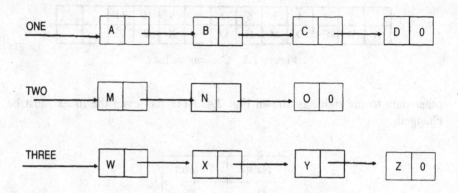

**Figure 2.5** Three linked lists.

The binary search functions can be obtained by computing midpoints of the list. The following discussion describes the binary search process. The midpoint between array elements 1 and 5 in the above linear list is array element 3. But in the linked list there is no way to find the node midway between two other nodes so a binary search is impossible.

*Circular Lists.* In *circular lists* the pointer cell of the last node is not null. It points the first node. This is shown in Fig. 2.7(a).

*Doubly Linked List.* The basic difficulty of a linked list or circular list is that we may only move in one direction. To move in both directions we introduce

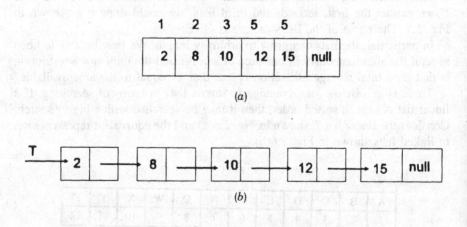

**Figure 2.6(a)** A list. **(b)** Linked list.

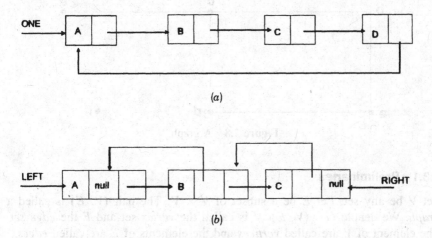

**Figure 2.7(a)**  Circular linked list. **(b)** Doubly linked list.

the concept of *doubly linked list*. The nodes in a doubly linked list have two links, LLINK, for left link and RLINK for right link, and every list has pointers to the left end and right end. Thus a typical doubly linked list looks like the structure shown in Fig. 2.7(b).

Note that there is one linked list found by following RLINK to a node and another list can be found by following LLINK to a node. It is particularly easy to delete a node in a linked list. The links allow you to find all different nodes. Suppose a node $X$ has left and right adjacent nodes.

The node $X$ may be deleted by the following instructions:

$$RLINK(LLINK(X)) = RLINK(X)$$
$$LLINK(RLINK(X)) = LLINK(X)$$

This is seen to produce the following doubly linked list structure, which effectively bypasses $X$. The two lists in the doubly linked list may themselves be circular.

To insert a node containing a desired data item, we first must get an unused node. For this purpose we keep a special linked list called the *free list*, which holds nodes that are not currently used. Such a list may be initialized when memory is first allocated for nodes.

## 2.3  GRAPHS AND TREES

This section introduces an important data structure, the graph model, and explains various types of graphs and some properties which are used in later chapter.

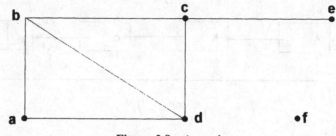

**Figure 2.8**   A graph.

### 2.3.1 Preliminaries

Let $V$ be any set. Let $E$ be a subset of $V \times V$. The pair $(V, E)$ is called a *graph*. We denote $G = (V, E)$. $V$ is called the *vertex* set and $E$ the *edge set*. The element of $V$ are called *vertices* and the elements of $E$ are called *edges*.

Let $V = \{a, b, c, d, e, f\}$ $E = \{(a, b), (b, c), (c, d), (c, e), (a, d), (b, d)\}$. The graph $G = (V, E)$ can be represented by the Fig. 2.8. If $e = (v_1, v_2)$ is an edge, then we say that *e incidents* on $v_1$ and $v_2$. In such case $v_1$ and $v_2$ are said to be *adjacent* vertices. An edge $(v, v)$ is called a *self edge*. If $e_1 = (v_1, v_2)$ and $e_2 = (v_1, v_2)$, then $e_1$ and $e_2$ are said to be *parallel edges*. A graph having no *parallel edge* and no self edge is called a *simple graph*. If the vertex set is an infinite set then the graph is called an *infinite graph*. Otherwise the graph is said to be a *finite graph*. A graph may have its edge set to be empty. Such a graph is called a *null graph*. A vertex in which no edge incidents is called an *isolated vertex*. The number of edges incident on a vertex $v$ is called the *degree* of $v$. In the graph represented in Fig. 2.8, $f$ is an isolated vertex.

The degrees of the vertices are given below.

| Vertex | $a$ | $b$ | $c$ | $d$ | $e$ | $f$ |
|--------|-----|-----|-----|-----|-----|-----|
| degree | 2   | 3   | 3   | 3   | 1   | 0   |

A vertex whose degree is 1 is called a *pendant vertex*. In our graph $e$ is a pendant vertex. We usually denote the number of vertices and the number of edges by $n$ and $m$, respectively. We are interested in the sum of the degrees of all the vertices. Each edge incidents on two vertices; so the presence of each edge contributes 2 to sum of the degrees. Hence we have the following observations:

1. *The sum of the degrees of all the vertices is 2 m.*
2. *The number of vertices of odd degree is always even.*

**Regular and Complete Graphs.** A graph in which all the vertices are of equal degree is called a *regular graph*. If a simple graph has $n$ vertices, at the

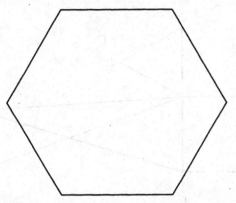

**Figure 2.9**   A regular graph of degree 2.

most $n(n-1)/2$ edges are possible. A graph with all possible edges is called a *complete graph*. $K_n$ denotes a complete graph with $n$ vertices (and $n(n-1)/2$ edges). Notice that $K_n$ is a regular graph of degree $n-1$. This is illustrated in Figs. 2.9 and 2.10.

**Walk, Path, Cycle.** Let $G = (V, E)$ be a simple graph. Let $v_1$, $v_2$, $v_3$, $v_4$ ... , $v_k$ be some vertices of $G$, and $v_i$ is adjacent to $v_{i+1}(1 \le i \le k)$. We say that this sequence $v_1, v_2 \ldots v_k$ is a walk from $v_1$ to $v_k$ if no edge appears more than once in the sequence. $v_1$ is called the *starting* point and $v_k$ is called the *terminus*. In the above definition of a walk some $v_i$ and $v_j$ may be the same for distinct $i$ and $j$. Consider a walk $v_1, v_2, \ldots v_k$. We say that the walk starts from $v_1$, travels through $v_2, v_3, \ldots v_{k-1}$, and finally reaches $v_k$. If $v_1 = v_k$ the walk is called a *closed walk*. A walk which is not closed is said to be *open*. A walk in which no vertex appears more than once is called a *path*. A closed walk in which no vertex appears more than once is called a *cycle* or *circuit*. In other words, a circuit is a closed path.

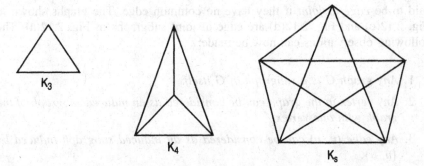

**Figure 2.10**   Some completed graphs.

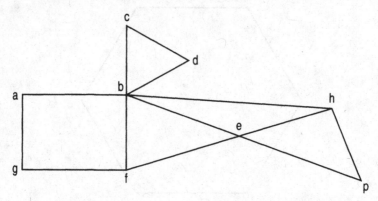

**Figure 2.11**   A graph to illustrate paths and walks.

In Fig. 2.11, a, b, c, d, b, e, f, is a walk. It is not a path because b is repeated a, b, c, d, is a path from a to d. Also note that c, b, e, p, h, e, b, d is neither a path nor a walk. It is not a walk because the edge (b, e) appears twice in the sequence (once from b to e and then from e to b). a, b, e, f, g, a is a cycle. In a cycle an edge joining two nonconsecutive vertices is called a *chord*. In the cycle a, b, e, f, g, a in Fig. 2.11, (b, f) is a chord of the cycle a, b, e, f, g, a.

**Subgraph.** Let $G = (V, E)$ be a graph. Let $V'$ be a subset of $V$ and $E'$ a subset of $E$ such that all the edges in $E'$ incident only on vertices of $V'$. $G' = (V', E')$ is called a *subgraph* of G. The graph shown in Fig. 2.12 (b) is a subgraph of the graph in Fig. 2.12(a). In a graph G, for any two vertices u and v if there is a path from u to v, the graph G is called a *connected graph*. In a disconnected graph, a maximal connected subgraph is called a *connected component* or *component*. Let $V'$ be a subset of V. Let $E'$ be the collection of all edges of G, which have both end vertices in $V'$. $G' = (V', E')$ is called the *induced subgraph* of G induced by $V'$. The graph in Fig. 2.12(b) is not an induced subgraph of Fig. 2.12(a). The graph in Fig. 2.12(c) and Fig. 2.12(d) are induced subgraphs, induced by {1,5,4} and {2,3,4}, respectively. Two subgraphs are said to be *edge disjoint* if they have no common edge. The graphs shown in Fig. 2.12(c) and Fig. 2.12(d) are edge disjoint subgraphs of Fig. 2.12(a). The following observations can now be made:

1. *Any graph G is a subgraph of G itself.*
2. *Any vertex in the graph can be considered as an induced subgraph of the graph with one vertex.*
3. *Any edge (u, v) can be considered as an induced subgraph induced by {u, v}.*
4. *The relation "subgraph of" is reflexive, antisymmetric and transitive.*

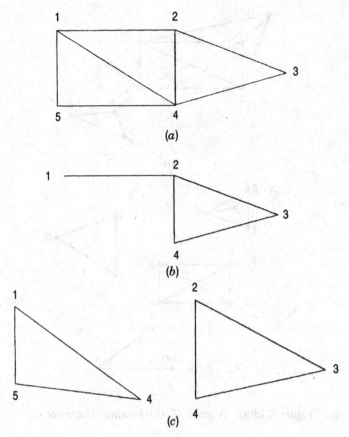

**Figure 2.12(a)**   A graph $G$. **(b)** A subgraph $G$. **(c)** Subgraph induced by $\{1,4,5\}$.

**Homeomorphism.** Let $G$ be a graph. Let $v_1$, $v_2$, $v_3$, be a path and the degree of $v_2$ is 2 in $G$. $(v_1, v_2)$ and $(v_2, v_3)$ are called *series edges*. The operation of replacing the two edges $(v_1, v_2)$, and $(v_2, v_3)$, by a single edge $(v_1, v_3)$ and removing the vertex $v_2$ is called the *merging* of series edges. If $(u, v)$ is an edge, the operation of introducing a new vertex $w$ and making it adjacent to both $u$ and $v$ and then removing the original edge $(u, v)$ is called *insertion of a vertex of degree 2*. Two graphs $G_1$ and $G_2$ are said to be *homeomorphic* if one can be obtained from the other using finite number of operations merging of series edges and/or insertion of a vertex of degree 2.

A complete subgraph is called a *clique*. A clique that is not a subgraph of any other clique is called a *maximal clique*. Consider the graph shown in Fig. 2.13(a). Its maximal clique are shown in Fig. 2.13(b).

**Isomorphism.** Two graphs $G = (V, E)$ and $G' = (V', E')$ are said to be *isomorphic* if there is a bijection between $V$ and $V'$ in such a way that two vertices

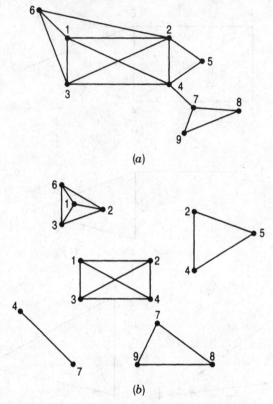

**Figure 2.13(a)**   A graph $G$. **(b)** Maximal cliques of $G$.

of $V$ are adjacent if and only if the corresponding vertices in $V'$ are adjacent. If two graphs are isomorphic to each other,

1. They have equal number of vertices.
2. They have equl number of edges.
3. They have equal number of vertices with the given degree.

Notice that the above three conditions are necessary but not sufficient. It is an interesting research problem to find simple and efficient criterion to check whether two given graphs are isomorphic. This problem is called the *isomorphism problem*.

### 2.3.2   Euler and Hamiltonian Graphs

This section introduces two special types of graphs that have applications in various fields. The Euler graphs were defined by Euler, who defined the graph models motivated by the famous Konigsberg bridge problem.

For a graph $G = (V, E)$, a closed walk traversing every edge of the graph (exactly once) is called *Euler line* or *Euler's Walk*. There are graphs that do not contain *Euler line*. For example, the complete graphs with four vertices $K_4$ do not have a Euler line. A graph that has a Euler line is called a *Euler's graph*.

**THEOREM 2.3.1 (Euler's Theorem)** *A connected graph is Euler if and only if the degree of every vertex is even.*

The proof of the theorem is not difficult. Since the walk is closed and every edge must be traversed exactly once, whenever the walk reaches a vertex through one edge it must depart from the vertex through another edge. Euler's theorem follows from this fact. The following theorem can also be proved easily from the definition of Euler line.

**THEOREM 2.3.2** *A graph is Euler if and only if its edges set E can be partitioned as $E = E_1 \cup E_2 \cup \ldots \cup E_k$ such that each $E_i$ constitutes a cycle.*

An open walk traversing all the edges once and only once is called an *open Euler line* or *unicursal line*. A graph having a Unicursal line is called a *unicursal graph*. It is easy to verify the following theorem.

**THEOREM 2.3.3** *A graph is unicursal if and only if it contains exactly two vertices of odd degree.*

A sequential polynomial algorithm to check whether a graph is Euler can be developed using Theorem 2.3.1. We can check whether the degree of each vertex is even. If the degree of each vertex is even, we shall conclude that the graph is Euler. Similarly a polynomial algorithm to check whether a graph is unicursal can be developed counting the number of vertices of odd degree.

**Hamiltonian Graphs.** A closed walk traversing every vertex once and only once is called a *Hamiltonian circuit*. This definition resembles the Euler's line definition, except that a Euler line traverses the edges exactly once, but the Hamiltonian circuit traverses the vertices exactly once. $K_4$ is Hamiltonian, but not Eulerian. IF $C_1$ and $C_2$ are two circuits having exactly one common vertex, then $C_1 \cup C_2$ is Eulerian, but not Hamiltonian. The necessary and sufficient condition for the existence of a Euler line for a connected graph has been given in Theorem 2.3.1 and Theorem 2.3.2. However, the necessary and sufficient condition for the existence of a Hamiltonian circuit for a connected graph is still unsolved. Though the problem has the origin from the Irish mathematician Sir William Rowan Hamilton in 1859, it still remains open.

### 2.3.3 Trees

A connected graph having no cycles is called a *tree*. The following statements are equivalent.

1. $G$ is a tree.
2. There is exactly one path between any two vertices of $G$.
3. $G$ is connected and it contains $n$ vertices and $n - 1$ edges.
4. $G$ is minimally connected.
5. $G$ has no cycles and $G$ has $n$ vertices and $n - 1$ edges.

Any tree has at least two pendant vertices. The length of a path is the number of edges it has. The length of the longest path from a vertex $v$ to any other vertex is called the *eccentricity* or *diameter* of $v$ and is denoted by $E(v)$.

$$E(v) = \text{Max}\{d(v, u)/u \in V\},$$

where $d(v, u)$ represents the length of the path from $v$ to $u$. In a tree $T$, the vertex having minimum eccentricity is called a $v$ to $u$ *center* of the tree. A tree contains one or two centers. In Fig. 2.14(a), the eccentricities of all the vertices are given. 3 and 5 are the vertices that have the minimum eccentricity. So, this graph has two centers, 3 and 5. The eccentricity of the center is called the *radius* of the tree. The length of the longest path in the tree is called the

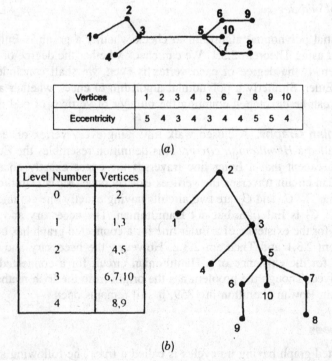

| Vertices | 1 | 2 | 3 | 4 | 5 | 6 | 7 | 8 | 9 | 10 |
|---|---|---|---|---|---|---|---|---|---|---|
| Eccentricity | 5 | 4 | 3 | 4 | 3 | 4 | 4 | 5 | 5 | 4 |

(a)

| Level Number | Vertices |
|---|---|
| 0 | 2 |
| 1 | 1,3 |
| 2 | 4,5 |
| 3 | 6,7,10 |
| 4 | 8,9 |

(b)

**Figure 2.14(a)**   Tree with radius = 3 and diameter = 5. **(b)** A rooted tree.

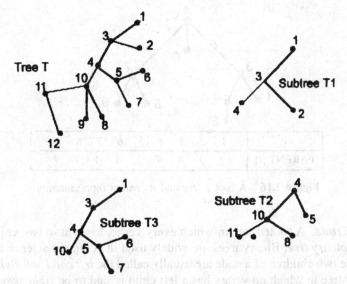

**Figure 2.15** A tree and some of its subtrees.

*diameter* of the tree. For the tree given in Fig. 2.14(a), the radius is 3 and the diameter is 5. We can designate a vertex of the tree as its root. If a vertex is designated as the *root* of the tree, the tree is called a *rooted tree.*

Consider the tree given in Fig. 2.14(a). If we designate 2 as the root of the tree, the tree can be redrawn, as in Fig. 2.14(b). For a rooted tree, *level numbers* can be defined to each of the vertices as follows: The root is assigned level number 0. The vertices adjacent to the root are called the *children of the root,* and they are assigned the level number 1. The root is called the *parent of its children.*

In our tree 1 and 3 are the children of 2. IF a vertex $v$ is at level $i$, any other adjacent vertex $u$ which is not the parent of $v$ is assigned level $i + 1$. Such a node will be called a *child* of $v$. If the maximum level number of a rooted tree is $k$ then its height or depth is defined to be $k + 1$.

The tree in Fig. 2.14(b) is of height 5. A connected subgraph of a tree is called a *subtree.* Figure 2.15 shows a tree and some of its subtrees. A rooted tree is usually represented by its parent relation. IF $T = (V, E)$ is rooted tree with root $r$, it is represented by the array PARENT (1 :n) (n is the number of vertices) defined by

PARENT($i$) = the parent of $i$, if $i$ is not the root.

PARENT($r$) = $r$, where, $r$ is the root.

In some cases the PARENT of the root is defined as $-1$. A tree and its PARENT representation are shown in Fig. 2.16.

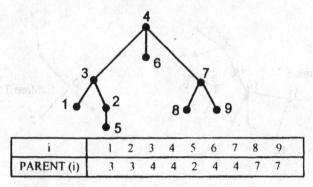

| i | 1 | 2 | 3 | 4 | 5 | 6 | 7 | 8 | 9 |
|---|---|---|---|---|---|---|---|---|---|
| PARENT (i) | 3 | 3 | 4 | 4 | 2 | 4 | 4 | 7 | 7 |

**Figure 2.16**   A root a tree and its parent representation.

**Binary Trees.** A rooted tree in which every vertex has atmost two children is called a *binary tree*. Binary trees are widely used in computer science applications. The two children of a node are usually called the *left child* and *right child*. A binary tree in which no vertex has a left child is said to be *right skewed*. We define a left-skewed binary tree similarly. Figure 2.17 shows a *left-skewed* and *right-skewed* binary tree. Consider the binary tree shown in Fig. 2.18. In level number 0, the root alone is there. In level 1, there are two vertices. In level number 2 there are 4 vertices, and in level number 3 there are 8 vertices. This observation leads to the following theorem.

**THEOREM 2.3.5**

a) *In binary tree there are at the most $2^i$ vertices at level $i$;*

b) *The maximum number of vertices in a tree of height $k$ is $2^k - 1$.*

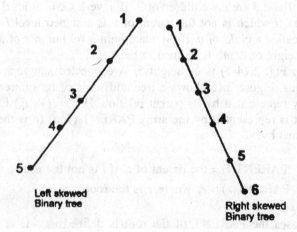

Left skewed
Binary tree

Right skewed
Binary tree

**Figure 2.17**   Skewed binary trees.

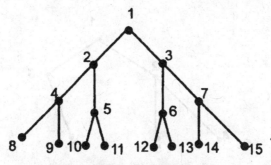

**Figure 2.18** A full binary tree.

*Proof.* The proof of (a) is on induction on the level number the result is true for $i = 0$. If the result is true for a level $i$, there are at most $2^i$ vertices in level $i$. Each of those vertices can produce at the most two children for the level $i + 1$. So, the maximum numbers of vertices at the level $i + 1$ is $2^{i+1}$. Hence the result (a) follows by induction on $i$. The proof of (b) is based on the following numerical result

$$2^0 + 2^1 + 2^2 \ldots + 2^{k-1} = 2^k - 1$$

A tree of height $k$ with all the $2^k - 1$ nodes is called a *full binary tree*. In a full binary tree nodes can be numbered serially as follows: The root is assigned the serial number 1. The nodes at level 1 are numbered as 2 and 3 from left to right. After assigning serial numbers for all the nodes at level $i - 1$, the consecutive numbers are assigned for all the nodes at level $i$ from left to right. In Fig. 2.18, a full binary tree of height 3 and the serial numbering of its vertices are given. The following theorem can be easily verified for any full binary tree.

**THEOREM 2.3.6** *In a full binary tree serially numbered,*

  a) *The left child of node i is 2i.*
  b) *The right child of node i is 2i + 1.*
  c) *The parent of i is [i/2].*

In a full binary tree, if some highest numbered vertices are removed, it is called a *complete binary tree*. Figure 2.19(a) shows a complete binary tree. Figure 2.19(b) is a full binary tree and Figure 2.19(c) is not a complete binary tree. In a complete binary tree the numbering is continuous and coincides with the numbering of the full binary tree of the same height. Theorem 2.3.6. holds for any complete binary tree. Consider a binary tree in which every pendant vertex is assigned a positive weight. Let $l_i$ and $w_i$ denote the level number

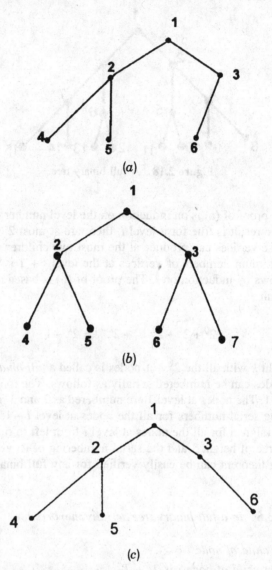

**Figure 2.19(a)** A complete binary tree. **(b)** A full binary tree. **(c)** An incomplete binary tree.

and weight of a pendant vertex. Consider the sum $\sum l_i w_i$, where the sum is taken over all pendant vertices. This sum is called the *weighted path length*. For example, consider the binary tree shown in Fig. 2.20. It has 6 pendant vertices $d$, $q$, $g$, $p$, $r$, and $f$. They are given and weights 5, 10, 7, 3, 4, and 8, respectively. The weights and the level numbers are shown in the following table.

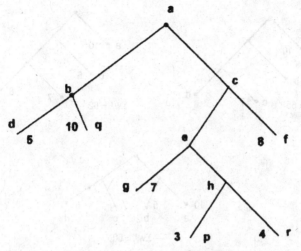

**Figure 2.20**   A tree with weighted path length = 95.

| Pendent Vertex | Weight | Level No. | $l_i w_i$ |
|:---:|:---:|:---:|:---:|
| $d$ | 5 | 2 | 10 |
| $q$ | 10 | 2 | 20 |
| $g$ | 7 | 3 | 21 |
| $p$ | 3 | 4 | 12 |
| $r$ | 4 | 4 | 16 |
| $f$ | 8 | 2 | 16 |
| | | $\sum l_i w_i$ | 95 |

Given $n$ pendant vertices and their weights, construction of a binary tree which minimizes the weighted path length is an interesting problem. It has applications in decision tree and optimal code construction problems. Some binary trees and their weighted path lengths are shown in Fig. 2.21.

**Spanning Trees.**   Let $G = (V, E)$ be a connected simple graph. A cycle-free, connected subgraph $T = (V, E')$ with all the vertices of $G$ is called a *spanning tree*. A graph $G$ and some of its spanning trees are shown in Figs. 2.22(a) to 2.22(d).

Consider six cities, which are shown in Fig. 2.23(a). The distance between the cities are represented by the weight of the edges. If a communication network has to be installed among the cities, it is sufficient if we establish the link along the edges of the spanning tree shown in Fig. 2.23(b). The cost of installation of the communication wires between two cities is proportional to

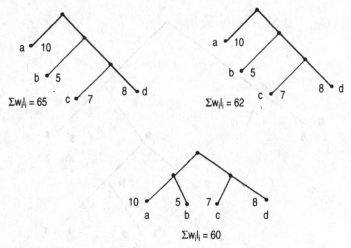

**Figure 2.21**   Some binary trees and their weighted path lengths.

the cost of the distance between them and, hence, the cost of the edge in the graph. So, the total cost of installation is proportional to the sum of the weights of the edges. So we must find the spanning tree that has its sum of the weights of the edges minimum. We define the weight of the spanning tree as the sum of the weights of the its edges. Given an undirected graph, finding the *minimum weight spanning tree* is a very interesting problem. The minimum weight spanning tree is also called the *minimum cost spanning tree* or *shortest spanning tree*. Every connected graph has a spanning tree of G. T has $n-1$ edges. These $n-1$ edges of the tree are called the *branches*. The non-tree edges are called the *chords*. If G is a disconnected graph, it has more than one component. In this case, we can find one spanning subtree for each component and the collection of such spanning subtrees are called the *spanning forest* of G. Figure 2.25 shows a *spanning forest* of the disconnected graph given in Fig. 2.24.

Let G be a graph with $n$ vertices, $m$ edges, and $c$ components. The spanning forest of G contains $n-c$ branches and there are $m-n+c$ chords. We define the *rank of the graph* as the number of branches and the *nullity of the graph* as the number of chords. For the graph shown in Fig. 2.25(a), $n = 15$, $m = 18$, $c = 3$,

$$rank = n - c = 15 - 3 = 12;$$
$$nullity = m - n + c = 18 - 15 + 3 = 6.$$

Notice that rank + nullity = number of edges. Also observe that for a connected graph, $n-1$ is the rank and $m-n+1$ is the nullity. Consider a connected graph G and a spanning tree T. Let $e$ be a chord. If we include $e$ in T, it will create a cycle. Let the cycle be

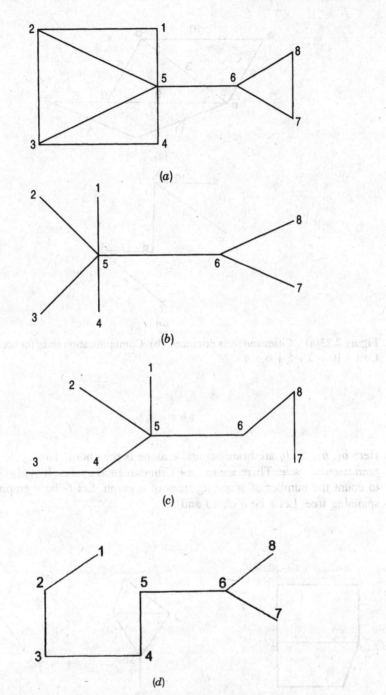

**Figure 2.22(a)** A graph G. **(b)** Spanning Tree $T_1$. **(c)** Spanning tree $T_2$. **(d)** Spanning tree $T_3$.

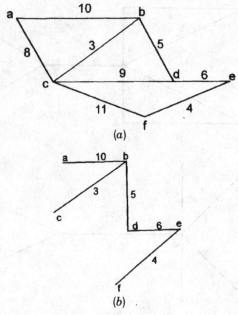

**Figure 2.23(a)** Cities and their distances. **(b)** Communication links for six cities. Total Cost = 10 + 3 + 5 + 6 + 4 = 28.

$$eb_1 b_2 \ldots b_t.$$

Here $b_1, b_2, \ldots b_t$ are branches and $e$ alone is the chord. This cycle is called a *fundamental cycle*. There are $m - n + 1$ fundamental cycles. It is also interesting to count the number of spanning trees of a graph. Let $G$ be a graph and $T$ its spanning tree. Let $e$ be a chord and

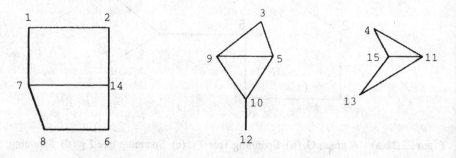

**Figure 2.24** A disconnected graph $G$.

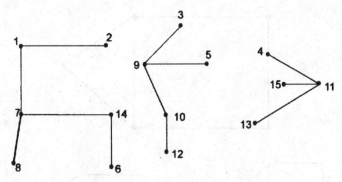

**Figure 2.25**   A spanning forest of $G$.

$$eb_1 b_2 \ldots b_t$$

be its fundamental cycle. By including $e$ to $T$ and removing from $T$ any $b_i$ we get a different spanning tree (call it $\{T_i(e)\}$). For every chord $e$ we can find these spanning trees $\{T_i(e), i = 1, 2, \ldots, t\}$. It is observed that any spanning tree can be obtained by repeating this operation on the given spanning tree $T$. A graph $G$ and all its spanning trees are given in Figs. 2.26(a) through 2.26(c). The operation, including a chord to the spanning tree and deleting a branch from its fundamental circuit, is called *cycle interchange*. It is noted that, given any two spanning trees $T_1$ and $T_2$ of the same graph $G$, one can be obtained from the other by a finite number of cycle interchanges. The number of cycle interchanges needed to get one spanning tree from the other is equal to the number of edges in one spanning tree that are not in the other.

We define

$$d(T_1, T_2) = \text{number of cycle interchanges needed to get } T_2 \text{ from } T_1$$
$$= \text{number of edges in } T_1 \text{ which are not in } T_2.$$

We can also observe that $d(T_1, T_2)$ satisfies the following properties for a metric:

1. $d(T_1, T_2) \geq 0$ and $d(T_1, T_2) = 0$ if and only if $T_1 = T_2$.
2. $d(T_1, T_2) = d(T_2, T_1)$.
3. $d(T_1, T_2) < d(T_1, T_3) + d(T_3 + T_2)$ for any spanning tree $T_3$ other than $T_1$ or $T_2$.

Also, $d(T_1, T_2)$ cannot exceed rank of the graph or nullity of the graph. Let $G$ be a connected graph and $T$ be the collection of all the spanning trees of $G$. A graph can be formulated using $T$ as a vertex set. Let the graph be denoted

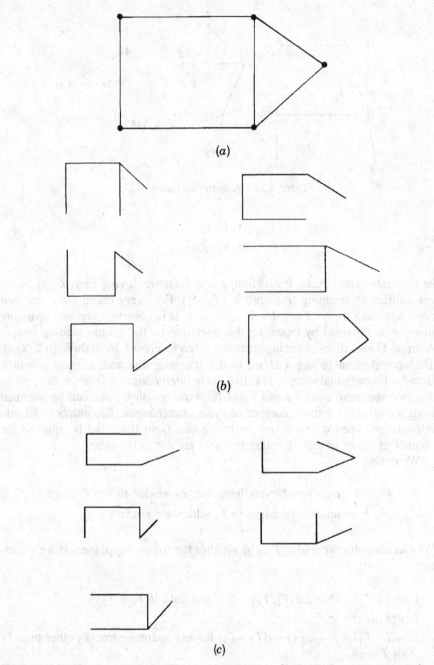

**Figure 2.26(a)**   A graph $G$. **(b)** Some spanning trees of $G$. **(c)** Some more spanning trees of $G$.

by $G_T = (T, E_T)$, where two vertices $T_1$ and $T_2$ or $T$ are joined by an edge if and only if $d(T_1, T_2) = 1$. The graph $G_T$ is called the *tree graph* of $G$.

### 2.3.4 Graph Traversal

In order to visit all the vertices of a graph, there must be some systematic way so that no vertex is left unvisited. There are two methods for traversing the vertices:

1. Breadth First Search (BFS); and
2. Depth First Search (DFS).

For traversing the graph, the starting vertex is known. Let $v$ be the starting vertex. The BFS starts by visiting the vertex $v$. After visiting $v$, all its adjacent vertices are visited in some defined order. Let the adjacent vertices of $v$, be $v_1 v_2$, ... $v_d$. After visiting these vertices, we must visit all the unvisited vertices that are adjacent to these vertices. The procedure is repeated until all the vertices of the graph are visited. In the depth first search technique, we start from $v$. Then we visit an adjacent vertex $v_1$ of $v$. Now visit an unvisited vertex adjacent to $v_1$. At some stage, if $v_i$ has no unvisited vertex adjacent to it, backtrack and come to $v_{i-1}$ and visit an unvisited vertex adjacent to it. The procedure is repeated until we backtrack to $v$ and all its adjacent vertices are visited. The traversal forms a spanning tree for $G$. A graph $G$, its BFS spanning tree, and its DFS spanning trees are shown in Figs. 2.27(a) to 2.27(c). In the BFS spanning tree

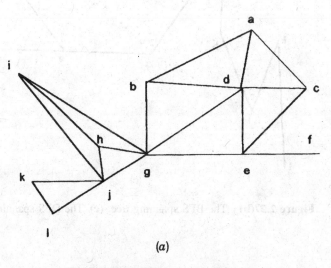

(a)

**Figure 2.27(a)** A graph.

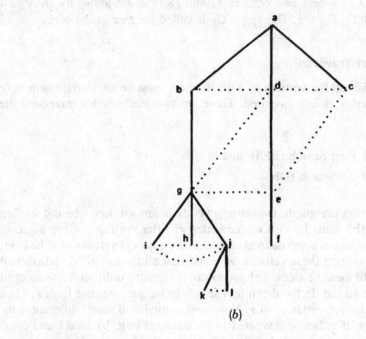

(b)

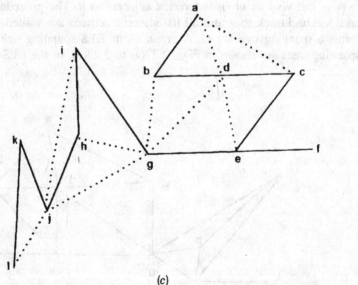

(c)

**Figure 2.27(b)** The BFS spanning tree. **(c)** The DFS spanning tree.

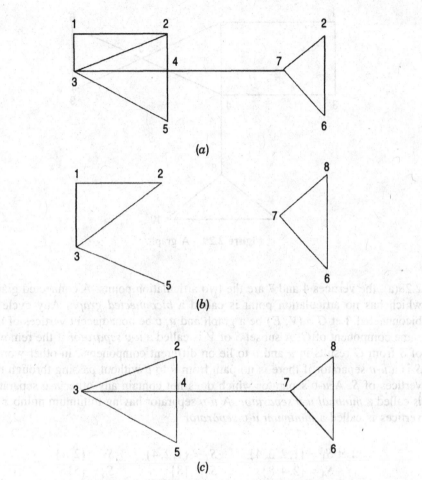

**Figure 2.28(a)** Graph $G$. (b) Graph $G$-4. (c) Graph $G$-1.

the dotted lines represent the chords and the bold lines are the branches. In the BFS spanning tree notice that every chord joins vertices either at the same level or at consecutive levels. This property can be effectively used to solve several problems in graph theory.

## 2.3.5 Connectivity

If $G = (V, E)$ is a graph and $v \in V$, $G - v$ represents the graph induced by $V - \{v\}$. This is illustrated in Figs. 2.28(a) to 2.28(c). Let $G = (V, E)$ be a graph with $k$ components, $a \in V$. If $G - a$ has more than $k$ components, $a$ is called an *articulation point*. In a connected graph a vertex whose removal disconnects the graph is called an articulation point. In the graph shown in Fig.

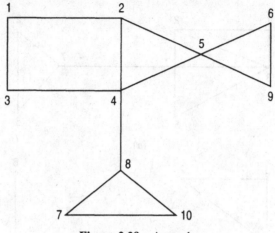

**Figure 2.29**   A graph.

2.28(a), the vertices 4 and 7 are the two articulation points. A connected graph which has no articulation point is called a *biconnected graph*. Any cycle is biconnected. Let $G = (V, E)$ be a graph and $u, v$ be nonadjacent vertices of the same component of $G$. A subset $S$ of $V$ is called a *u-v separator* if the removal of $S$ from $G$ results in $u$ and $v$ to lie on different components. In other words, $S$ is a *u-v* separator if there is no path from $u$ to $v$ without passing through the vertices of $S$. A *u-v* separator which does not contain any other *u-v* separator is called a *minimal u-v separator*. A *u-v* separator having minimum number of vertices is called a *minimum u-v-separator*.

$$\text{Let } S_1 = \{1, 2, 3, 4\} \qquad S_2 = \{1, 2, 4\} \qquad S_3 = \{2, 4\}$$
$$S_4 = \{2, 4, 8\} \qquad S_5 = \{8\} \qquad S_6 = \{5\}$$

Each of $S_1, S_2, S_3, S_4, S_5$, and $S_6$ is a 7-6 separator in the graph $G$ of Fig. 2.29. But $S_3$ is a minimal 7-6 separator. Similarly $S_5$ and $S_6$ are also minimal 7-6 separator. $S_5 = \{8\}$ and $S_6 = \{5\}$ are two minimum 7-6 separators.

Let $G = (V, E)$ be a connected graph; $S$ be a subset of $V$. If $G-S$ is disconnected, $S$ is called a *separator* of $G$. A separator $S$ is called a *minimal separator* if whenever, $S'$ is subset of $S$, $S'$ is not a separator. A minimal separator of minimum cardinality is called a *minimum separator*. The cardinality of a minimum separator is defined to be the vertex connectivity of the graph. In other words the *vertex connectivity* of a connected graph is the minimum number of vertices to be removed from the graph, in order to make the remaining graph disconnected. Notice that if a graph has an articulation point, the vertex connectivity of the graph is 1. A graph with vertex connectivity 1 is called a *separable graph*. A nonseparable graph is also called a *biconnected graph*. For a *biconnected graph* the vertex connectivity is at least 2. A connected graph with vertex connectivity

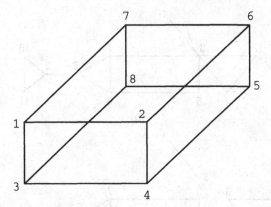

**Figure 2.30** A triconnected graph.

of at least 3 is called a *triconnected graph*. In other words, a triconnected graph is a connected graph in which the removal of any one or two vertices does not make it disconnected. Observe that any triconnected graph is biconnected and a biconnected graph is connected. A connected graph with vertex connectivity at least $k$ is said to be *k-connected* ($k$ is a positive integer). The following results immediately follow:

1. *A connected graph is biconnected if and only if for any two vertices u and v, there are at least two edge disjoint paths from u to v.*

2. *A connected graph is triconnected if and only if for two vertices u and v, there are at least three edge disjoint paths from u to v.*

3. *A connected graph is k-connected if and only if for any two vertices u and v there are at least k edge disjoint paths from u to v.*

The graph shown in Figs. 2.28(a) and 2.29 are connected, but not biconnected. Any cycle $C_n$ is biconnected. Figure 2.30 shows a triconnected graph. If $d$ denotes the minimum degree in a graph $G$, vertex connectivity of $G$ is at the most $d$.

We have already seen that a disconnected graph has more than one connected component. (A connected component is a maximal connected subgraph.) Similarly, we are defining the biconnected component as a maximal biconnected subgraph of the graph. If the graph itself is biconnected, there is only one biconnected component. Otherwise, the biconnected components can be found. Figure 2.31(b) shows the biconnected components of the graph shown in Fig. 2.31(a). The biconnected components are also called *blocks*. A graph $G$ in which every *block* is a complete subgraph is called a *block graph*. Figure 2.32(a) shows a block graph. The biconnected components of a graph $G$ can be found by the following operation:

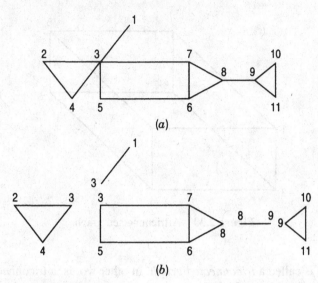

**Figure 2.31(a)** A graph $G$ which is connected but not biconnected. **(b)** Biconnected components of $G$.

1. If $G$ has no articulation point, $G$ itself is the only biconnected component.
2. For every articulation point $a \in V$ do the following: Let $V_1, V_2, V_3 \ldots V_S$ denote the sets of vertices in the different components of $G - \{a\}$. Let $G_i$ = graph induced by $V_i \cup \{a\}(i = 1,2,3, \ldots s)$.

These definitions and procedures can be generalized for $k$-connected components ($k \geq 2$). A block graph can be represented by its Block-Cut vertex tree representation (BC-tree). For example, consider the block graph shown in Fig. 2.32(a). Its blocks are

$$B_1 = \{1, 2\}, \; B_2 = \{2, 3, 4, 5\}, \; B_3 = \{5, 6, 7\}, \; B_4 = \{5, 9\}, \; B_5 = \{5, 8\}$$
$$B_6 = \{8, 10\}, \; B_7 = \{10, 11\}, \; B_8 = \{10, 12, 13\}, \; B_9 = \{4, 14\}$$

The cut-vertices are 2,4,5,8, and 10. The vertex set of the BC-tree consists of the blocks and the cut vertices. A block and a cut vertex are joined by an edge only when the vertex is contained in the block. The BC-tree of the block graph depicted in Fig. 2.32(a) is given in Figure 2.32(b).

## 2.3.6 Planar Graphs

The graph $G$ has been defined as a pair of two sets $V$ and $E$, where $V$ is any (nonempty) set and $E$ is a subset of $V \times V$. Any graph can be pictorially represented in more than one way. Figure 2.33 shows some pictorial representation of the graph $G = (V, E)$, where

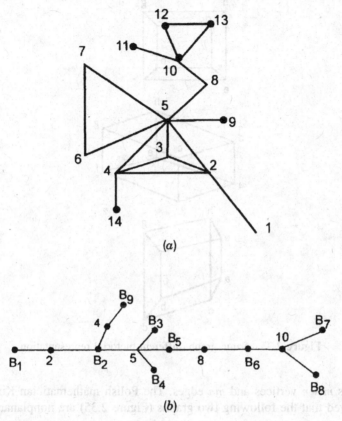

**Figure 2.32(a)** Block graph. **(b)** The BC-tree of block graph shown in Fig. 2.32(a).

$$V = \{a, b, c, d, e, f, g, h\}$$
$$E = \{(a, b), (b, c), (c, d), (d, a), (e, f), (f, g), (g, h), (h, e), (a, e), (b, f),$$
$$(c, g), (d, h)\}$$

The interest is to draw a graph on the two-dimensional plane so that no two edges intersect each other. It is evident that we cannot draw all the graphs in the plane in such a way that no two edges intersect. A graph is said to be *planar* if it can be drawn in a two-dimensional plane without its edges intersecting. Figure 2.34 shows some simple examples of planar graphs. A graph $G = (V, E)$ is said to be bipartite if $V$ can be partitioned into $V_1$ and $V_2$, such that every edge of $G$ joins a vertex of $V_1$ and a vertex of $V_2$. Notice that a bipartite graph contains no cycle of odd length. A complete bipartite graph is a bipartite graph in which every vertex of $V_1$ is adjacent to all the vertices of $V_2$. A complete bipartite graph with $m$ vertices in $V_1$ and $n$ vertices in $V_2$ is denoted by $K_{m,n}$. Notice that

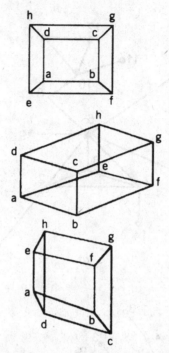

**Figure 2.33** Same graph, different pictorial representation.

$K_{m,n}$ has $m + n$ vertices and $mn$ edges. The Polish mathematician Kuratowski has proved that the following two graphs (Figure 2.35) are nonplanar.

1. The complete graph with 5 vertices ($K_5$).
2. The complete bipartite graph $K_{3,3}$.

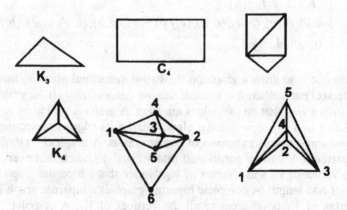

**Figure 2.34** Some planar graphs.

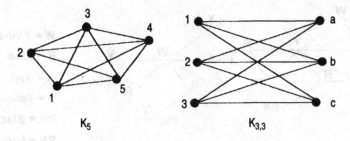

**Figure 2.35** Kuratowski's graphs.

Observe that both the Kuratowski's graphs are regular, and nonplanar. Also notice that they are minimal nonplanar graphs with respect to the number of vertices, as well as the number of edges.

Consider the planar graph $G$ drawn in a plane (without its edges intersecting). The graph divides the plane into several regions. Figure 2.36 shows a planar graph and the region $R_1, R_2 \ldots R_6$.

It is easy to observe the following results:

1. *Any simple planar graph can be embedded in a plane such that every edge is drawn as a straight line segment.*

2. *A planar graph can be embedded in a plane such that any specified region can be made the infinite region.*

3. *Any planar graph can be embedded in a sphere and any graph that can be embedded in a sphere is a planar graph.*

If $G$ is a connected planar graph with $n$ vertices and $m$ edges, then it generates $m - n + 2$ regions. For example, in Fig. 2.36, $n = 13$, $m = 17$, and the number of regions is $m - n + 2 = 17 - 13 + 2 = 6$. Also, we can prove that, for a planar

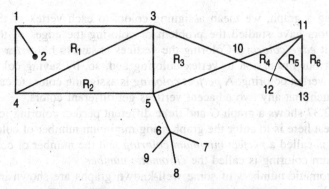

**Figure 2.36** A planar graph with six regions.

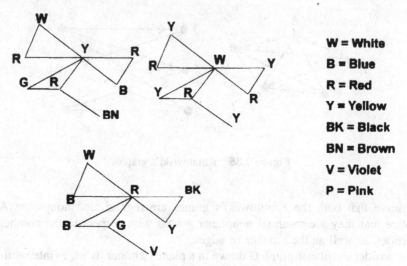

| | |
|---|---|
| **W** = White | |
| **B** = Blue | |
| **R** = Red | |
| **Y** = Yellow | |
| **BK** = Black | |
| **BN** = Brown | |
| **V** = Violet | |
| **P** = Pink | |

**Figure 2.37**   A graph with three perfect colorings.

graph, $m \leq 3n-6$. This is a necessary condition, but not sufficient. Kuratowski's second graph is a nonplanar graph, satisfying this condition. A necessary and sufficient condition for a graph $G$ to be planar is that $G$ does not contain either of Kuratowski's two graphs or any other graph homeomorphic to either of them. An *outerplanar graph* is a planar graph that has a planar embedding in which all the vertices of the graph lie on the exterior region (infinite region). A *maximal outer planar (mop)* graph is an outer planar graph in which addition of an edge between any pair of nonadjacent vertices result in a nonouterplanar graph. A mop graph is Hamiltonian.

### 2.3.7   Coloring and Independence

By *coloring* a graph, we mean assigning colors to each vertex of the graph. Some authors have studied the problem of coloring the edges of the graph. They call it *edge coloring*. Coloring the vertices is said to be *vertex coloring*. We restrict our discussion to vertex coloring and, so, by saying coloring, we mean only vertex coloring. A *perfect coloring* is assigning colors to each of the vertices, such that any two adjacent vertices get different colors.

Figure 2.37 shows a graph $G$ and three different perfect coloring for $G$. The main interest here is to color the graph using minimum number of colors. Such a coloring is called a *perfect minimum coloring* and the number of colors used for minimum coloring is called the *chromatic number*.

The chromatic numbers of some well-known graphs are shown in the following table:

| S. No | Graph | Chromatic Number |
|-------|-------|------------------|
| 1 | $K_n$ | $n$ |
| 2 | Tree | 2 |
| 3 | A graph with no edge | 1 |
| 4 | A cycle of even length | 2 |
| 5 | A cycle of odd length | 3 |
| 6 | Bipartite graph | 2 |

A complete subgraph is called a *clique*. A clique $C$ with $r$ vertices, is called an *r-clique*. A clique $C$ is said to be *maximal* if there exists no other clique that properly contains $C$. The maximal clique of the greatest cardinality is called the *maximum clique*. The number of vertices in the maximum clique is called the *clique number*. In order to color an $r$-clique, we need $r$ colors. So, chromatic number $\geq$ clique number.

### 2.3.8  Clique Covering

A *clique cover* of a graph $G = (V, E)$ is a partition of $V$ into $V_1, V_2, \ldots, V_k$, such that each $V_i$ is a clique. We show here two different clique covering of the graph $G$ shown in Fig. 2.38.

**Clique covering 1:**

$V_1 = \{1\}$
$V_2 = \{10\}$
$V_3 = \{2, 8, 9\}$
$V_4 = \{6, 7\}$
$V_5 = \{3, 4, 5\}$

**Clique covering 2:**

$V_1 = \{1, 2\}$
$V_2 = \{3, 4, 5\}$
$V_3 = \{6, 7, 8\}$
$V_4 = \{9, 10\}$

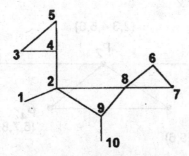

**Figure 2.38**   A graph with clique covering $\{1, 2\}$, $\{3, 4, 5\}$, $\{6, 7, 8\}$, $\{9, 10\}$.

The *size of a clique* cover $\{V_1, V_2, \ldots V_k\}$ refers to the number of partitioned sets $k$. The clique cover of minimum size is called the *minimum clique cover*. A set of vertices $X$ of a graph $G = (V, E)$ is called an *independent set* if any two vertices of $X$ are not adjacent in $G$. Independent sets are also called *stable sets*. A maximal independent an $V$ set is an independent set $X$, where $X \cup \{v\}$ is not independent set for any vertex $v$ not in $X$. The maximal independent set of largest cardinality is called the *maximum independent set*.

For the graph shown in Figure 2.38, some independent sets are shown below:

$$X_1 = \{1, 4, 8, 10\} \qquad X_2 = \{1, 10, 6, 3\} \qquad X_3 = \{8, 4\} \qquad X_4 = \{1, 7, 10\}$$

Among these, $X_1$ and $X_2$ are maximum independent sets. All the vertices of an independent set can be colored with the same color. Each vertex of a clique needs to be colored with a distinct color.

### 2.3.9   Intersection Graph

Let F be a family of subsets. From the family F, we construct a graph $G = (V, E)$ as follows: The vertex set $V$ has one–one correspondence with F. Two vertices of $V$ are adjacent if and only if the corresponding subsets in F have a nonempty intersection. The graph $G$ constructed in this manner from $P$ is called the *intersection graph of* F.

Let $F = \{P_1, P_2, P_3, P_4, P_5\}$, where $P_1 = \{1, 2, 3\}$, $P_2 = \{2, 3, 4, 5, 6\}$, $P_3 = \{5, 6\}$, $P_4 = \{6, 7, 8, 9\}$, and $P_5 = \{4, 10\}$. The intersection graph of F is shown in Fig. 2.39. Let $(v_1, v_2, \ldots v_k, v_1)$ be a cycle of a graph. Any edge joining two nonconsecutive vertices $V_i$ and $V_j$ is called a *chord*.

### 2.3.10   Chordal Graphs

A vertex $x$ is said to be *simplicial* if ADJ$(x)$, which is the collection of all vertices that are adjacent to $x$, is a clique. A graph is *chordal* if every simple cycle of length greater than three has a chord. An ordering of the vertices $v_1, v_2, \ldots, v_n$ is called a *perfect elimination ordering* (PEO) or *perfect elimination scheme*

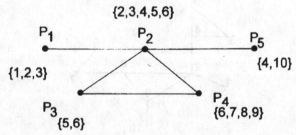

**Figure 2.39**   Intersection graph of $F = \{P_1, P_2, P_3, P_4, P_5\}$.

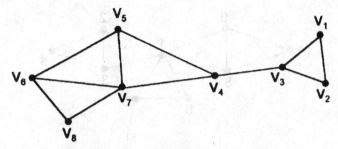

**Figure 2.40** A chordal graph and a PEO.

(PES) if and only if $v_i$ is simplicial in the graph induced by $\{v_i, v_{i+1}, \ldots v_n\}$ for all $i$. For example, a chordal graph $G$ and one PEO are shown in Fig. 2.40.

In this graph, $\{v_5, v_7, v_8\}$ is a $v_4-v_6$ separator and $\{v_5, v_7\}$ is a minimal $v_4 v_6$ separator. Let $A = \{1\}$, $B = \{1\}$, $C = \{1,2\}$, $D = \{2,3\}$, $E = \{3,4\}$, $F = \{4,5\}$, $G = \{3,4,5\}$, and $H = \{5\}$. Consider the family of set $\mathsf{F} = \{A, B, C, D, E, F, G, H\}$. The intersection graph of $\mathsf{F}$ is the graph given in Fig. 2.40, with the association $v_1 = A$, $v_2 = B$, $v_3 = C$, $v_4 = D$, $v_5 = E$, $v_6 = F$, $v_7 = G$, and $v_8 = H$.

Chordal graphs are intersection graphs of subtrees of a tree. That is to say, there is an undirected tree $T$, a family of subtrees $\mathsf{F} = \{S_1, S_2, \ldots S_n\}$, and a bijection from $\mathsf{F}$ to $V$ with the property that two vertices are adjacent in $G$, if and only if their corresponding subtrees share a common node. Given a chordal graph $G$, this tree $T$ can be constructed by assigning the vertex set of $T$ isomorphic to the collection of maximal cliques of $G$ and formulating the edges in such a way that, for every vertex $v$ of $G$, the nodes corresponding to the cliques containing $v$ induce a subtree in $T$. The tree thus constructed is called a *clique tree* of chordal graph $G$. For example, consider the chordal graph $G$ shown in Fig. 2.41(a). The graph has vertex set $V = \{1,2,3,4,5,6,7,8,9,10\}$. The maximal cliques are $C_1 = \{1,2,3\}$, $C_2 = \{2,3,4\}$, $C_3 = \{1,5,6\}$, $C_4 = \{5,7\}$, $C_5 = \{1,8,9\}$, and $C_6 = \{8,9,10\}$. The clique tree of $G$ is shown in Fig. 2.41(b). Chordal graphs have application in various fields, including solution of sparse systems of linear equations, study of evolutionary trees, facility location problems, and acyclic relational database theory. The following characterizations are well known for chordal graphs.

**THEOREM 2.3.10.1.** *The following are equivalent:*

1. *$G$ is Chordal.*
2. *$G$ has a PEO.*
3. *$G$ can be obtained by the following recursive construction rules:*
   a. *Start with any clique as the base graph. A clique is a chordal graph.*
   b. *To a chordal graph H, add a new vertex and make it adjacent to a clique subgraph of H.*

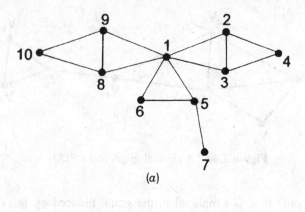

(a)

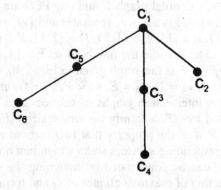

**Figure 2.41(a)** A chordal graph G. **(b)** A clique tree of G.

4. *Every minimal separator of G induces a clique in G.*

5. *G is the intersection graph of subtrees of a tree.*

6. *Every induced subgraph of G is either a clique or contains two nonadjacent simplicial vertices.*

7. *Every connected induced subgraph of G with two or more vertices contains at most n − 1 cliques.*

The sequential algorithms for chordal graph recognition make use of various procedures called *PEO schemes* to generate a PEO if it exists.

The following are some such PEO schemes in the literature:

1. Lexicographic Breadth First Search (LBFS).

2. Maximum Cardinality Search (MCS).

3. Maximal Element in Component (MEC).

4. Maximum Cardinality neighbourhood in Component (MCC)

The following theorem establishes the importance of the PEO schemes in the recognition of chordal graphs.

**THEOREM 2.3.10.2** *A graph G is chordal if and only if an ordering of the vertices of G, generated by any of the PEO schemes LBFS, MCS, MEC, and MCC is a PEO. Furthermore, G can be so tested for chordality in $O(m + n)$ times.*

Thus the PEO has emerged as the key technique in sequential algorithms for chordal graphs and its study has yielded important algorithmic ideas in the sequential realm. However, the researchers in parallel algorithms largely abandoned the use of PEO. Chandrasekhar and Iyengar have given an NC parallel algorithm to recognize chordal graphs using the minimal clique separators. Edenbrandt has also given a similar approach for this problem. However, NC parallel algorithms for PEO have been given by Naor, Naor, and Schäffer, and independently by Dahlhaus and Karpinski. Both these algorithms require $O(n^4)$ processors. Klein has given a better algorithm for the problem, which works in $O(\log^2 n)$ time, using only linear number of processors in CRCW PRAM.

*Path Graphs.* The intersection graph representation of the chordal graphs has motivated the researchers to study some more classes of intersection graphs. Monma and Wei have studied several classes of intersection graphs arising from families of paths in a tree. A path is called a *vertex path* if it is considered as a collection of vertices. Two vertex paths are said to have a nonempty intersection if they have a common vertex. A path, considered as a collection of edges, is called an *edge path*. The intersection of two edge paths is nonempty if the paths have a common edge. The intersection graph of a family of undirected vertex paths in an undirected tree is called an *undirected vertex path graph* or *UV graph*. In the terminology of Monma and Wei, the tree can be directed, or rooted-directed, giving rise to directed, undirected, or rooted-directed graphs, respectively. Thus six types of path graphs are possible, because of the three ways of directing the tree and two different ways of considering paths (vertex path or edge path). They are

1. Directed vertex path graph (DV graph);
2. Undirected vertex path graph (UV graph);
3. Rooted-directed vertex path graph (RDV graph);
4. Directed edge path graph (DE graph);
5. Undirected edge path graph (UE graph); and
6. Rooted-directed edge path graph (RDE graph).

Monma and Wei showed that any graph in these six classes can be represented by an appropriate type of clique tree, whose nodes are labeled with cliques of G. A linear time-sequential algorithm was given by Dietz to recognize RDV graphs. In order to recognize UV graphs, Gavril gave the first algorithm, which works on the intersection representation in $O(n^4)$ time. A faster algorithm to recognize UV graphs in $O(mn)$ time was given by Scäffer. An NC parallel algorithm to recognize UV graphs has been given by Xavier.

**Interval Graphs.** A graph is said to be an *interval graph* if it is the intersection graph of a family of intervals along the real line. The following theorem characterizes interval graphs.

**THEOREM 2.3.10.3**    *The following are equivalent:*

   a. *G is an interval graph.*
   b. *G is the intersection graph of a collection of intervals of the real line.*
   c. *G is a chordal graph and its maximal cliques can be linearly ordered, such that for every vertex x of G, the maximal cliques containing x occur consecutively.*

Figure 2.42 shows an interval graph, its interval representation, and the linear ordering of its maximal cliques. It's maximal cliques are $C_1 = \{a, b, c\}$, $C_2 = \{c, d, g\}$, $C_3 = \{c, e, g\}$, and $C_4 = \{c, f, g\}$. Booth and Lucker demonstrated that the interval graph recognition can be done sequentially in $O(m + n)$ time. They introduced a data structure called *PQ-tree* (see Fig. 2.43). The PQ-tree is a very useful data structure, which can represent all possible linear orientations of the maximal cliques of an interval graph. A PQ-tree is a rooted-oriented tree, which has three types of nodes.

   1. *Leaves:* The leaves of a PQ-tree are the elements under processing. In a interval graph recognition, the leaves represent the maximal cliques of the graph.
   2. *P-nodes:* The P-nodes are internal nodes that have at least two children and are represented by circles.
   3. *Q-nodes:* These Q nodes are internal nodes that have at least two children and are represented by rectangles.

Two PQ-trees $T$ and $T'$ are equivalent (denoted by $T \equiv T'$ if there is a sequence composed of the following transformations, which turns $T$ into $T'$.

   1. Arbitrarily permute the order of the children of a P-node.
   2. Reverse the order of the children of a Q-node.

Clearly $\in$ is an equivalence relation. For any ordered tree $T$, the *frontier* of a node $v$ of $T$ is defined to be the sequence of leaves that are descendants of $v$, where a leaf $a$ occurs before leaf $b$ in the sequence, if and only if there is a common ancestor $c$ of $a$ and $b$, such that the child of $c$ on the path from before the child of $c$ on the path from $c$ to $b$. In other words, the frontier of a vertex $v$ is

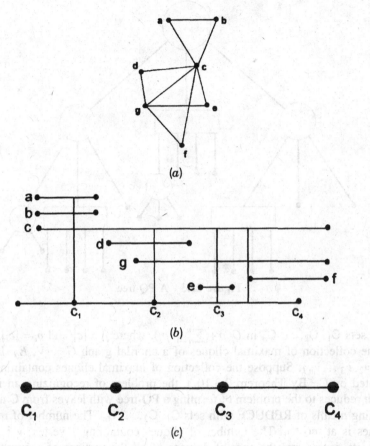

**Figure 2.42(a)** Interval graph $G$. **(b)** Interval representation of $G$. **(c)** Linear ordering of maximal of $G$.

the sequence of leaves visited by a traversal of the subtree rooted at $\nu$. If $T$ is an ordered tree, then FRONTIER($T$) = FRONTIER(root($T$)). We define, for a PQ-tree $T$, CONSISTENT($T$) = {FRONTIER($T'$): $T' \in T$}. That is, CONSISTENT of $T$ is the collection of all possible sequence of leaves represented by the PQ-tree $T$. Now we have the following result, which can be easily verified:

**THEOREM 2.3.10.3**    *If $Z$ and $Z'$ are PQ-trees, and $Z \equiv Z'$, if and only if CONSISTENT($Z$) = CONSISTENT($Z'$).*

Let $T$ be a PQ-tree, whose leaf nodes are elements of a set C. Let C' be a subset of C. Booth and Lueker have given a procedure REDUCE, such that CONSISTENT (REDUCE($T$, $C'$)) = {$\sigma \in$ CONSISTENT($T$): the members of C are consecutive in $\sigma$}. They have also shown that REDUCE can be called

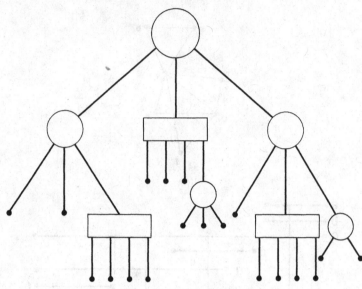

**Figure 2.43** A PQ-tree.

on $n$ sets $C_1$, $C_2$, ... $C_n$ in $O(p + \sum_{i=1}^{n} p_i)$, where $p = |c|$ and $p_i = |c_i|$. Let $C$ be the collection of maximal cliques of a chordal graph $G = (V, E)$. Let $V = \{v_1, v_2, v_3 \dots v_n\}$. Suppose the collection of maximal cliques containing $v_i$ be denoted by $C_i$. By Theorem 2.3.10.3, the problem of recognizing an interval graph reduces to the problem of forming a PQ-tree with leaves from $C$ and performing $n$ calls of REDUCE with sets $C_1$, $C_2$, ... $C_n$. The number of maximal cliques is at most $n$. The number of cliques containing a vertex, $v$ is, at the most, its degree and the sum of degrees of all the vertices of a graph is $2m$. The maximal cliques of a chordal graph can be found in $O(m + n)$ time. Hence an interval graph can be recognized in $O(m + n)$, time sequentially.

Klein and Reif designed another operation—MREDUCE $(\{C_1, C_2, \dots C_k\})$, which reduces the PQ-tree $T$, with respect to all the sets $C_i$ simultaneously. They have also given a parallel implementation for the case where the $C_i$ are pairwise disjoint. Their algorithm runs in $O(\log n)$ time, using $O(n)$ processors.

### 2.3.11  Some More Intersection Graphs

Scheinerman has characterized the class of intersection graphs. He defines a graph operation called *vertex expansion*. A Graph $G$ with vertex $v$ expanded is the same graph as $G$, except it also contains a new vertex $v'$, which is adjacent to $v$ and to every neighbor of $v$. We state his result as follows:

**THEOREM 2.3.11.1**  F *is a class of intersection graphs if and only if all the following hold:*

   i. *F is hereditary; that is, every induced subgraph of a graph in F is also in F.*

   ii. *F is closed under vertex expansion.*

   iii. *If $G_1$ and $G_2$ are in F, then there is a graph $G \in F$, such that $G_1$ and $G_2$ are induced subgraphs of G. The vertex sets of $G_1$ and $G_2$ may intersect.*

A graph $G$ is said to be *perfect* if, for every induced subgraph $H$, the size of the maximum independent set and the size of the minimum clique cover are equal. Several intersection graphs such as interval graphs, UV graphs, RDV graphs, and chordal graphs are perfect. In this section we review some more intersection graphs.

**Circle Graphs.** Circle graphs are intersection graphs of a family of chords in a circle. The problem of recognizing circle graphs efficiently was open for many years and solved by three groups of independent researchers at nearly the same time.

**Parity and Distance–Hereditary Graphs.** If for every pair of vertices $a$ and $b$ in $G$, all the induced paths from $a$ to $b$ have the same length, then we call $G$ a distance–hereditary graph. An induced path from a vertex $a$ to $b$ is said to be of *even parity* if it is of even length. Similarly an odd *parity path* is defined. In a graph $G$, for any two vertices $a$, $b$ if all the induced paths between $a$ and $b$ are of same parity then $G$ is called a *parity graph*. By Theorem 2.3.11.1, both the graphs defined above are intersection graphs.

**Circular-Arc Graphs.** The intersection graph of a set of arcs of a circle is called a *circular-arc graph*. Every interval graph is a circular-arc graph. However, there are *circular arc graphs* that are not even chordal graphs.

### 2.3.12 Matching Problems in Graphs

Given a graph $G = (V, E)$, a *matching* is a set of edges $M$, such that no two edges in $M$ incident on the same vertex. If an edge $(u, v) \in M$, we say that $u$ and $v$ are matched in $M$. A *maximal matching* is a matching that is not properly contained in another matching. A matching with maximum number of edges is called a *maximum matching*. A *perfect matching* of $G = (V, E)$ is a matching $M$, which matches all the vertices of $G$ except possibly one. That is, $M$ is a perfect matching if and only if $|M| = [n/2]$. A perfect matching does not exist for some graphs. When the edges of the graph have associated weights, we can define the *cost of the matching* as the sum of the costs of edges in $M$. When a perfect matching exists, one may be interested in finding the perfect matching with minimum cost (or maximum cost). The matching problem has applications in several situations. Workers may be matched to jobs, machines to parts, players to teams, and so forth.

Wu and Manber have introduced a generalization of the matching problem. Let $G = (V, E)$ be a weighted graph. A *path-matching* in $G$ is a set of simple paths with distinct end vertices. Thus a matching is a special case of a path-matching, in which all the paths consist exactly of one edge.

A path matching $P$ of $G$ is said to be *perfect* if $|P| = [n/2]$. If $G$ contains odd number of vertices, a perfect path-matching leaves exactly one vertex unmatched. If $G$ has even number of vertices, all the elements of $G$ are matched in a perfect path-matching. A path-matching $P$ of $G$ in which any two matching paths are edge disjoint is called an *edge disjoint path matching*. Wu and Manber have proved that.

**LEMMA 2.3.11.2**   *Every undirected graph has at least one edge disjoint perfect path matching.*

As an application of path matching, let us assume that $G$ models a network of computers, such that each vertex corresponds to a computer and each edge corresponds to a link of communication. Each link is associated with a cost (e.g., load, tariff, delay). Suppose further that we want to organize a tournament among the computers, such that each computer is paired with another one and they perform some competition together. The competition may correspond to some computation task in which both computers are involved. A path represents the pairing of the computers corresponding to the end vertices. We now list some variations of the path matching problem.

**Min-Sum Path Matching.** Let $G = (V, E)$ be a weighted graph and $P$ be a perfect path matching of $G$. The cost of a path is the sum of the weights of all the edges in the path. The sum of all the costs of the paths in $P$ is called the *cost-sum* of $P$. The problem of finding the perfect path matching with minimum cost sum is called the *Min-Sum Path Matching Problem*. Assume an $O(n)$ sequential algorithm to find the min-sum path matching for trees. For general graphs, there is a min-sum path matching that contains only paths with, at most, two edges each. This can be obtained by computing all shortest paths (with at most two edges) and finding a minimum matching.

**Min-Max Path Matching.** The max-cost of a perfect path matching $P$ is the maximum cost of paths in $P$. The perfect path matching, which has minimum max-cost, is called the *min-max perfect path matching*. This problem is also called the *bottle-neck problem*. We call the edge disjoint perfect path matching *DP-Matching*. Wu and Manber have given an $O(n \log d \log w)$ time-sequential algorithm to find the min-max DP-Matching for integer weighted trees, where $d$ is the maximum degree of a vertex and $w$ is the maximum cost of an edge. Xavier (1995) has given a parallel algorithm for finding the min-max DP-matchings of a tree.

## 2.3.13 Centrality in Graphs

The distance between two vertices $u$ and $v$ of a graph $G$ is the minimum number of edges in a path from $u$ to $v$ and is denoted by $d(u, v)$. If $G$ is a weighted graph, then $d(u, v)$ is the length of the shortest path from $u$ to $v$. The *distance* of a vertex $v$ is defined to be the sum of distances from $v$, to all the vertices and is denoted by $d(v)$. That is,

$$d(v) = \sum_{u \in V} d(v, u)$$

Each vertex of $G$, which has minimum distance, is called a *median* of $G$. Each tree contains either one or two medians and, if two, then they are adjacent.

A *branch* at vertex $v$ of a tree $T$ is a maximal subtree containing $v$ as a leaf node. The *branch weight* of a vertex $v$, denoted by $B(v)$, is defined to be the maximum number of edges in any branch at $v$. Equivalently, the branch weight of a vertex $v$ is the maximum number of vertices in any component of $T - v$. Each vertex of $T$, at which the branch weight function is minimized, is called a *centroid* of $T$. For any tree $T$, a vertex is a median if and only if it is a centroid.

The problem of finding the center, median, and centroid, have applications in facility location problem. For example, suppose the vertices of a graph $G$ represent several villages and the edges represent the roads connecting them. The weights of the edges represent the distance between the villages. Suppose we want to select a village for constructing a hospital for the use of all the villages. Evidently, if we select a center of $G$ for the hospital site, we can minimize the maximum distance to be traveled by a patient. If the vertices represent the various branch offices of a company and the management wants to locate a vertex for the venue of the annual meeting, we may be interested in choosing a median, because it will minimize the total travel allowance to be paid to the branch managers. Slater has proposed to generalize these concepts, so that the facility is located in a structure instead of a single vertex. He has proposed the central path structures.

***Central Path.*** The distance from a vertex $v$ to a path $P$ is defined as

$$d(v, P) = \text{Min}\{d(v, u)/u \in P\}.$$

The eccentricity of a path $P$ is defined as

$$e(P) = \text{Max}\{d(v, P)/v \in V\}.$$

A path $P$ with minimum eccentricity is called a *central path* if any other path with the same minimum eccentricity is longer than $P$. The distance sum of a path $P$ is defined as

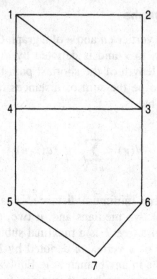

**Figure 2.44** A graph $G$.

$$d(P) = \sum_{v \in V} d(v, P).$$

A path with minimum distance sum is called a *core* of $G$. NC parallel algorithms to find the core of a tree network has been given by two independent group of researchers.

## 2.3.14 Domination Theory

Consider a graph $G = (V, E)$. A set of vertices $D$ is called a *dominating* set of $G$, if every vertex not in $D$ is adjacent to some element of $D$. We say that $D$ is dominating the graph $G$. Consider the graph shown in Fig. 2.44. Two of its dominating sets are $D_1 = \{1, 4, 7\}$ and $D_2 = \{1, 5\}$.

This has a number of very different types of applications. Consider a company having seven executives. If the interpersonal relationship between two executives $i$ and $j$ is good, we draw an edge between $i$ and $j$. Consider the graph shown in Fig. 2.44, which represents the interpersonal relationship among the seven executives of the company.

Suppose the company wants to appoint a committee to execute a project which needs the cooperation of the seven executives of the company. Then the members in the committee must have good relationships with the people not in the committee. In other words, for every person not in the committee, there must be at least one person in the committee who is having good relationship with the former. So the committee is a dominating set.

The *minimal dominating* set is a dominating set that does not contain any other dominating set. The *minimum dominating* set is minimal dominating set of least cardinality. The cardinality of the minimum dominating set is called the *domination number* of the graph. Notice that every maximal independent set is a dominating set. If a dominating set is a cycle, it is called a *dominating cycle*. Similarly, a *complete (independent) dominating* set is a dominating set that is also complete (independent). The strong domination number of a graph $G = (V, E)$ is the least integer $s$, for which every set of $s$ vertices of $G$ is a dominating set.

A set of vertices $D$ is said to be a *k-dominating set* (where $k$ is a positive integer) if each $v$ in $V$-$D$ is adjacent to at least $k$ members of $D$. If $(x, y)$ is an edge such that degree of $x \geq$ degree of $y$, then we say that $x$ *strongly dominates* $y$ and $y$ *weakly dominates* $x$. The concept of strong and weak domination also appears in the literature. A dominating set that has no isolated vertex is called a *total dominating* set. In other words, a subset $D$ of $V$ is called a total dominating set if every vertex of $G$ is adjacent to at least one vertex of $D$. A domatic partition of $G = (V, E)$ is a partition of $V$, all of whose classes are dominating sets in $G$. The maximum number of classes of a domatic partition of $G$ is called the *domatic number* of $G$. This concept has been introduced and studied by Cockayne and Hedetnemi (1977). Neeralagi (1988) has defined the odd (even) dominating set of a graph $G = (V, E)$, as a set of vertices $D$, such that every vertex in $V$-$D$ is at an odd (even) distance from some vertex in $D$.

Slater, Banger, and Barkauskas have studied the concept of efficient domination. A set $D$ of vertices in a graph $G = (V, E)$ is an *efficient dominating set* if every vertex $u$ in $V$-$D$ is adjacent to exactly one vertex in Cockayne et al. (1988) also has studied efficient domination in graphs.

## 2.3.15 Some Graph Problems

This section introduces some graph problems, for which algorithms are studied in the literature.

1. **Maximum Independent set problem.** Find the maximum independent sets of the graph $G$.
2. **Minimum Coloring Problem.** Find the chromatic number of the graph.
3. **Maximum Clique Problem.** Find a clique of maximum size in the given graph $G$.
4. **Minimum Clique Cover Problem.** Find a minimum clique cover of the given graph $G$.
5. **Isomorphism Problem.** Given two graphs $G$ and $G'$, verify whether $G$ and $G'$ are isomorphic.
6. **Subgraph Isomorphism Problem.** Given two graphs $G$ and $G'$, where

G has more vertices than $G'$, verify whether $G$ has any induced subgraph isomorphic to $G'$.

7. **Maximal Common Subgraph Problem.** Let $G$, $G'$ be two graphs. It is obvious that $G$ as well as $G'$ have subgraphs isomorphic to $K_2$. If $G''$ is a graph such that $G$ and $G'$ have induced subgraphs isomorphic to $G''$, we say that $G''$ is a *common subgraph* of $G$ and $G'$. Given $G$ and $G'$, find the common subgraph of $G$ and $G'$, containing maximum number of vertices.

8. **Hamiltonian Problem.** Verify whether a graph $G$ has a Hamiltonian circuit.

9. **Domination Problems.** Given a graph $G$, find a minimal dominating set, total dominating set, dominating cycle, connected dominating set, dominating clique, etc.

10. **Connected Components.** Given a graph $G$, verify whether $G$ is connected; if $G$ is not connected, find the connected components of $G$. Similarly verifying whether a graph is biconnected and, if not, find the biconnected components of $G$.

11. **Matching Problem.** Given a graph $G$, the problem of finding the maximum matching is called the matching problem.

12. **Path Matching Problems.** The problem of finding the path matching with minimum cost is one variation of the problem. The problem of minimizing the maximum weight of the paths in the path matching is another variation of the problem.

13. **Longest Path Problem.** Find the longest simple path in the given graph. In a tree, the longest path is also called the *diameter*.

14. **Core and Two Core.** The core of a weighted graph is a path which minimizes the sum of the distances of all the vertices from the path. Two-core is a pair of paths which minimizes the sum of the distances of all the vertices from anyone of the paths.

15. **Path Covering Problem.** A path covering of a graph $G$ is a collection of simple paths, such that each vertex of $V$ is in a path. Find the minimum number of paths to cover the graph.

16. **Recognition Problems.** Restricted classes of graphs are very important in the process of designing efficient algorithms. The structural properties of these restricted classes of graphs are exploited to design parallel and sequential algorithm. The recognition problems for various restricted classes of graph have received considerable importance in the literature.

## BIBLIOGRAPHY

Bondy, J. A., and Murty, U. S. R. (1976) *Graph Theory with Applications*, North-Holland, New York.

Joseph, J. J. (1972). *Introduction to Parallel Algorithms*, Addison-Wesley, Reading, MA.

Johnson, D. S. (1985). The NP-completeness column: An ongoing guide. *J. Algorithms*. **6**, 434–451.

Klein, P. N. (1988). Efficient Parallel Algorithms for Planar, Chordal and Interval Graphs. TR 426 (Ph.D. Thesis) Laboratory for Computer Science, MIT, Cambridge, MA.

Samy, A., Arumugam, G., Devasahayam, M. P., and Xavier, C. (1991). Algorithms for Intersection Graphs of Internally Disjoint Paths in Trees, *Proceedings of National Seminar on Theoretical Computer Science, IMSC*, Madras, India, Report 115, pp. 169–178.

Berge, C. and Chvatal, C. eds. (1984). *Topics on Perfect Graphs, Annals of Discrete Mathematics*, **21**.

Sekharan, N. C. (1985). New Characterizations and Algorithmic Studies on Chordal Graphs and k-Trees, M.Sc. (Engg.) thesis, School of Automation, Indian Institute of Science, Bangalore.

Chandrasekharan, N. and Iyengar, S. (1988). NC Algorithms for Recognizing Chordal Graphs and k-Trees, *IEEE Transactions on Computers*, **37(10)**.

Joseph, J. A. (1992). *Introduction to Parallel Algorithms*, Addison-Wesley, Reading, MA.

Kelly, D. (1985). Comparability graphs. In I. Rival, ed., *Graphs and Order*, pp. 3–40. D. Reidel, Dordrecht. (NATO ASI series C, v. 14.)

Klein, P. N. (1988). Efficient Parallel Algorithms for Chordal graphs, *Proc. 29th IEEE Symposium on Foundation of Computer Section* pp. 150–161.

Klein, P. N. (1988). Efficient Parallel Algorithms for Planar, Chordal and Interval Graphs, TR 426 (Ph.D. thesis), Laboratory for Computer Science, MIT, Cambridge, MA.

Kozen, D., Vazirani, U. V., and Vazirani, V. V. (1985). NC Algorithms for Comparability Graphs, Interval Graphs and Unique Perfect Matchings. In *Fifth Conference on Foundations of Software Technology and Theoretical Computer Science*, pp. 496–503, New York and Berlin. (Springer Lecture Notes in Computer Science 206.)

Moitra, A. and Iyengar, S. S. (1987). Parallel Algorithms for Some Computational Problems, *Advances in Computers*, **26,** 93–153.

Manacher, G. K. (1992) Chord Free Path Problems on Interval Graphs, *Computer Science and Informatics*, **22,(2)** 17–24.

Mohring, R. H. (1984). Algorithmic Aspects of Comparability Graphs and Interval Graphs. In Ivan Rival, ed., *Graphs and Order*, pp. 41–101. D. Reidel, Dordrecht (Nato ASI series C, v. 147.)

Xavier C. and Arumugam, G. (1994). Algorithms for Parity Path Problems in Some Classes of Graphs, *Computer Science and Informatics*, **24(4)** 50–54.

Xavier, C. (1995). Sequential and Parallel Algorithms for Some Graph Theoretic Problems (Ph.D. thesis). Madurai Kamaraj University.

## CHAPTER 3

# Paradigms for Parallel Algorithms

In sequential computing a processor manipulates the data stored in an appropriate data structure. The way in which this change has to take place is written in the form of an algorithm. This paradigm must shift for parallel computing. In the parallel computing our paradigm must be entirely different. This chapter deals with various paradigms used so far in constructing parallel algorithms. In designing sequential algorithms, if the time complexity of the algorithms is $O(n)$, then it is considered to be a good algorithm. In the parallel case, if an algorithm takes $O(n)$ time, it is not considered to be a good one. The parallel algorithms that work in $O(\log^k n)$ time for sufficiently small positive integer $k$, using polynomial number of processors, are considered to be good algorithms. These algorithms are said to belong to NC class. In order to design NC parallel algorithms, we introduce certain paradigms in this chapter. If we want to design a parallel algorithm for a new problem, we can try to solve it, using any of paradigms that we study here. If it cannot be solved in parallel, using any of the paradigms, then we can design a new paradigm, depending upon the nature of the problem. The purpose of this chapter is only to introduce some well-known paradigms.

## 3.1 BINARY TREE PARADIGM

The concept of binary tree has already been introduced in Chapter 2. A complete binary tree with $n$ leaves is of height $\lceil \log n \rceil$. We can bravely use this property in the design of parallel algorithms. Suppose there are $n$ data items, corresponding to the $n$ pendant (leaf) vertices of a complete binary tree. We will process them in parallel and get partial results at the non-leaf nodes. We proceed bottom up, and reach the root in $\lceil \log n \rceil$ time. This is illustrated in this section.

***Sum of n Numbers.*** Consider the problem of summation of $n$ numbers. It takes $O(n)$ time for a single processor to sum $n$ numbers. Let us see how we can use more processors to reduce the computing time. Assume that $n = 2^k$. Here, dividing the data into two groups when $n = 8$, we have

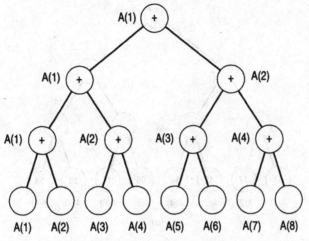

**Figure 3.1** Sum of $n = 8$ numbers.

Group I : $A(1) \quad A(3) \quad A(5) \quad A(7)$
Group II : $A(2) \quad A(4) \quad A(6) \quad A(8)$

Each group contains four elements. So, we employ $n/2$ processors. (i.e., 4 processors). Now the corresponding elements are added by these four processors simultaneously and stored in $A(1)$, $A(2)$, $A(3)$, and $A(4)$ respectively. This is shown in Figure 3.1. This is illustrated in Fig. 3.2(a) through 3.2(d), using the sample data shown below:

$A(1) \quad A(2) \quad A(3) \quad A(4) \quad A(5) \quad A(6) \quad A(7) \quad A(8)$

$51 \quad\quad 17 \quad\quad 42 \quad\quad 34 \quad\quad 85 \quad\quad 11 \quad\quad 19 \quad\quad 54$

At the first stage we do the following operations:

$$A(1) \leftarrow A(1) + A(2) = 68$$
$$A(2) \leftarrow A(3) + A(4) = 76$$
$$A(3) \leftarrow A(5) + A(6) = 96$$
$$A(4) \leftarrow A(7) + A(8) = 73.$$

In general, for $i = 1$ to $4$, we do the following operations:

$$A(i) \leftarrow A(2i - 1) + A(2i).$$

Then, in the second stage, we evaluate

$$A(1) \leftarrow A(1) + A(2) = 144 \qquad A(2) \leftarrow A(3) + A(4) = 169$$

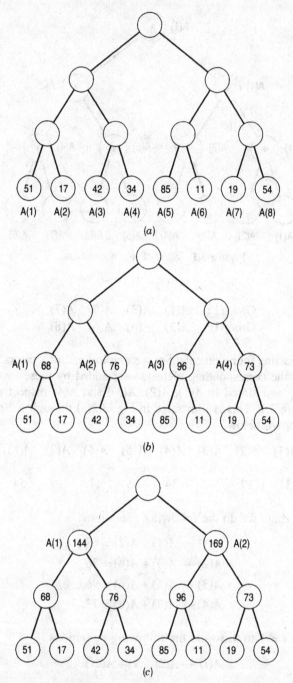

**Figure 3.2(a)**   Initial values. **(b)** Stage 1. **(c)** Stage 2.

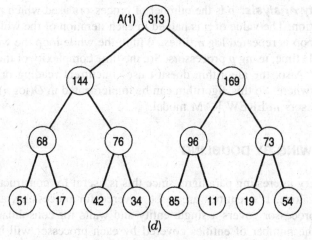

*(d)*

**Figure 3.2(d)** Stage 3.

That is, we evaluate for $i = 1$ to 2

$$A(i) \leftarrow A(2i - 1) + A(2i)$$

At the third stage we evaluate

$$A(1) \leftarrow A(1) + A(2) = 313.$$

This is done by the following parallel algorithm:

**Algorithm SUM**
  **Input:** Array $A(1:n)$ where $n = 2^k$.
  **Output:** The sum of the values of the array stored in $A(1)$.

BEGIN

1. $p = n/2$
2. While $p > 0$ do
3. For $i = 1$ to $p$ do in parallel
4. $A(i) = A(2i - 1) + A(2i)$
5. End parallel
6. $p = [p/2]$
7. End while

END

***Complexity Analysis.*** $p$ is the number of processors used which is $n/2$ at the initial iteration. The value of $p$ is halved in each iteration of the while loop. So, the while loop is repeated $\log n$ times. Within the while loop the works can be done in $O(1)$ time, using $p$ processors. So, the time complexity of this algorithm is $O(\log n)$. Also, the algorithm doesn't use concurrent reading or concurrent writing anywhere. So this algorithm can be implemented in $O(\log n)$ time using $O(n)$ processors in EREW RAM model.

## 3.2 GROWING BY DOUBLING

This is a very interesting paradigm, since this is useful for constructing parallel algorithms alone. If $n$ entities are to be covered for processing, at the initial step each processor covers a single entity and waits for consolidation. At the first step, the number of entities covered by each processor will be two, and at the second stage it will be 4, and at the third stage it is 8, and so on. At every step the number of entities covered is double the entities covered at the previous step.

The summation of $n$ numbers can be viewed as an example for growing by doubling. At the first step, each processor finds the sum of two numbers.

$$P_1 \text{ evaluates } x_1 + x_2$$
$$P_2 \text{ evaluates } x_3 + x_4$$
$$\dots\dots\dots\dots\dots\dots\dots\dots$$
$$\dots\dots\dots\dots\dots\dots\dots\dots$$
$$P_{n/2} \text{ evaluates } x_{n-1} + x_n$$

At the second step,

$$P_1 \text{ evaluates } (x_1 + x_2) + (x_3 + x_4)$$
$$P_2 \text{ evaluates } (x_5 + x_6) + (x_7 + x_8)$$
$$\dots\dots\dots\dots\dots\dots\dots\dots$$
$$\dots\dots\dots\dots\dots\dots\dots\dots$$
$$P_{n/4} \text{ evaluates } (x_{n-3} + x_{n-2}) + (x_{n-1} + x_n)$$

Here at every step, the total number of entities added by the processor is double the number of entities added at the previous step. This enables a processor to cover all the $n$ entities in $\log n$ time. The "ranking a list" problem given below is another example for growing by doubling.

## 3.3 POINTER JUMPING

The linked list representation is extensively used as a data structure for most of the classical problems. If we want to reach the end of the linked list from the

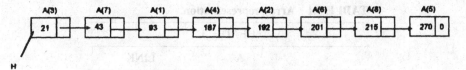

**Figure 3.3**   Linked list of 8 entries.

head, $O(n)$ time is needed in the sequential case. The pointer jumping technique provides a method to reach the end in $O(\log n)$ time. This is illustrated in the following example:

**List Ranking Problem.**  Let $A(1:n)$ be an array of numbers. They are in a linked list in some order. LINK($i$) denotes the index of the number next to $A(i)$. LINK(3) = 7 means that in the linked list $A(7)$ is the number next to $A(3)$. LINK($i$) = 0 if $A(i)$ is the last entry in the linked list. The variable HEAD contains the index of the first number. *The rank of the number is defined to be its distance from the end.* The last number in the linked list has the rank 1 and the next one has rank 2, and so on. The first entry of the linked list is of rank $n$. Figure 3.3 gives a linked list with 8 entities.

Table 3.1 shows the array representation of the linked list shown in Fig. 3.3. We are interested in finding rank of each entry. A sequential algorithm for this problems traverses the whole list from the start to the end. So it takes $O(n)$ time. An algorithm is given below.

**Algorithm Sequential List**
Ranking
   **Input:** $A(1:n)$, LINK $(1:n)$, HEAD
   **Output:** RANK $(1:n)$

BEGIN
   $p$ = HEAD
   $r = n$
   RANK($p$) = $r$
   Repeat
      $p$ = LINK($p$)
      $r = r - 1$
      RANK $(p)$ = $r$
   until LINK($p$) is not equal to 0.
END

We would like to develop a parallel algorithm for this. We introduce a new variable NEXT($i$). Initially NEXT($i$) = LINK($i$). That is, NEXT($i$) initially denotes the index of its right neighbor. At the next step we shall have

**TABLE 3.1  Array representation.**

| | HEAD = 3 | |
| --- | --- | --- |
| i | A | LINK |
| 1 | 93 | 4 |
| 2 | 192 | 6 |
| 3 | 21 | 7 |
| 4 | 187 | 2 |
| 5 | 270 | 0 |
| 6 | 201 | 8 |
| 7 | 43 | 1 |
| 8 | 215 | 5 |

$$\text{NEXT}(i) = \text{NEXT}(\text{NEXT}(i)).$$

Now NEXT($i$) denotes the entry at distance 2. Similarly, at the next stage, NEXT($i$) will denote the entry at distance 4, that is, NEXT($i$) grows by doubling. So, in [log $n$] stages we can reach the last entry and, hence, the ranking will be complete. The complete parallel algorithm is given below.

**Algorithm List Ranking**
   **Input:** $A(1:n)$, LINK $(1:n)$, HEAD
   **Output:** RANK $(1:n)$

BEGIN
   1. For $i = 1$ to $n$ do in parallel
         RANK $(i) = 1$
         NEXT $(i) = $ LINK $(i)$
      End Parallel
   2. For $k = 1$ to [log $n$] do
      2a. For $i = 1$ to $n$ do in parallel
         If NEXT $(i)$ is not zero
               RANK $(i) = $ RANK $(i) + $ RANK(NEXT($i$))
               NEXT $(i) = $ NEXT (NEXT($i$))
         Endif
      End Parallel
   Endfor
END

***Complexity Analysis.*** Here in step 1, $O(n)$ processors can be used to work in $O(1)$ time. Step 2 is repeated $0(\log n)$ times. Step 2(a) requires $O(m)$ processors to complete in 0(1) time. So, the overall complexity of the parallel algorithm is $O(\log n)$ time, using $O(n)$ processors. Step 1 can be executed using an EREW PRAM. Step 2 can also be implemented in an EREW PRAM. So the model needed for this algorithm is EREW PRAM.

Let us illustrate the working of this algorithm, using the example already shown in this section. The illustration is shown in Figs. 3.4(a) through 3.4(d).

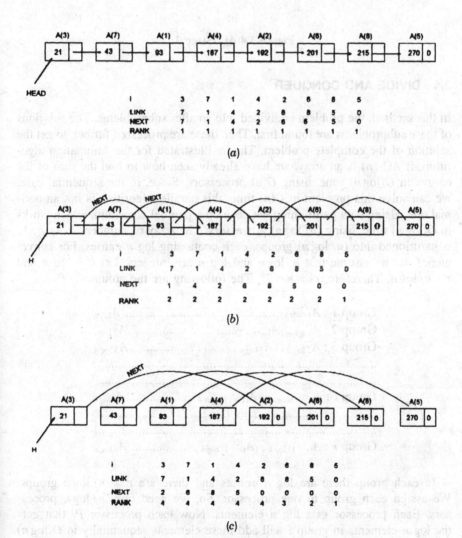

**Figure 3.4(a)** Initial stage. **(b)** Stage 1. **(c)** Stage 3.

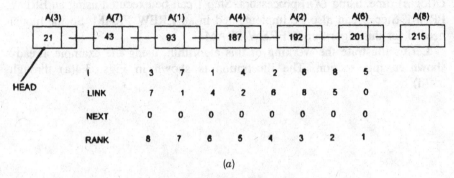

(a)

**Figure 3.4(d)** Stage 3.

## 3.4 DIVIDE AND CONQUER

In this method, the problem is divided into smaller subproblems. The solutions of these subproblems are found first. Then these are processed further, to get the solution of the complete problem. This is illustrated for the summation algorithm. If $A(1:n)$ is an array, we have already seen how to find the sum of the entires in $O(\log n)$ time, using $O(n)$ processors. Since, in the sequential case, we can solve this problem in $O(n)$ time, this parallel algorithm is not an optimal one. Using data partitioning we develop a parallel algorithm, which works in $O(\log n)$ time, using $(n/\log n)$ processors. The array of numbers $A_1 A_2 \ldots A_n$ is partitioned into $(n/\log n)$ groups, each containing $\log n$ entries. For convenience, let us assume that $n/\log n$ and $\log n$ are integers. Let $k = \log n$ and $r = n/\log n$. Therefore, $rk = n = 2^k$. The following are the groups:

$$\text{Group 1} : A_1 A_2 A_3 \ldots\ldots\ldots\ldots\ldots\ldots\ldots\ldots\ldots A_{\log n}$$
$$\text{Group 2} : A_{\log n + 1} A_{\log n + 2} \ldots\ldots\ldots\ldots\ldots\ldots A_{2 \log n}$$
$$\text{Group 3} : A_{2 \log n + 1} A_{2 \log n + 2} \ldots\ldots\ldots\ldots\ldots A_{3 \log n}$$
$$\ldots\ldots\ldots\ldots\ldots\ldots\ldots\ldots\ldots\ldots\ldots\ldots\ldots\ldots\ldots\ldots$$
$$\ldots\ldots\ldots\ldots\ldots\ldots\ldots\ldots\ldots\ldots\ldots\ldots\ldots\ldots\ldots\ldots$$
$$\text{Group } i : A_{(i-1) \log n + 1} A_{(i-1) \log n + 2} \ldots\ldots\ldots\ldots A_{i \log n}$$
$$\ldots\ldots\ldots\ldots\ldots\ldots\ldots\ldots\ldots\ldots\ldots\ldots\ldots\ldots\ldots\ldots$$
$$\ldots\ldots\ldots\ldots\ldots\ldots\ldots\ldots\ldots\ldots\ldots\ldots\ldots\ldots\ldots\ldots$$
$$\text{Group } r : A_{(r-1) \log n + 1} A_{(r-1) \log n + 2} \ldots\ldots\ldots\ldots A_{r \log n}$$

In each group there are $\log n$ entries and there are $r = n/\log n$ groups. We assign each group to one processor. So, we need only $n/\log n$ processors. Each processor gets $\log n$ elements. Now each processor $P_i$ that gets the $\log n$ elements in group $i$ will add these elements sequentially in $O(\log n)$ time and stores in a variable called $B_i$. Now there are only elements, $B_1$, $B_2$,

... $B$, $n/\log n$. Using the algorithm shown in Section 3.1, we now add these entries in $o(\log(n/\log n))$ time, using $o(n/\log n)$ processors. We know that $o(\log n/\log n) = 0(\log n - \log\log n) = O(\log n)$. So this method solves the summation problem in $O(\log n)$ time, using $o(n/\log n)$ processors. Hence, this is the optimal algorithm for this problem. The algorithm is formally presented below:

**Algorithm Optimal-Sum**
   **Input:** an array of numbers $A(1:n)$
   **Output:** The sum of these numbers in a variable called SUM.
   1. For $i = 1$ to $n/\log n$ do in parallel
   2. Using the sequential method find the sum of $A_{(i-1)\log n+1}$, $A_{(i-1)\log n+2}$, ... $A_{i\log n}$ and store the result in variable $B_i$.
   3. End parallel
   4. Find the sum of $B_1$, $B_2$, ... $B$ $n/\log n$ and store in the variable SUM.
   5. End optimal sum.

*Complexity Analysis.* In the above algorithm, step 2 is done using the sequential summation algorithm in $O(\log n)$ time. So, steps 1 to 3 can be implemented in $O(\log n)$ time, using $o(n/\log n)$ processors only. Step 4 can be done using the parallel algorithm shown in Section 3.1 in $o(\log(n/\log n))$ time, using processors in EREW PRAM model. So the complexity of the above algorithm is $O(\log n)$ time, using $o(n/\log n)$ processors in EREW PRAM. Hence this algorithm is optimal. The divide-and-conquer technique just explained can also be used to find the minimum/maximum of the entries of the array $A(1:n)$. The algorithm, very similar to the one given above, will solve the problem in $O(\log n)$ time using $o(n/\log n)$ processors in EREW PRAM model.

## 3.5 PARTITIONING

In the divide-and-conquer approach, we divide the problem in to subproblems and solve the subproblems concurrently. Then we consolidate the results of the subproblems to get the result of the final problem. That is, the divide-and-conquer technique consists of the following steps:

   **Step 1:** Divide the problem into subproblems $P_1$, $P_2$, ... $P_s$, and solve them concurrently and get the solutions $S_1$, $S_2$, ... $S_s$.
   **Step 2:** Consolidate $S_1$, $S_2$, ... $S_s$, to get the solution of the original problem.

In partitioning technique, we pay more attention to the process of dividing the problem into subproblems. We carefully divide the problem into subproblems $P_1$, $P_2$ ... $P_s$, in such a way that, when subproblems $P_1$, $P_2$, ... $P_s$ are solved concurrently, the solution of the original problem is already available. In other words, we divide the problem into $P_1$, $P_2$, ... $P_s$, in such a way that step 2 of the divide-and-conquer strategy is not necessary. This is illustrated using the merging problem.

**Merging Problem.** Let $A(1:n)$ and $B(1:n)$ be two sorted arrays. That is, $A_1 \leq A_2 \leq \ldots \leq A_n$ and $B_1 \leq B_2 \leq \ldots B_n$. We want to merge these two arrays into a single array $C(1:2n)$, such that $C_1 \leq C_2 \leq \ldots \leq C_{2n}$. For example, if $A = (1,5,9,12)$ and $B = (2,3,15,19)$, we want to merge these two arrays to get $C = (1,2,3,5,9,12,15,19)$. For convenience, let $n = 2^k$ and $n/\log n = r$. We further assume that both $k$ and $r$ are integers. We know that the following sequential algorithm merges the two arrays in $O(n)$ time.

**Algorithm Sequential Merge**
**Input:** Two sorted arrays $A(1:n)$ and $B(1:n)$.
**Output:** $C(1:2n)$, such that $C_1 \leq C_2 \leq \ldots C_{2n}$.

1. Let $A_{n+1} = B_{n+1} = \infty$
2. $i = 1; j = 1; k = 1$
3. While $k \leq 2n$ do
4. If $A_j < B_j$, then
   $$C_k = A_i$$
   $$i = i + 1$$
   else
   $$c_k = B_j$$
   $$j = j + 1$$
   end if
5. $k = k + 1$
6. end while
7. End sequential merge

Our approach to the problem partitions the sorted array. A into $r = n/\log n$ groups, each having $k = \log n$ elements as follows:

Group 1 : $A_1 A_2 A_3$ .................................... $A_k$
Group 2 : $A_{k+1} A_{k+2} A_{k+3}$ ................ $A_{2k}$
.........................................................................
.........................................................................
Group $i$ : $A_{(i-1)k+1} A_{(i-1)k+2}$ ................... $A_{ik}$
.........................................................................
.........................................................................
Group $r$ : $A_{(r-1)k+1} A_{(r-1)k+2}$ ................ $A_{rk}$

We now find $r$ integers $j(1), j(2), \ldots j(r)$, such that

$j(1)$ is the greatest index, such that $A_k \geq B_{j(1)}$

$j(2)$ is the smallest index, such that $A_{2k} \geq B_{j(2)}$

...............................................................................................

$j(i)$ is the smallest index, such that $A_{ik} \geq B_{j(i)}$

...............................................................................................

...............................................................................................

$j(r)$ is the smallest index, such that $A_{rk} \geq B_{j(r)}$

This has now partitioned the array $B(1:n)$ into $r$ groups, as follows:

Group 1 : $B_1, B_2 \ldots B_{j(1)}$

Group 2 : $B_{j(1)+1}, B_{j(1)+2} \ldots B_{j(2)}$

.............................................................................................

.............................................................................................

Group $i$ : $B_{j(i-1)+1}, B_{j(i-1)+2}, \ldots \ldots \ldots B_{j(i)}$

.............................................................................................

.............................................................................................

Group $r$ : $B_{j(r-1)+1}, B_{j(r-1)+2}, \ldots \ldots \ldots B_{j(r)}$

Now we observe the following: Every entry of group 1 of A is less than or equal to every entry of group 2, 3, ... of $B$. If group 1 of A and group 1 of B are merged separately, it is guaranteed that the elements have reached their final position in the final sorted array $C(1:n)$. This holds for the other groups also. So, we assign processor $i(1 \leq i \leq r)$ to group $i$ of A and group $i$ of B. Processor $i$ sequentially merges group $i$ of A and group $i$ of B.

Now let us formally present our parallel algorithm.

**Algorithm Merge**

  **Input:** Two sorted arrays $A(1:n)$ and $B(1:n)$. Assume that

$$n = 2^k, \log n = k,$$

**Output:** The merged array $C(1:2n)$

1. for $i = 1$ to $r$ do in parallel.
2. Using binary search find the index.

$$j(i) = \text{Max}\{t, \text{ such that } A_{ik} \geq B_t\}$$

3. Using sequential method merge the two arrays

$$A((i-1)k + 1 : ik) \text{ and } B(j(i-1) + 1 : j(i)).$$

4. End parallel
5. end Merge

In order to illustrate the above algorithm, consider the arrays $A = (1, 5, 15, 18, 19, 21, 23, 24, 27, 29, 30, 31, 32, 37, 42, 49)$ and $B = (2, 3, 4, 13, 15, 19, 20, 22, 28, 29, 38, 41, 42, 43, 48, 49)$. Here $n = 16 = 2^4$ log $n = k = 4$. $r = n/\log n = 4$. We divide $A$ into 4 groups ($r = 4$).

| A | 1, 5, 15, 18 | 19, 21, 23, 24 | 27, 29, 30, 31 | 32, 37, 42, 45 |
|---|---|---|---|---|
| Group | Group 1 | Group 2 | Group 3 | Group 4 |

The $j(i)$ values are found as $j(1) = 5$, $j(2) = 8$, $j(3) = 10$, and $j(4) = 15$. The groups of $B$ are appended to the above table and shown below:

| Group | Group 1 | Group 2 | Group 3 | Group 4 |
|---|---|---|---|---|
| A | 1, 5, 15, 18 | 19, 21, 23, 24 | 27, 29, 30, 31 | 32, 37, 42, 49 |
| B | 2, 3, 4, 13, 15 | 19, 20, 22 | 28, 29 | 38, 41, 42, 43, 48, 49 |

When we merge the subarrays $A$ and $B$ groupwise,

Group 1 gives $C(1:9) = (1, 2, 3, 4, 5, 13, 15, 15, 18)$
Group 2 gives $C(10:16) = (19, 19, 20, 21, 22, 23, 24)$
Group 3 gives $C(17:22) = (27, 28, 29, 29, 30, 31)$
Group 4 gives $C(23:32) = (32, 37, 38, 41, 42, 42, 43, 48, 49, 49)$.

Hence we get the final array

$$C(1:32) = (1, 2, 3, 4, 5, 13, 15, 15, 18, 19, 19, 20, 21,$$
$$22, 23, 24, 27, 28, 29, 29, 30, 31, 32, 37, 38, 41, 42,$$
$$42, 43, 48, 49, 49)$$

**Complexity Analysis.** Step 2 can be implemented using binary search in $O(\log n)$ time. The time taken to implement step 3 depends on the $A$ and $B$ subarrays. $A((i-1)k+1:ik)$ is of size $k$. The size of $B(j(i-1)+1:j(i))$ is not known. If its size is also less than or equal to $k$, then step 3 of the algorithm can be implemented by the processor $i$ sequentially in $O(\log n)$ time. If the size of $B(j(i-1)+1:j(i))$ is greater than $k$, we must repeat the same partitioning technique one more recursive iteration with $B$ first and $A$ next. Thus step 3 can be completed in $O(\log n)$ time sequentially by the processor $i$. So, the algorithm can be implemented in $O(\log n)$ time, using $O(n/\log n)$ processors in EREW PRAM.

## 3.6 SUMMARY

In this chapter some important paradigms have been introduced. In order to illustrate these paradigms, some simple parallel algorithms have also been developed. The binary tree paradigm exploits the structure of the binary tree. Data are suitably distributed and processing done so as to give efficient parallel algorithms. Another paradigm pointer jumping was introduced in Section 3.2. It has been fully explained with a suitable example. The divide-and-conquer and partitioning methods are also explained, using simple interesting examples.

## BIBLIOGRAPHY

Akl, S. G. (1989) *The Design and Analysis of Parallel Algorithms*, Prentice-Hall, Englewood Cliffs, NJ.

Brassard, G and Brately, P. (1988) *Algorithmics: Theory and Practice*, Prentice-Hall, Englewood Cliffs, NJ.

Dekel, E., Nassimi D., and Sahni, S. (1987) Parallel Matrix and Graph Algorithms, *Siam. J. Computing*, **10**, 657–675.

Joseph, J. A. (1992) An Introduction to Parallel Algorithms, Addison-Wesley, Reading, MA.

Moitra, A. and Iyengar, S. S. (1987) Parallel Algorithms for Some Computational Problems in Advances in Computers, Academic Press, New York, pp. 93–153.

Quinn, M. J. (1987) Designing Efficient Algorithms for Parallel Computers, McGraw-Hill, New York.

## EXERCISES

**3.1.** Given a set $S = \{p_1, p_2, p_3, \ldots p_n\}$ of $n$ points in a two-dimensional plane, the planar convex hull of $S$ is the smallest convex polygon containing these $n$ points. Develop a divide-and-conquer parallel algorithm to find the sequence in which we must join the points so as to get the boundry of the convex hull.

**3.2.** Consider the following recursive approach to find the partial sums:
1. $x_1, x_2, \ldots x_n$ is the given array.
2. Find the partial sum of

$$x_1, x_2, \ldots, x_{n/2}, \text{and call them}$$

$$z_1, z_2, \ldots, z_{n/2}$$

That is, $z_i = x_1 + x_2 + \ldots + x_i$, where $i \geq n/2 + 1$

3. For $i \leq n/2$,     $s_i = z_i$
4. For $i > n/2$,     $s_i = z_i + z_{n/2}$

Develop a nonrecursive algorithm to find the partial sums of an array, using the above technique.

**3.3.** Let $A$ be a $n \times n$ lower triangular matrix, such that $n$ is a power of 2. Assume that $A$ is nonsingular. Let $A$ be partitioned into four blocks, as follows:

$$A = \begin{pmatrix} A_{11} & 0 \\ A_{21} & A_{22} \end{pmatrix}$$

In the above representation, $A_{11}$, $A_{21}$ and $A_{22}$ are each an $(n/2 \times n/2)$ matrix. The inverse of the whole matrix $A$ is

$$A^{-1} = \begin{bmatrix} A_{11}^{-1} & 0 \\ -A_{22}^{-1}A_{21}A_{11}^{-1} & A_{22}^{-1} \end{bmatrix}$$

Develop a divide-and-conquer algorithm to find the inverse of a lower triangular matrix $A$, using the above method.

**3.4.** $A$ is Boolean array of size $n$. We want to find the smallest index $i$, such that $A(i)$ is true.
a) Develop a CREW parallel algorithm.
b) Develop a CRCW parallel algorithm.

**3.5.** Let $X(1:n)$ be an array of $n$ numbers. The left match of an entry $x_i$ is the element $x_k$ (if it exists), where $k$ is largest index, such that $1 \leq k \leq i$ and $x_k < x_i$. Similarly, we can define the right match of an entry $x_i$. Develop a parallel algorithm to find the left match and right match of each entry of the array.

**3.6.** Develop an algorithm, using partitioning method, to find the minimum entry of an array $A(1:n)$. Verify if the time is $O(\log n)$, using $O(n/\log n)$ processors.

**3.7.** Draw the binary tree representation of the working of the algorithm developed in exercise 3.6 for $n = 16$.

## CHAPTER 4

# Simple Parallel Algorithms

In this chapter we study certain simple problems and illustrate how parallel algorithms are designed to solve them.

## 4.1 SCALAR PRODUCT OF TWO VECTORS

Let $a = (a_1, a_2 \ldots a_n)$; $b = (b_1, b_2 \ldots b_n)$ be two vectors. The scalar product of the two vectors is given by $a_b = a_1 b_1 + a_2 b_2 + \ldots + a_n b_n$. Our focus here is to design a parallel algorithm to find the scalar product of two vectors. This is similar to the sum of the array entries algorithm. The two arrays $a[1:n]$ and $b[1:n]$ are available in the shared common memory. The final value of $a.b$ is to be stored in another variable $c_1$.

The following algorithm describes the paradigm.

**Algorithm Scalar Product**
**Input:** Arrays $a[1:n]$ and $b[1:n]$
**Output:** The value of the scalar product to be stored in variable $c_1$

BEGIN
   1. For $i = 1$ to $n$ do in parallel
   2. $c_i = a_i \overset{*}{} b_i$
   3. End parallel
   4. $p = n/2$
   5. While $p > 0$ do
   6. For $i = 1$ to $p$ do in parallel
   7. $c_i = c_i + c_{i+p}$
   8. End parallel
   9. $p = [p/2]$
  10. End while
END

In this algorithm, steps 1–3 can be implemented $O(1)$ time using $O(n)$ processors. Steps 4–10 is nothing but sum of an array. So the above algorithm can be implemented on a EREW PRAM in $O(\log n)$ time, using $O(n)$ processors. The result will be available at $c_1$. Using the divide-and-conquer approach explained in Chapter 3, Section 3.4, this problem can be solved in $O(\log n)$ time, using $O(n/\log n)$ processors. This is left to the reader as an exercise. In the next example, we illustrate the design of parallel algorithm to a more popular application—matrix multiplication.

## 4.2 MATRIX MULTIPLICATION

Matrix multiplication plays a major role in several important problems. If $A$ is a matrix of order $m \times n$, and $B$ is a matrix of order $n \times p$, the product $C = AB$ can be evaluated and it will be of order $m \times p$. The entry in the $i$th row and $j$th column of $C$, $C(i,j)$ is obtained by the scalar product of the $i$th row of $A$ and the $j$th column of $B$. That is,

$$C(i,j) = (a_{i1}, a_{i2} \ldots a_{in}) \begin{pmatrix} b_{ij} \\ b_{2j} \\ \vdots \\ b_{nj} \end{pmatrix}$$

$$C(i,j) = \sum_{k=1}^{n} a_{ik}b_{kj}$$

The outline of the algorithm is given below.

**Algorithm Matrix-Multiply**
  **Input:** The matrices $A$ and $B$.
  **Output:** The product matrix $C$.

  BEGIN
  1. For $i = 1$ to $m$ do in parallel
  2.          For $j = 1$ to $p$ do in parallel
  3.                  Evaluate $C(i,j)$
  4.          End Parallel
  5. End Parallel
  END

Here step 3 must be explained further. Evaluation of $C(i,j)$ is the scalar product of two vectors. It can be done by the following segment. A temporary local variable $T(1:n)$ for each processor is used, to store the value $A(i,k) * B(k,j)$.

3.1　For $k = 1$ to $n$ do in Parallel
3.2　　　　　　　　$T(k) = A(i, k) * B(k, j)$
3.3　End parallel
3.4　$p = n/2$
3.5　While $p > 0$ do
3.6　　　　　　For $k = 1$ to $p$ do in Parallel
3.7　　　　　　　　$T(k) = T(2k - 1) + T(2k)$
3.8　　　　　　End Parallel
3.9　　　　　　$p = \lceil p/2 \rceil$
3.10　End while
3.11　$C(i, j) = T(1)$

**Complexity Analysis.** The above segment contains two parts. In the first part the values $A(i, k) * B(k, j)$ are first evaluated. Then, in the second part, these values are added to get the $C(i, j)$ value. A temporary local variable $T(1 : n)$ is used for the purpose of multiplying and adding. In this segment of the algorithm, steps 3.1 to 3.3 take $O(1)$ time, using $O(n)$ processors. Steps 3.4 to 3.11 are same as the algorithm SUM, and so they take $O(\log n)$ time, using $O(n)$ processors. Step 3 is placed inside two nested parallel loops and, hence, the complexity of the algorithm is $O(\log n)$ time, using $O(mnp)$ processors. In particular, when $A$ and $B$ are square matrices, this runs in $O(\log n)$ time, using $O(n^3)$ processors. The value $A(i, j)$ is needed to evaluate $C(i, 1)$, $C(i, 2) \ldots C(i, n)$. Since $C(i, 1)$, $C(i, 2) \ldots C(i, n)$ are evaluated in parallel by different groups of processors, $A(i, j)$ will be concurrently read by more than one processor. So the above algorithm needs a CREW PRAM model. If we use the divide-and-conquer approach illustrated in Chapter 3, Section 3.4. The problem can be solved in $O(\log n)$ time, using $O(n^3 / \log n)$ processors. The example described in the following section deals with a more interesting problem.

## 4.3 PARTIAL SUMS

Let $A(1 : n)$ be an array of numbers. The partial sums of the array is defined by

$$PS(i) = \sum_{j=1}^{i} A(j) \qquad (1 \leq i \leq n)$$

Let us use the binary tree paradigm to evaluate the partial sums $PS(i)$ ($1 \leq i \leq n$). Using the algorithm to sum the array values, we can only determine $PS(n)$. We are going to modify the algorithm to get the partial sums. Consider Fig. 4.1, which illustrates the summation algorithm for $n = 8$. $S(i, j)$ denotes the $j$th node a level $h - i$, counted from left to right. Initially we assign $S(o, i) = A(i)$. Then we find $S(1, i)$ by adding the values of its children. $S(1, 1)$, $S(1,$

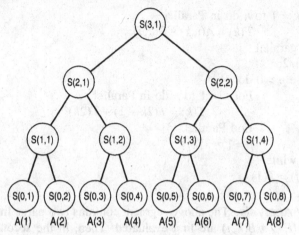

**Figure 4.1**  $S(i, j)$ values in the tree.

2), $S(1, 3)$, and $S(1, 4)$ are obtained at the first time slab in parallel. $S(2, 1)$ and $S(2, 2)$ are obtained at the second time slab, and $S(3, 1)$ is obtained at third time slab. The process is complete in the bottom-up traversal in $O(\log n)$ time, where $n$ is the length of the array. Evaluation of $S$ values is illustrated in Figs. 4.2(a) through 4.2(d). Now, $S(3, 1)$ is the sum of all the entires of the array.

$S(2, 1)$ is the sum of the first four elements. In order to get the partial sums, we introduce another variable, PS. The partial sums will be $PS(0, 1)$, $PS(0, 2)$, ..., $PS(0, n)$ at the end. These values are determined by a traversal from the root to the leaf of the binary tree. From the $S$ values, PS values are determined as follows:

Start with $PS(3, 1) = S(3, 1)$. Coming to the next level,

$$PS(i, j) = \begin{cases} S(i, j) & \text{if } j = 1 \\ PS(i + 1, \lfloor j/2 \rfloor) + S(i, j) & \text{if } j \text{ is } odd \text{ and } j > 1 \\ PS(i + 1, j/2) & \text{if } j \text{ is } even. \end{cases}$$

The procedure is illustrated here for an array with eight entries.

| $i$ | 1 | 2 | 3 | 4 | 5 | 6 | 7 | 8 |
|---|---|---|---|---|---|---|---|---|
| $A(i)$ | 23 | 38 | 40 | 73 | 91 | 39 | 48 | 63 |

The values $S(i, j)$ are determined by traversing the binary tree bottom up. This is shown in Figure 4.2(d). After evaluating $S(i, j)$, we evaluate $PS(i, j)$ (using the formula given above) by traversing the binary tree from the top towards

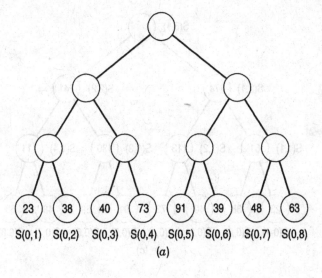

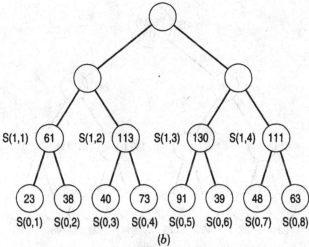

**Figure 4.2(a)** Initial stage. **(b)** Stage 1.

the bottom. It is shown in Fig. 4.3(a) through 4.3(d). $S$ values are given outside and the $PS$ values are given inside each node. In the evaluation of $PS(i,j)$, it is easy to note that $PS(i, 1)$, $PS(i, 2)$, ... could be found in parallel. Also note that $PS(i,j)$ is used to evaluate $PS(i - 1, 2j)$ and $PS(i - 1, 2j + 1)$ concurrently. So this needs a CREW PRAM. The algorithm is given below.

**Algorithm Partial-Sum**
  **Input:** The array of numbers $A(1 : n)$.
  **Output:** Partial Sums $PS(0, 1 : n)$.

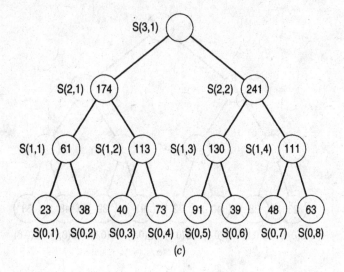

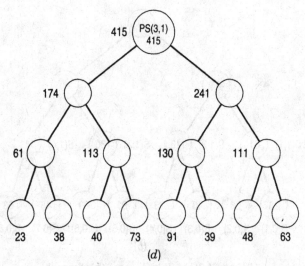

**Figure 4.2(c)**   Stage 2. **(d)** Stage 3.

BEGIN (*i* denotes level number and *p* the number of nodes at that level.)
0. Copy $A(i)$ to $S(0, i)$ for $1 \leq i \leq n$ in parallel
1. $p = n$
2. For $i = 1$ to $[\log n]$ do
3.     $p = [p/2]$
4.     For $j = 1$ to $p$ do in parallel
5.         $S(i,j) = S(i - 2, 2j) + S(i - 1, 2j - 1)$
6.     End Parallel
7. End for

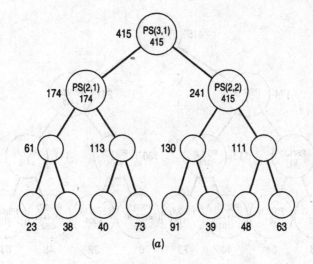

(a)

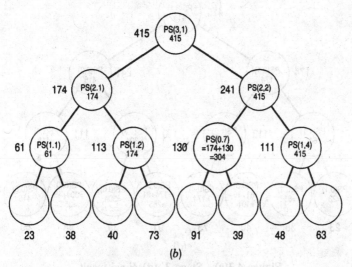

(b)

**Figure 4.3(a)** Stage 1. **(b)** Stage 2.

8. $PS([\log n], 1) = S([\log n], 1)$
9. $h = 1$
10. For $i = [\log n] - 1$ down to 0 do
11.     $p = 2p$
12. For $j = 1$ to $p$ do in parallel
13. Case
        $j = 1$: $PS(i, j) = S(i, j)$

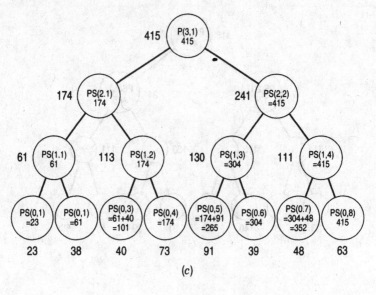

(c)

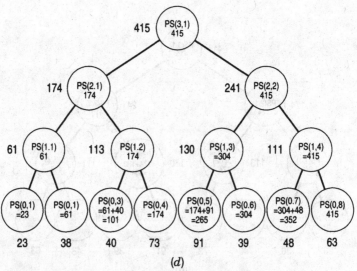

(d)

**Figure 4.3(c)** Stage 3. **(d)** Final result.

$j$ = even: $PS(i,j) = PS(i + 1, j/2)$
Else: $PS(i,j) = PS(i + 1, [j/2]) + S(i,j)$
Endcase
14.   End parallel
15. End for
END

*Complexity Analysis.* Step 0 takes $O(1)$ time, using $O(n)$ processors. Steps 2–7 need $O(\log n)$ time, using $O(n)$ processors. Steps 10–15 also take $O(\log n)$ time, using $O(n)$ processors. So the complexity of this algorithm is $O(\log n)$ time, using $O(n)$ processors. From the formulas for $PS(i, j)$, it is observed that $PS(i, j)$ is used in the calculation of $PS(i - 1, 2j - 1)$, as well as $PS(i - 1, 2j)$, which are evaluated in parallel. So we need a concurrent read memory. But concurrent write is not used anywhere in the program. So we need a CREW PRAM model to implement this algorithm.

## 4.4 BINOMIAL COEFFICIENTS

The binomial coefficient $\binom{n}{4}$ is given by the formula

$$\binom{n}{r} = \frac{\lfloor n}{\lfloor r \lfloor (n - r)}.$$

The problem here is to find all the binomial coefficients

$$\binom{n}{0}, \binom{n}{1}, \binom{n}{2}, \ldots, \binom{n}{n}.$$

Let us write the binomial coefficients in the form of a triangular table. For simplicity, let us denote $\binom{n}{r}$ by $C_{nr}$

$$
\begin{array}{lllll}
C_{00} \\
C_{10} & C_{11} \\
C_{20} & C_{21} & C_{22} \\
C_{30} & C_{31} & C_{32} & C_{33} \\
C_{40} & C_{41} & C_{42} & C_{43} & C_{44} \\
\cdots & \cdots & \cdots & \cdots & \cdots \\
\cdots & \cdots & \cdots & \cdots & \cdots
\end{array}
$$

This can also be put in the form of a square table:

$$
\begin{array}{lllllll}
C_{00} & C_{11} & C_{22} & C_{33} & C_{44} & C_{55} & \cdots \\
C_{10} & C_{21} & C_{32} & C_{43} & C_{54} & \cdots & \cdots \\
C_{20} & C_{31} & C_{42} & C_{53} & \cdots & \cdots & \cdots \\
C_{30} & C_{41} & C_{52} & \cdots & \cdots & \cdots & \cdots \\
C_{40} & C_{51} & \cdots & \cdots & \cdots & \cdots & \cdots \\
C_{50} & \cdots & \cdots & \cdots & \cdots & \cdots & \cdots
\end{array}
$$

If this dimensional array is represented by $P$, then we observe that $P = (i, j) = C_{i+j-1,j}$, $\quad i \geq 1$, $\quad j \geq 0$.

Now, using the fact that $\binom{n}{r} = \binom{n-1}{r} + \binom{n-1}{r-1}$, we get $P(i,j) = P(i-1, j) + P(i-1, j-1)$. Using this result repeatedly on $P(i-1, j)$, we get

$$P(i,j) = \sum_{k=1}^{i} P(k, j-1).$$

We have the $P$ values in the following table

| | | | | | |
|---|---|---|---|---|---|
| $C_{00}$ | $C_{11}$ | $C_{22}$ | $C_{33}$ | $C_{44}$ | $C_{55}$ |
| $C_{10}$ | $C_{21}$ | $C_{32}$ | $C_{43}$ | $C_{54}$ | |
| $C_{20}$ | $C_{31}$ | $C_{42}$ | $C_{53}$ | | |
| $C_{30}$ | $C_{41}$ | $C_{52}$ | | | |
| $C_{40}$ | $C_{51}$ | | | | |
| $C_{50}$ | | | | | |

The value of cell $(i, j)$ is reached by adding all the cells of the previous column upto the $i$th row. Notice that $P(i, 0) = C_{i-1,0} = \binom{i-1}{0} = 1$. Also, $P(1, j) = C_{jj} = 1$. That is, all the first-row entries and the first-column entries are ones. The procedure first fills the first column entries by ones. Then it finds the partial sums of the first column entries, and fills the next column. This procedure is repeated.

**Algorithm Binomial-Coeff**
   **Input:** A positive integer $n$.
   **Output:** The binomial Coefficients $\binom{n}{0}, \binom{n}{1}, \ldots, \binom{n}{n}$.

BEGIN
   1. For $i = 1$ to $n + 1$ do in Parallel
   2. $P(i, 0) = 1$
   3. End parallel
   4. For $j = 1$ to $n$ do
   5. Find the partial sums of the $(j - 1)$th column entries using PARTIAL SUM algorithm and store in $j$th column. That is,

$$P(i,j) = \sum_{k=1}^{i} P(k, j-1) \quad \text{where } i = 1 \text{ to } n - j + 1$$

   6. End for
   7. OUTPUT the result as $P(n + 1, 0), P(n, 1), P(n - 1, 2), \ldots, \ldots$
END

**TABLE 4.1   Initial values.**

|   | 0 | 1 | 2 | 3 | 4 | 5 | 6 |
|---|---|---|---|---|---|---|---|
| 1 | 1 |   |   |   |   |   |   |
| 2 | 1 |   |   |   |   |   |   |
| 3 | 1 |   |   |   |   |   |   |
| 4 | 1 |   |   |   |   |   |   |
| 5 | 1 |   |   |   |   |   |   |
| 6 | 1 |   |   |   |   |   |   |
| 7 | 1 |   |   |   |   |   |   |

*Complexity Analysis.* Steps 1–3 can be done in constant time, using $O(n)$ processors. Step 5 could be done in $O(\log n)$ time, using $O(n)$ processors. So steps 4–6 need $O(n \log n)$ time, using $O(n)$ processors. This can be implemented in a CREW PRAM model, because of the use of Partial Sum Algorithm. Now let us see how the algorithm works. Suppose $n = 6$ is the input given. The $P$ table is formed in six iterations. At the initial stage, the values are shown in Table 4.1.

At iteration 1, the first column values are formed by partial sums, as shown in Table 4.2. Subsequent iterations are shown in Tables 4.3 to 4.7. In Table 4.7, the lower-left to top-right diagonal entries give the values of $\binom{6}{0}$, $\binom{6}{1}$, $\binom{6}{2}$, $\binom{6}{3}$, $\binom{6}{4}$, $\binom{6}{5}$, and $\binom{6}{6}$ as 1, 6, 15, 20, 15, 6, and 1, respectively.

## 4.5   RANGE MINIMA PROBLEM

Let $A(1:n)$ be an array of $n$ numbers. The minimum of these elements can be determined in $O(\log n)$ time, using $O(n)$ processors in EREW PRAM. The

**TABLE 4.2   Values at stage 1.**

|   | 0 | 1 | 2 | 3 | 4 | 5 | 6 |
|---|---|---|---|---|---|---|---|
| 1 | 1 | 1 |   |   |   |   |   |
| 2 | 1 | 2 |   |   |   |   |   |
| 3 | 1 | 3 |   |   |   |   |   |
| 4 | 1 | 4 |   |   |   |   |   |
| 5 | 1 | 5 |   |   |   |   |   |
| 6 | 1 | 6 |   |   |   |   |   |
| 7 | 1 |   |   |   |   |   |   |

**TABLE 4.3   Values at stage 2.**

|   | 0 | 1 | 2 | 3 | 4 | 5 | 6 |
|---|---|---|----|---|---|---|---|
| 1 | 1 | 1 | 1  |   |   |   |   |
| 2 | 1 | 2 | 3  |   |   |   |   |
| 3 | 1 | 3 | 6  |   |   |   |   |
| 4 | 1 | 4 | 10 |   |   |   |   |
| 5 | 1 | 5 | 15 |   |   |   |   |
| 6 | 1 | 6 |    |   |   |   |   |
| 7 | 1 |   |    |   |   |   |   |

same problem can also be solved on $0(1)$ time, using $0(n^2)$ processors in CRCW PRAM (refer Chapter 3). The range minima problem can be stated as follows: Given any $i$ and $j$, such that $1 \le i < j \le n$, find the minimum entry of the elements $A_i$, $A_{i+1}$, ... $A_j$.

When $i = 1$ and $j = n$, the range minima problem reduces to the simple problem of finding the minimum of the array. We are interested in preprocessing the array and so store the data in a suitable form, so that the range minima query can be efficiently answered. As an example, consider the array $A = (8, 3, 4, 5, 2, 11, 15, 17, 19, 7, 16, 5, 9, 10, 2, 8)$. The range minima of some ranges are shown in Table 4.8.

In order to proceed further, let us now define two terms, *prefix minima* and *suffix minima* of an array. For an array $a_1$, $a_2$, ... $a_n$, the prefix minima is an array $p = (p_1, p_2, \ldots, p_n)$, where $p_i = \min \{a_1, a_2, \ldots a_i\}$. That is, $p_i$ is the minimum of the first $i$ elements of the array. Similarly, the suffix minima is

**TABLE 4.4   Values at stage 3.**

|   | 0 | 1 | 2 | 3 | 4 | 5 | 6 |
|---|---|---|----|----|---|---|---|
| 1 | 1 | 1 | 1  | 1  |   |   |   |
| 2 | 1 | 2 | 3  | 4  |   |   |   |
| 3 | 1 | 3 | 6  | 10 |   |   |   |
| 4 | 1 | 4 | 10 | 20 |   |   |   |
| 5 | 1 | 5 | 15 |    |   |   |   |
| 6 | 1 | 6 |    |    |   |   |   |
| 7 | 1 |   |    |    |   |   |   |

**TABLE 4.5   Values at stage 4.**

|   | 0 | 1 | 2 | 3 | 4 | 5 | 6 |
|---|---|---|---|---|---|---|---|
| 1 | 1 | 1 | 1 | 1 | 1 |   |   |
| 2 | 1 | 2 | 3 | 4 | 5 |   |   |
| 3 | 1 | 3 | 6 | 10 | 15 |   |   |
| 4 | 1 | 4 | 10 | 20 |   |   |   |
| 5 | 1 | 5 | 15 |   |   |   |   |
| 6 | 1 | 6 |   |   |   |   |   |
| 7 | 1 |   |   |   |   |   |   |

defined to be the sequence $S = (s_1, s_2, \ldots s_n)$, where $s_i$ is the minimum of the last $i$ elements of the original array.

That is,

$$s_1 = \min\{a_n\}$$
$$s_2 = \min\{a_{n-1}, a_n\}$$
$$s_3 = \min\{a_{n-2}, a_{n-1}, a_n\}$$
$$\cdots\cdots\cdots\cdots\cdots\cdots\cdots$$
$$\cdots\cdots\cdots\cdots\cdots\cdots\cdots$$
$$s_i = \min\{a_{n-i+1}, \ldots a_n\}$$

For example, if the original array is $A = (8, 3, 4, 5, 2, 11)$, then the prefix and suffix minima are $P = (8, 3, 3, 3, 2, 2)$ and $S = (11, 2, 2, 2, 2, 2)$. Consider the array $A$ with $n$ elements (assume that $n = 2^k$). In order to solve the range minima problem, we first construct a complete binary tree with $n$

**TABLE 4.6   Values at stage 5.**

|   | 0 | 1 | 2 | 3 | 4 | 5 | 6 |
|---|---|---|---|---|---|---|---|
| 1 | 1 | 1 | 1 | 1 | 1 | 1 |   |
| 2 | 1 | 2 | 3 | 4 | 5 | 6 |   |
| 3 | 1 | 3 | 6 | 10 | 15 |   |   |
| 4 | 1 | 4 | 10 | 20 |   |   |   |
| 5 | 1 | 5 | 15 |   |   |   |   |
| 6 | 1 | 6 |   |   |   |   |   |
| 7 | 1 |   |   |   |   |   |   |

**TABLE 4.7   Final values.**

|   | 0 | 1 | 2 | 3 | 4 | 5 | 6 |
|---|---|---|---|---|---|---|---|
| 1 | 1 | 1 | 1 | 1 | 1 | 1 | 1 |
| 2 | 1 | 2 | 3 | 4 | 5 | 6 |   |
| 3 | 1 | 3 | 6 | 10 | 15 |   |   |
| 4 | 1 | 4 | 10 | 20 |   |   |   |
| 5 | 1 | 5 | 15 |   |   |   |   |
| 6 | 1 | 6 |   |   |   |   |   |
| 7 | 1 |   |   |   |   |   |   |

leaf nodes. The leaf nodes are denoted by the labels $(0, 1)$, $(0, 2)$, $(0, 3)$, ... $(0, n)$. The nodes at the next level are denoted by the labels $(1, 1)$, $(1, 2)$, $(1, 3)$, ... , $(1, n/2)$. The nodes at the next level are labeled as $(2, 1)$ $(2, 2)$ ... $(2, n/4)$. Similarly, all the nodes are labeled. This is illustrated Fig. 4.4.

The leaf nodes contain the given data $A(1 : n)$. That is, the node with label $(0, i)$ contains the value $A_i$. This is shown in Fig. 4.5 for the array $A = (8, 3, 4, 5, 2, 11, 15, 17)$ with eight elements.

Each internal node $v$ contains the prefix minima and the suffix minima of the leaves of the subtree rooted at $v$. For example, consider the internal node $(2, 2)$. The leaves of the subtree rooted at $(2, 2)$ are $(A_5, A_6, A_7, A_8) = (2, 11, 15, 17)$. The prefix and suffix minima of this subarray are $P = (2, 2, 2, 2)$ and $S = (17, 15, 11, 2)$. So the internal node $(2, 2)$ contains the two arrays, $P = (2, 2, 2, 2)$ and $S = (17, 15, 11, 2)$. The contents of other nodes are shown in Fig. 4.6. How are we to determine $P$ and $S$ arrays? Now let us see how to find the $P$ and $S$ arrays for each node $(h, i)$. This is done in the bottom-up manner. For all the nodes in level 1, $P$ and $S$ have only two elements each. If $(1, i)$ is a node at level 1, its left child is $(0, 2i - 1)$, and its right child is $(0, 2i)$. They contain $A_{2i-1}$ and $A_{2i}$, respectively.

Let $x = \min \{A_{2i-1}, A_{2i}\}$. Then the $P$ and $S$ arrays corresponding to the internal node $(0, i)$ are:

**TABLE 4.8   Some range minima values.**

| Range | | | |
|---|---|---|---|
| i | j | Entries | Minimum |
| 3 | 8 | 4, 5, 2, 11, 15, 17 | 2 |
| 9 | 12 | 19, 7, 16, 5 | 5 |
| 5 | 11 | 2, 11, 15, 17, 19, 7, 16 | 2 |

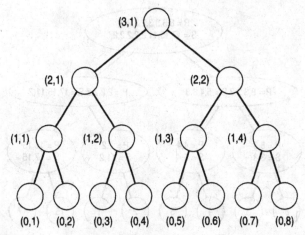

**Figure 4.4**  A complete binary tree with the labels for its nodes.

$$P_{o,i} = A_{2i-1}, x$$
$$S_{o,i} = A_{2i}, x$$

When the height is greater than 1, the left child and the right child of the node $(h, i)$ are $(h - 1, 2i - 1)$ and $(h - 1, 2i)$. We determine $P_{h,i}$ as follows:

1. $P_{h,i}$ is obtained by concatenating the two lists $P_{h-1, 2i-1}$ and $P_{h-1, 2i}$.
2. Every entry $x$ of the second half of $P_{h,i}$ is replaced by the minimum of $x$ and the last entry of the first half.

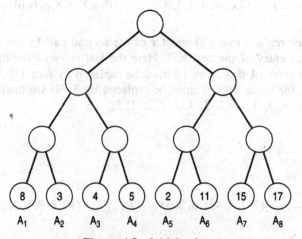

**Figure 4.5**  Initial values.

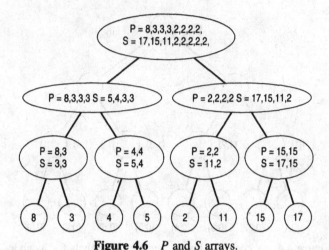

**Figure 4.6**   *P* and *S* arrays.

This process is illustrated by two examples below:

**Example 1**

As an example, consider two values,

$$P_{h-1,2i-1} = (7,7,4,4,4,3,3,3); \text{ and}$$
$$P_{h-1,2i} = (10,8,8,8,8,8,6,6).$$

In the first step, we concatenate these two arrays to get $P_{h,i}$.

$$P_{h,i} = (7,7,4,4,4,3,3,3, \qquad 10,8,8,8,8,8,6,6)$$

Now we must replace every element $x$ of the second half by the minimum of $x$ and the last entry of the first half. Here the last entry of the first half is 3. So the ninth entry of this array 10 must be replaced by min $\{10,3\}$, which is 3. Similarly, the tenth entry 8 must be replaced by 3. So we finally get $P_{h,i} = (7, 7, 4, 4, 4, 3, 3, 3 \qquad 3, 3, 3, 3, 3, 3, 3, 3)$.

**Example 2**

Suppose

$$P_{h-1,2i-1} = (7,7,4,4,4,3,3,3) \qquad P_{h-1,2i} = (10,8,8,8,2,2,1,1).$$

In this case, we concatenate the two arrays first and get

$$P_{h,i} = (7,7,4,4,4,3,3,3 \quad 10,8,8,8,2,2,1,1).$$

Now replacing every element $x$ of the second half by the minimum of $x$ and the last entry of the first half, we get

$$P_{h,i} = (7,7,4,4,4,3,3,3 \quad 3,3,3,3,2,2,1,1).$$

The method of obtaining $S$ array is also similar. For a node $(1, i)$ in the level 1, the $S$ array is $S_{1,i} = (A_{2,i}, x)$, where $x = $ Min $\{A_{2i-1}, A_{2i}\}$. Then, for nodes of height $h > 1$, we first concatenate $S_{h-1,2i}$ and $S_{h-1,2i1}$.

Notice that $S_{h-1,2i}$ comes as the first half and $S_{h-1,2i-1}$ comes as the second half of $S_{h-1}$. Now we can replace every entry $x$ in the second half by the minimum of $x$ and the last entry of the first half.

When the prefix and suffix arrays $P$ and $S$ are known for all the nodes $(h, i)$, the range minima problem can be solved in constant time as follows: Let $i$ and $j$ be two integers, such that $1 \le i < j \le n$. In the complete binary tree find the node $(h, k)$ which is the lowest common ancestor of nodes $(0, i)$ and $(0, j)$. Since the tree is complete, this can be found in constant time. We determine the minimum $m$ of the entries $A_i, A_{i+1}, A_{i+2}, \ldots A_j$ from the arrays, $S_{h-1,2k-1}$ and $P_{h-1,2k}$.

Let $x$ be the entry in $S_{h-1,2k-1}$ corresponding to the node $(0, i)$ and $y$ be the entry in $P_{h-1,2k}$ corresponding to the node $(0, j)$. Min $\{x, y\}$ is the minimum entry of $A_i, A_{i+1}, \ldots A_j$. So, if the $P$ and $S$ arrays are known for each node, then the range minima problem can be answered in constant time. For example, consider the numbers represented in Figure 4.5. Suppose $i = 3$ and $j = 7$. The lowest common ancestor of these two nodes is the root node. So, we must consider the $S$ array of its left child and the $P$ array of its right child. they are

$$S = 5,4,3,3; \text{ and}$$

$$P = 2,2,2,2.$$

The entry corresponding to $i$ in $S$ is the third entry, whose value is 3 and the entry corresponding to $j = 7$ in $P$ is the third entry whose value is 2. So the solution is the min $\{3, 2\}$, which is 2.

**Complexity Analysis.** Given the array $A(1:n)$, the binary tree and the $S$ and $P$ values of each node can be found in $O(\log n)$ time, using $O(n \log n)$ processors. When this preprocessing work is completed, the range minima query for any $i$ and $j$ $(1 \le i < j \le n)$ can be answered in $O(1)$ time.

The Range Minima problem has a number of applications. This problem is applied in the lowest common ancestor problem for trees (see Chapter 5).

## BIBLIOGRAPHY

Cole, R. and Vishkin, U. (1989) Faster Optimal Prefix Sums and List Ranking, *Information and Computing*, **81(3)**, 344–352.

Kruskal, Rudolph C. L., and Snir, M. (1985) The Power of Parallel Prefix, *IEEE Transactions on Computers*, **C-34(10)**, 965–968.

Valiant, L. G., Skyum, S., Berkowitz, S., and Rackoff, C. (1983) Fast Parallel Computation of Polynomials Using Few Processors, *SIAM Journal of Computing*, **12(4)**, 641–644.

## EXERCISES

**4.1.** Let $A(0:n-1)$ be an array of sorted numbers. For a given index $i$, left match of $A(i)$ is the biggest integer $k$, such that $0 \leq k < i$ and $A(k) < A(i)$. Develop an algorithm to find the left match of each entry of an array in $O(1)$ time, using $O(n^2)$ processors.

**4.2.** A $(0:n-1)$ is an array of integers. Write an algorithm to find the smallest index $k$, such that $A(k)$ is positive, and which works in $O(\log n)$ time. Develop an $O(1)$ time algorithm to solve this problem.

**4.3.** $X$ is a Boolean array of size $n$. Develop an algorithm to find the largest index $k$, such that $X_k$ is false in $O(1)$ time, using CRCW PRAM.

**4.4.** Let $X$ and $Y$ be two arrays of sizes $n$ and $m$, respectively. Rank $(a:X)$ is the number of entries of $X$ that are less than or equal to $a$. We define rank $(X:Y)$ as the array $(r_1, r_2, r_3 \ldots r_n)$, such that $r_1 = \text{rank}\ (x_i:Y)$. Develop a parallel algorithm to find rank $(X:Y)$.

**4.5.** A matrix $A$ is said to be symmetric if $A(i,j)$ and $A(j,i)$ are equal for every $i$ and $j$.

  a) Develop an algorithm to check whether a matrix is symmetric, which uses CREW PRAM. What is the time complexity of your algorithm?

  b) Develop an algorithm to check whether a matrix symmetric, which uses CREW PRAM. What is the time complexity of your algorithm.

**4.6.** Develop an algorithm to add two matrices each of order $n \times m$. Verify whether your algorithm works in $O(1)$ time, using $O(mn)$ processors.

**4.7.** A matrix is called a lower triangular matrix if all its upper diagonal entries are zeros. Given a matrix $A$, we want to find whether it is lower triangular or not. Develop an $O(1)$ time algorithm, using a CREW PRAM model.

**4.8.** Given a matrix of order $n \times n$, develop an algorithm to find the sum of all the entries of the row. What is the time and processor complexity of your algorithm?

**4.9.** Let $A(0:n-1)$ be an array of $n$ numbers. The range sum problem is to find the sum of the entries $A(i)$, $A(i+1)$, $A(j)$; for any given $i$ and $j$, such that $0 <= i < j <+ = n - 1$. When $i = 0$ and $j = n - 1$, the problem is ordinary summation problem. Develop a method that finds the range sum for all possible $i$ and $j$ values.

**4.10.** Let $A(1 : n)$ be an array of numbers. Let $B(1 : m)$ be another array of numbers, such that $m < n$. We want to verify whether $B$ forms a subarray of $A$. For example, suppose $A = (2, 1, 7, 5, 120,     5, 2, 7, 1, 1, 8)$ and $B = (5, 120, 5, 2)$. Then $B$ is a subarray of $A$. If $B = (1, 2, 7, 5)$, then $B$ is not a subarray of $A$.

a) Develop a parallel algorithm to verify whether $B$ is a subarray of $A$, which works in $0(\log n)$ time, using CREW PRAM.

b) Develop a parallel algorithms for the same problem on a CRCW PRAM.

**4.11.** Develop a parallel algorithm that considers an array $A(0 : n - 1)$ of numbers as an input, and evaluates the number of occurrences of a given number in the array. For example, if $A = (1, 2, 3, 1, 4, 1, 2, 1, 3, 2, 3, 3)$, then 1 appears 4 times, 2 appears 3 times, 3 appears 4 times. Develop a parallel algorithm to have $A(0 : n - 1)$ and a value $x$ as input and the number of occurrences of $x$ in the array.

**4.12.** If $A(0 : n - 1)$ is an array of numbers, the mode of this array is the value that appears the most frequently. That is, if $A = (1, 2, 3, 4, 1, 5, 1, 7, 1, 9, 2, 8, 1, 3)$, then 1 appears 5 times, 2 appears 2 times, 3 appears 2 times, 4 appears once, and so on. Since 1 appears the most frequently (5 times), the mode of this array is 5. Develop a parallel algorithm to find the mode of the given array 1.

# ALGORITHMS FOR GRAPH MODELS

## CHAPTER 5

# Tree Algorithms

In this chapter we are going to study some fundamental algorithms on trees. We have already studied Eulerian graphs and Euler's circuits. A tree has no circuit. Further, the pendant vertices of trees have degree 1, which is odd. So, a tree is not an Eulerian graph. However, we define the Euler circuit of a tree in a slightly different way, and study the method of determining the Euler's circuit of the tree.

## 5.1 EULER CIRCUITS

Let $T = (V, E)$ be a graph. Let $T'$ be the directed graph obtained by replacing each edge $(u, v)$ of $T$ by two directed arcs $\langle u, v \rangle$ and $\langle v, u \rangle$. The directed graph $T'$ is Eulerian. The Euler circuit of $T'$ is said to be the Euler circuit of $T$. Assume that the tree is represented in terms of its adjacency list. For example, the adjacency list of the tree in Fig. 5.1, which is shown in Table 5.1.

We represent the Euler circuit of the tree as a list of directed arcs. The Euler circuit is

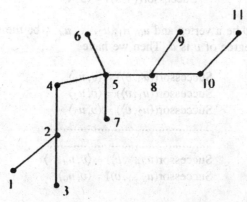

**Figure 5.1** A tree.

**TABLE 5.1 Adjacency list of the tree shown in Fig. 5.1.**

| Vertex (v) | adj (v) |
|---|---|
| 1 | 2 |
| 2 | 1, 3, 4 |
| 3 | 2 |
| 4 | 2, 5 |
| 5 | 4, 6, 7, 8 |
| 6 | 5 |
| 7 | 5 |
| 8 | 5, 9, 10 |
| 9 | 8 |
| 10 | 8, 11 |
| 11 | 10 |

$$\{\langle 1,2\rangle\langle 2,3\rangle\langle 3,2\rangle\langle 2,4\rangle\langle 4,5\rangle\langle 5,6\rangle\langle 6,5\rangle\langle 5,7\rangle \quad \langle 7,5\rangle\langle 5,8\rangle\langle 8,9\rangle\langle 9,8\rangle\langle 8,10\rangle$$
$$\langle 10,11\rangle\langle 11,10\rangle\langle 10,8\rangle\langle 8,5\rangle\langle 5,4\rangle\langle 4,2\rangle\langle 2,1\rangle\}$$

This list is represented in the form of its successor function. That is, *successor* is a bijection from the set of directed arcs of $T'$ to itself. The successor function completely specifies the Euler circuit. So the problem of finding the Euler circuit of the tree reduces to the problem of finding the successor function. The successor function is defined as follows: Consider the vertex 5. The vertices adjacent to 5 arc 4, 6, 7, and 8. If we see the Euler circuit, we find that

$$\text{Successor}(\langle 4,5\rangle) = \langle 5,6\rangle$$
$$\text{Successor}(\langle 6,5\rangle) = \langle 5,7\rangle$$
$$\text{Successor}(\langle 7,5\rangle) = \langle 5,8\rangle$$
$$\text{Successor}(\langle 8,5\rangle) = \langle 5,4\rangle.$$

In general, let $v$ be a vertex and $u_0, u_1, u_2, \ldots u_{d-1}$ be the vertices adjacent to $v$, where the degree of $v$ is $d$. Then we have

$$\text{Successor}(\langle u_0, v\rangle) = \langle v, u_1\rangle$$
$$\text{Successor}(\langle u_1, v\rangle) = \langle v, u_2\rangle$$
$$\text{Successor}(\langle u_2, v\rangle) = \langle v, u_3\rangle$$
$$\cdots\cdots\cdots\cdots\cdots\cdots\cdots\cdots\cdots\cdots\cdots\cdots\cdots$$
$$\cdots\cdots\cdots\cdots\cdots\cdots\cdots\cdots\cdots\cdots\cdots\cdots\cdots$$
$$\text{Successor}(u_{d-2}, v\rangle) = \langle v, u_{d-1}\rangle$$
$$\text{Successor}(u_{d-1}, v\rangle) = \langle v, u_0\rangle.$$

That is,

$$\text{Successor}(\langle u_i, v \rangle) = \langle v, u_{i+1(\mathrm{mod}\, d)} \rangle.$$

Consider a tree represented by its adjacency list with some additional pointers. For any arc $\langle u_i, v \rangle$, we can find $\langle v, u_{i+1(\mathrm{mod}\, d)} \rangle$ in $0(1)$ time. Hence, we have the following parallel algorithm to find the Euler circuit of a tree which works in $0(1)$ time using $0(n)$ processors is EREW PRAM.

**Algorithm Euler Circuit**
 **Input:** A tree $T$ represented by its adjacency list with some additional pointers.
 **Output:** Successor $(\langle u, v \rangle)$ for every arc $\langle u, v \rangle$.
 1. For every arc $\langle u, v \rangle$, do step 2 in parallel.
 2. Successor $(\langle u, v \rangle) = \langle v, w \rangle$, where $w$ occurs next to $u$ in the ordered list of vertices adjacent to $v$. If $u$ appears last in the list of vertices adjacent to $v$, then $w$ is the first node in the list.

Having developed an algorithm to find the Euler circuit of a tree in $0(1)$ time, we can solve several interesting problems on trees using Euler circuits. Let us first study how to convert a tree into a rooted tree having root at a given vertex $v$.

## 5.2 ROOTING A TREE

A rooted tree is a tree having a vertex as its root and all other vertices as its descendants. A rooted tree can be represented by its parent function. The tree $T$ shown in Fig. 5.1 can be converted into a rooted tree with root 4, as shown in Fig. 5.2. Now, instead of representing this rooted tree by adjacency list, we usually represent the tree by its parent relation, as shown in Table 5.2.

Now our aim is to determine the parent function from the adjacency list. We use the Euler circuit for this purpose. Given the adjacency is $p(2) = 4$. $\langle 2, 1 \rangle$

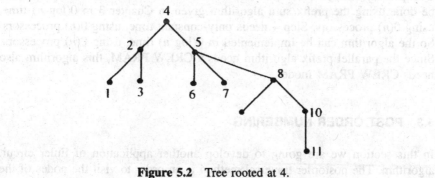

**Figure 5.2** Tree rooted at 4.

**TABLE 5.2   Parent relation.**

| Vertex | 1 | 2 | 3 | 4 | 5 | 6 | 7 | 8 | 9 | 10 | 11 |
|--------|---|---|---|---|---|---|---|---|---|----|----|
| Parent | 2 | 4 | 2 | 4 | 4 | 5 | 5 | 5 | 8 | 8  | 10 |

appears before $\langle 1, 2 \rangle$. So $p(1) = 2$, $\langle 2, 3 \rangle$ appears before $\langle 3, 2 \rangle$. So, $p(3) = 2$, $\langle 4, 5 \rangle$ appears before $\langle 5, 4 \rangle$. So, $p(5) = 4$.

Now we must see how to verify that one arc appears before the other. We assign a weight of 1 to each arc. We find the prefix sum of the weights of the arcs. If prefix sum of $\langle u, v \rangle$ is less than the prefix sum of $\langle v, u \rangle$, it means that $\langle u, v \rangle$ appears first and so we assign $p(v) = u$. Let us now formally present the parallel algorithm for rooting a tree.

**Algorithm Rooting**
   **Input:**
   1. A tree $T$ defined by the adjacency lists.
   2. Euler tour of $T$ defined by the successor function.
   3. A special vertex $r$.
   **Output:**

For each vertex $v = r$, the parent $p(v)$ in the rooted tree $T$ with root $r$.

   1. Identify the last vertex $v$ in the list of vertices adjacent to $r$ and set successor $(\langle u, r \rangle) = 0$.
   2. Assign weight 1 to each arc $\langle u, v \rangle$.
   3. Find the prefix sum of the weights of the arcs in the list given by the successor function.
   4. For each arc $\langle u, v \rangle$, do the following in parallel: If the weight of $\langle u, v \rangle$ is less than the weight of $\langle v, u \rangle$, then set $p(v) = u$.
   5. End ROOTING.

***Complexity Analysis.*** Steps 1 and 2 can be done in constant time. Step 3 can be done using the prefix sum algorithm given in Chapter 3 in $O(\log n)$ time, using $O(n)$ processors. Step 4 needs only constant time, using $O(n)$ processors. So the algorithm can be implemented in $O(\log n)$ time, using $O(n)$ processors. Since the parallel prefix algorithm needs a CREW PRAM, this algorithm also needs CREW PRAM model.

## 5.3   POST ORDER NUMBERING

In this section we are going to develop another application of Euler circuit algorithm. The postorder traversal method is an order to visit the nodes of the

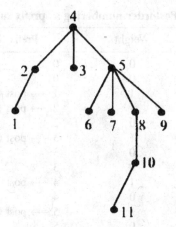

**Figure 5.3**  A tree.

tree. The postorder traversal of a tree $T$ with root $r$ consists of the postorder traversal of the subtrees of $r$ from left to right, followed by the root $r$. For example, consider the simple tree shown in Fig. 5.3. Here 4 is the root. The children of 4 are 2, 3, and 5. The postorder traversal of this tree is, 1, 2, 3, 6, 7, 11, 10, 8, 9, 5, 4.

The post order numbering is the function which gives the rank of the vertex in the post order traversal sequence. For example, the post order numbering is given by, post(1) = 1; post(2) = 2; post(3) = 3; post(6) = 4; post(7) = 5; post(11) = 6; post(10) = 7; post(8) = 8; post(9) = 9; post(5) = 10; post(4) = 11 (see Table 5.3).

The post order numbering can be found using the Euler circuit. In the Euler circuit, whenever we travel along the arc $\langle v, p(v) \rangle$, we have just traversed the vertex $v$. This is achieved by the following steps:

1. For every arc $\langle u, v \rangle$, if $u$ is the parent of $v$, then assign weight 0 to $\langle u, v \rangle$; and if $v$ is the parent of $u$, assign the weight 1 to $\langle u, v \rangle$.
2. Perform the prefix sum of the weights of the arcs as per the list specified by the successor function of the Euler circuit.
3. For every vertex $v$, post($v$) is the prefix sum of the arc $\langle v, p(v) \rangle$.
4. Post order numbering of the root is $n$, where $n$ is the number of vertices in the tree.

**TABLE 5.3  Post order numbering.**

| v | 1 | 2 | 3 | 4 | 5 | 6 | 7 | 8 | 9 | 10 | 11 |
|---|---|---|---|---|---|---|---|---|---|----|----|
| post (v) | 1 | 2 | 3 | 11 | 10 | 4 | 5 | 8 | 9 | 7 | 6 |

**TABLE 5.4  Postorder numbering as prefix sum.**

| Euler's Path | Weight | Prefix Sum |
|---|---|---|
| $\langle 4,2 \rangle$ | 0 | 0 |
| $\langle 2,1 \rangle$ | 0 | 0 |
| $\langle 1,2 \rangle$ | 1 | $1 \longrightarrow$ post $(1) = 1$ |
| $\langle 2,4 \rangle$ | 1 | $2 \longrightarrow$ post $(2) = 2$ |
| $\langle 4,3 \rangle$ | 0 | 2 |
| $\langle 3,4 \rangle$ | 1 | $3 \longrightarrow$ post $(3) = 3$ |
| $\langle 4,5 \rangle$ | 0 | 3 |
| $\langle 5,6 \rangle$ | 0 | 3 |
| $\langle 6,5 \rangle$ | 1 | $4 \longrightarrow$ post $(6) = 4$ |
| $\langle 5,7 \rangle$ | 0 | 4 |
| $\langle 7,5 \rangle$ | 1 | $5 \longrightarrow$ post $(7) = 5$ |
| $\langle 5,8 \rangle$ | 0 | 5 |
| $\langle 8,10 \rangle$ | 0 | 5 |
| $\langle 10,11 \rangle$ | 0 | 5 |
| $\langle 11,10 \rangle$ | 1 | $6 \longrightarrow$ post $(11) = 6$ |
| $\langle 10,8 \rangle$ | 1 | $7 \longrightarrow$ post $(10) = 7$ |
| $\langle 8,5 \rangle$ | 1 | $8 \longrightarrow$ post $(8) = 8$ |
| $\langle 5,9 \rangle$ | 0 | 8 |
| $\langle 9,5 \rangle$ | 1 | $9 \longrightarrow$ post $(9) = 9$ |
| $\langle 5,4 \rangle$ | 1 | $10 \longrightarrow$ post $(5) = 10$ |

The procedure is illustrated in Table 5.4 for the tree shown in Fig. 5.3. The Euler path, the weights, and the prefix sum, are shown in Table 5.4. We formally present the algorithm below:

**Algorithm Postorder Numbering**
  **Input:**
  1. The rooted tree $T = (V, E)$ with root $r$ given by the Parent relation $p(v)$.
  2. The Euler circuit of $T$.
  **Output:** For every vertex $v$, the post order numbering post$(v)$.
  1. For every arc $\langle u, v \rangle$ do in parallel
     If $u = p(v)$, assign the weight 0, else assign the weight 1 to the arc $\langle u, v \rangle$.
     End Parallel.
  2. Find the prefix sum of the list of weights specified by the successor function.
  3. For every vertex $v$ do in parallel.
     post$(v)$ = prefix sum of the arc $\langle v, p(v) \rangle$
     End parallel.
  4. $p(r) = n$.
  5. End Post order Numbering

***Complexity Analysis.*** The algorithm can be implemented in $0(\log n)$ time with $0(n)$ processors in CREW PRAM.

## 5.4   NUMBER OF DESCENDANTS

The number of descendants for each vertex can be obtained from the prefix sum of the weights of arcs determined in the post order numbering algorithm. The number of descendants of a vertex $v$ is the number of vertices in the maximal subtree with $v$ as the root. It is the difference between the prefix sum of $\langle p(v), v \rangle$ and the prefix sum of $\langle v, p(v) \rangle$. For example, for the tree shown in Fig. 5.3, observe from the table of prefix sums that the prefix sum of $\langle 4, 5 \rangle$ and $\langle 5, 4 \rangle$ are 3 and 10, respectively. So the number of descendants of vertex 5 are 10 − 3 = 7. That is, the maximal subtree with 5 as root has 7 vertices. (The vertices 5, 6, 7, 8, 9, 10, and 11 are these seven vertices.) The prefix sums of the arcs $\langle 5, 8 \rangle$ and $\langle 8, 5 \rangle$ are 5 and 8, respectively. So number of descendants for 8 is three (they are the vertices 8, 10, and 11).

## 5.5   LEVEL OF EACH VERTEX

The root has level number 0. We travel along the Eulers path; when we travel along the arc $\langle p(v), v \rangle$, the level numbers of $p(v)$ is 1 less than two level number of $p(v)$. When we travel along $\langle v, p(v) \rangle$, the level number of $v$ is 1 more than the level number of $p(v)$. When we travel along $\langle v, p(v) \rangle$, the level number of $p(v)$ is 1 less than the level number of $v$. So, let us assign the weight +1 to all arcs of the form $\langle p(v), v \rangle$ and −1 to all the arc of the form $\langle v, p(v) \rangle$. Now perform the prefix sum on the list defined by the Euler path. Then level $(v)$ is the prefix sum of the arc $\langle p(v), v \rangle$. This illustrated in Table 5.5 for the tree shown in Fig. 3.

## 5.6   LOWEST COMMON ANCESTOR

In this section we are going to study a very interesting and useful problem on rooted trees. In a rooted tree $T$ with root $r$, the vertices on the path from a vertex $v$ to $r$ are said to be the ancestors of $v$. Given two vertices $u$ and $v$, the common ancestor of $u$ and $v$ which is farthest from the root is called the *lowest common ancestor* of $u$ and $v$ and is denoted by LCA $(u, v)$. For example, in the rooted tree shown in Fig. 5.3, LCA (2, 6) = 4; LCA (6, 10) = 5; LCA (7, 11) = 5; LCA (8, 11) = 8.

When $T$ itself is a simple path, the lowest common ancestor of two vertices $u$ and $v$ is the vertex $u$ or $v$ which is nearer to the root. The lowest common ancestor problem can be easily solved for complete binary trees also. If $T$ is a complete binary tree, first label the nodes using in order traversal. Now if $u$ and $v$ are the labels of two vertices, the lowest common ancestor of $u$ and $v$ is found by the following steps:

**TABLE 5.5    Level number.**

| Euler's Path | Weight | Prefix Sum |
|---|---|---|
| $\langle 4,2 \rangle$ | 1 | $1 \longrightarrow$ level(2) = 1 |
| $\langle 2,1 \rangle$ | 1 | $2 \longrightarrow$ level(1) = 2 |
| $\langle 1,2 \rangle$ | $-1$ | 1 |
| $\langle 2,4 \rangle$ | $-1$ | 0 |
| $\langle 4,3 \rangle$ | 1 | $1 \longrightarrow$ level(3) = 1 |
| $\langle 3,4 \rangle$ | $-1$ | 0 |
| $\langle 4,5 \rangle$ | 1 | $1 \longrightarrow$ level(5) = 1 |
| $\langle 5,6 \rangle$ | 1 | $2 \longrightarrow$ level(6) = 2 |
| $\langle 6,5 \rangle$ | $-1$ | 1 |
| $\langle 5,7 \rangle$ | 1 | $2 \longrightarrow$ level(7) = 2 |
| $\langle 7,5 \rangle$ | $-1$ | 1 |
| $\langle 5,8 \rangle$ | 1 | $2 \longrightarrow$ level(8) = 2 |
| $\langle 8,10 \rangle$ | 1 | $3 \longrightarrow$ level(10) = 3 |
| $\langle 10,11 \rangle$ | 1 | $4 \longrightarrow$ level (11) = 4 |
| $\langle 11,10 \rangle$ | $-1$ | 3 |
| $\langle 10,8 \rangle$ | $-1$ | 2 |
| $\langle 8,5 \rangle$ | $-1$ | 1 |
| $\langle 5,9 \rangle$ | 1 | $2 \longrightarrow$ level(9) = 2 |
| $\langle 9,5 \rangle$ | $-1$ | 1 |
| $\langle 5,4 \rangle$ | 1 | 2 |

1. Express $u$ and $v$ as binary numbers. Let $i$ be the first bit position from left where $x$ and $y$ disagree.

2. Let the left most $i - 1$ bits of $x$ and $y$ that are identical be $b_1, b_2, b_3 \ldots b_{i-1}$.

3. The lowest common ancestor of $u$ and $v$ has the label $b_1 b_2 b_3 \ldots b_{i-1}$ $1\ 0\ 0 \ldots 0$. For example, suppose $u = 47$ and $v = 61$

$$u = 101111$$

$$v = 111101$$

Scanning from left to right, they disagree at the second place. So the lowest common ancestor of $v = 47$ and $v = 61$ is 110000. That is, LCA (47, 61) = 48.

**LCA of a General Rooted Tree.** The method of finding the LCA of a general rooted tree is studied in this section. This method uses the Euler circuit of the tree. First we find the Euler circuit of the tree which begins from the root. The Euler circuit must be had as a list of arcs.

In this list replace every arc $\langle u, v \rangle$ by the vertex $v$. Then, finally, include the root at the very beginning. The list thus obtained is called the *Euler array* A. For example, the Euler array of the rooted tree given in Fig. 5.3 is A = (4, 2,

**TABLE 5.6** l(v) and r(v) values.

| Vertex v | 1 | 2 | 3 | 4 | 5 | 6 | 7 | 8 | 9 | 10 | 11 |
|----------|---|---|---|---|---|---|---|---|---|----|----|
| l(v)     | 3 | 2 | 6 | 1 | 8 | 9 | 11 | 13 | 19 | 14 | 15 |
| r(v)     | 3 | 4 | 6 | 21 | 20 | 9 | 11 | 17 | 19 | 16 | 15 |

1, 2, 4, 3, 4, 5, 6, 5, 7, 5, 8, 10, 11, 10, 8, 5, 9, 5). This array must be viewed as

$$A = (a_1, a_2, \ldots, a_m).$$

Let $B = (b_1, b_2, b_3, \ldots b_m)$, where $b_i$ is the level number of vertex $a_i$ in the tree $T$. For the tree shown in Fig. 5.3,

$$B = (0, 1, 2, 1, 0, 1, 0, 1, 2, 1, 2, 1, 2, 1, 2, 3, 4, 3, 2, 1, 2, 1).$$

We further define two more arrays, $l(v)$ and $r(v)$. For every vertex $v$, $l(v)$ is the index of the leftmost occurrence of $v$ in the array $A$, and $r(v)$ is the index of the rightmost occurrence of $v$ in the array $A$. For the tree shown in Fig. 5.3, $l(v)$ and $r(v)$ are shown in Table 5.6.

$$\text{Index} = (1, 2, 3, 4, 5, 6, 7, 8, 9, 10, 11, 12, 13, 14, 15, 16, 17, 18, 19, 20, 21)$$
$$A = (4, 2, 1, 2, 4, 3, 4, 5, 6, 5, 7, 5, 8, 10, 11, 10, 8, 5, 9, 5, 4)$$
$$B = (0, 1, 2, 1, 0, 1, 0, 1, 2, 1, 2, 1, 2, 3, 4, 3, 2, 1, 2, 1, 0)$$

We begin the Euler's path from the root and proceed as per the depth first search method. So we proceed to a vertex $v$ only from its parent first. So, in the leftmost appearance $a_i = v$, we have level $(a_{i-1}) + 1 = $ level $(a_i)$. Similarly, we go back from $v$ to parent of $v$, only after visiting all the nodes in the subtree rooted at $v$. If we go back from $v$ to its parent, we shall never come back to $v$. So, in the rightmost appearance $a_j = v$, we shall have $a_{j+1} = $ parent of $v$. Thus we have the rightmost appearance $a_j = v$, if and only if level $(a_j) - 1 = $ level $(a_{j+1})$. Hence, we have the following results:

**THEOREM 5.1**

1. *Given the array A, the element $a_i = v$ is the leftmost appearance of $v$ in A, if and only if level $(a_{i-1}) + 1 = $ level $(a_i)$.*
2. *The element $a_j = v$ is the rightmost appearance of $v$ in A, if and only if level $(a_i - 1 = $ level $(a_{i+1})$.*

Due to the depth-first procedure adopted in the Euler circuit, we have the following results:

**THEOREM 5.2**

1. *u is an ancestor of v, if and only if $l(u) < l(v) < r(u)$.*
2. *If u is not an ancestor of v and v is not an ancestor of u, we say that u and v are not related. u and v are not related if and only if either $r(u) < l(v)$ or $r(v) < l(u)$.*

When $u$ is an ancestor of $v$, the LCA$(u, v) = u$. When $u$ and $v$ are not related, we find LCA$(u, v)$ using the $B$ array. We observe that LCA$(u, v)$ appears in the path from $u$ to $v$. When $u$ and $v$ are not related, assume, without loss of generality, that $r(u) < l(v)$. Now LCA$(u, v)$ lies in the Euler's path between the rightmost appearance of $u$ and the leftmost appearance of $v$. This part of the Euler path visits only the vertices in the path from $u$ to $v$ and their descendants. So, the vertex having least level number in this part of the Euler's path is the LCA$(u, v)$. Hence we have the following result:

**THEOREM 5.3** *If $r(u) < l(v)$ then LCA$(u, v)$ is the vertex with minimum level over the interval $r(u)$ to $l(v)$.*

Now we summarize the method explained above, and present it formally as an algorithm:

**Algorithm LCA**
  **Input:**

1. A rooted tree $T$ in terms of parent relation.
2. Two nodes $u$ and $v$.

  **Output:** LCA$(u, v)$.

1. Find the Euler path beginning from the root.
2. In the Euler path, replace every arc $(u, v)$ by vertex $u$ and insert root at the beginning and get the array $A$.
3. Find array $B = (b_1, b_2, \ldots, b_m)$, where $b_i$ = level number of $a_i$, the $i$th entry of $A$.
4. For every vertex $x$ of $T$. Find $l(x)$ and $r(x)$, using the arrays $A$ and $B$.
5. If $l(u) < l(v) < r(u)$, then set LCA$(u, v) = u$ and return.
6. If $l(v) < l(u) < r(v)$, then set LCA$(u, v) = v$ and return.
7. If $r(u) < l(v)$ set $i = (r(u)$ and $j = l(v)$, else set $i = r(v)$ and $j = l(u)$.
8. Choose the index $k$ that is minimum in $\{b_i, b_{i+1}, b_{i+2}, \ldots b_j\}$.
9. LCA$(u, v) = a_k$.

  End LCA.

***Complexity and Analysis.*** As we have already studied, the Euler path can be found in constant time. The level number of a vertex also can be found in 0(1) time.

Hence $l(x)$ and $r(x)$ can also be found in 0(1) time. This shows that steps 1–4 can be done in 0(1) time. Step 5, 6, and 7 are simple 0(1) step instructions. Step 8 is the range minima problem. We have already studied that, by a preprocessing of the array, the range minima query can be answered in 0(1) time. But the preprocessing takes 0(log $n$) time with 0($n$ log $n$) processors. Hence the overall complexity of LCA problem is 0(log $n$) time, using 0($n$ log $n$) processors.

## 5.7   TREE CONTRACTION

Tree contraction is a systematic method to contract a binary tree and represent it as a complete tree with only three nodes. This has immediate application in arithmetic expression evaluation. In this section we study tree contraction algorithm and then, in the next section, we study its application to arithmetic expression evaluation. For example, consider the arithmetic expression (2 * $x$ + 4 * $y$)/(2 + $a$). This is represented as a binary tree shown in Fig. 5.4(a). Each interval node represents an operation and each leaf represents an operand. In

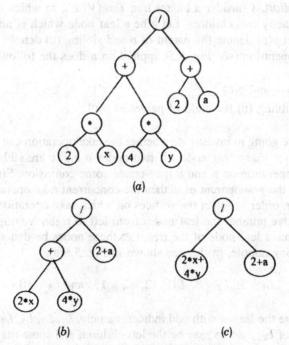

(a)

(b)          (c)

**Figure 5.4(a)**   (2 * $x$ + 4 * $y$)/(2 + $a$). **(b)** Contracted tree. **(c)** Contracted tree.

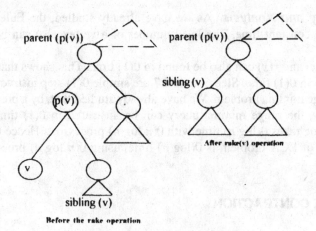

parent (p(v))  parent (p(v))

sibling (v)

p(v)

v

sibling (v)

After rake(v) operation

Before the rake operation

**Figure 5.5** Rake operation.

order to evaluate this expression, the values $2 * x$, $4 * y$ and $2 + a$ are first evaluated. (See Fig. 5.4(b)). Then $2 * x$ and $4 * y$ are added (see Fig. 5.4(c)). Finally, the value $2 * x + 4 * y$ is divided by $2 + a$. (See Fig. 5.4(c)). Here the original tree is contracted to the final tree, which gives the value of the expression. In order to contract a tree, we introduce an operation called *rake*.

**Rake Operation.** Consider a binary tree $T = (V, E)$, in which every internal vertex has exactly two children. Let $v$ be a leaf node which is not the child of the root $r$. Let $p(v)$ denote the parent of $v$ and sibling $(v)$ denote the sibling of $v$. The rake operation (see Fig. 5.5) applied on $u$ does the following works:

1. Remove $v$ and $p(v)$.
2. Make sibling $(v)$ the child of parent of $p(v)$.

Now we are going to investigate whether the rake operation can be performed concurrently for many leaf nodes. If two nodes $u$ and $v$ are siblings, the concurrent rake operation on $u$ and $v$ may create some confusion. Similarly, if the parent of $u$ is the grandparent of $v$, then the concurrent rake operation may create conflict. In order to select the vertices on which rake operation can be done concurrently, we number the leaf nodes from left to right, leaving the leftmost and the rightmost leaf node of the tree. Let these nodes be denoted by $L_1$, $L_2$, $L_3$, ... $L_n$. For example, in the tree shown in Fig. 5.6(a).

$$L_1 = 5; \ L_2 = 8; \ L_3 = 12; \ L_4 = 13; \ \text{and} \ L_5 = 10.$$

Let $L_{odd}$ denote the leaves with odd indices, namely, $L_1, L_3, L_5, L_7, \ldots$ . Among the elements of $L_{odd}$, some may be the left children and some may be the right children of their respective parents. We rake all the elements of $L_{odd}$ which

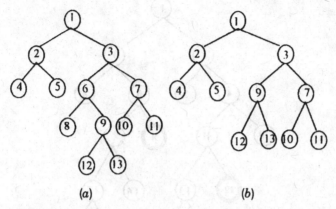

**Figure 5.6(a)** Before the operation rake (8). **(b)** After the operation rake (8).

are left children of their respective parents. Then we rake others. For example, in the tree shown in Fig. 5.6(a), $L_{odd} = (L_1, L_3, L_5) = (5, 12, 10)$. Among the members of $L_{odd}$, 5 is a right child of its parent and 12 and 10 are left children. First we do the rake operation on 12 and 10 concurrently. After this we do the rake operation on 5. That is, we do the rake operation on the nodes of $L_{odd}$ which are left children of their parents first, and then we rake the right children of $L_{odd}$. The process is illustrated using the tree shown in Fig. 5.7. Figure 5.7(a) shows a tree with 10 leaf nodes. In iteration 1, $L$ has 8 leaves

$$L = (12, 14, 15, 5, 8, 16, 18, 19)$$
$$L_{odd} = (12, 15, 8, 18)$$

Among the members for $L_{odd}$, 12, 8 and 18 are left children and 15 is a right child. So, we first rake on 12, 8 and 18 concurrently and then rake on 15 (see Fig. 5.7(a), (b), and (c)). In every figure, the nodes which are to be raked next are shown bold. Now for iteration 2 we have four members in $L$.

$$L = (14, 5, 16, 19);$$
$$L_{odd} = (14, 16).$$

Here 16 is a left child and 14 is a right child. So, first we rake 16 and then 14 (see Fig. 5.7(c), (d), and (e)). Now in iteration 3, we have $L = (5, 19)$ and $L_{odd} = (5)$. So we rake 5 only (see Fig. 5.7(e) and (f)). Finally, for the last iteration, we have $L = (19)$ and $L_{odd} = (19)$. After raking 19 we finally get the three-node complete binary tree in Fig. 5.7(g).

Notice that there were 8 members in $L$ at the beginning. For each iteration, the number of entries in $L$ is halved. So, if there are $n$ leaf nodes in $L$ initially, we reach a complete tree with 3 nodes in O(log $n$) iterations. Each iteration consists

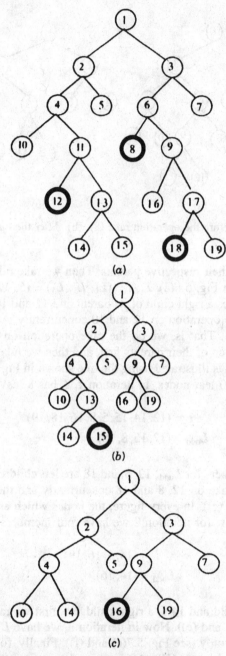

**Figure 5.7(a)**   A tree. For iteration − 1, $L$ = (12, 14, 15, 15, 8, 16, 18, 19) $L_{odd}$ = (12, 15, 8, 18). **(b)** After doing rake on 12, 8, and 18 concurrently. We are going to do rake on 15. **(c)** After doing rake on 15. Now for iteration-2 $L$ = (14, 5, 16, 19) $L_{odd}$ = (14, 16). We do rake on the left child 16 and then for the right child 14.

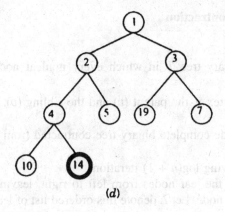

(d)

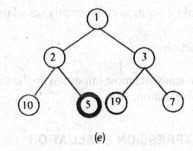

(e)

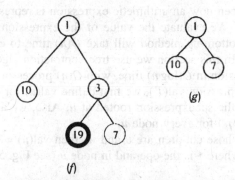

(g)

(f)

**Figure 5.7(d)** After doing rake operation on 16. Next we do rake on 14. **(e)** After the rake operation on 14. Now *m* for iteration 3, we have the new values $L = (5, 19)$ $L_{odd}$ = (5), we do rake on 5. **(f)** After doing rake on 5. Now for the last iteration, $L = (19)$ and $L_{odd} = (19)$ W do rake on 19. **(g)** After doing rake on 19. We have got ten final tree with 3 nodes.

of two steps. Each can be executed in constant time with $0(n)$ processors. So, the overall time complexity of this tree contraction algorithm is $0(\log n)$, with $0(n)$ processors in EREW PRAM. We now give the formal presentation of the tree contraction algorithm.

**Algorithm Tree Contraction**
**Input:**

1. A rooted binary tree $T$ in which every nonleaf node has exactly two children.
2. For every vertex $v$, the parent $(v)$ and the sibling $(v)$.

**Output:** A 3-node complete binary tree contracted from the original tree.

1. Do the following $\log(n + 1)$ iterations.
   1.1. Number the leaf nodes from left to right, leaving the leftmost and the rightmost node. Let $L$ denote this ordered list of leaves, which are left children.
   1.2. Apply the rake operation concurrently on all the nodes of $L_{\text{odd}}$ which are right children.
2. End Tree Contraction.

Now we are going to study the most important application of tree contraction, arithmetic expression evaluation.

## 5.8 ARITHMETIC EXPRESSION EVALUATION

We have already seen how an arithmetic expression is represented as a binary tree (see Fig. 5.4). We evaluate the value of the expression from the bottom of the tree. This bottom-up method will take $O(n)$ time to evaluate the value of the expression. In this section we use tree contraction algorithm to find the value of the expression in $O(\log n)$ time, with $O(n)$ processors. In order to find the value of the expression val$(T)$, we first define val$(u)$ for any internal node $u$, as the value of the subexpression rooted at $u$. Also, we associate a pair of real numbers $(p_u, q_u)$ for every node $u$.

If $u$ is a node whose children are $v$ and $w$, then val$(u) = \{p_v \text{val}(v) + q_v\} * \{p_w \text{val}(w) + q_w\}$, where $*$ is the operand in node $u$ (see Fig. 5.8). For example,

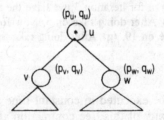

**Figure 5.8** A tree with $(p, q)$ values.

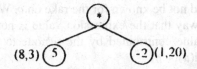

**Figure 5.9** A small tree with $(p, q)$ values.

consider the tree shown in Fig. 5.9. The value of the expression is $\{8 * 5 + 3\}$ $* \{(-2) * 1 + 20\} = (43) * (18) = 774$.

Initially for an ordinary expression tree, we assign $(p, q) = (1, 0)$ for every node. When a node $v$ is subject to rake operation, we adjust the $(p, q)$ values of nodes in the resultant tree, in such a way that the final value of the expression is not affected. Consider the tree shown in Fig. 5.10. Suppose the operation at the node $u$ is $*$ and leaf node $u$ contains a constant $c$.

Now we are going to rake the node $v$. After the rake operation on $v$, the resultant tree is shown in Fig. 5.10(b). Notice that the value of $w$ is the same as $X$ as before the rake, but the pair $(p_w, q_w)$ has now changed into $(p'_w, q'_w)$.

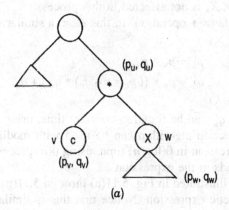

(a)

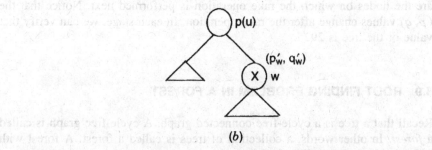

(b)

**Figure 5.10(a)** The tree before rake operation. **(b)** The tree after rake on $v$.

So, the value of $X$ need not be known for the rake on $v$. We are going to choose $p'_w$ and $q'_w$, in such a way that the expression value is not affected. Before the rake operation, the value contributed by the $u$ node to the evaluation at the parent of $u$ is $p_u * \text{val}(u) + q_u$

That is,

$$p_u\{p_v * c + q_v) * (p_w * X + q_w)\} + q_u,$$

which is equal to

$$\{p_u * (p_v * c + q_v) * p_w\} * X + \{p_u * (p_v * c + q_v) * q_w + q_u\}.$$

If we want to preserve the same value after the rake operation also, we must have

$$p'_w = p_u * (p_v * c + q_v) * p_w;$$
$$q'_w = p_u * (p_v * c + q_v) * q_w + q_u.$$

The value at $w$, $X$, is not affected in this process.

Suppose $u$ contains + operation. In this case, a similar derivation will give

$$p'_w = p_w * p_u;$$
$$q'_w = p_u * \{(p_v * c + q_v) * q_w\} + q_u.$$

Hence $p'_w$, and $q'_w$ can be found in constant time, using the above formulas. So the tree contraction algorithm can be used with modifications to evaluate an arithmetic expression in $0(\log n)$ time, using $0(n)$ processors, where $n$ is the number of operands in the expression.

The process is illustrated in Fig. 5.11(a) through 5.11(g). Figure 5.11(a) represents an arithmetic expression. Notice that this is similar to the tree shown in Fig. 5.7(a). The rake operations performed in Fig. 5.7(a) through 5.7(g) are performed in Fig. 5.11(a) through 5.11(g), in the same order. The bold nodes are the nodes on which the rake operation is performed next. Notice that the $(p, q)$ values change after the rake operation. In each stage, we can verify that value of the tree is 2925.


## 5.9  ROOT FINDING PROBLEM IN A FOREST

Recall that a tree is a cycle-free connected graph. A cycle-free graph is called a *forest*. In other words, a collection of trees is called a forest. A forest with 12 nodes is shown in Fig. 5.12.

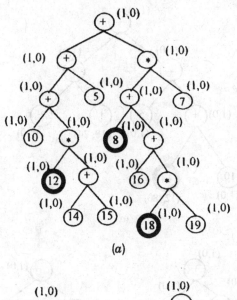

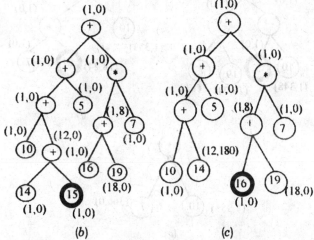

**Figure 5.11(a)**  The tree $T$ representing the arithmetic expression Val($T$) = {10 + (12 * (14 + 15) + 5} + {(8 + (16 + 18 * 19))) * 7} = 2925. **(b)** After rake on 12, 8, 18. **(c)** After rake on 15.

Let $R(v)$ denote the root of the tree in which the node $v$ is a member. For our example shown in Fig. 5.12, the $R$ values are given in Table 5.7.

We are going to develop an algorithm using the pointer jumping method, to find $R(v)$ for each node $v$. We start by choosing $R(v)$ = parent($v$) for every node $v$ in parallel. If $R(v)$ is the root, then we must have $R(R(v)) = R(v)$.

Until we get $R(R(v)) = R(v)$, we assign $R(v) = R(R(v))$. The working is

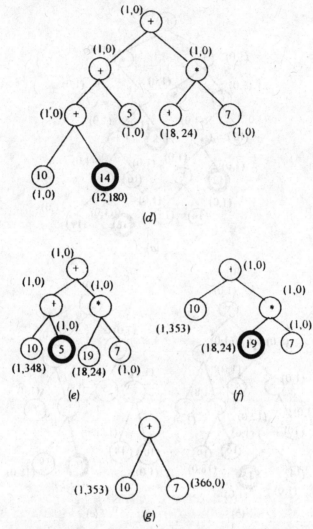

**Figure 5.11(d)**   After rake on 16. **(e)** After rake on 14.
**(f)** After rake on 5. **(g)** val($T$) = {10 + 353} + {7 * 366} = 2925.

illustrated, using the forest shown in Fig. 5.13. The value of $R(i)$ at each stage
are tabulated in Table 5.8.

The parallel algorithm is shown below:

**Algorithm Find-Root**
   **Input:**   A forest represented by the array PARENT $(1:n)$.
   **Output:**   $R(1:n)$.

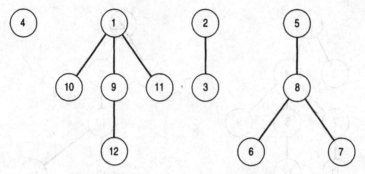

**Figure 5.12**  A forest and its parent relation.

BEGIN
  1. For $i = i$ to $n$ do in parallel
  2.    $R(i) = \text{PARENT }(i)$
  3.    while $R(i)$ and $R(R(i))$ are not equal do
  4.    $R(i) = R(R(i))$
  5. Endwhile
  6. End Parallel
END

**Complexity Analysis.** Clearly the number of processors needed is $O(n)$. The while loop in steps 3–5 is repeated at the most $[\log n]$ times. This is because of the following reason: First $R(v) = \text{PARENT}(v)$. So, $R(v)$ gives the ancestor of $v$ at a distance 1 from $v$ toward the root. Whenever we assign $R(R(v))$, the distance is doubled. So, the whole height of the tree is traversed $[\log h]$ times, where $h$ is the height of the tree. But $h \leq n$ and, hence, the computing time of the algorithm, is $O(\log n)$. When step 4 is executed, two read operation take place. One is $R(i)$ and the other is $R(R(i))$. $R(i)$ values may be equal for two different $i$ values. So a concurrent read takes place. However, concurrent write never takes place. So this algorithm can be implemented in a CREW PRAM model.

## 5.10  PATHS TO THE ROOT

We present the problem of finding the path between every node and the root in an arbitrary tree as another example for the pointer jumping paradigm.

**TABLE 5.7  Root array for the forest in Fig. 5.12.**

| v | 1 | 2 | 3 | 4 | 5 | 6 | 7 | 8 | 9 | 10 | 11 | 12 |
|------|---|---|---|---|---|---|---|---|---|----|----|----|
| R(v) | 1 | 2 | 2 | 4 | 5 | 5 | 5 | 5 | 1 | 1  | 1  | 1  |

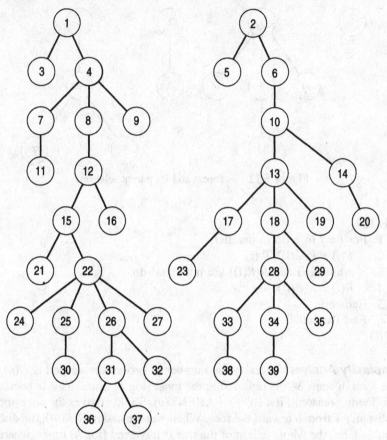

**Figure 5.13**   A forest with 39 nodes.

Let $T = (V, E)$ be a rooted tree with root $r$ represented by the
PARENT relation.

PARENT$(v)$ = parent of vertex $v$ in the tree if $v$ is not the root
         = $r$ if $v = r$, the root.

Initially we have a path of length 1 only from every vertex to its parent.
At the next stage, all the paths of length at most 2 toward the root are found.
Then all the paths of length at most 4 toward the roots are found. Proceeding in
this manner, the paths from every vertex to the root are found in [log $h$] steps,
where $h$ is the height of the tree. The paths are represented by the variable
PATH. PATH $(v)$ is the path constructed from $v$ to the root. It is a sequence of
(adjacent) vertices. At one stage, suppose that

**TABLE 5.8 Root finding for the forest in Fig. 5.13.**

| | R(v) | | | | | R(v) | | | |
|---|---|---|---|---|---|---|---|---|---|
| v | Initial | Stage-1 | Stage-2 | Stage-3 | v | Initial | Stage-1 | Stage-2 | Stage-3 |
| 1 | 1 | 1 | 1 | 1 | 21 | 15 | 12 | 4 | 1 |
| 2 | 2 | 2 | 2 | 2 | 22 | 15 | 12 | 4 | 1 |
| 3 | 1 | 1 | 1 | 1 | 23 | 17 | 13 | 6 | 2 |
| 4 | 1 | 1 | 1 | 1 | 24 | 22 | 15 | 8 | 1 |
| 5 | 2 | 2 | 2 | 2 | 25 | 22 | 15 | 8 | 1 |
| 6 | 2 | 2 | 2 | 2 | 26 | 22 | 15 | 8 | 1 |
| 7 | 4 | 1 | 1 | 1 | 27 | 22 | 15 | 8 | 1 |
| 8 | 4 | 1 | 1 | 1 | 28 | 18 | 13 | 6 | 2 |
| 9 | 4 | 1 | 1 | 1 | 29 | 18 | 13 | 6 | 2 |
| 10 | 6 | 2 | 2 | 2 | 30 | 25 | 22 | 12 | 1 |
| 11 | 7 | 4 | 1 | 1 | 31 | 26 | 22 | 12 | 1 |
| 12 | 8 | 4 | 1 | 1 | 32 | 26 | 22 | 12 | 1 |
| 13 | 10 | 6 | 2 | 2 | 33 | 28 | 18 | 10 | 2 |
| 14 | 10 | 6 | 2 | 2 | 34 | 28 | 18 | 10 | 2 |
| 15 | 12 | 8 | 1 | 1 | 35 | 28 | 18 | 10 | 2 |
| 16 | 12 | 8 | 1 | 1 | 36 | 31 | 26 | 15 | 1 |
| 17 | 13 | 10 | 2 | 2 | 37 | 31 | 26 | 15 | 1 |
| 18 | 13 | 10 | 2 | 2 | 38 | 33 | 28 | 13 | 2 |
| 19 | 13 | 10 | 2 | 2 | 39 | 34 | 28 | 13 | 2 |
| 20 | 14 | 10 | 2 | 2 | | | | | |

$$PATH(1) = (1, 2, 7)$$
$$PATH(7) = (7, 9, 3).$$

We denote

$$PATH(1)//PATH(7) = (1, 2, 7, 9, 3).$$

The symbol // is used two connect to paths having a common end to form a longer path. We also define another variable, $ANC(v)$ (ancestor). Initially, $ANC(v) = PARENT(v)$, and $PATH(v) = (v, PARENT(v))$.

At the next stage, we find the longer path from $v$ toward the root by the operation:

$$PATH(v) = PATH(v)//PATH(ANC(v)).$$

We update the ANC values:

$$ANC(v) = ANC(ANC(v)).$$

This finds the ancestor at a longer distance. Note that the PATH from $v$ to ANC($v$) has now been constructed. We once again double the length of the path as

$$PATH(v) = PATH(v)//PATH(ANC(v)).$$

For every vertex, this process gives the path from the vertex to the root in [log $h$] steps, where $h$ is the height of the tree. The process is illustrated below by an example. Consider the tree shown in Fig. 5.14(a). The *height* of the tree is 4. The tree is represented by the PARENT relation. Initially we have the paths and the ancestor value as in Fig. 5.14(b). Figure 5.14(c), (d), and (e) show the position of after stages 1 and 2, respectively. After stage 2, PATH(1), PATH(2), PATH(3), PATH(4), PATH(5), PATH(6), PATH(9), PATH(10), and PATH(12) are the same as in stage 1, because their corresponding ANC values are the root 3. We must extend the path only for the vertices $v$, for which ANC($v$) is not the root. The parallel algorithm is shown below.

**Algorithm Tree-Path**
  **Input:** $T = (V, E)$ is given in the form of PARENT ($v$) for each $v$.
  **Output:** PATH($v$) for each $v \in V$.

BEGIN
  1. For all $v \in V$ do in parallel
     ANC($v$) = PARENT($v$)PATH($v$) = ($v$, PARENT($v$))
     End Parallel
  2. Repeat the following steps [log $h$] times where $h$ is the height of the tree. If $h$ is not given its maximum value $n - 1$ must be considered where $n$ is number of vertices.
    2.1. For all $v \in V$ do in Parallel
    2.2. If ANC($v$) is not root
       PATH($v$) = PATH($v$)//PATH(ANC($v$))
       ANC($v$) = ANC (ANC($v$))
    2.3. Endif
    2.4. End Parallel
END Tree Path

This algorithm works in $O(\log h)$ time, using $O(n)$ processor. This needs CREW PRAM model, because ANC($v$) may be the same for more than one vertex $v$.

## 5.11 CONVERTING A TREE INTO A BINARY TREE

The commonly used data structure to represent a tree is a single-dimensional array PARENT, which gives the parent of the vertex.

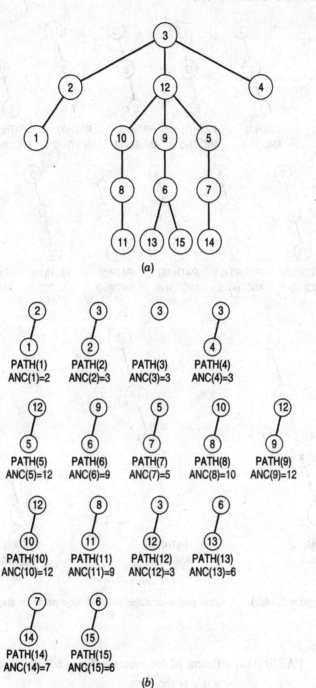

**Figure 5.14(a)**  A tree $T$. **(b)** Initial stage $T$.

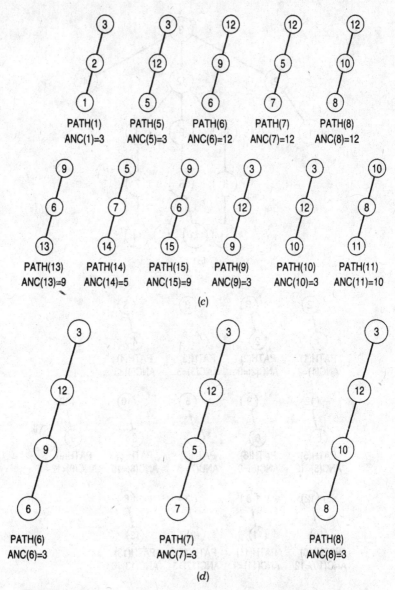

Figure 5.14(c) A some paths in stage 1. (d) Some paths in stage 2.

PARENT($u$) = Parent of the vertex $u$ if $u$ is not the root

= $u$ if $u$ is the root.

For example, consider the tree given in Fig. 5.15. The PARENT relation is shown in Table 5.9. Unfortunately, this data structure will be highly inefficient

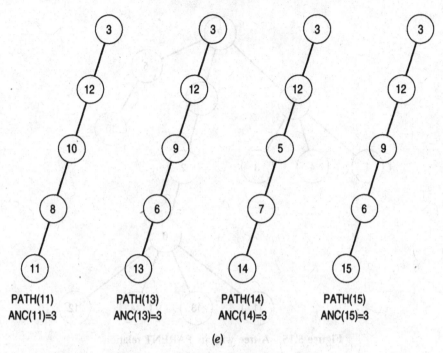

PATH(11)  PATH(13)  PATH(14)  PATH(15)
ANC(11)=3  ANC(13)=3  ANC(14)=3  ANC(15)=3

(e)

**Figure 5.14(e)**  Some paths in stage 2.

for processing the tree structure. So, a tree is converted into a binary tree. Only after converting into a binary tree, the operations are performed efficiently. For practical convenience, let us represent the nodes by integers 1, 2 ... n. For any node i, all its children are arranged in such a way that the indices of the children increase from left to right. So, the leftmost child has the smallest index. The method of transforming a tree into a binary tree is as follows: Let i be a node. Let $i_1, i_2, \ldots i_k$ be the children of i, such that $i_1 < i_2 < i_3 \ldots < i_k$. In the binary tree:

> left child of i is $i_1$;
> right child of $i_1$ is $i_2$;
> right child of $i_2$ is $i_3$;
> ...        ...
> right child of $i_{k-1}$ is $i_k$.

This is illustrated in Fig. 5.16. A binary tree is represented by three single-dimensional arrays, PARENT, LCHILD, and RCHILD each indexed by the vertices:

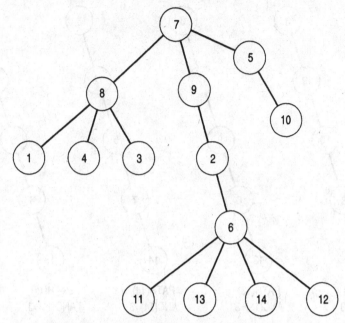

**Figure 5.15**   A tree with its PARENT relation.

LCHILD($i$) = left child of $i$ in the binary tree;

RCHILD($i$) = right child of $i$ in the binary tree.

When a tree is converted into a binary tree, we have seen that the child of $i$ with the smallest index is chosen as the left child of $i$. The right of a node $i$ is the sibling of $i$, with least index higher than $i$.

LCHILD($i$) = child of $i$ having least index;

RCHILD($i$) = sibling of $i$ having least index but greater than $i$.

More formally, we can write

$$\text{LCHILD}(i) = \begin{cases} j \text{ if } j = Min\{k/Parent(k) = i\} \\ o \text{ if } no \ vertex \ exists, \ such \ that \ its \ Parent \ is \ i. \end{cases}$$

$$\text{RCHILD}(i) = \begin{cases} j \text{ if } j = Min\{k > i/Parent(i) = Parent(k)\} \\ o \text{ if } no \ vertex \ exists, \ such \ that \ Parent(i) = Parent(k). \end{cases}$$

Figure 5.17 is a tree and its binary tree representation. The PARENT, LCHILD, and RCHILD values are given in Table 5.10.

In order to evaluate the LCHILD and RCHILD values, we must first sort

**TABLE 5.9** Parent relation.

| Vertex | PARENT |
|:------:|:------:|
| 1 | 8 |
| 2 | 9 |
| 3 | 8 |
| 4 | 8 |
| 5 | 7 |
| 6 | 2 |
| 7 | 7 |
| 8 | 7 |
| 9 | 7 |
| 10 | 5 |
| 11 | 6 |
| 12 | 6 |
| 13 | 6 |
| 14 | 6 |

the nodes to ascending order. That is, the nodes must be sorted in such a way
that the LCHILD and RCHILD are evaluated easily. The parallel algorithm to
output LCHILD and RCHILD array is given below.

**Algorithm Binary-Tree**
　**Input:** PARENT(1: n).
　**Output:** LCHILD (1: n), RCHILD(1: n).

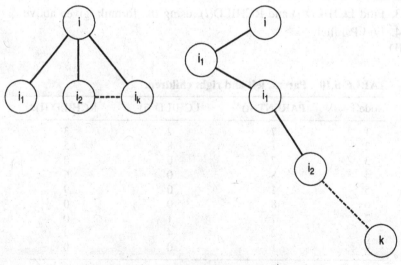

**Figure 5.16** Transforming into a binary tree.

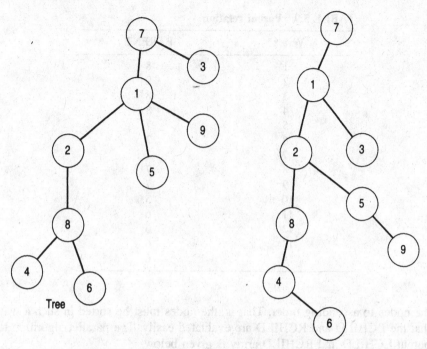

**Figure 5.17** A tree its binary tree representation.

BEGIN
1. Arrange the nodes in a convenient order so that the evaluation can be done efficiently
2. For $i = 1$ to $n$ do in parallel
3. Find LCHILD($i$) and RCHILD($i$), using the formula given above
4. End Parallel.
END

**TABLE 5.10  Parent, left and right children.**

| Node i | PARENT (i) | LCHILD (i) | RCHILD (I) |
|--------|------------|------------|------------|
| 1 | 7 | 2 | 3 |
| 2 | 1 | 8 | 5 |
| 3 | 7 | 0 | 0 |
| 4 | 8 | 0 | 6 |
| 5 | 1 | 0 | 9 |
| 6 | 8 | 0 | 0 |
| 7 | 7 | 1 | 0 |
| 8 | 2 | 4 | 0 |
| 9 | 1 | 0 | 0 |

The above algorithm can be implemented in $O(\log n)$ time, using $O(n)$ processors in a CREW PRAM model.

## 5.12 DIAMETER OF ALL THE VERTICES OF A TREE

In this section we study the parallel algorithm to find the diameter of all the vertices of a tree. The diameter of a vertex $v$ of a tree $T$ is the vertices of a tree. The diameter of a vertex $v$ of a tree $T$ is the length of the longest path from $v$ to any other vertex in $T$.

That is,

$$dia(v) = Max\{d(v, w), w \in T\},$$
where $d(v, w)$ means the shortest distance from $v$ to $w$.

The algorithm is designed based on two properties of trees. They are first stated and proved.

**THEOREM 5.12.1** *Let $T = (V, E)$ be a tree and $u, v$ be two vertices of $T$, such that*

$$Max \{d(i, u), d(i, v)\} \le d(u, v) \qquad \text{for every } i \in V.$$

*Then, for any vertex $i \in V$, $dia(i) = Max\{d(i, u), d(i, v)\}$ In particular, the path from $u$ to $v$ is one of the longest paths in $T$.*

*Proof.* A simple observation of the statement makes it clear that $u$ and $v$ must be leaf nodes. Let $i$ and $j$ be two arbitrary vertices of $T$. We are going to prove that

$$d(i, j) \le Max\{d(i, u), d(i, v)\}.$$

If this proved, then, since $j$ is an arbitrary vertex of $T$ the $dia(i) = Max\{d(i, u), d(i, v)\}$ and, hence, the proof will be complete. Now let us prove that

$$d(i, j) \le Max\{d(i, u), d(i, v)\}.$$

Let $w$ be a vertex in the path from $u$ to $v$ which is nearest to $j$. By hypothesis, we have $d(j, v) \le d(u, v)$. Therefore,

$$\begin{aligned}
d(j, w) &= d(j, v) - d(v, w) \le d(u, v) - d(v, w) \\
&\le d(u, w) + d(v, w) - d(v, w) \\
&= d(w, u)
\end{aligned}$$

Similarly, by using the fact that

$$d(j,u) \le d(u,v),$$

we can also show that

$$d(j,w) \le d(w,v).$$

We are going to use the two results

$$d(j,w) \le d(w,u)$$
$$d(j,w) \le d(w,v),$$

obtained just now to achieve our goal.

## Case 1

Suppose the path from $u$ to $v$ and the path from $i$ to $j$ have some common vertices. Notice that

$$d(i,w) + d(w,u) = d(i,u)$$
$$d(i,w) + d(w,v) = d(i,v).$$

We have, in the former case,

$$\begin{aligned} d(i,j) &= d(i,w) + d(w,j) \\ &\le d(i,w) + d(w,u) \\ &= d(i,u) \end{aligned}$$

In the latter case, we have

$$\begin{aligned} d(i,j) &= d(i,w) + d(w,j) \\ &\le d(i,w) + d(w,v) \\ &= d(i,v) \end{aligned}$$

So we have

$$d(i,j) \le Max\{d(i,u), d(i,v)\}$$

## Case 2

Suppose the path from $u$ to $v$ and the path from $i$ to $j$ do not share any common vertex. Let $j'$ be the vertex in the path from $i$ to $j$ which is nearest to $w$. Then it is easy to see that

$$d(j',j) \leq d(j,w) \leq d(w,u)$$

Therefore,

$$d(i,j) = d(i,j') + (d(j',j)$$
$$\leq d(i,j') + d(w,u)$$
$$\leq d(i,j') + d(j',w) + d(w,u)$$
$$= d(i,u).$$

Similarly, we can show that $d(i,j) \leq d(i,v)$. So, in both cases we have the result

$$d(i,j) \leq \text{Max}\{d(i,u), d(i,v)\}.$$

Hence the proof of the theorem is complete.

**THEOREM 5.12.2.** *Let $T$ be a tree and let $u$ be a vertex of $T$. Then for any vertex $k$ such that $dia(u) = d(u, k)$, thee is a longest path of the tree $T$, with $k$ being one of its end points.*

*Proof.* Consider the tree $T$ as a rooted tree with $u$ as its root. As per the choice of $k$ in the statement of the theorem, $k$ is a leaf node. Let $v, w$ be two vertices of $T$. Let $j_1$ be the lowest common ancestor of $v$ and $w$.

## Case 1

Suppose $j$ is an ancestor of $k$. This case we have by the choice of $k$.

$$d(j,v) \leq d(j,k);$$
$$d(j,w) \leq d(j,k).$$

Also note that

$$d(v,k) = d(v,j) + d(j,k)$$

or

$$d(w,k) = d(w,j) + d(j,k).$$

Thus

$$d(v,w) = d(j,v) + d(j,w)$$
$$\leq \text{Max}\{d(v,k), d(w,k)\}.$$

## Case 2

Suppose $j$ is not an ancestor of $k$. Let $j_1$, be the lowest common ancestor of $k$ and $j$. Then we have

$$d(v,j) < d(v,j_1)$$

and

$$d(w,j) < d(w,j_1).$$

By condition on $k$, we further have

$$d(v,j_1) \leq d(j_1,k).$$

Thus

$$\begin{aligned}
d(v,w) &= d(v,j) + d(w,j) \\
&< d(v,j_1) + d(w,j_1) \\
&\leq d(k,j_1) + d(w,j_1) \\
&= d(w,k).
\end{aligned}$$

Also, we can show that $d(v,w) \leq d(v,k)$. Hence $d(v,w) \leq \text{Max}\{d(w,k), d(v,k)\}$. In Cases 1 and 2, we have proved that

$$d(v,w) \leq \text{Max}\{d(w,k), d(v,k)\}.$$

From this, the result of the theorem follows immediately. Now we are ready to describe the algorithm to find the diameter of all the vertices of a tree $T$.

**Algorithm Diameter**
  **Input:**   Tree $T = (V, E)$.
  **Output:**   dia(i) for each $i \in V$.

BEGIN
  1. Choose an arbitrary vertex $i \in V$ and compute $\{d(i,j)/j \in V\}$.
  2. Find the maximum of the set $\{d(i,j)/j \in V\}$ and the vertex $u$, such that $d(i,u)$ is the maximum. So, dia(i) = $d(i,u)$.
  3. Compute $\{d(u,w)w \in V\}$.
  4. Choose the maximum of $\{d(u,w)/w \in V\}$ and find the vertex $v \in V$, such that dia(u) = $d(u,v)$.
  5. Compute $\{d(v,i)/i \in V\}$.
  6. For each vertex $j \in V$ do in parallel
  7.     $dia(j) = Max\{d(u,j), d(v,j)\}$
  8. End parallel
END

In a tree, given the distance of one vertex, from all other vertices it can be computed in $O(\log n)$ time, using $O(n/\log n)$ processors. Similarly, the maximum of integers can be obtained in $O(\log n)$ time, using $O(n/\log n)$ processors. So the algorithm DIAMETER works in $O(\log n)$ time, using $O(n/\log n)$ processors.

## 5.13 FURTHEST NEIGHBORS IN TREES

Let $T = (V, E)$ be a tree where every edge is having a real valued positive weight. A vertex $v$ is called a *furthest neighbor* of a vertex $u \in V$ if

$$dia(u) = d(u, v),$$

where $d(u, v)$ represents the sum of the weights of edges of the path from $u$ to $v$, and $dia(u)$ denotes the diameter of $u$. Notice that a vertex can have more than one furthest neighbor. For example, in the tree given in Fig. 5.18, vertex $u$ has three furthest neighbors $x$, $y$, and $z$. A furthest neighbor of each vertex in any graph can be computed by computing the transitive closure of the adjacency matrix of the graph. The transitive closure can be computed in $O(\log^2 n)$ time using $O(n^3)$ processors. But, in the case of trees, Ghosh and Maheswari (1992)

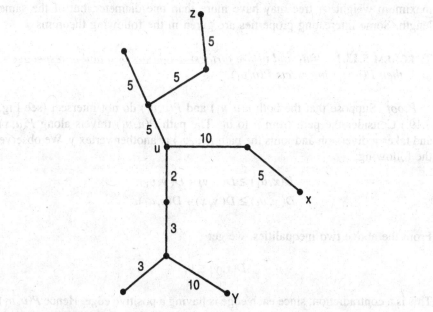

**Figure 5.18** $x$, $y$, and $z$ are the furthest neighbors of vertex $u$.

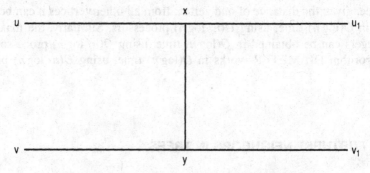

**Figure 5.19** $P(u, u_1)$ and $P(v, v_1)$ are disjoint.

have shown that, if the longest path in the tree is between two vertices $u$ and $v$, then a furthest neighbor of each vertex is either $u$ or $v$. Using this property, efficient parallel algorithms have been designed in this section.

Let us first define some notations for the development of the algorithm. $P(u, v)$ denotes the unique path in the tree from $u$ to $v$.

$$D(u, v) = \text{Distance between } u \text{ and } v$$
$$= \text{sum of the weights of edge in } P(u, v)$$

$P(u, v) \cap P(x, y)$ denotes the maximal path common to $P(u, v)$ and $P(x, y)$. A diameter of the tree $T$ is dfined to be the longest path, that is, the path with maximum weight. A tree may have more than one diameter, but of the same length. Some interesting properties are given in the following theorems

**THEOREM 5.13.1** *If $u_1$ and $v_1$ are furthest neighbors of $u$ and $v$, respectively, in $T$, then $P(u, u_1)$ intersects $P(v, v_1)$.*

*Proof.* Suppose that the both $p(u, u_1)$ and $P(v, v_1)$ do not intersect (see Fig. 5.19.) Consider the path from $u$ to $v_1$. The path $P(u, v_1)$ travels along $P(u, x)$ and takes a diversion and joins the path $P(v, v_1)$ at another vertex $y$. We observe the following:

$$D(x, u_1) \geq D(x, y) + D(y, v_1);$$
$$D(y, v_1) \geq D(y, x) + D(x, u_1).$$

From the above two inequalities, we get

$$D(x, y) \leq 0.$$

This is a contradiction, since each edge is having a positive edge. Hence $P(u, u_1)$ and $P(v, v_1)$ intersect.

**COROLLARY 5.13.2** *The path between a vertex and one of its furthest neighbors always intersects all diameters of the tree.*

**THEOREM 5.13.3** *Let $P(u, v)$ be a diameter of the tree $T = (V, E)$. Then, for any vertex $x \in V$, either $u$ or $v$ is a furthest neighbor of $x$.*

*Proof.* Let $P(u, v)$ be a diameter and $x \in v$ be an arbitrary vertex. Let $y$ be a furthest neighbor of $x$. It is enough if we prove that

$$D(x, y) = D(x, u) orD(x, y) = D(x, v).$$

As per corollary, $P(x, y)$ and $P(u, v)$ intersect, let

$$P(x, y) \cap P(u, v) = P(p, q).$$

Let $p$ be a vertex in $P(u, q)$. We see that

$$D(q, v) \geq D(q, y).$$

This is because $P(u, v)$ is a diameter. Also, since $y$ is a furthest neighbor of $x$, we have

$$D(q, y) \geq D(q, v)$$

From the above discussion, we conclude that

$$D(q, y) = D(q, v).$$

Hence we have

$$D(x, y) = D(x, v).$$

The proof is complete.

If we know a diameter $P(u, v)$ of the tree $T$, we can compute the furthest neighbor of each vertex $x$ of $T$ by comparing $D(x, u)$ and $D(x, v)$. So, our method must first find a diameter. Theorem 5.12.2 suggests the procedure to find a diameter. The above results give the following procedure to find a diameter of the tree:

1. Let $x$ be an arbitrary vertex.
2. Let a furthest neighbor of $x$ be $y$.
3. Let a furthest neighbor of $y$ be $z$.
4. $P(y, z)$ is a diameter of $T$.

If a diameter $P(y, z)$ is found, then, for any vertex $u \in V$, further neighbors of

$$u = \begin{cases} y & \text{if } D(y, u) \geq D(z, u) \\ z & \text{otherwise.} \end{cases}$$

It is possible to prove that the above method can be implemented in $O(\log n)$ time, using $O(n/\log n)$ processors.

## BIBLIOGRAPHY

Akl, S. G. (1989) *The Design and Analysis of Parallel Algorithms*, Prentice-Hall, Englewood Cliffs, NJ.

Samy, A. A., Arumugam, G., Devasahayam, M. and Xavier, C. (1991) Algorithms for Intersection Graphs of Internally Disjoint Paths in Trees, *Proceedings of National Seminar on Theoretical Computer Science*, IMSC, Madras, India, Report 115, pp. 169–178.

Arnborg, S., Lagergren, J., and Seese, D. (1989) Problems Are Easy for Tree-Decomposable Graphs, in T. Lepistoo and A. Salomaa, ed., *15th ICALP*, pp. 335–351.

Arikati, S. R., and Pandurangan, C. (1989) Linear Algorithms for Parity Path Problems on Circular Arc Graphs. Workshop on Algorithms and Data Structures, Ottawa, Canada.

Albacea, E. A. (1994) Parallel Algorithm for Finding a Core of a Tree Network, *Information Processing Letters*, **51** 223–226.

Berge, C., and Chvatal, C. ed. (1984) Topics on Perfect Graphs, *Annals of Discrete Mathematics*, **21**.

Bondy, J. A., and Murty, U. S. R. (1976) *Graph Theory with Applications*, North-Holland, New York.

Bandelt, H. J. and Mulder, H. M. (1986) Distance–Hereditary Graphs. *Journal of Combinational Theory*, Series B, **41**, 182–208.

Bouchet, (1988) Transforming Trees by Successive Local complementation. *Journal of Graph Theory*, **12**, 195–207.

Chen, Z. Z. (1992) A Simple Parallel Algorithm for Computing the Diameters of All Vertices in a Tree and Its Applications, *Information Processing Letters*, **42** 243–248.

Ghosh, S. K., and Maheswari, A. (1992) An Optimal Parallel Algorithms for Computing the Furthest Neighbours in a Tree, *Information Processing Letters*, **44**, 155–160.

Nykanen, M. and Ukkonen, E. (1994) Finding Lowest Common Ancestors in Arbtitrarily Directed Trees, *Information Processing Letters*, **50**, 307–310.

Wu, S. and Mamber, U. (1988) Algorithms for Generalised Matching, Technical Report Tr 88-39, Department of Computer Science, University of Arizona.

Wu, S. and Manber, U. (1992) Path Matching Problems, *Algorithmica*, **8**, 89–101.

Xavier, C. and Arumugam, G. (1994) Algorithms for Parity Path Problems in Some Classes of Graphs, *Computer Science and Informatics*, **24(4)** 50–54.

Xavier, C. (1995) Sequential and Parallel Algorithms for Some Graph Theoretic Problems (Ph.D. Thesis), Madurai Kamaraj University. Madurai, India.

Yannakakis, M. (1981) Computing the Minimum Fill-In is NP-Complete. *SIAM J. Alg. and Disc. Methods*, **2**, 77–79.

## EXERCISES

**5.1.** Let $T$ be a tree represented in the form of its adjacency list. The adjacency list is just a linear list. Develop an algorithm to determine the Euler Tour.

**5.2.** The preorder traversal of a tree consists of a traversal of the root $r$, followed by the preorder traversal of each of the subtrees of $r$ from left to right. Develop a parallel algorithm to obtain the preorder number of each vertex $v$ in $O(\log n)$ time, using EREW PRAM model.

**5.3.** Let $T = (V, E)$ be a tree. It is also given $s(v)$, the next sibling of $v$ for each vertex and $fc(v)$, the first child of $v$ for each vertex. From these two values, we want to find the parent of each vertex $v$. Develop a parallel algorithm for this.

**5.4.** The inorder traversal of a rooted binary tree consists of the inorder traversal of the left subtree of the root $r$, followed by the traversal of $r$, followed by the inorder traversal of the right subtree of $r$. Develop on $O(\log n)$ time algorithm to find the inorder number of each vertex.

**5.5.** In a binary tree each vertex $v$ has a weight $w(v)$. For each vertex $v$, $S(v)$ is the sum of the weights of all the vertices in the subtree rooted at $v$. Develop a parallel algorithm to find $S(v)$ for each vertex $v$.

**5.6.** A vertex $v$ is said to be a centroid of the tree $T$ if the removal of $v$ results in subtrees each of size less than or equal to $n$ (where $n$ is the number of vertices originally in $T$). Develop an algorithm that works in $O(\log n)$ time on a EREW PRAM.

**5.7.** Let $T$ be a tree. We want to root the tree such that the height of the tree is minimum. Develop a parallel algorithm to choose a vertex $v$ and root the tree $T$, with $v$ as the root so that $T$ is of minimum height.

**5.8.** Let $T$ $(V, E)$ be a rooted tree with root $r$. Let size$(v)$ be the number of vertices in the subtree rooted at $v$. Develop a parallel algorithm to find size$(v)$ for each vertex $v$.

**5.9.** Let $X(1 : n) = (x_1, x_2, \ldots, x_n)$ be an array of distinct numbers. A pair $(a_i, a_j)$ is said to be a matching pair if $i < j$ and $a_i < a_j$. Develop a parallel algorithm to identify all the matching pairs of this array.

**5.10.** Let $T$ be a rooted tree. For each vertex $v$, the number of descendants of $v$ is denoted by des$(v)$. Develop a parallel algorithm to find des$(v)$ for each vertex $v$.

## CHAPTER 6

# Graph Algorithms

Graphs are used to represent a number of real-life situations. Even social applications, such as personal relationships among the staff of an institution, can be represented using graphs, and studied. Transportation systems, communication systems, job scheduling, and facility supply problems are some useful areas which are represented and analyzed using graph models. After the invention of computers, the study of graph theory got an acceleration and the algorithmic graph theory was rigorously studied. The researchers have developed efficient algorithms for various graph problems. In recent years, the design and analysis of parallel algorithms for graph problems is considered to be a very useful area of research.

## 6.1 SIMPLE GRAPH ALGORITHMS

In this section, parallel algorithms are developed for a number of simple graph problems. In order to make the reader comfortable, some easy graph problems are first considered. Let us first start from the problem of determining the degree of each vertex. Whenever a problem is considered, the data structure assumed plays a major role in the design of algorithms. In our first study, let us assume that a graph is represented in terms of its adjacency matrix. The following theorem proposes how an algorithm must be designed for finding the degree of each vertex of a graph.

**THEOREM 6.1** *Let $G = (V, E)$ be a simple graph. Let n and m be the number of vertices and the number of edges in the graph. Let the vertices be denoted by the integers from 1 to n. Let A be the adjacency matrix of G. The degree of the vertex i is*

$$d(i) = \sum_{j=1}^{n} A(i,j).$$

*Proof.* As per the definition of the adjacency matrix,

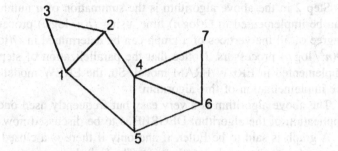

**Figure 6.1** A graph G.

$$A(i,j) = \begin{cases} 1 & \text{if } i \text{ is adjacent } j \\ O & \text{otherwise} \end{cases}$$

So $\sum_{j=1}^{n} A(i,j)$ gives the number of edges incident on $i$. Hence the proof is complete. For example, consider the graph shown in Fig. 6.1. Its adjacency matrix is

$$\begin{pmatrix} 0 & 1 & 1 & 0 & 1 & 0 & 0 \\ 1 & 0 & 1 & 1 & 0 & 0 & 0 \\ 1 & 1 & 0 & 0 & 0 & 0 & 0 \\ 0 & 1 & 0 & 0 & 1 & 1 & 1 \\ 1 & 0 & 0 & 1 & 0 & 1 & 0 \\ 0 & 0 & 0 & 1 & 1 & 0 & 1 \\ 0 & 0 & 0 & 1 & 0 & 1 & 0 \end{pmatrix}$$

The degree of vertex $i$ is given by the row sum of the $i$th row of the adjacency matrix. That is, $d(1) = 3$; $d(2) = 3$; $d(3) = 2$; $d(4) = 4$; $d(5) = 3$; $d(6) = 3$; $d(7) = 2$. The following is a parallel algorithm to find the degree of each vertex of a graph.

**Algorithm Degree**
 **Input:** $A(1:n, 1:n)$ adjacency matrix.
 **Output:** The degree $d(1:n)$.

BEGIN
 1. For $i = 1$ to $n$ do in parallel
 2. $d(i) = \sum_{j=1}^{n} A(i,j)$
 3. End parallel
END

Step 2 in the above algorithm is the summation of $n$ numbers and hence it can be implemented in $O(\log n)$ time, using $O(n/\log n)$ processors. Hence the degree of all the vertices of a graph can be determined in $O(\log n)$ time, using $O(n^2/\log n)$ processors. Notice that the parallelization of steps 1 to 3 can be implemented in EREW PRAM model. So, the EREW model can be used for the implementation of this algorithm.

The above algorithm is a very easy but frequently used one. An interesting application of the algorithm DEGREE is to be discussed now.

A graph is said to be Euler, if and only if there is a closed walk traversing every edge of the graph exactly once. The Euler's theorem says that a graph is Euler, if and only if it has no vertex of odd degree. So, in order to verify whether a graph is Euler, it is necessary and sufficient to verify whether the graph has no odd degree vertex. So, the following algorithm determines whether a graph is Euler. $eu$ is a Boolean Array, indexed by the vertices such that $eu(v)$ = true, if degree of $v$ is even and $eu(v)$ = false, otherwise. If $eu(v)$ is true for all the vertices, then the graph is Euler.

**Algorithm Euler**
   **Input:**   A graph $G = (V, E)$.
   **Output:**   The value of Boolean variable EULER.

BEGIN
   1. Find the degree of each of the vertex of $G$.
   2. For each vertex $v$ of $G$ do in parallel.
   3. If $d(v)$ is odd
          $eu(v)$ = false
      else
      $eu(v)$ = true
      endif
   4. End Parallel
   5. EULER = Boolean AND of all the $eu(v)$.
END

In the above algorithm, step 1 can be executed by implementing the algorithm DEGREE. Steps 2 to 4 can be done in $O(1)$ time, using $O(n)$ processors. Step 5 performs the AND operation of $n$ Boolean values. The complexity of this step depends upon the type of the PRAM model. If it is EREW PRAM model, it needs $O(n)$ processors and $O(\log n)$ time. This step can be implemented in ERCW PRAM in $O(1)$ time, using $O(n)$ processors. So, the overall complexity of the algorithm is $O(\log n)$ time and $O(n^2)$ processors, irrespective of the type of the PRAM model used, whether EREW or ERCW model.

Another application of the DEGREE algorithm is problem of verifying whether a set of vertices form a clique. When the adjacency matrix $A$ is given, let $C$ be a subset of vertices of the given graph $G = (V, E)$. For any vertex $v$, $\sum_{u \in c} A(v, u)$ gives the number of vertices of $C$ adjacent to $v$. So, $C$ is a clique, if and only if $\sum_{u \in C} A(v,u) = |C| - 1$ for each vertex $v \in C$. So, the following algorithm can verify whether $C$ forms a clique. In the algorithm, $dc(v)$ denotes the number of vertices in $C$ adjacent to $v$. $C$ is a clique, if and only if $dc(v) = |C| - 1$. So, if $C$ has $k$ vertices, then $C$ is a clique, if and only if $dc(v) = k - 1$ for every vertex $v$ of $C$. In order to check this, we find $d = \sum_{v \in C} dc(v)$. Then $d$ is equal to twice the number of edges in $C$. So, $C$ is a clique, if and only $d = k(k - 1)$. We now present the formal algorithm.

**Algorithm Clique-EW**
   **Input:**
      1. Adjacency matrix $A$.
      2. Set $C$ of vertices.
   **Output:**  Boolean value CLIQUE

BEGIN (Let $k$ denote $|C|$)
    1. For each vertex $v \in C$ do in Parallel
    2. $dc(v) = \sum_{u \in C} A(u,v)$
    3. End Parallel
    4. $d = \sum_{v \in C} dc(v)$
    5. If $d = k(k - 1)$ then
        CLIQUE = True
    else
        CLIQUE = False
    End if
END

In this algorithm, steps 1–3 takes $O(\log k)$ time using $O(k^2)$ processors. Step 4 can also be implemented in $O(\log k)$ time, using only $O(k)$ processors. So, this algorithm, which needs an EREW PRAM model for implementation, works in $O(\log k)$ time, using $O(k^2)$ processors. If the PRAM model is ERCW, then the problem can be solved in $O(1)$ time, using $O(k^2)$ processors. The algorithm is given below.

**Algorithm Clique-CW**
   **Input:**
      1. Adjacency matrix $A$ of the graphs $G = (V, e)$.
      2. A set of vertices $C$.
   **Output:**  The Boolean value CLIQUE

BEGIN
   Let $k$ be the number of vertices in $C$.
    1. CLIQUE = True
    2. For each $v, u \in C$ such that $v \neq u$ do in Parallel
    3. If $A(v,u) = 0$ then
        CLIQUE = False

      End if
    4. End Parallel
END

In the above algorithm, for each pair of vertices $u$, $v$ of $C$, a separate processor verifies if $A(u,v) = 0$. If so, it returns the 'False' value to the Boolean variable CLIQUE. Here there is every possibility of more than one processor trying to write on the same location CLIQUE. When the conflict arises during concurrent write, it can be resolved arbitrarily. So, a given set of vertices can be verified whether it forms a clique in constant time using $O(k^2)$ processors, where $k$ is the number of vertices in the given set. From the simple problems that we have seen so far, let us move on to a very important problem in graphs theory.

## 6.2 PARALLEL CONNECTIVITY ALGORITHMS

The Breadth-First Search and Depth-First Search are two important search techniques for the graphs. They are also used for checking whether a graph is connected components. Given a graph, finding all its connected components is a very interesting problem. In the graph shown in Fig. 6.2. There are four connected components. Parallel algorithms have been developed by various authors for finding the connected components of undirected graphs. All these algorithms can be broadly classified according to two major criteria.

1. The basic techniques used; and
2. The format of the input.

In all the algorithms developed so far, the basic technique used is one among the following three: (1) Breadth-First Search; (2) Transitive Closure; (3) Vertex Collapse. The most common form of the input is adjacency matrix. The popularity of the adjacency matrix is because it allows graph-theoretic problems to be stated and solved in terms of matrix manipulation problems. This works very well for dense graphs, but for sparse graphs this may lead to inefficient

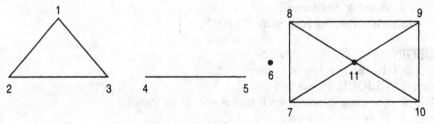

**Figure 6.2** A disconnected graph.

algorithms, so, quite often, adjacency list forms of input is used. While most of the algorithms for finding connected components are very general, some of them are more suitable for sparse or dense graphs.

### 6.2.1   Breadth-First Search (BFS)

The BFS of a graph proceeds by first visiting a vertex, say $v$. After visiting $v$, all the vertices at distance 1 from $v$ are visited and then all the vertices at distance 2, and so on, until all the vertices are visited. For example, consider the graph shown in Fig. 6.5(a). If the BFS starts from 1, we first visit 1. Then 2 and 3 are visited. Then, since 4 and 5 are adjacent to 2 to 3, they are not visited. Then we visit 6. No more vertices adjacent to 5 and 4 are yet to be visited. So we visit the vertex adjacent to 6. That is, we visit 7 next. Then the vertices 8 and 9, adjacent to 7, are visited. In order to know how BFS can be parallelized, let us introduce some definitions.

Let $G = (V, E)$ be a graph. Let $x \in V$ and $k$ be an integer, such that $0 \le k \le \lceil \log n \rceil$ where $n$ is the number of vertices. $T(v, k)$ denotes the tree with $v$ as root and the vertices which are reachable from $v$ through a path less than or equal to $2^k$. Figure 6.3 shows a graph and $T(u, 0)$, $T(u, 1)$, and $T(u, 2)$. Let $G = (V, E)$ be a graph. $T = (V_T, E_T)$ be a rooted tree which is a subgraph of $G$. $T$ is said to preserve the BFS property, if, for any two vertices $u, v \in V_T$, $(u, v) \in E$ implies $u$ and $v$ are either at the same level or at adjacent levels in $T$. Figure 6.4 illustrated the BFS property. $T(v, k)$ is called a *k-tree* of $G$. If $T(v, k)$ preserves the BFS property, it is called $k$-BFS tree. Now let us see how BFS can be parallelized. $T(v, 0)$ contains $v$ as root and all its neighbors as

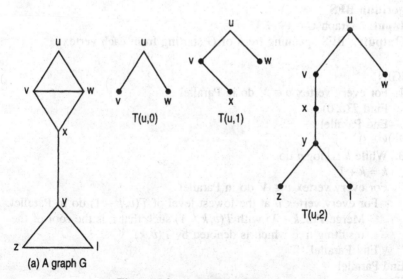

(a) A graph G

**Figure 6.3**   A graph and $T(u, i)$.

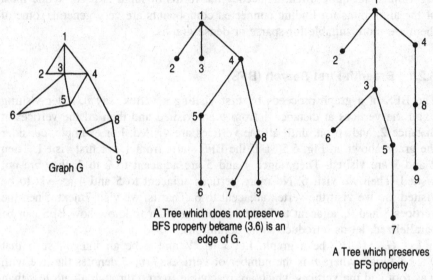

Graph G

A Tree which does not preserve BFS property became (3.6) is an edge of G.

A Tree which preserves BFS property

**Figure 6.4** A graph and trees to illustrate BFS property.

its children. For every vertex $u$ of $T(v,0)$, we must merge $T(u,0)$ with $T(v,0)$ to get $T(v,1)$. In general, for every $k$ such that $1 \leq k \leq \log n$, we must do the following: For every vertex $u$ at the lowest level of $T(v, k-1)$, merge $T(u, k-1)$ with $T(v, k-1)$, such that $v$ is the root of the resulting tree. The following is a parallel algorithm to get the BFS spanning tree $T(v, \log n)$ for every vertex $v$.

**Algorithm BFS**
  **Input:**   Graph $G = (V, E)$.
  **Output:**  BFS spanning trees of $G$ starting from each vertex.

BEGIN
  1. For every vertex $v \in V$ do in Parallel
     Find $T(v, 0)$
     End Parallel
  2. $k = 0$
  3. While $k \leq \lceil \log n \rceil$ do
     $k = k + 1$
     For every vertex $v \in V$ do in Parallel.
        For every vertex $u$ at the lowest level of $T(v, k-1)$ do in Parallel.
          Merge $T(u, k-1)$ with $T(v, k-1)$ such that $v$ is the root of the
          resulting tree which is denoted by $T(v, k)$
        End Parallel
     End Parallel
END

The above algorithm is illustrated in Figs. 6.5(a) through 6.5(d). The merging of the trees $T(u, k-1)$ with $T(v, k-1)$ will take $O(\log n)$ time. The while loop of the algorithm is repeated $\log n$ times. So, the parallel algorithm for BFS takes $O(\log^2 n)$ time. There are two nested parallel loops in the algorithm. And it can be proved that merging takes $O(n)$ processors. So, totally, the algorithm needs $O(n^3)$ processors.

## 6.2.2   Connected Components Using BFS

$T(v, \lceil \log n \rceil)$ is the BFS spanning tree of $G$ with root $v$. Let $P(u, v)$ denote the parent of $u$ in $T(v \lceil \log n \rceil)$. If $G$ is not a connected graph, what is the output of BFS algorithm described above? In this case, $T(v, \lceil \log n \rceil$ will not be the spanning tree or spanning forest of $G$. $T(v, \lceil \log n \rceil$ will only be the spanning tree of the connected component of $G$ containing $v$. For simplicity, let BFS($v$) denote $T(v, \lceil \log n \rceil)$. If $G$ is not connected, then $P(u, v)$ is defined only for the vertices $u$ which are reachable from $v$. Let us denote that $P(u, v) = \infty$ if $u$ is not reachable from $v$. In short,

$$P(u, v) = \begin{cases} \text{Parent of } u \text{ in BFS}(v) & \text{if } u \text{ is a vertex of BFS}(v) \\ \infty & \text{otherwise} \end{cases}$$

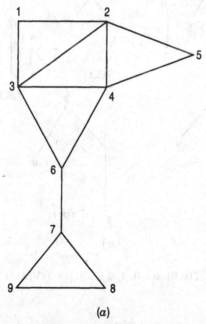

(a)

**Figure 6.5(a)**   An undirected graph G.

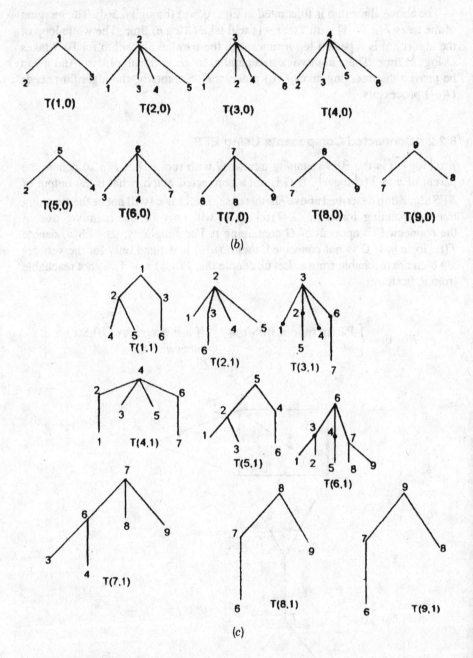

(b)

(c)

**Figure 6.5(b)** $T(v, 0)$, $v = 0, 1, 2 \ldots 9$. (c) $T(V, 1)$, $V = 1, 2, \ldots 9$.

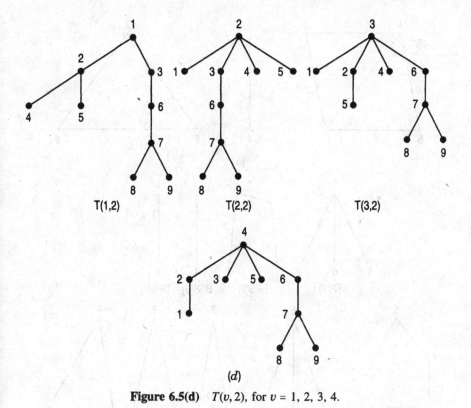

**Figure 6.5(d)** $T(v,2)$, for $v = 1, 2, 3, 4$.

For convenience, let us denote the vertices by $1, 2, 3 \ldots n$. Let us define the connectivity matrix by

$$C(i,j) = \begin{cases} \infty & \text{if } P(i,j) = \infty \\ i & \text{otherwise.} \end{cases}$$

In the connectivity matrix the $j$th column will contain the value $j$ at the vertices that belong to the component containing $j$. The component number of a vertex $j$ is the smallest vertex in the component containing $j$. It is the smallest entry of the $j$th column. Consider the graph shown in Fig. 6.6(a), and their BFS trees, which are shown in Fig. 6.6(b). The matrices $P(i,j)$ and $C(i,j)$ are given below:

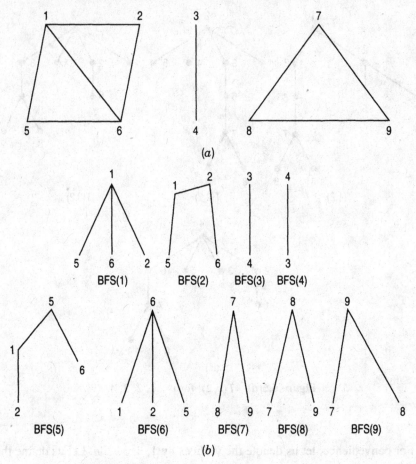

**Figure 6.6(a)** Graph G. **(b)** BFS trees obtained.

| P | 1 | 2 | 3 | 4 | 5 | 6 | 7 | 8 | 9 |
|---|---|---|---|---|---|---|---|---|---|
| 1 | 1 | 2 | ∞ | ∞ | 5 | 6 | ∞ | ∞ | ∞ |
| 2 | 1 | 2 | ∞ | ∞ | 1 | 6 | ∞ | ∞ | ∞ |
| 3 | ∞ | ∞ | 3 | 4 | ∞ | ∞ | ∞ | ∞ | ∞ |
| 4 | ∞ | ∞ | 3 | 4 | ∞ | ∞ | ∞ | ∞ | ∞ |
| 5 | 1 | 1 | ∞ | ∞ | 5 | 6 | ∞ | ∞ | ∞ |
| 6 | 1 | 2 | ∞ | ∞ | 5 | 6 | ∞ | ∞ | ∞ |
| 7 | ∞ | ∞ | ∞ | ∞ | ∞ | ∞ | 7 | 8 | 9 |
| 8 | ∞ | ∞ | ∞ | ∞ | ∞ | ∞ | 7 | 8 | 9 |
| 9 | ∞ | ∞ | ∞ | ∞ | ∞ | ∞ | 7 | 8 | 9 |

| C | 1 | 2 | 3 | 4 | 5 | 6 | 7 | 8 | 9 |
|---|---|---|---|---|---|---|---|---|---|
| 1 | 1 | 1 | ∞ | ∞ | 1 | 1 | ∞ | ∞ | ∞ |
| 2 | 2 | 2 | ∞ | ∞ | 2 | 2 | ∞ | ∞ | ∞ |
| 3 | ∞ | ∞ | 3 | 3 | ∞ | ∞ | ∞ | ∞ | ∞ |
| 4 | ∞ | ∞ | 4 | 4 | ∞ | ∞ | ∞ | ∞ | ∞ |
| 5 | 5 | 5 | ∞ | ∞ | 5 | 5 | ∞ | ∞ | ∞ |
| 6 | 6 | 6 | ∞ | ∞ | 6 | 6 | ∞ | ∞ | ∞ |
| 7 | ∞ | ∞ | ∞ | ∞ | ∞ | ∞ | 7 | 7 | 7 |
| 8 | ∞ | ∞ | ∞ | ∞ | ∞ | ∞ | 8 | 8 | 8 |
| 9 | ∞ | ∞ | ∞ | ∞ | ∞ | ∞ | 9 | 9 | 9 |

The component number of a vertex $j$ is got the minimum of the $j$th column in $C$ matrix. For the graph shown in Fig. 6.6(a), this is shown below:

Vertex :                   1   2   3   4   5   6   7   8   9

Component Number :   1   1   3   3   1   1   7   7   7.

The parallel algorithm designed for CREW model based on the above method is given below:

**Algorithm CC-BFS**
  **Input:**   The Graph $G = (V, E)$.
  **Output:**   Component number of each number $v$.

BEGIN
    1. Using ALGORITHM BFS construct the BFS trees BFS($v$)
        for each $v \in V$ in Parallel.
    2. For $i = 1$ to $n$ do in Parallel
        For $j = 1$ to $n$ do in Parallel
            If $P(i, j) = \infty$ then
            $C(i, j) = \infty$
            else
            $C(i, j) = i$
        End if
        End Parallel
    3. For $j = 1$ to $n$ do in parallel
        Comp($j$) = Min $\{C(i, j), i = 1, 2, \ldots n\}$
        End Parallel
END

The complexity of the BFS algorithm is $O(\log^2 n)$ with $O(n^3)$ processors. Step 2 takes $O(1)$ time using $O(n^2)$ processors. Choosing the minimum could be done in $O(\log n)$ time using $O(n)$ processors. So step 3 takes $O(\log n)$ time $O(n^2)$ processors. So the total time taken for this algorithm is $O(\log^2 n)$ using $O(n^3)$ processors in CREW PRAM model.

### 6.2.3 Transitive Closure Matrix

From the adjacency matrix $A$ of a graph $G = (V, E)$, its transitive closure matrix can be obtained by evaluating $(A + I)^n$. Let us denote it by $R = (A + I)^n$. Also note that

$$R(i,j) = \begin{cases} 1 & \text{if } i \text{ and } j \text{ are in the same component in } G \text{ adjacent,} \\ 0 & \text{otherwise.} \end{cases}$$

Now the component number of a vertex $i$ is the smallest index $j$ such that $R(i,j) = 1$. The parallel algorithm is shown below:

**Algorithm CC-TRC**
**Input:** The adjacency matrix $A(i,j)$ of a graph.
**Output:** The component number of each vertex.

BEGIN
    1. Obtain the transitive closure matrix $R$ from the adjacency matrix.
    2. For $i = 1$ to $n$ do in Parallel
        $\text{Comp}(i) = \text{Min}\{j/R(i,j) = 1\}$
        End Parallel
END

The complexity of the algorithm depends upon the complexity of the matrix multiplication algorithm. For CRCW PRAM model it will take $O(\log n)$ time with $(n^3)$ processors for computing $R$. The computing time and the number of processors for computing $R$ in a CREW PRAM model is $O(\log^2 n)$ and $O(n^3)$, respectively. Since step 2 requires only $O(\log n)$ time with $O(n^2)$ processors, the overall computing time is as follows:

| Model | Time | Processors |
|-------|------|------------|
| CRCW | $O(\log n)$ | $O(n^3)$ |
| CREW | $O(\log^2 n)$ | $O(n^3)$ |

### 6.2.4 Vertex Collapse

The vertex collapse approach to find the connected components of a graph was first suggested by Hirschberg in 1976. The adjacent nodes are combined to form "supernodes". The supernodes are repeatedly joined into *their* supernodes. The process is repeated until each component is represented by a supernode. It has been shown that this final stage is reached in $[\log n]$ repetitions. Each process consists of three stages.

1. The lowest-numbered neighboring supernode of each node is obtained.
2. Each supernode root is connected to the root of the lowest-numbered neighboring supernode.
3. All the newly connected supernodes are collapsed into larger supernodes.

Initially every node is considered its supernode, $sup(i)$ denotes the supernode of $i$, and $nbr(i)$ denotes the smallest-numbered neighboring supernode of $i$. A high-level description of the algorithm is given below:

BEGIN
   1. For $i = 1$ to $n$ do
         $sup(i) = i$;
   2. For $k = 1$ to $[\log n]$ do
   2(a) For $i = 1$ to $n$ do
         Compute the lowest numbered neighboring supernode and call
         it $nbr(i)$. If $i$ has no neighboring supernode assign $nbr(i) = sup(i)$
         end for
   2(b) For $i = 1$ to $n$ do
         Among all vertices whose supernode is $i$ choose the vertex $j$
         with minimum $nbr(j)$ value.
         Assign $nbr(i) = nbr(j)$
         If there is no such vertex assign $nbr(i) = sup(i)$
            $sup(i) = nbr(i)$
   2(c) For $p = 1$ to $[\log n]$ do
         For $i = 1$ to $n$ do
            $nbr(i) = nbr(nbr(i))$
         end for
         end for
   2(d) For $i = 1$ to $n$ do
         $sup(i) = \text{Min } \{nbr(i), sup(nbr(i))\}$
         end for
 END

The input is the adjacency matrix $A(1:n, 1:n)$ of the graph and the output is $sup(i)$, which finally gives the lowest-numbered vertex of the component in which $i$ is a member. The algorithm is illustrated in Figs. 6.7(a) through 6.7(e). A complete parallel algorithm for CREW PRAM model is given below:

**Algorithm CC-VC**
  **Input:**  The adjacency matrix $A[1:n, 1:n]$.
  **Output:**  $sup[1:n]$. In the final result $sup(i)$ will be the smallest

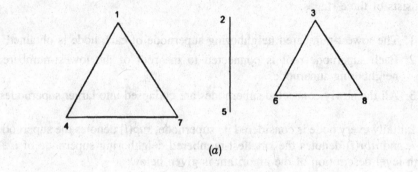

(a)

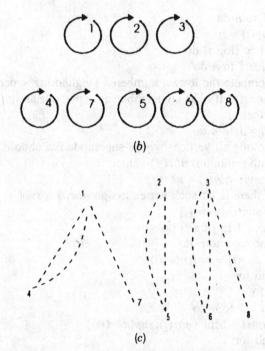

(b)

(c)

**Figure 6.7(a)** The original graph. **(b)** Initialization $sup(i) = i$. **(c)** Iteration 1 $nbr(i)$.

numbered vertex such that $i$ and $sup(i)$ belong the same component.

BEGIN
    1. For $i = 1$ to $n$ do in parallel

        $sup(i) = i$

    End Parallel

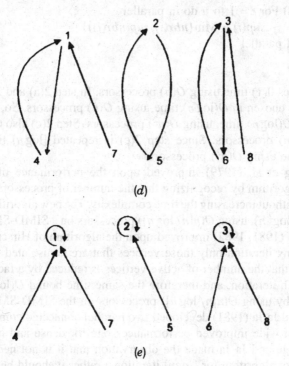

**Figure 6.7(d)** Iteration 1 $nbr(i) = sup(i)$. **(e)** Iteration 1 $sup(i)$.

2. For $k = 1$ to $[\log n]$ do
    2(a) For $i = 1$ to $n$ do in parallel
        $nbr(i) = $ Min $\{sup(j)/A(i,j) = 1$ and $1 \le j \le n\}$
        If $nbr(i)$ does not exist
            $nbr(i) = sup(i)$
        end if
        end parallel
    2(b) For $i = 1$ to $n$ do in Parallel
        $nbr(i) = $ Min$\{nbr(j)/sup(j) = i$ and $nbr(j) = j\}$
        If no such vertex $j$ exists then
            $nbr(i) = sup(i)$
        end if
        $sup(i) = nbr(i)$
    End Parallel
    2(c) For $p = 1$ to $[\log n]$ do
        For $i = 1$ to $n$ do in Parallel
            $nbr(i) = nbr(nbr(i))$
        end parallel
        end for

2(d) For $i = 1$ to $n$ do in parallel
$$sup(i) = \text{Min}\{nbr(i), sup(nbr(i))\}$$
end parallel
END

Step 1 takes $O(1)$ time using $O(n)$ processors. In step 2(a) and 2(b), the minimum can be chosen in $O(\log n)$ time, using $O(n)$ processors. So, step 2(a) and 2(b) require $O(\log n)$ time, using $O(n^2)$ processors. Step 2(c) also takes $O(\log n)$ time and $O(n)$ processors. Since step 2(c) is repeated [$\log n$] times, it takes $O(\log^2 n)$ time using $O(n^2)$ processors.

Hirschberg et al. (1979) improved upon the performance of the original Hischberg algorithm by recognizing that the number of processors required can be reduced without increasing the time complexity. The new algorithm has a complexity of $O(\log^2 n)$, using $O(n[n/\log n])$ processors on a SIMD-SM-R model.

Chin et al. (1981, 1982) improved upon the algorithm of Hirschberg by considering in any iteration only those vertices that are nonisolated supervertices. This implies that the number of active vertices is reduced by a factor of at least two after each iteration, and therefore the same time bound $O(\log^2 n)$ can still be achieved by using $O(n[n/\log n])$ processors on the SIMD-SM-R model.

Savage and Ja Ja (1981) developed two parallel connected components algorithms that provide improved performances one for dense and one for sparse graphs. Savage and Ja Ja made the observation that it is not necessary to run the Hirschberg algorithm for [$\log n$] iterations; rather it should be run until two consecutive iterations produce the same result. In that case, the running time of the algorithm can be made $O(\log n * \min\{\log n, d/2\})$, where $d$ is the diameter of the graph. When $d < 2\log n$ (i.e., for dense graphs), this algorithm is faster than the original. When the graph is dense, this algorithm requires $O(n^3/\log n)$ processors to obtain time complexity $O(\log n \log d)$.

When the graph is sparse, the number of processors required can be reduced by organizing the input in the form of the adjacency list rather than the adjacency matrix. Certain reorganization of the original Hirschberg algorithm then leads to an algorithm with time complexity $O(\log^2 n)$, using $O((m + n)\log n)$ processors, where $m$ is the number of edges in the graph.

Nath and Maheshwari (1982) consider the problem of finding the connected components on a weaker model that does not permit simultaneous reading from the same memory location by different processors. Their algorithm is based on the one due to Hirschberg et al. (1979), but it avoids read conflicts by organizing the intermediate data structure as a chain (which avoids read conflicts) when children access nonroot parents) and by keeping multiple copies of data. This algorithm has complexity $O(\log^2 n)$ time with $n$ processors on an SIMD-SM model.

Shiloach and Vishkin (1982) consider a stronger model. SIMD-SM-RW. The processors are allocated by considering each undirected edge to be two directed edges, and each vertex and each directed edge is allocated one processor. In contrast to the Hirschberg algorithm, it is no longer required that each connected component be identified by its lowest-numbered member vertex; this allows the algorithm to utilize the power of this model by letting the vertices try simultaneous 'hooking' instead of connecting to minimum-numbered neighboring root. This allows one of the two $\log^2 n$ factors to be replaced by a $\log n$ factor. The other $\log^2 n$ factor is replaced by a $\log n$ factor by reorganization that allows the path compression step to be done twice in each iteration, rather than $O(\log n)$ times.

Awerbuch and Shiloach (1983) improved upon the results of Shiloach and Vishkin (1982) to obtain an $O(\log n)$ time complexity, connected components algorithm using $2m$ processors for the SIMD-SM-RW model. Wyllie (1979) uses vertex collapse to obtain an $O(\log^2 n)$ algorithm, using $O(n + 2m)$ processors on synchronized MIMD-TC-R model. For sparse graphs this is a very efficient algorithm. A vertex $x$ can be collapsed into vertex $y$ by making any edge incident to $x$ become incident to $y$ instead. Each edge is viewed as a pair of two directed edges, and the input is in the form of an adjacency list matrix. This input is converted in constant time, so that each vertex has a circular doubly linked list with a list header. The list consists of two type of elements: directed edge elements and dummy elements. At all times edge elements are separated by at least one dummy element. Each directed edge element contains (in addition to the forward and backward pointer) the number of vertices to which this directed edge is incident and a pointer to its 'brother' directed edge (the oppositely oriented directed edge representing the same undirected edge). The structure of the directed element allows for efficient collapse of two vertices, into one vertex and the use of dummy elements permits simultaneous collapse of different vertices.

## 6.3 BICONNECTED COMPONENTS

A vertex of a connected graph $G$ is called an *articulation point* if $G-v$ is disconnected. If a graph has no articulation point, it is called a *biconnected graph*. The graph shown in Fig. 6.8(a) is biconnected, whereas the one shown in Fig. 6.8(b)

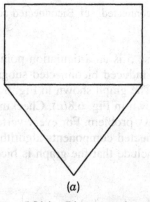

(a)

**Figure 6.8(a)** Biconnected graph.

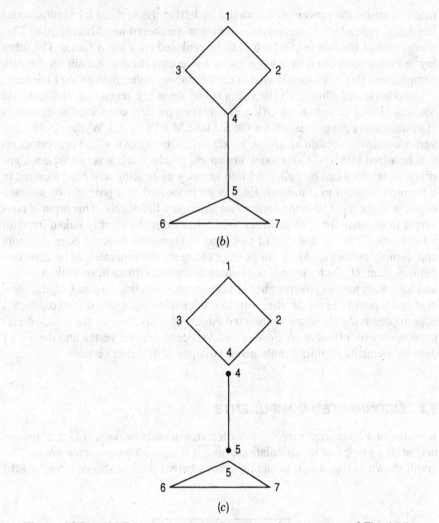

**Figure 6.8(b)** NOT biconnected. **(c)** Biconnected components of Fig. 6.8(b).

is not biconnected, because 5 is an articulation point (4 is also another articulation point). A maximal induced biconnected subgraph is called *biconnected component* of the graph. The graph shown in Fig. 6.8(b) has three biconnected components. They are shown in Fig. 6.8(c). Checking a graph for biconnectivity is an interesting but easy problem. For every vertex $v$, verify whether $G$-$v$ is connected, using the connected components algorithm. If the result is positive for every $v \in V$, then conclude that the graph is biconnected.

BEGIN
    For every $v \in V$ do in parallel

> if $G$-$v$ is connected
>     $BCC(v) = 0$
> else
>     $BCC(v) = 1$
> endif
> end parallel
> $BCC(G) = \sum_{v \in V} BCC(v)$
> If $BCC(G) = 0$, then $G$ is biconnected, otherwise not biconnected.
END

In order to verify the connectivity of $G$-$v$, we can use $CC$-$VC$ algorithm described in the previous section. The complete algorithm is described below:

**Algorithm BCC**
  **Input:**  Adjacency matrix of the graph $A[i:n, i:n]$.
  **Output:**  The Boolean value BCC which is TRUE if $G$ is
        biconnected and FALSE otherwise.

BEGIN
  1. For $i = 1$ to $n$ do in parallel
     1(a) Construct $A_i[1:n-1, 1:n-1]$ from $A$ by deleting the $i$th
          row and the $i$th column
     1(b) Using $CC$-$VC$ algorithm verify whether $A_i$ represents
          a connected graph.
     1(c) If it represents a connected graph assign $B(i) = 0$
            else
              $B(i) = 1$
            End if
     End Parallel
  2. $S = \sum_{i=1}^{n} B(i)$
  3. If $S = O$ then $BCC$ = TRUE
     else
          $BCC$ = FALSE
     End if
END

**Complexity Analysis.** Step 1a should be done in $O(1)$ time using $O(n^2)$ processors. $CC$-$VC$ algorithms to check the connectivity takes $O(\log^2 n)$ time, using $O(n^2)$ processors. Step 1 here is done for $n$ vertices in parallel. So, step 1 takes $O(\log^2 n)$ time, using $O(n^2)$ processors. In step 2, the summation can be done in $O(\log n)$ time, using $O(n)$ processors. So, the complexity of the algorithm $BCC$ is $O(\log^2 n)$ time using $O(n^3)$ processors. This algorithm can be modified to get all the biconnected components of the graph.

## 6.4 SPANNING TREES

Spanning trees are very useful in the application of several problems such as communication network, transportation modeling, and so on. When the cities are represented by vertices and edges represent the communication lines or roads connecting the cities, a spanning tree is very useful in studying the problem. When the edges are assigned a weight, the spanning tree of the graph having minimum total weight is a very important application. It is called the *minimum cost spanning tree* of the graph.

This section deals with the problem of finding the minimum cost spanning tree of a graph in which the edges are weighted. There are three methods to find the minimum cost spanning tree of a connected simple weighted graph.

1. Prim's method;
2. Kruskal's method; and
3. Sollin's method.

In Prim's method, the spanning tree is constructed by starting from a single vertex and selecting one vertex at a time and including it to the spanning tree, such that the total weight is minimized. Kruskal's method selects edges one after the other, in such a way that total cost is minimized. In this section we study Sollins's algorithm.

***Sollin's Algorithm.*** The graph is represented by the two dimensional array COST defined by

$$\text{COS T}(u, v) = \begin{cases} \text{weight of edge } (u, v) \text{ if } (u, v) \text{ is an edge} \\ \infty \quad \text{if } u = v \\ \infty \quad \text{if } (u, v) \text{ is not an edge} \end{cases}$$

Sollins algorithm starts by considering all the vertices of the given graph as isolated ones. So, the $n$ vertices of the graph are considered as $n$ trees with one vertex each. Let us denote these $n$ trees by $T_{1o}, T_{2o}, \ldots T_{no}$. This is said to constitute the forest

$$F^i = \{T_{1o}, T_{2o}, \ldots T_{no}\}.$$

For each tree $T_{io}$, we are interested in selecting an edge $(u, v)$ with minimum cost, such that $u \in T_{io}$ and $v \in T_{jo}$ for some distinct $i$ and $j$. When these edges selected are used and trees joined, we will have at the most, half the number of trees in the next iteration.

In general, in the $i$th iteration,

$$F_i = \{T_{1i}, T_{2i}, \ldots T_{ni}\}.$$

For each $T_{ij}$, we must select a minimum cost edge $(u, v)$, such that $u \in T_{ki}$ and $v \in T_{ji}$ for some distinct $k$ and $j$ and use the edge to join the trees $T_{ki}$ and $T_{ji}$. The resulting forest is denoted by $F_{i+1}$. From the above discussion it is clear that the forest $F_{i+1}$ contains, at the most, half the number of trees as in $F_i$. When we get a single tree in some iterations, we can stop the procedure and that is the minimum cost spanning tree. As the number of trees is halved in each iteration, the minimum cost spanning tree is obtained in not more than $\log n$ iterations. The parallel algorithm using Sollin's method is given below.

**Algorithm Sollin**
   **Input:**   The graph $G = (V, E)$ represented by its cost array
               $COST(u, v)$ where $u, v \in V$.
   **Output:**  Minimum cost spanning tree of $G$.

BEGIN
   1. $F_0 = (V, \Phi)$
   2. $i = O$
   3. While there is more than one tree in $F_i$ do
   4. For each tree $T_j$ in forest $F_i$ do in Parallel
   5. Choose the minimum weight edge $(u, v)$ joining some
      vertex $u$ in $T_j$ to a vertex $v$ in some other tree $T_k$ in
      forest $F_i$.
   6. Form the forest $F_{i+1}$ by joining all $T_j$ and $T_k$ of $F_i$ with the
      corresponding selected edges:
   7. $i = i + 1$
   8. End Parallel
   9. End While

The above algorithm is not a complete one. It needs to be explained how steps 4 to 6 have to be implemented in parallel. The technique used by Savage and Ja Ja (1981) is described below: The forest $F_i$ contains several trees. A tree is represented by its parent relation. Another data structure NEAR($u$) is used to denote the vertex of another tree which is nearest to $u$. ROOT is another data structure which gives the root of the tree to which the node belongs to. The parallel version of the implementation is given below:

**Algorithm Sollin-1**
   **Input:**   The weighted graph $G = (V, E)$ represented by weight
               matrix $W(u, v)$.
   **Output:**  Minimum cost spanning tree of $G$.

BEGIN
    1. For each $u \in V$ do in parallel
    2. ROOT($i$) = $i$
    3. End parallel
    4. Over = False
    5. While not (over) do
    6. For each $u \in V$ do in parallel
    7. NEAR($u$) = $v$ such that ROOT($u$) different from ROOT($v$)
       and $W(u, v)\lambda$ = Min $\{W(u, w)/w \in V\}$
    8. End parallel
    9. For each component $k$ of the forest $F_i$ do in parallel.
  10. Choose a vertex $u$ such that $W(u, \text{NEAR}(u))$ is minimum
      overall vertices of $k$.
  11. End parallel
  12. Combine the new edges and create the new forest $F_{i+1}$
  13. For each vertex $u \in V$ do in parallel
  14. Search ROOT($u$)
  15. If ROOT($u$) = ROOT($v$) for all $u, v \in V$ then over = true.
  16. End Parallel.
  17. End while.
END

Steps 1–3 is simple operation, which could be completed in $O(1)$ time using $O(n)$ processors. The forest $F_{i+1}$ of next iteration has, at the most, half the number of trees in $F_i$. So, the while loop from step 5 to 17 is repeated $\log n$ times, step 7 chooses the nearest vertex and, hence, using a suitable data structure and maintaining the edges in the descending order of its weights, the binary search technique could be used. Hence step 7 takes $O(\log n)$ time. Steps 6–8 is a parallel loop and it can be completed in $O(\log n)$ time, using $O(n)$ processors. Steps 9–11 is a parallel loop, within which step 10 takes $O(\log n)$ time using $O(n)$ processors. Similarly, steps 12 to 16 is a parallel loop. Steps 14 and 15 can be implemented in $O(\log^2 n)$ time, using a data structure proposed by Ja Ja using $O(n)$ processors. Hence Sollin's algorithm can be implemented in parallel in $O(\log^2 n)$ time, using $O(n^2)$ processors. The PRAM model needed for implementation is CREW.

## 6.5 SHORTEST PATH PROBLEM

Consider a weighted directed graph $G = (V, E)$, in which each edge is associated with a nonnegative weight. The weight of edge $(i, j)$ is denoted by $w_{ij}$. Assume that $w_{ij} = 0$ for all $i \in v$. If $(i, j)$ is not an edge, $w_{ij} = \infty$. The length of a path is the sum of the weights of the edges in the path. The shortest path from vertex $i$ to $j$ is the path from $i$ to $j$ having least length. A shortest path is represented by the path length and by the ordered set of vertices (or ordered set of edges)

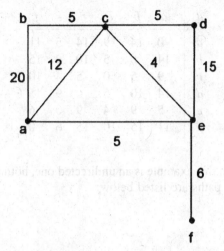

**Figure 6.9** A weighted graph.

the path is going through. The all-pair shortest path problem finds the shortest path between each ordered pair of vertices $(i,j)$. The following data structure is used to develop an algorithm for the all pair shortest path problem.

Define $d_{ij}$ = shortest path from $i$ to $j$ which is to be determined finally.

$p_{ij}$ = the predecessor of $j$ in the shortest path from $i$ to $j$.

For example, consider the graph given in Fig. 6.9. The graph is represented by its weight matrix $(w_{ij})$, given below.

| $W$ | $a$ | $b$ | $c$ | $d$ | $e$ | $f$ |
|---|---|---|---|---|---|---|
| $a$ | 0 | 20 | 12 | $\infty$ | 5 | $\infty$ |
| $b$ | 20 | 0 | 5 | $\infty$ | $\infty$ | $\infty$ |
| $c$ | 12 | 5 | 0 | 5 | 4 | $\infty$ |
| $d$ | $\infty$ | $\infty$ | 5 | 0 | 15 | $\infty$ |
| $e$ | 5 | $\infty$ | 4 | 15 | 0 | 6 |
| $f$ | $\infty$ | $\infty$ | $\infty$ | $\infty$ | $\infty$ | 60 |

The shortest paths between any two vertices is given by the following matrix:

| $d$ | $a$ | $b$ | $c$ | $d$ | $e$ | $f$ |
|-----|-----|-----|-----|-----|-----|-----|
| $a$ | 0 | 14 | 9 | 14 | 5 | 11 |
| $b$ | 14 | 0 | 5 | 10 | 9 | 15 |
| $c$ | 9 | 5 | 0 | 5 | 4 | 10 |
| $d$ | 14 | 10 | 5 | 0 | 9 | 15 |
| $e$ | 5 | 9 | 4 | 9 | 0 | 6 |
| $f$ | 11 | 15 | 10 | 15 | 6 | 0 |

Since the graph in this example is an undirected one, both the above matrices are symmetric. The paths are listed below:

Path $(a, b) = a\ e\ c\ b$
Path $(a, c) = a\ e\ c$
Path $(a, d) = a\ e\ c\ d$
Path $(a, e) = a\ e$
Path $(a, f) = a\ e\ f$
Path $(b, c) = b\ c$
Path $(b, d) = b\ c\ d$
Path $(b, e) = b\ c\ e$
Path $(b, f) = b\ c\ e\ f$
Path $(c, d) = c\ d$
Path $(c, e) = c\ e$
Path $(c, f) = c\ e\ f$
Path $(d, e) = d\ c\ e$
Path $(d, f) = d\ c\ e\ f$
Path $(e, f) = e\ f$.

From the above paths we can find the $p_{ij}$ values for each vertex pair $(i, j)$. The above data structure is efficiently used in the Floyd Warshall algorithm, which we are going to study now. To start with, let us have

$$d_{ij} = \begin{cases} w_{ij} & \text{if } (i, j) \in E \\ \infty & \text{if } (i, j) \text{ is not an edge} \\ 0 & \text{if } i = j \end{cases}$$

$$P_{ij} = i \text{ for all } i \text{ and } j.$$

The above initialization means that the direct distance alone has been considered first. Now we are going to compare this distance $d_{ij}$ with sum of the distance of $i$ to an intermediate vertex $k$ and the distance of $k$ to $j$. If $d_{ij}$ is bigger, then we prefer the path through $k$. The above updation can be done through each vertex $k$. The Floyd-Warshall algorithm is given below:

## Algorithm Floyd-Warshall
**Input:** The graph represented by its weight matrix $(w_{ij})$.
**Output:** $(d_{ij})$ and $(P_{ij})$ matrices.

BEGIN
    1. For $i = 1$ to $n$ do in parallel
    2. For $j = 1$ to $n$ do in parallel
    3. $d_{ij} = w_{ij}$
    4. $p_{ij} = i$
    5. End parallel
    6. End parallel
    7. For $k = 1$ to $n$ do
    8. For each pair $(i, j)$ where $0 < i, j \le n$ and $i, j \ne k$ do in parallel
    9. If $d_{ij} > d_{ik} + d_{kj}$ then
          $d_{ij} = d_{ik} + d_{kj}$
          $p_{ij} = p_{kj}$
        endif
   10. End parallel
   11. End for
   12. Output $p$ and $d$ matrices.
END

It is clear that the above algorithm needs $O(n)$ time using $O(n^2)$ processors, using an CREW PRAM model. Gayraud and Authir (1991) have suggested another parallel implementation, which runs in $O(n^3/p + np)$ time, using $P$ processors. In their algorithm they consider the line-oriented approach of this algorithm. In the algorithm at the $k$th iteration, updation of the $i$th line (row) of the $(d_{ij})$ and $(P_{ij})$ matrix is given as separate procedure called LMOD$(i, k)$. Steps 7 to 11 can be written as follows:

BEGIN
    7. For $k = 1$ to $n$ do
    8. For $i = 1$ to $n$ $(i \ne k)$ do in parallel
     9. LMOD$(i, k)$
   10. End parallel
   11. End for.
END

The procedure LMOD is given below:

**Procedure LMOD** *(i, k)*

BEGIN
  For $j = 1$ to $n$, $j = i$ and $j = k$ do in parallel
    if $d_{ij} > d_{kj}$ then
      $d_{ij} = d_{ik} + d_{kj}$
      $P_{ij} = P_{kj}$
    end if
  End Parallel
END

## BIBLIOGRAPHY

Samy, A. A., Arumugam, G., Devasahayam, M. P. and Xavier, C. (1991) Algorithms for Intersection Graphs of Internally Disjoint Paths in Trees, *Proceedings of National Seminar on Theoretical Computer Science*, IMSC, Madras, India, Report 115, pp. 169–178.

Berge, C. and Chatval, C. (1984) *Topics on Perfect Graphs. Annals of Discrete Mathematics*, **21.**

Sekharan, N. C. (1985) New Characterizations and Algorithmic Studies on Chordal Graphs and k-Trees, (M.Sc. (Engg.) Thesis), School of Automation, Indian Institute of Science, Bangalore, India.

Sekharan, N. C. and Iyengar, S. S. (1988) NC Algorithms for Recognizing Chordal Graphs and *k*-trees, *IEEE Transactions on Computers*, **37(10).**

Ja Ja, J. (1992) *Introduction to Parallel Algorithms*, Addison-Wesley, Reading, MA.

Kelly, D. (1985) Comparability Graphs. In I. Rival, ed., *Graphs and Order*, D. Reidel, pp. 3–40. (NATO ASI series C, v14.)

Klein, P. N. (1988) Efficient Parallel Algorithms for Chordal Graphs, Proc. 29th IEEE symposium on foundation of Computer Section (1988) pp. 150–161.

Klein, P. N. (1988) Efficient Parallel Algorithms for Planar, Chordal and Interval Graphs, TR 426 (Ph.D. thesis) Laboratory for Computer Science, MIT, Cambridge, MA.

Kozen, D., Vazirani, U. V. and Vazirani, V. V. (1985) NC Algorithms for Comparability Graphs, Interval Graphs and Unique Perfect Matchings. In *Fifth Conference on Foundations of Software Technology and Theoretical Computer Science*, 496–503, New York and Berlin, pp. 496–503. (Springer Lecture Notes in Computer Science, 206.)

Moitra, A. and Iyengar, S. S. (1987) Parallel Algorithms for Some Computational Problems, *Advances in Computers* **26,** Academic Press, New York, pp. 93–153.

Manacher, G. K. (1992) Chord Free Path Problems on Interval Graphs, *Computer Science and Informatics*, **22(2),** 17–24.

Mohring, R. H. (1984) Algorithmic Aspects of Comparability Graphs and Interval Graphs. In I. Rival, ed., *Graphs and Order*, pp. 41–101, D. Reidel. (NATO ASI series C. v. 147.)

Xavier, C. and Arumugam, G. (1994) Algorithms for Parity Path Problems in Some Classes of Graphs, *Computer Science and Informatics*, **24(4)**, 50–54.

Xavier, C. (1995) Sequential and Parallel Algorithms for Some Graph Theoretic Problems (Ph.D. thesis), Madurai Kamaraj University, India.

## EXERCISES

**6.1.** A topological sort can be defined as follows: Given a directed acyclic graph $G = (V, E)$ with $n$ vertices, assign label $l$ to vertex $v$ from $\{1, 2, \ldots, n\}$, such that $l(u) < l(v)$ whenever $(u, v) \in E$. Develop a parallel algorithm to perform a topological sort on $G$.

**6.2.** A trail of a connected graph $G$ is a sequence $W = (e_1 = (v_0, v_1), e_2 = (v_1, v_2), \ldots, e_{k-1} = (v_{k-2}, v_{k-1}), e_k = (v_{k-1}, v_k))$, such that all the edges are distinct. A Euler trail traverses every edge of $G$.

**6.3.** Let $G = (V, E)$ be a bipartite graph whose maximum degree $\Delta = 2^l$, for some positive integer $l$.

    **a.** Show how to divide $G$ into two bipartite graphs $G_1$ and $G_2$, each of maximum degree $\Delta/2$. Your algorithm should run in $O(\log n)$ time, using $O(|E| + |V|)$ operations.

    **b.** A $k$-edge coloring of $G$ is an assignment of colors to the edges from the colour set $\{1, 2, \ldots, k\}$, such that $c(e) \neq c(g)$ whenever $e$ and $g$ share a vertex. Use the algorithm for part(a) to find a $\Delta$-edge coloring of $G$. State the resource bounds needed by your algorithm.

**6.4.** Let $G = (V, E)$ be an undirected graph given by its adjacency lists. A Euler partition is a partition of $E$ into edge-disjoint paths (including cycles) $\{pi\}$, such that each vertex of odd degree is the endpoint of exactly one path (with two distinct endpoints), and no vertex of even degree can appear as the endpoint of such a path. Show how to obtain a Euler partition in $O(\log n)$ time, using a linear number of operations. *Hint:* Start by making the graph Eulerian.

**6.5.** Suppose you are given an undirected graph $G = (V, E)$ together with a vector $D$, such that $D(u) = D(v)$, if and only if $u$ and $v$ are in the same connected component. Develop an efficient parallel algorithm to determine the number $k$ of connected components, and to generate a separate list of the vertices in each connected component.

**6.6.** We have seen three different ways to represent a graph $G = (V, E)$: the adjacency matrix, a set of adjacency lists, and an unordered set of edges. Develop an $O(\log n)$ time parallel algorithm to convert one representation into another, where $|V| = n$. What is the total number of operations used in each case?

**6.7.** Given an undirected, connected graph $G$ with $n$ vertices, develop a detailed $O(\log n)$ time algorithm to determine an arbitrary spanning tree of $G$. The total number of operations used by your algorithm must be $O((n + m) \log n)$, where $m$ is the number of edges of $G$. Assume that the input is given as a sequence of edges. Do not use the priority CRCW PRAM for your algorithm.

**6.8.** An undirected graph $G = (V, E)$ is bipartite if there exists partition of $V$, $V = V_1 \cup V_2$, such that each edge has one endpoint in $V_1$ and the other in $V_2$. Develop an $O(\log n)$ time algorithm to find such a partition whenever it exists. *Hint:* Start by determining a spanning tree of $G$.

**6.9.** A cut vertex $v$ of a connected, undirected graph $G = (V, E)$ is a vertex whose removal leaves $G$ disconnected.

    **a.** Show that $v$ is a cut vertex if and only if it belongs to more than one block.

    **b.** Develop an efficient parallel algorithm to determine all the cut vertices of $G$.

**6.10.** Let $G = (V, E)$ be a connected graph. Recall that a bridge is an edge $e$ whose removal leaves $G$ disconnected. Develop a parallel algorithm to determine all the bridges of $G$. The complexity bounds of your algorithm should match those of either of the connected components algorithms. *Hint:* Start by determining a spanning tree of $G$.

## CHAPTER 7

# NC Algorithms for Chordal Graphs

If the time complexity of a parallel algorithm is $O(\log^k n)$ and uses polynomially many processors on $n$, where $n$ is the size of the input and $k$ is a constant, the algorithm is said to belong to NC class. In this chapter we study some NC algorithms for chordal graphs. Chordal graphs play a major role in the class of data structures. Several NP complete problems can be solved in linear time if the input graph is chordal. Chordal graphs have already been introduced in Chapter 2. Chordal graphs are an important subclass of perfect graphs which are graphs in which the maximum clique size and the chromatic number are equal. Chordal graphs have applications in several areas, including Gaussian elimination and data bases. We first list a characterization of chordal graphs.

**THEOREM 7.1** *A graph $G = (V, E)$ is chordal, if and only if every minimal separator of $G$ induces a clique in $G$.*

*Proof.* Let $u$, $v$ be two nonadjacent vertices of a chordal graph $G = (V, E)$. Let $S$ denote the minimal separator of $u$ and $v$. If $S$ contains only one vertex, then $S$ induces clique, otherwise let $x$, $y$ be any two vertices of $S$. If $x$ and $y$ are adjacent for every pair of vertices of $S$, then $S$ induces a clique. Suppose $x$ and $y$ be two nonadjacent vertices of $S$. Since $S$ is minimal $u$, $v$ separator $u$, $x$, $v$, $y$ are four vertices of a cycle which has no chord. This contradicts the chordality and so every pair of vertices of $S$ are adjacent. So, $S$ induces a clique. Conversely, suppose every minimal separator is a clique. Let $v_1, v_2, \ldots, v_k, v_1$ be a chordless cycle. $v_1$ and $v_3$ are two nonadjacent vertices and the minimal separator contains $v_2$, as well as at least one of the vertices $v_4, v_5, \ldots, v_k$. That is, the minimal separator contains $v_2$ and $v_i$ where $4 \leq i \leq k$. But $v_2$ and $v_i$ are not adjacent and, hence, the minimal separator does not induce a clique. The contradiction proves the result.

## 7.1 CHORDAL GRAPH RECOGNITION

In order to develop an algorithm for chordal graph recognition, let us introduce some notations: If $u$ and $v$ are two nonadjacent vertices of $G$, let us denote $G_u = G - Adj(u)$.

$C_{uv}$ = component of $G_u$ containing $v$.

$M_{uv} = \{x : x \in adj(u) \text{ and } x \text{ is adjacent to some vertex in } C_{uv}\}$.

For example, consider the graph shown in Fig. 7.1(a). The graph $G_u$, is shown in Fig. 7.1(b). The component of $G_u$, containing $v$ is denoted by $C_{uv}$ and is shown in Fig. 7.1(c). $M_{uv}$ is the set of vertices in $adj(u)$ which are adjacent to some vertex of $C_{uv}$. In the graph shown in Fig. 7.1(a), $M_{uv} = \{6, 3\}$. $M_{uv}$ is a minimal uv separator. Now let us prove a result.

**THEOREM 7.2**   *The graph G is chordal if and only if $M_{uv}$ is a clique for every pair of nonadjacent vertices u and v.*

*Proof.* Before proving the result, let us show first that $M_{uv}$ is a uv separator, and if $M_{uv}$ contains a pair of nonadjacent vertices, then G has a chordless cycle of length at least four. It is clear that $G - M_{uv} - \{u\}$ contains $C_{uv}$. Any $x$ in $G - M_{uv} - \{u\}$ and not in $C_{uv}$ is not connected to the vertices $C_{uv}$. So, $C_{uv}$ separates $u$ and all the vertices of $C_{uv}$. In particular, $M_{uv}$ is a uv separator in G. We claim that if $M_{uv}$ contains a nonadjacent pair of vertices, then G contains a chordless cycle of length at least four.

Let $x$ and $y$ be two nonadjacent vertices in $M_{uv}$. Let $x$ and $y$ be adjacent to $r$ and $s$, respectively, in $C_{uv}$. Let $r a_1 a_2 a_3 \ldots a_p s$ be a shortest chordless path in $Cv_{uv}$. Then $uxr a_1 a_2 \ldots a_p syu$ is a chordless cycle of length at least four in G.

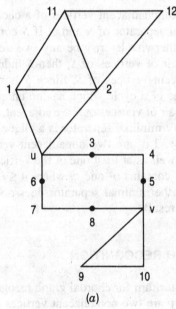

(a)

**Figure 7.1(a)**   Graph G.

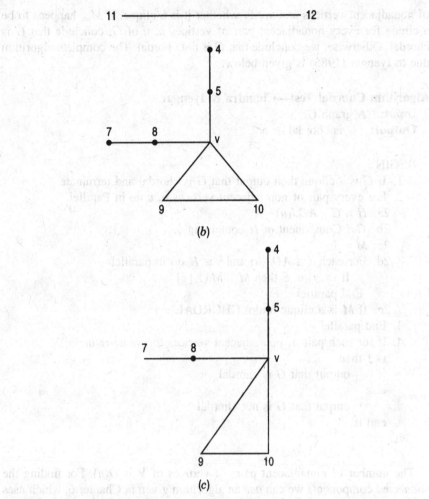

**Figure 7.1(b)**  The graph $G_{uv}$. **(c)** $C_{uv}$ = Component of $G_{uv}$ containing $v$.

Now let us prove Theorem 7.2. Let $G$ be chordal and contain more than one clique. Suppose $M_{uv}$ is not a clique. Then it contains a pair of nonadjacent vertices. Therefore, the discussion of the previous pair implies that $G$ contains a chordless cycle of length at least four. This contradicts the fact that $G$ is chordal. So, $M_{uv}$ is a clique. Conversely, suppose $M_{uv}$ is a clique for every pair of nonadjacent vertices. Suppose $G$ is not chordal. Then there exists a chordless cycle $v_1, v_2, \ldots v_k$. Let $u = v_1$ and $v = v_3$. Then $M_{uv}$ contains $\{v_2, v_4\}$, which is not a clique. This contradicts the fact that $M_{uv}$ is clique for every nonadjacent pair $uv$. So, $G$ is chordal.

In order to verify whether a graph is chordal, we can find for $M_{uv}$ every pair of nonadjacent vertices and verify whether it is a clique. If $M_{uv}$ happens to be a clique for every nonadjacent pair of vertices $u$, $v$ of $G$, conclude that $G$ is chordal. Otherwise, we conclude that $G$ is not chordal. The complete algorithm due to Iyengar (1985) is given below:

**Algorithm Chordal Test—Chandra & Iyengar**
**Input:** A graph $G$.
**Output:** $G$ is chordal or not.

BEGIN
   1. If $G$ is a clique then output that $G$ is chordal and terminate.
   2. For every pair of non adjacent vertices $u$, $v$ do in Parallel.
     2a. $H = G - ADJ(u)$
     2b. $C$ = Component of $H$ containing $v$.
     2c. $M = \Phi$
     2d. For each $x \in ADJ(u)$ and $y \in H$ do in parallel
         If $(x, y) \in E$ then $M = M \cup \{x\}$
       End parallel
     2e. If $M$ is a clique return CHORDAL = 1
   3. End parallel
   4. If for each pair of non adjacent vertices the value returned
     is 1 then
         output that $G$ is chordal
     else
         . output that $G$ is not chordal
     end if
END

The number of nonadjacent pairs of vertices of $V$ is $O(n)$. For finding the connected components we can use an algorithm given in Chapter 6, which uses $O(\log n)$ time using $O(n^2)$ processors. Also, step 2d needs $O(n^2)$ processors. So, this algorithm can be implemented in $O(\log n)$ time, using $O(n^4)$ processors. The model of the PRAM required is CREW. The method adopted to recognize a chordal graph can be applied to recognize another interesting subclass of graphs $k$-trees.

**_k-Trees._** The class of $k$-trees is an important subclass of chordal graphs. The definition and some properties are shown below:
   DEFINITION: A graph is a $k$-tree if it can be obtained by the following recursive construction rules.

   1. Start with any clique with $k$ elements as a basis graph. A clique with $k$ elements is a $k$-tree.
   2. To any $k$ tree $H$, add a new vertex and make it adjacent to all the vertices

of a clique sub graphs of $H$ with $k$ elements and form a clique with $k + 1$ elements.

Now we list a characterization theorem for $k$-trees.

**THEOREM 7.3** *The following are equivalent:*

1. $G = (V, E)$ *is a $k$-tree.*
2. *(a) $G$ is connected.*
   *(b) $G$ has a $k$-clique, but not $(k + 2)$ clique.*
   *(c) Every minimal vertex separator is a $k$-clique.*
3. *(a) $G$ is chordal.*
   *(b) $|E| = k|V| - k(k + 1)/2$.*
   *(c) $G$ has a $k$-clique, but no $(k + 2)$ clique.*
4. *(a) $G$ is connected.*
   *(b) $|E| = k|V| - k(k + 1)/2$.*
   *(c) Every minimal vertex separator of $G$ is a $k$-clique.*

The proof of the above theorem is a systematic verification, and so is left to the reader as an exercise.

***Chandra and Iyengar's Algorithm for k-Tree Recognition.*** The NC algorithm for recognizing $k$-trees is similar to the one for recognizing chordal graphs, but different, in the sense that it makes use of minimal separators. We need the following preliminary results:

**THEOREM 7.4** *Let $G$ be a noncomplete chordal graph. Let $x$ be a simplicial vertex in $G$ and $H = (U, F) = G - \{x\}$. Then for any nonadjacent pair of vertices $u$ and $v$ of $H$, no minimal $uv$ separator contains $x$.*

*Proof.* If $H$ is a clique, then the lemma is vacuously true. Assume $H$ is not a clique. Let $u$ and $v$ be nonadjacent vertices. Both $u$ and $v$ cannot be adjacent to $x$, otherwise $u$ and $v$ would themselves have to be adjacent to each other. Therefore, at most one of the vertices $u$ and $v$ is adjacent to $x$. Two cases arise.

**Case 1**

Without loss of generality, let $u$ be adjacent to $x$. Then $v$ is not adjacent to $x$. Let $S$ be a minimal $uv$ separator contained in $\{x\} \cup ADJ(x) - \{u\}$. Let $C_1$ and $C_2$ be the connected components of $G - S$ containing the vertices $u$ and $v$, respectively. Then $C_1 \cap C_2 = \Phi$. Also no vertex in $C_2$ is adjacent to $x$, because $x$ is a simplicial vertex. Furthermore, no vertex in $C_2$ is adjacent to $u$. This is because if there is a vertex $z$ in $C_2$ adjacent to $u$, then $u$ and $v$ will be connected by a path in $G - S$, unless $z$ is adjacent to $x$ also. But we know that no vertex in $C_2$ is adjacent to $x$. So all the vertices in $C_2$ are adjacent to a subset of $ADJ(x) - \{u\}$. Therefore, $u$ and $v$ can be separated by $R = (ADJ(x) - \{u\}) \cap ADJ(C_2)$. Furthermore, it is easy to see that $R$ is also the only minimal $uv$ separator contained in $ADJ(x) - \{u\} \cup \{x\}$. If any minimal $uv$ separator $S$ is to contain $x$, then it should be a subset of $ADJ(x) \cup \{x\} - \{u\}$. But we have seen that the only minimal $uv$ separator in $ADJ(x) \cup \{x\} - \{u\}$ is $R$, which does not contain $x$. Therefore, the lemma holds.

## Case 2

Both $u$, $v$ are not adjacent to $x$. Let $S$ be a minimal $uv$ separator contained in $\{x\} \cup ADJ(x)$. Let $C_1$ and $C_2$ be the connected components of $G$-$S$ containing the vertices $u$ and $v$, respectively. Again, no vertex in either $C_1$ or $C_2$ is adjacent to $x$. So the only minimal $uv$ separator contained in $ADJ(x) \cup \{x\}$ are $ADJ(x) \cap ADJ(C1)$ and $ADJ(x) \cap ADJ(C2)$, neither of which contains the vertex $x$. As in the previous case, we can see that the lemma holds. We give below a new characterization of $k$ trees.

**THEOREM 7.5** *A graph $G = (V, E)$ is a k-tree if and only if*

    a: *For every nonadjacent pair of vertices u and v of G, there exists a minimal uv separator which is a k clique; and*

    b: $m = kn - k(k + 1)/2$.

*Proof.* (ONLY IF): If $G$ is a clique then it is a *k-tree*, trivially. If $G$ is not a clique, then for every pair of nonadjacent vertices $u$ and $v$, the minimal separator of $G$ is a $k$ clique. Furthermore, $m = kn - k(k + 1)/2$.

(IF): The condition a) alone implies that $G$ is chordal. Therefore, it is enough to show that $G$ has a $k$ clique, but no $(k + 2)$ clique. This we show below: It is easy to see that if $G$ is a clique, it cannot be a $(k + 2)$ clique. Therefore, assume that $G$ is not a clique. Then $G$ has a $k$-clique because it will have a minimal separator. We show by induction on the number of vertices that $G$. All graphs having $1, 2, 3$, and $4$ vertices don't have $(k + 2)$ cliques. Assume that all graphs having fewer than or equal to $n - 1$ vertices and satisfying conditions (a) and (b) do not have cliques. Consider a graph $G$ on $n$ vertices and satisfying conditions (a) and (b). Because $G$ is chordal, there exists a simplicial vertex $x$ in $G$. Let $H = (U, F) = G - \{x\}(U, F) = G - \{x\}$ and $W = \{x\} \cup ADJ(x)$. Now $|U| = n - 1$ and $|w| \leq n - 1$, otherwise $G$ would be a clique. Now we consider two cases here.

## Case 1

Suppose $H$ is a clique with $n-1$ vertices. The conditions (a) and (b) are satisfied by $H$. By the induction hypothesis, $H$ does not have a $k + 2$ clique. Since $G$ is not a clique, there exists at least one vertex in $U$ not adjacent to $x$. Furthermore, all the minimal $zx$ separators, where $z \in ADJ(x)$ are nothing but itself. Since $G$ satisfies condition (a), $ADJ(x)$ has to be a $k$ clique. This implies that in $G$ there is at least one $k_1$ clique but no $k + 2$ clique.

## Case 2

$H$ is not a clique. In $G$, for every nonadjacent pair of vertices $w, z \in U$, there exists a minimal separator which is a $k$ clique. Since $x$ cannot be in any such minimal $wz$ separator, $H$ satisfies condition (a). Consider the recursive construction of the graph $G$ starting from the maximal clique $W$. Let $y$ be a vertex to be added next in this recursive construction process. The vertex $y$ is not adjacent to $x$, but adjacent to a clique in $ADJ(x)$. Furthermore, any minimal $xy$ separator is contained in $ADJ(x)$. If either $|ADJ(x)|$ or $|ADJ(y)| < k$, then there exists a minimal $xy$ separator of size less than $k$ in $G$, which is a contradiction to our assumption. If both $|ADJ(y)|$ and $|ADJ(x)|$ are less than $k$, then again a similar contradiction arises. Therefore, $|ADJ(y)| = |ADJ(x)| = k$. Hence, $H$ has $m - k = k(n - 1) - k(k + 1)/2$ edges. So $H$ satisfies condition (b) also. By the induction hypothesis, $H$ does not contain a $(k + 2)$ clique. By the above facts, $G$ also does not contain a $(k + 2)$ clique.

The following sequential algorithm tests whether a graph $G$ is a $k$-tree or not. The body of this algorithm is similar to that of the Chordal Test algorithm.

### Algorithm $k$-tree Test—Chandra and Iyengar
**Input:** A graph $G$ with $n$ vertices and in edges.
**Output:** If $G$ a $k$-tree.

```
BEGIN
   1. If the equation m = kn − k(k + 1)/2 does not have a positive
      integer root ≤ n for k, G is not a k tree, Terminate
      End if
   2. Let k < n be a positive integer root of the above equation
   3. For every non adjacent unordered pair of vertices u and v of V do
   4. Gᵤ = G − ADJ(u)
   5. Cᵤᵥ = the component of Gᵤ containing v
   6. Mᵤᵥ = {x : x ∈ ADJ(u) and x is adjacent to some vertex in Cᵤᵥ
   7. If Mᵤᵥ induces a k-cliques in G then continue
      else
      G is not a k tree
      terminate
      End if
   8. End for
   9. G is a k tree
END
```

The correctness of the above algorithm is established below.

**THEOREM 7.6** *The graph G is a k tree if and only if*

1. $m = kn - k(k + 1)/2$; *and*
2. $M_{uv}$ *(in the algorithm) induces a k clique for all nonadjacent pairs of vertices u and v of G.*

*Proof.* (IF): It is easy to see that $M_{uv}$ is a minimal $uv$ separator in $G$. Furthermore, the condition of Theorem 7.5 is satisfied. By Theorem 7.5, $G$ is a $k$ tree.

(ONLY IF): Let $G$ be a $k$ tree. Then clearly $m = kn - k(k+1)/2$ and therefore $k$ will have a positive integer value in any solution to this equation. Furthermore, $G$ is not a clique, it can be easily shown that the above equation can have at most one positive integer root less than $n$ for $k$. Now, assume that for some nonadjacent pair of vertices $u$ and $v$, $M_{uv}$ is not $k$ clique. Then because $M_{uv}$ is a minimal separator, it is not a $k$ tree contradicting the assumption. The proof of the following result is straightforward.

**THEOREM 7.7** *The algorithm k-tree Test correctly tests if G is a k tree or not.*

Along the same lines as the NC algorithm for recognizing chordal graphs, the sequential algorithm $k$-tree test can be parallelized into an NC algorithm. Therefore, we have the following theorem:

**THEOREM 7.8** *There exists parallel algorithm for recognizing k-trees which takes $O(\log n)$ time and makes use of $O(n^4)$ processors.*

**Naor, Naor, and Schaffer's Algorithm.** Naor, Naor, and Schaffer (1989) have worked on the parallel algorithm for chordal graphs and designed a number of NC algorithms for chordal graphs. Let us start with their chordal graph recognition algorithm. The main advantage of their algorithm is that the correctness of the algorithm easily follows from the definition of chordal graphs as graphs that contain no induced chordless cycles of lengths greater than 3. A secondary advantage is that on sparse graphs it uses asymptotically fewer processors. The following notations are used in the algorithm.

$N(v)$ = set of vertices adjacent to $v$.

$G - v$ = graph induced by $V - \{v\}$.

If $W V, G - W$ = graph induces by $V - W$

The parallel algorithm follows only from the following theorem.

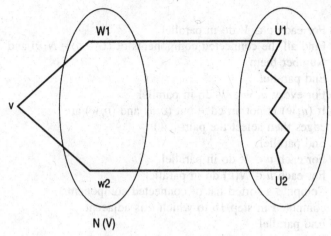

**Figure 7.2**   A circuit is formed.

**THEOREM 7.9**   *A graph $G = (V, E)$ is not chordal if and only if it contains a vertex $v$ with the property that a connected component of $(G - v) - N(v)$ is adjacent to two vertices of $N(v)$ which are not adjacent to each other.*

*Proof.* Let $G = (V, E)$ be a graph such the there exists a vertex $v$ such that $w_1, w_2 \in N(v)$ and they are adjacent to a connected component of $(G-v)-N(v)$ and $w_1$ is not adjacent to $w_2$ (see Fig. 7.2). Let $u_1$ and $u_2$ be the vertices of the connected component such that $w_1, w_2$ are adjacent to $u_1$ and to $u_2$, respectively. Now $w_1$, $v$ and $w_2$ belong to a chordless cycle of length greater than three. So, $G$ is not a chordal graph.

Conversely, suppose $G$ is not a chordal graph. Let $v_1, v_2, \ldots v_k, v_1$ induce a chordless cycle of length $k > 4$. Consider the vertex $v_1$. In $(G - v_1) - N(v_1)$ the vertices $v_3, v_4, \ldots v_{k1}$ lie in the same connected component $v_2$ and $v_k$ are in $N(v_1)$, such that they are adjacent to the connected component of $(G-v_1)-N(v_1)$ having $v_3, v_4, \ldots v_{k-1}$ and $v_2$ is not adjacent to $v_k$. Hence the proof is complete.

By Theorem 7.9, in order to verify whether $G$ is chordal, we can verify whether $G$ has any vertex $v$ satisfying the condition of Theorem 7.9. For each vertex $v$ we must first find $(G - u) - N(v)$ and all its connected components. Then for every pair $(u, w)$ of nonadjacent vertices of $N(v)$ we verify whether any component is adjacent to both $u$ and $w$. If any such component is adjacent, we conclude that $G$ is not chordal. The parallel algorithm is given below:

**Algorithm Chordal Test—Naor, Naor, and Schaffer**
   **Input:**   A simple undirected graph $G = (V, E)$.
   **Output:**   Is $G$ chordal?

BEGIN
1. (a) For each $v \in V$ do in parallel
   (b) Find all the connected components of $(G - v) - N(v)$ and Number them.
   (c) End parallel
2. (a) For every $u, w \in V$ do in parallel
   (b) If $(u, w)$ is not an edge but $(v, u)$ and $(v, w)$ are edges then select the pair$(u, w)$.
   (c) End parallel.
3. (a) For each $v \in V$ do in parallel
   (b) For each $u \in N(v)$ do in parallel
   (c) Compute a sorted list of connected components computed in step 1b to which $u$ is adjacent.
   (d) End parallel.
   (e) End parallel.
4. (a) For every vertex $v \in V$ do in parallel.
   (b) For every pair of vertices $u, w \in N(v)$ such that $(u, w)$ is not adjacent do in parallel.
   (c) Verify if there is an entry in the list of connected components to which both $u$ and $w$ are adjacent. If so, conclude $G$ is not chordal.
   (d) End parallel
   (e) End parallel
5. (a) If step 4c does not declare that $G$ is not chordal for any pair $(u, w)$ and $v \in V$ then conclude that $G$ is chordal.

END

**Complexity Analysis.** In step 1 we can use the connected components algorithm presented in Chapter 6, which uses $O(n^2)$ processors and works in $O(\log_n^2)$ time in a CREW PRAM. In step 1 we are doing the work in parallel for all the $n$ vertices. So, step 1 can be implemented in $O(\log n)$ time, using $O(n^3)$ processors. The complexity of step 2.2 depends upon the data structure used to represent the graph. If the graph is represented in terms of its adjacency matrix, step 2.2 can be described as follows:

> If $(A(u, w) = 0$ and $A(v, u) = 1$ and $A(v, w) = 1)$ then select
>
> the pair $(u, w)$
>
> end if.

This needs only $O(1)$ time. However the adjacency matrix representation is inefficient in other processing areas. If the graph is represented in the form of its adjacency list case 2.2 needs $O(\log n)$-time using $O(m)$ processors. ($m$ is the number of edges in the graph $G$). So, step 2 can be implemented in $O(\log n)$

time using $O(mn)$ processors. Step 3.3 takes $O(\log_n^2)$ time for a single processor. Steps 3.2 to 3.4 is a parallel loop. The number of times this loop is executed is the degree of $v$. Since sum of the degree of all the vertices is $2m$, the step 3 can be implemented in $O(\log_n^2)$ time using $O(mn)$ processors. Step 4 can be implemented in $O(\log n)$ time using $O(mn^2)$ processors as follows: To every triple $(v, u, w)$ such that $v$ is adjacent to $u$ and $w$ and $u$ are not adjacent to each other, assign one processor to every component on the list of components which we compute for the pair $(u, w)$ in step 3. The total length of component lists for all pairs $(u, w)$ is $O(mn)$. To each entry on such a list assign at the most $n - 2$ processors, one for each choice of $w$. The total number of processors is $O(mn^2)$. A processor corresponding to entry $C$ for the triple $(v, u, w)$ does a binary search for $C$ on the component list of $(v, w)$ and records the result (1 if it finds $C$ and $O$ otherwise). For each fixed value of $v$, all processors corresponding to triples with $v$ as the first component do a Boolean OR of their results. This leaves $n$ Boolean values for step 5. Step 5 can be implemented in $O(\log n)$ time with $O(n)$ processors by just doing a Boolean OR of the $n$ values computed in step 4. So, the overall complexity of the algorithms is $O(\log^2)$ time using $O(mn^2)$ processors. This uses a CREW PRAM model.

Naor, Naor, and Schaffer (1980) have also designed NC parallel algorithm for the following problems:

1. To list all maximal cliques of a chordal graph.
2. To find the optimal coloring of a chordal graph.
3. To find the tree representation of a chordal graph.
4. To find the maximum independent set of a chordal graph.
5. To find the minimum clique cover of a chordal graph.

## 7.2 MAXIMAL CLIQUES OF CHORDAL GRAPHS

Let us first see the algorithm to find all maximal cliques in a chordal graph. A chordal graph can have at the most $n$ maximal cliques. Let us first define a *bi-clique*.

A graph $G = (V, E)$ is defined to be a *bi-clique* if its vertex set $V$ can be partitioned into two sets $A$ and $B$ such that the graphs induced by $A$ as well as $B$ are cliques. The divide-and-conquer method is used to find all the maximal cliques of a general chordal graph $G$. $G$ is divided into two arbitrary disjoint subsets $A$ and $B$ of almost equal size. The maximal cliques of the graphs induced by $A$ and $B$ are computed recursively. Then for each pair of maximal cliques $p$ of $G_A$ and $GAB$ all the maximal cliques in the induced subgraph $G_{A \cup B}$ which is a bi-clique. The above process might have generated duplicates of maximal cliques occurring in more than one bi-clique. The important procedure needed for determining all the maximal cliques from the above discussion is the procedure for evaluating all the maximal cliques of a bi-clique. Let $G = (V, E)$

be the chordal graph for which we are interested in evaluating all the maximal cliques. Let $V = A \cup B$ be a partition of the vertices of $G$, such that $|A|$ and $|B|$ are almost equal. Let $P$ and $Q$ be maximal cliques of $G_A$ and $G_B$, respectively, where $G_A$ denotes the graph induced by $A$. $P \cup Q$ induces a bi-clique and it is denoted by $G_{PUQ}$. For $v \in Q$, we denote $N_Q(v) = \{w \in Q : (v, w)$ is an edge in $P \cup Q\}$. Similarly, for $V \in Q$, we denote $NP(v) = \{w \in P - (v, w)$ is an edge in $P \cup Q\}$.

It is very interesting to note that the $\{N_Q(v) : v \in P\}$ is ordered by inclusion. This means that, for any two vertices $v_1$, $v_2 \in P$, either $N_Q(v_1)N_Q(v_2)$ or $N_Q(v_2)N_Q(v_1)$.

**THEOREM 7.10** *The collection $\{N_Q(v) : v \in P\}$ is ordered by set inclusion.*

*Proof.* Suppose $u$ and $v$ are two vertices of $P$ such that neither $N_q(u)Nq(v)$ nor $N_q(v)N_q(u)$. Let $w_1 \in N_Q(u)$ but $w_1N_Q(v)$. Similarly, $w_2$ be a vertex in $N_Q(v)$ but not in $N_Q(u)$. As $w_1$ and $w_2$ are two vertices of $Q$ they are adjacent. Since $u$ and $v$ are in $P$, they are adjacent (see Fig. 7.3). But the selection of $w_1$ and $w_2$ implies that $u$ is not adjacent to $w_2$ and $v$ is not adjacent to $w_1$. Hence $u - v - w_2 - w_1$ induce a chordless cycle. Hence contradiction to the fact that $G$ is chordal. So the proof of the theorem is complete.

**COROLLARY 7.11** Let $C = C_P \cup C_Q$ be any maximal clique of the chordal biclique $G_{PUQ}$, where $Cp$ $P$ and $CQ$ $Q$ are both nonempty. Then $Cp$ is the smallest set in the collection $\{N_P(x) | x \in C_Q\}$ and $CQ$ is the smallest set in the collection $\{NQ(x) | x \in CP\}$.

The above two results imply the following parallel algorithm to generate all the maximal cliques of $G$ occurring in a biclique.

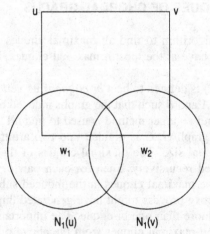

**Figure 7.3** A circuit is formed.

**Algorithm Biclique—MC**
  **Input:**  Graph $G$, $AV$ and $BV$, such that
         $A \cup B = V$, $A \cap B = \Phi$
         Clique $PA$,
         Clique $QB$.
  **Output:**  List of cliques occurring in $G_{PUQ}$ which are maximal
         cliques in $G$.

BEGIN
  1. Compute $\{N_Q(v) : v \in P\}$.
  2. Sort these sets with set inclusion and sort the vertices
     of $P$ according to this order.
  3. Compute $\{N_P(u) : u \in Q\}$.
  4. Sort these vertices with set inclusion and sort the
     vertices of $Q$ according to this order.
  5. Find the vertices $v_i$ in the list $P$ such that $N_Q(v_i)$ is a
     proper superset of $N_Q(v_{i+1})$.
  6. Each vertex $v$ chosen in step 5 yields a different maximal
     clique $QA(v) \cup QB(v)$. $QA(v)$ consists of $v$ and every
     vertex of $P$ with the same or larger neighbor set in $Q$.
     That is,

$$QA(v) = \{v\} \cup \{w : NQ(w)NQ(v)\}.$$

     Given $QA(v)$, we can find $QB(v)$ by Corollary 7.11 we
     may also need to include the cliques $P$ and $Q$.
  7. Decide which maximal cliques of the biclique $G_{PUQ}$ are
     maximal cliques in $G$.
END

Before discussing the complexity of the above algorithm, let us first see how
we can implement step 7. Let us first define a notation: If $v \notin P \cup Q$, $u(P, v) =$
highest vertex in the sorted list of vertices $P$, such that $N_Q(u(P, v))N_Q(v)$. There
may not exist any vertex satisfying the above defined condition. In such a case,
$u(P, v)$ does not exist for $v$. In a similar way, $u(Q, v)$ is also defined.

**THEOREM 7.12**  *Let $C$ be a clique that is maximal in $G_{PUQ}$, such that*

  1. $C \cap P \neq \Phi$.
  2. $C \cap Q \neq \Phi$.
  3. *For every $v \notin P \cup Q$, contains almost one of $u(P, v)$ or $u(Q, v)$.*

*Then $C$ is also a maximal clique in $G$.*

The reader can refer Naor, Naor, and Schaffer (1989) for a proof of Theorem 7.12.

Based on the above theorem, we can implement step 7 of the algorithm Bi-Clique-MC. Now let us discuss the complexity of the algorithm Bi-Clique-MC.

**Complexity Analysis.** Steps 1 to 4 can be implemented in $O(\log n)$ time using $O(n^2)$ processors. Step 5 can be implemented in constant time, using the same number of processors. In step 6, $QA(v)$ is a prefix of $P$. The size of $QA(v)$ is the rank of $v$ in $P$. The set $QB(v)$ is the same as $NQ(v)$. Thus for each clique $Q(v)$ we can then compute its size in $O(\log n)$ time with one processor. For each member of $Q(v)$, we can then assign one processor for listing the output. So, it can be done in $O(\log n)$ time, using $O(m + n)$ processors. $u(P, v)$ and $u(Q, v)$ can be determined in $O(\log n)$ time, using $O(n^2)$ processors. So, step 7 can be implemented in $O(\log n)$ time, using $O(n^2)$ processors.

Having seen the procedure for obtaining all the maximal cliques of a bi-clique, let us formally state the NC algorithm to find all the maximal cliques of a graph.

**Algorithm Max-Cliques**
   **Input:**   Graph $G = (V, E)$.
   **Output:**   List of maximal cliques of $G$.

BEGIN
   1. Let $V = A \cup B$,
      where $A \cap B = \Phi$ and $|A| = |B|$ (approx.).
   2. Compute all the maximal cliques of $G_A$ and $G_B$ recursively.
   3. For every pair of maximal cliques $P$ of $G_A$ and $Q$ of $G_B$
      compute all the maximal cliques of $G$ in the induced
      subgraph $G_{PUQ}$ which is a bi-clique.
   4. Eliminate duplicate cliques occurring in more than one
      bi-clique.
   END

As we are halving the number of vertices in each recursive call, there will be $O(\log n)$ recursive calls.

We use Bi-Clique-MC algorithm in each recursive call. The elimination of duplicate cliques takes $O(\log_n^2)$ time, using $O(n^4)$ processors. Hence all the maximal cliques of a chordal graph can be computed in $O(\log^3 n)$ time, using $O(n^4)$ processors.

**Some Subclasses of Chordal Graphs.** C. Xavier et al. (1990) have defined two classes of intersection graphs of a family of paths in trees. A family of paths in a tree $T$ is said to be *perfect* if no vertex of $T$ is an internal vertex of more than one path of the family. The intersection graph of a perfect family of vertex paths in a tree is called a *perfect vertex path graph* or *PV graph*. A family of paths in a tree $T$ is said to be *compact* if no edge of $T$ is in more than one path of the family. The intersection graph of a compact family of vertex paths in a tree is called a *compact vertex path graph* or *CVgraph*. We observe that CV graphs form a proper subcollection of RD graphs and PV graphs, a proper subcollection of DV graphs.

## 7.3 CHARACTERIZATION OF CV GRAPHS

From the very definition, a PV graph is a UV graph. A PV graph need not be an RDV graph and an RDV graph need not be a PV graph. A CV graph need not be an interval graph and every interval graph need not be a CV graph. We present below several characterizations of CV groups.

**THEOREM 7.13** *For any graph G the following are equivalent.*

a. *G is the intersection graph of a family F of edge-disjoint paths in some tree $T_1$.*

b. *G is the intersection graph of a family F of edge-disjoint subtrees of some tree $T_2$.*

c. *There exists a tree T with $V(T) = C(G)$ s.t. $F = \{T[C_v(G)]|v \in V\}$ is an edge-disjoint family of paths of T.*

d. *G contains neither $K_4 - e$ nor $C_n$, $n \geq 4$ as an induced subgraph. Note that $K_4 - e$ is the graph obtained by the removal of one edge from $K_4$, the complete graph with 4 vertices. $C_n$ is a cycle with n vertices.*

e. *G is a block graph.*

f. *$|H|C(G)| = |B(G)|A$ tree T satisfying (3) is called a CV clique tree for G.*

The proof of the theorem is left as an exercise to the reader.

Let $G$ be a $CV$ graph and $C$ be a separating clique of $G$. Let $G_i = G[V_i \cup C]$, $1 \leq i \leq r$, $r \geq 2$ be the separated subgraphs.

**PROPOSITION 7.14** *$W(G_i)$ is a singleton set, $1 \leq i \leq r$.*

*Proof.* Clearly, $W(G_i)$ is nonempty. If $|W(G_i)| \geq 2$, then it is easy to show that $G_i$ contains $K4 - e$ as an induced subgraph, a contradiction to the fact that $G$ is a block graph.

**COROLLARY 7.15** *G is a CV graph if each separated subgraph is a CV graph.*

*Proof.* Necessity is trivial. For sufficiency, let each separated subgraph $G_i$, $1 \le i \le r$, be a $CV$ graph. So each $G_i$ is a block graph. Again by Proposition 7.14, each $W(G_i)$ is a singleton set. Hence $G$ is a block graph. So $G$ is a $CV$ graph.

**Recognition Algorithm for CV-Graph.** We now suggest a linear time algorithm to recognize a $CV$ graph and to construct an intersection model if the graph is a $CV$ graph.

**Algorithm $CV$ test**
  **Input:**  A graph $G = (V, E)$ in adjacency list representation.
  **Output:**  'No' if $G$ is not a $CV$ graph. Otherwise a $CV$ clique tree
        $T$ for $G$.

BEGIN
   1. If $G$ is not a block graph, then output 'No'.
   2. Find all clique of $G$. Let $C_1, C_2 \ldots , C_r$ be the cliques of $G$.
   3. Find the set $\{C_{i1}, C_{i2}, \ldots , C_{iri}\}$ of cliques containing $v_i$,
      $1 \le i \le n$
   4. $T = T(V_o, E_o)$, where $V_o$ is the set of all clique of $G$ and
      $Eo = \Phi$
   5. For $i: = 1$ to $n$ do
   6. $T = T(V_i, E_i)$, where $V_i = V_o$ and
   7. $E_i = E_{i-1} \cup \{G_i, G_{ij}, 1 < j < r_i - 1\}$
   8. If $r_i > 1$ return else $E_i = E_{i-1}$
   9. End for
END

## 7.4  PATH GRAPH RECOGNITION

In this section we present an $NC$ parallel algorithm to recognize UV graphs (path graphs) developed by C. Xavier. We adapt an entirely different strategy from that adapted to recognize chordal graphs. We begin with the following two simple facts.

*Fact 7.16  If G is a UV graph and v is a vertex of G, the nodes of the clique tree T corresponding to the cliques of G containing v induce a path in T.*

*Fact 7.17  In an interval graph, the maximal cliques can be linearly ordered such that for any vertex v, the cliques containing v are consecutive in the linear ordering. In other words, the clique tree of an interval graph is a path and for every vertex v the nodes corresponding to the cliques containing v form a subpath.*

If $G$ is a UV graph, we prove in Theorem 7.19 that the union of maximal cliques of $G$ containing a vertex $v$ of $G$ induce an interval graph. For every vertex $v$ of $G$ we check in parallel if the graph induced by the union of maximal cliques of $G$ containing $v$ is an interval graph. If it fails for any one of the vertices, we conclude that $G$ is not a UV graph. If it succeeds for each vertex $v$ of $G$ then we formulate a $PQ$-tree representation of the corresponding interval graph. From these $PQ$-tree representations, we try to formulate a clique tree of $G$. If we fail to formulate, we conclude that $G$ is not a UV graph. The procedure of formulating a clique tree of $G$ is involved and we do it step by step. Section 7.4.1 gives the fundamental definitions and some simple facts necessary for the development of the algorithm. An outline of the algorithm is then explained in Section 7.4.2. A detailed algorithm, its correctness, and complexity analysis are presented in the subsequent sections.

### 7.4.1  Some Definitions and Facts

We now begin with some notations used in the development of the algorithm. In the rest of this section we are going to deal with only maximal cliques. So, hereinafter a clique will mean only a maximal clique. Also we assume that $G$ is a chordal graph and $T$ its clique tree representation. If capital alphabet $C$ is a clique in $G$, the corresponding small letter $c$ represents the node in $T$ corresponding to $C$. The vertices of the clique tree $T$ are referred as nodes.

If $a$ is a vertex of $G$ let $C_a$ denote the collection of cliques of $G$ that contain $a$. In other words,

$$C_a = \{C/C \text{ is a clique of } G \text{ and } a \in C\}.$$

Let $G_a$ denote the graph induced by the union of all cliques in $C_a$. If $a$ and $b$ are two vertices of $G$, $C_{a+b}$ and $C_{ab}$ denote $C_a \cup C_b$ and $C_a \cap C_b$, respectively. The graphs induced by the union of all cliques in $C_{a+b}$ and $C_{ab}$ are denoted by $G_{a+b}$ and $G_{ab}$, respectively. For example, consider the graph $G$ given in Figure 7.4(a). Its cliques are $C_1 = \{a,b,c,d\}$; $C_2 = \{e,d\}$; $C_3 = \{d,f,g\}$; $C_4 = \{d,g,h\}$; $C_5 = \{s,h,r\}$; $C_6 = \{h,r,p\}$; $C_7 = \{p,q\}$.

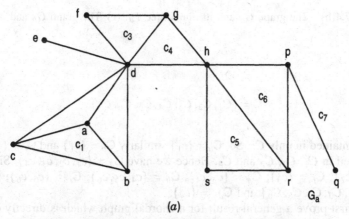

(a)

**Figure 7.4(a)**   A chordal graph $G$ to illustrate $G_a$.

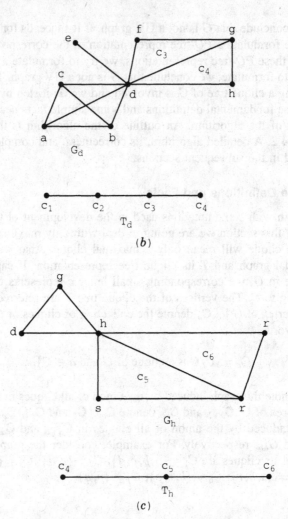

**Figure 7.4(b)** The graph $G_d$ and its clique tree $T_d$. **(c)** The graph $G_h$ and its clique tree $T_h$.

$$C = \{C_1, C_2, C_3, C_4, C_5, C_6, C_7\},$$

as is contained in only $C_1$. So, $C_a = \{c_1\}$ similarly $C_b = \{c_1\}$ and $C_c = \{c_1\}$ $d$ is contained in $C_1, C_2, C_3$ and $C_4$. Hence we have $C_d = \{c_1, c_2, c_3, c_4\}$. Similarly $C_e = \{c_2\}$; $C_f = \{c_3\}$; $C_g = \{c_3, c_4\}$; $C_h = \{c_4, c_5, c_6\}$; $C_r = \{c_5, c_6\}$; $C_{d+h} = \{C_1, C_2, C_3, C_4, C_5, C_6\}$ and $C_{dh} = \{c_4\}$.

We first prove a general result for a chordal graph which is directly or indirectly used in the development of the algorithm.

**THEOREM 7.18** *Let G be a chordal graph and T its clique tree representation. Every nonleaf node of T represents a separating clique of G.*

*Proof.* Let $c$ be a nonleaf node of $T$, such that $c_1$ and $c_2$ are adjacent to $c$. The cliques $C$, $C_1$ and $C_2$ are such that one is not contained in the other. So, there exists vertices $a$ and $b$, such that

$$a \in C_1 \text{ but } a \notin C \text{ and therefore } a \notin C_2;$$
$$b \in C_2 \text{ but } b \notin C \text{ and therefore } b \notin C_1.$$

We claim that every path of $G$ from $a$ to $b$ must go through a vertex of $C$. Let $P = a_1, a_2, a_3 \ldots, a_k$ be an arbitrary path from $a$ to $b$ where $a = a_1$ and $b = a_k$. Let $S_1, S_2, \ldots S_k$ denote the subtrees of $T$, corresponding to the vertices $a_1, a_2, \ldots a_k$.

Let $S = S_1 \cup S_2 \cup \ldots \cup S_k$. $S$ is a subtree of $T$, $c_1$ and $c_2$ are in $S$. Therefore, the entire path in $T$ from $c_1$ to $c_2$ is also in $S$. Hence $c \in S$, which implies $c \in S_i$ for some $i$ and so $a_i \in C$. Since $P$ is arbitrary, every path from $a$ to $b$ must pass through a vertex of $C$. This proves that $C$ separates $a$ and $b$. So, $C$ is a separating clique. We now state and prove a vital result, which forms the basis for the design of our algorithm.

**THEOREM 7.19** *If G is a UV graph, $G_a$ is an interval graph for every vertex $a$ of G.*

Before proving the theorem, let us examine an example that illustrates this result. Consider the chordal graph shown in Fig. 5.2(a). This graph has only 6 cliques. They are $C_1 = \{a, b, f, g\}$; $C_2 = \{b, f, g, h\}$; $C_3 = \{b, g, h, k\}$; $C_4 = \{f, g, h, d\}$; $C_5 = \{f, h, l\}$; and $C_6 = \{p, l\}$.

Here $g$ is contained in $C_1$, $C_2$, $C_3$, and $C_4$. So $\mathbf{C}_g = \{c_1, c_2, c_3, c_4\}$ and $G_g$ is shown in Fig. 7.5(b). It is not very difficult to check that $G_g$ is not an interval graph. So, $G$ is not an UV graph by Theorem 7.19.

*Proof of Theorem 7.19.* Let $P_a = c_1, c_2, \ldots c_k$ be the path in $T$ corresponding to the vertex $a$. Then $G_a = C_1 \cup C_2 \cup \ldots \cup C_k$. The cliques of $G_a$ are precisely $C_1, C_2, \ldots C_k$. We claim that the ordering $C_1 C_2 \ldots C_k$ is a linear ordering, such that, for any vertex $b$ of $G_a$, the cliques of $G_a$ containing $b$ appear consecutively. Let $b$ be an arbitrary vertex of $G_a$. The cliques of $G$ containing $b$ form a path in $T$. Let the path be $P_b = c'_1, c'_2, \ldots c'_r$.

Since $b \in G_a$, $P_a \cap P_b$ is nonempty. Since $T$ is a tree and $P_a$, $P_b$ are its two paths such that $P_a \cap P_b$ is nonempty, $P_a \cap P_b$ is a subpath of both $P_a$ and $P_b$. In particular, $P_a \cap P_b$ is a subpath of $P_a$. Let $P_a \cap P_b = c_i c_{i+1} \ldots c_{i+l}$. This precisely means that the cliques of $G_a$ containing $b$ are $C_i, C_{i+1}, \ldots C_{i+l}$. Hence $G_a$ is an interval graph.

The converse of Theorem 7.19 is not true. For example, consider the graph

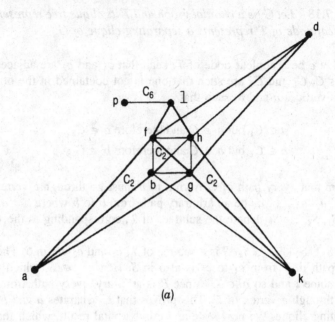

(a)

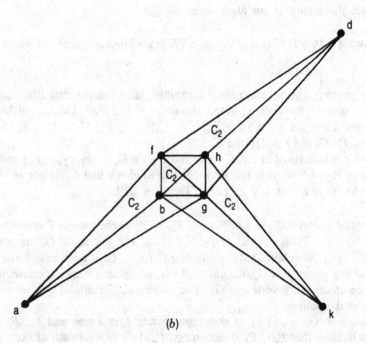

(b)

**Figure 7.5(a)**   A chordal graph $G$ to illustrate Theorem 7.19. **(b)** The graph $G_8$ which is not an interval graph.

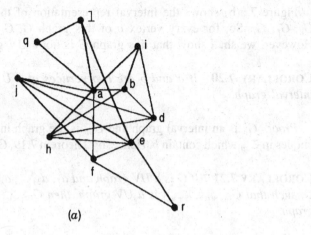

(a)

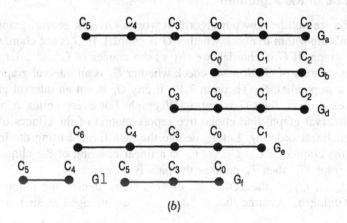

(b)

**Figure 7.6(a)**  A chordal graph $G$ which is not UV graph. **(b)** The interval representation of $Ga$, $Gb$, etc. of $G$.

given in Fig. 7.6(a). The following are its cliques: $C_0 = \{a,b,d,e,f\}$; $C_1 = \{a,b,d,e,h\}$; $C_2 = \{a,b,d,i\}$; $C_3 = \{a,b,d,e,f,j\}$; $C_4 = \{a,e,l\}$; $C_5 = \{a,l,q\}$; $C_6 = \{e,f,r\}$.

$$C_a = \{C_0, C_1, C_2, C_3, C_4, C_5\}$$
$$C_b = \{C_0, C_1, C_2\} \; C_d = \{C_0, C_1, C_2, C_3\}$$
$$C_e = \{C_0, C_1, C_3, C_4, C_6\} \; C_f = \{C_0, C_3, C_6\}$$
$$C_l = \{C_4, C_5\} \; C_q = \{C_5\} \; C_r = \{C_6\}$$
$$C_h = \{C_1\} \; C_i = \{C_2\} \; C_j = \{C_3\}.$$

Figure 7.6(b) shows the interval representation of the graphs $G_a$, $G_b$, $G_d$, $G_e$, $G_f$, $G_l$. So, for every vertex $v$ of this graph $G$, $G_v$ is an interval graph. However, we shall show that this graph $G$ is not a UV graph.

**COROLLARY 7.20** *If $a$ and $b$ are two vertices of a UV graph $G$, $G_{ab}$ is an interval graph.*

*Proof.* $G_a$ is an interval graph and $G_{ab}$ is the graph induced by the union of cliques in $C_{ap}$ which contain $b$. Hence, by Theorem 7.19, $G_{ab}$ is an interval graph.

**COROLLARY 7.21** *If $G$ is a UV graph and $a_1, a_2, \ldots a_k$, and $b$ are vertices of $G$, such that $G_{(a_1 + a_2 + \ldots + a_k)}$ is a UV graph, then $G_{(a_1 + a_2 + \ldots + a_k)}b$ is an interval graph.*

### 7.4.2 Outline of the Algorithm

In this section we outline how our algorithm works. Given a general graph $G$, we use Klein's algorithm to check whether $G$ is chordal. If $G$ is not chordal, $G$ is not a UV graph. If $G$ is chordal, we list all the cliques of $G$ and determine $G_a$ for every vertex $a$ of $G$. Now we check whether $G_a$ is an interval graph for each vertex $a$ in parallel. By Theorem 7.19, if any $G_a$ is not an interval graph for one vertex $a$ of $G$, then $G$ is not a UV graph. For every vertex $a$ of $G$, if $G_a$ is an interval graph, find clique tree representation of the cliques of $G_a$ and also their linear ordering. Let $T_a$ denote the path formed using the linear ordering of the cliques. If $C_1, C_2, \ldots C_k$ is a linear ordering of the cliques of the interval graph $G_a$, then $T_a$ denotes the path is $c_1, c_2, \ldots c_k$.

Let $\{a_1, a_2, \ldots a_n\}$ be the vertex set of $G$. Let $n_{a_i}$ denote the number of cliques containing $a_i$. Assume that $a_1, a_2 \ldots a_n$ are arranged in such a way that

$$n_{a_1} \geq n_{a_2} \geq \ldots \geq n_{a_n}.$$

First we want to do $n/2$ processes in parallel, combining two graphs $G_{a_i}s$ in each process and examining whether their union is a UV graph. More precisely, $G_{a_1 + a_2}$ is processed and checked whether it is a UV graph by one process; $G_{a_3 + a_4}$ is processed and checked whether it is a UV graph by another process, and so on. That is, the following work is done:

For $i = 1$ to $n/2$ do in parallel
    Check whether $G_{(a_{2i-1} + a_{2i})}$ is a UV graph.
End parallel.

When $n = 8$, the process is illustrated by Fig. 7.7. The procedure is formally stated below given in the form of an algorithm $NC$-UV $(G)$.

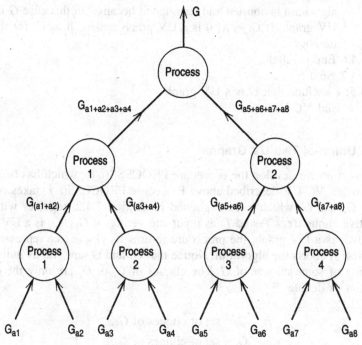

**Figure 7.7**  The process for $n = 8$.

**Algorithm NC-UV (G)**
  **Input:**   An undirected simple connected graph $G$.
  **Output:**  Is $G$ a UV graph?

  Step 1: Check if $G$ is chordal. If $G$ is not chordal abort the algo
           rithm because $G$ is not a UV graph.
  Step 2: List the cliques of $G$ and also list $G_a$ for every vertex $a$ of $G$
  Step 3: Arrange the vertices of $G$ as $a_1, a_2, \ldots a_n$ such that
           $$n_{a_1} \geq n_{a_2} \geq n_{a_3} \geq \ldots \geq n_{a_n}$$
           Assign $k_0 = n$
           Rename $G_{a_l}$ as $G_l$ for $1 \leq l \leq n$.
  Step 4:
    4.1 For $j = 1$ to $[\log n]$ do
    4.2 $k_j = k_{j-1}/2$
    4.3 For $i = 1$ to $k_j$ do in parallel.
    4.4 PROCESS $(2i - 1, 2i)$
         PROCESS $(i, j)$ is a procedure which takes the UV graphs $G_i$
         and $G_j$ and checks whether $G_i \cup G_j = G_{i+j}$ is a UV graph. If $G_{i+j}$
is a
         UV graph it returns the clique tree representation $T_{i+j}$ of $G_{i+j}$.
    4.5 If $G_{(2i-1)+2i}$ is not a UV graph the fact is informed and the entire

algorithm is aborted and terminated because, in this case $G$ is not a UV graph. If $G_{(2i-1)+2i}$ is a UV graph rename it as $G_i$ for the next iteration.

    4.6 End parallel

    4.7 Next $j$.

Step 5: Conclude that $G$ is a UV graph.

    End $NC$-UV

### 7.4.3  Union of Two UV Graphs

In this section we develop the procedure PROCESS($i, j$), which has been used in algorithm $NC$-UV described above Procedure PROCESS($i, j$) takes two UV graphs $G_i$ and $G_j$ which were explained in Section 7.4.2, together with their respective clique trees $T_i$ and $T_j$ as input and verifies if $G_i \cup G_j$ is a UV graph. If $G_i \cup G_j$ is a UV graph, the procedure returns its clique tree representation. Otherwise it aborts the algorithm. Notice that $G_i$ and $G_j$ are graphs induced by the union of some cliques of $G$. The cliques of $G_i$ or $G_j$ are only the cliques of $G$. Let us denote

$$C_i = \text{set of cliques of } G_i;$$

$$C_j = \text{set of cliques of } G_j.$$

Since $G_i \cap G_j$ is an induced subgraph of $G_i$ it is also a UV graph. In $G_j$ we remove all the nodes corresponding to the members of $C_i \cap C_j$ with all edges incident on them. This removal leaves a collection of subtrees of $T_j$. We try to join each such subtree of $T_j$ to $T_i$ and construct the clique tree of $G_i \cup G_j$. We first state the algorithm for the PROCESS($i, j$).

**Procedure PROCESS($i, j$)**

    **Input:**   Two UV graphs $G_i$ and $G_j$ and their respective clique tree representations $T_i$ and $T_j$.

    **Output:**  1. Is $G_i \cup G_j$ a UV graph?

                2. If $G_i \cup G_j$ is a UV graph, output the clique tree model of the graph.

    1. For every $C \in C_i \cap C_j$ do in parallel

    2. Let $c_1, c_2, \ldots c_s$ be the nodes adjacent to $c$ in $T_j$
       Such that $C_t \notin C_i \cap C_j$ ($1 \le t \le s$)

    3. Remove $c$ from $T_j$. This removal causes a forest of $s$ subtrees of $T_j$. Consider these trees as subtrees with roots $c_1, c_2, \ldots c_s$ respectively.

    4. End Parallel

    5. Let $R = $ set of subtrees (rooted) of $T_j$ left out after steps 1 to 4.

    6. For every element $ST$ of $R$ do the operation which where going ATTACH($ST, T_i$) explained in step-7.

7. ATTACH($St, T_i$) Let $c'$ be the root of $ST$. We try to join $ST$ to $T_i$ by creating an edge between $c'$ and a node $c$ of $T_i$ where $C' \cap G_i$ abort because $G_i \cup G_j$ is not a UV graph.
8. End for
9. End PROCESS

The procedure ATTACH($ST, T_i$) mentioned in step 7 of Procedure PROCESS($i, j$) is very much involved and needs defailed explanation. We shall do it after developing some additional results.

**Modifying the Clique Tree of a UV Graph.** Let $G$ be a UV graph and $T$ its clique tree representation. Let $C$ be a clique of $G$ and $v$ is a vertex of $C$. We first develop a procedure for the following:

*To check whether the clique tree $T$ can be modified such that $c$ is an end node of the path in $T$ corresponding to $v$ without losing its property of being a clique tree representation of the UV graph $G$. We explain this checking process in detail below.*

If $c$ is already a leaf node of $T$ or it is already an end node of the path of $v$ then we are done. So, assume that $c$ is not a leaf node and the path of $v$ in $T$ has $c$ as an internal node. Consider $T$ as a rooted tree with root $c$. Let the path of $v$ in $T$ be $c_l c_{l-1} \ldots c_2 c_1 c c_1' c_2' \ldots c_r'$.

## Case 1

Suppose there exists integers $i$ and $j (1 \le i \le l1 \le j \le r)$ such that $(C_i \cap C) \backslash C_j' \ne \Phi$ and $(C_j \cap C) \backslash C_i \ne \Phi$. Considering $C$ as a separating clique the cliques $c_i, c_j'$ are antipodal (Theorem 7.18). Hence we cannot rearrange $T$ in such a way that $c$ is a leaf node of the path of $v$ and still $T$ being a clique tree representation of the UV graph $G$. This can also be justified as follows: If $c$ is to be an endpoint of the path of $v$ in $T$, either $c_i$ must lie in the path from $c$ to $c_j'$ or $c_j'$ must lie in the path from $c$ to $c_i$.

$$\text{Let } a \in (C_i \cap C) \backslash C_j';$$
$$b \in (C_j' \cap C) \backslash C_i.$$

Since the path of $a$ passes through $c_i$ and $c$ but not through $c_j'$ we cannot rearrange such that $c_j'$ lies in the path from $c$ to $c_i$. Similarly since the path of $b$ passes through $c$ and $c_j'$ but not through $c_i$, we cannot rearrange such that $c_i$ lies in the path from $c$ to $c_j'$. Hence $T$ cannot be rearranged as required.

As an example, consider the graph $G$ given in Fig. 7.8. Its clique tree $T$ is also is given. Suppose we try to modify $T$ such that $c$ becomes an end node of the path corresponding to the vertex $b$. Here we have,

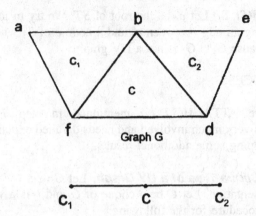

**Figure 7.8** Graph $G$ to illustrate the definition of MODIFY.

$$(C_1 \cap C)\backslash C_2 = \{f\};$$
$$(C_2 \cap C)\backslash C_1 = \{d\}.$$

So, the clique tree cannot be modified such that $c$ becomes an end node of the path corresponding to the vertex $b$.

### Case 2

Suppose, $C_1' \cap C$ $C_l'$. In this case, $C_l$ dominates $C_1'$ with reference to the separating clique $C$. We are now tempted to remove $c_1'$ from $c$ and make it a child of $c_l$. But we need to verify some more things before doing so. Suppose $C_1'$ is unattached to each child of $C_l$. In this case, we are free to remove $c_1'$ from $c$ and make it a child of $c_l$. *Suppose* $c_{l+1}$ is a child of $c_l$ and $C_{l+1} \cap C_1' \neq \Phi$. Notice that $C_{l+1} \cap C_1' \subseteq C$. In this case, if we want $c_1'$ to be made a child of $c_l$, we must remove $c_{l+1}$ and make it a child of some other node. Since $C_{l+1} \cap C_1' \neq \Phi$ and $C_{l+1} \cap C_i' \subseteq C$. We must only try to make $c_{l+1}$ a child of $c$. We can do so only if $C_{l+1} \cap C_l \subseteq C$. Hence for every child $c_{l+1}$ of $c$, for which $C_{l+1} \cap C_1' \neq \Phi$, verify if $C_{l+1} \cap C_1 \subseteq C$. If so, remove $c_{l+1}$ from $c_l$ and make $c_{l+1}$ a child of $c$. After removing all such $c_{l+1}$, we can remove $c_1'$ from $c$ and make it a child of $c_l$. For some child $c_{l+1}$, if $C_{l+1} \cap C_1' \neq \Phi$ and $C_{l+1} \cap C_l$ is not contained in $C$, we cannot remove $c_{l+1}$ from $c_l$ and, hence, it is not possible to make $c_1'$ a child of $c_l$. Also since $C_l$ dominates $C_1'$, we cannot modify the tree in such a way that $c_1'$ lies in the path from $c$ to $c_l$. This shows that we cannot modify the tree such that $c$ is an end node for the path of $v$ in $T$.

For example, consider the UV graph $G$ given in Fig. 7.9. This graph contains five cliques. They are $C_0 = \{a, b, d, f\}$, $C_1 = \{b, d, f, g\}$, $C_2 = \{d, f, h\}$, $C_3 = \{d, f, h\}$, $C_4 = \{d, i, j\}$, and $C_5 = \{f, k\}$.

A clique tree representation $T$ of this UV graph is given in Fig. 7.9(b). In

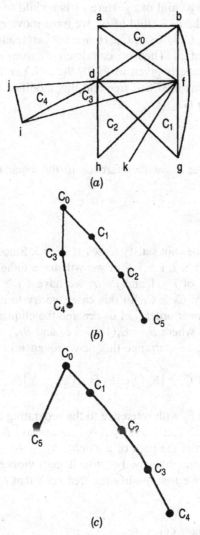

**Figure 7.9(a)** An UV graph to illustrate case 2. **(b)** A clique tree of G. **(c)** Modified clique tree.

the clique tree, the path corresponding to $d$ is $c_2, c_1, c_0, c_3, c_4$. Suppose we are interested in modifying the tree $T$, such that the path of $d$ in $T$ has $c_0$ as an end node.

Notice that $C_3$ is not antipodal with neither $C_1$ nor $C_2$, nor $C_5$ with reference to the separating clique $C_0$. Similarly $C_4$ is also not antipodal to any of the cliques $C_1$ or $C_2$ or $C_5$. Hence this does not come under Case 1. However, we find that $C_3 \cap C_0 \subseteq C_2 \cap C_0$. That is, $C_2 \geq C_3$ with reference to the separating clique $C_0$. So, we can try to make $c_3$ a child of $c_2$. In order do this, $C_3$ must be unattached to every child of $c_2$. Here $c_5$ is a child of $c_2$, but $C_5 \cap C_3 \neq \Phi$. So, if we want to make $c_3$ a child of $c_2$, we must move $c_5$ to some other place. Fortunately, we have $C_5 \cap C_2 \subseteq C_0$. Hence we can readily remove $c_5$ from $c_2$ and make it a child of $c_0$. Then we can delete $c_3$ from $c_0$ and make it a child of $c_2$. The modified tree is given in Fig. 7.9(c). Notice that $c_0$ is an end node of the path of $d$ in this modified tree and this modified tree $T$ is still a clique tree of the UV graph $G$.

## Case 3

Suppose $C_r'$ dominates $C_1$ with reference to the separating clique $C$. This is similar to Case 2.

## Case 4

Suppose the node $c$ does not satisfy Cases 1, 2, or 3. Since case 1 is not satisfied for any $i$ and $j$ ($1 \leq i \leq l, 1 \leq j \leq r$) we will have either $C_i \geq C_j'$ or $C_j' \geq C_i$. However in the case of $i = 1$ and $j = r$, we have $C_1 \geq C_r$. Similarly, when $i = 1$ and $j = l$ we have $C_1' \geq C_l$. In this case, we try to arrange $C_1, C_2, \ldots C_l$, $C_1', C_2', \ldots C_r'$ in a linear order. Let us rename the cliques as $B_1, B_2, B_3, \ldots B_l$, $B_{l+1}, B_{l+2}, \ldots B_{l+r}$, where $B_i = C_i (1 \leq i \leq l)$ and $B_{l+j} = C_j' (1 \leq j \leq r)$.

Now we are going to rearrange this new sequence in such a way that

$$|B_1 \cap C| \geq |B_2 \cap C| B_3 \cap C| \geq \ldots \geq |B_{1+r} \cap C|$$

Now check if $B_i \geq B_j$ with reference to the separating clique $C$ for every pair of integers $i$ and $j$, such that $1 \leq i, \leq j \leq l+r$. If we have $B_1 \geq B_2 \geq B_3 \geq \ldots B_{1+r}$, we may try to construct the path of $v$ as $cb_1, b_2 \ldots b_{l+r}$.

We cannot do it straightaway, because it may violate the path property of other vertices of $G$. We first modify the tree such that $c, b_1, b_2 \ldots b_{l+r}$ is the path of $v$ as follows:

1. Remove the edges $cc_1, c_1c_2, \ldots c_{l-1}c_l$.
2. Remove the edges $cc_1', c_1'c_2' \ldots c_{r-1}'c_r'$.
3. Add the new edges $cb_1, b_1b_2, b_2b_3, \ldots b_{l+r-1}b_{l+r}$.

We can easily verify that $T$ is still a tree after the above modification. We must verify if $T$ still satisfies the clique tree property for the UV graph $G$. For that we must check the following for every $i$ ($1 \leq i \leq 1 + r$). Assume $b_0 = c$.

If $B_{i-1} \geq B_i$, we can make $b_i$ a child of $b_{i-1}$, only if $B_i$ is unattached to every child $b$ of $b_{i-1}$. In case $B_i$ is attached to a child $B$ of $b_{i-1}$, we must try to remove $b$ and make it a child of some other node. Originally $b_i$ and $b_{i-1}$ were from the two sides of $c$. Hence, $B_i \cap B \neq \Phi$ implies that $C \cap B \neq \Phi$. So we can only make $b$ a child of $c$. For doing so, we want $B \cap B_{i-1} \subseteq C$. Hence whenever $B \cap B_i \neq \Phi$ verify if $B \cap B_{i-1} \subseteq C$ and, if so, make $b$ a child of $c$ and otherwise conclude that $T$ cannot be modified as we desire. Based on the above discussion, the procedure MODIFY can be formally described as follows:

**Procedure Modify** $(G, T, C, v)$
   **Input:**

1. A UV graph $G$.
2. Its clique tree representation $T$.
3. A clique $C$ of $G$.
4. A vertex $v$ of $C$.

**Output:**   Modified form of $T$ such that the path of $v$ in $T$ has $c$ as an end node and $T$ still satisfies the clique tree property for the UV graph $G$. If it is not possible to modify $T$ as required, return the original $T$ and inform that it is not possible to modify as desired.

Step 1:   Verify if $c$ is already an end node of the path of $v$ in $T$. If true return $T$, else let the path of $v$ in $T$ be $c_l c_{l-1} c_{l-2} \ldots c_2 c_1 c c_1' c_2' \ldots c_r'$. Consider $T$ as a rooted tree with root $c$.

Step 2:   For every $i \in \{1, 2, 3 \ldots l\}$ and $j \in \{1, 2, \ldots r\}$ do the following in parallel.

$$\text{If } (C_i \cap C) \backslash C_j' \neq \Phi$$
$$\text{and } (C_j' \cap C) \backslash C_i \neq \Phi,$$

then return with a message that $T$ cannot be modified.

Step 3:   If $C_1' \cap C \subseteq C_l$, then
   3.1   For every child $c_{l+1}$ of $c_l$ do in parallel
   3.2   If $C_{l+1} \cap C_1' \neq \Phi$ then
   3.3   If $(C_{l+1} \cap C_1) \backslash C \neq \Phi$ then Proceed to step 4.
      ELSE
   3.4   Delete the edge $c_{l+1} c_l$ and create a new edge $c_{l+1} c$ so that $c_{l+1}$ is a new child of $c$.
      End if
      End if
      End parallel
   3.5   Delete the edge $c_1' c$ and create a new edge $c_1' c_l$ so that $c_1'$ becomes a new child of $c_l$.
   3.6   Return $T$ successfully.
      End if

Step 4:   If $C_1 \cap C \subseteq C_r'$, then

4.1 For every child $C_{r+1}$ of $C_r$ do in parallel

4.2 If $C_{r+1} \cap C_1 \neq \Phi$ then

4.3 If $(C_{r+1} \cap C_1)\backslash C \neq \Phi$ then Proceed to step 5
ELSE

4.4 Delete the edge $c_{r+1}c_r$ and create a new edge $c_{r+1}c$ so that $c_{r+1}$ becomes a new child of $c$.
End if
End if
End parallel

4.5 Delete the edge $c_1c$ and create a new edge $c_1c'_r$ so that $c_1$ becomes a new child of $c'_r$

4.6 Return $T$ successfully
End if.

Step 5:

5.1 Form duplicate copies of the cliques $C_1C_2 \ldots C_lC'_1, C'_2 \ldots C'_r$ with new names $B_1, B_2, \ldots B_lB_{l+1}B_{l+2} \ldots B_{l+r}$ so that $B_i = C_i(1 \leq i \leq l)$ and $B_{l+j} = C'_j(1 \leq j \leq r)$. Let the corresponding nodes in $T$ be denoted by $b_1, b_2, \ldots b_{l+r}$ respectively.

5.2 Sort the cliques such that

$$|B_1 \cap C| \geq |B_2 \cap C| \geq \ldots \geq |B_{l+r} \cap C|$$

5.3 For $i = 1$ to $l$ and for $j = 1$ to $r$ do in parallel
Remove edges $c_{i-1}$ and $c'_{j-1}c'_j$. Here $C_0$ means $C$. While removing keep log of the operation because if we are not able to modify $T$ as desired we have to return the original $T$ with failure message.
End parallel

5.4 For $i = 1$ to $l + r$ do in parallel
Create a new edge $b_{i-1}b_i$ and reconstruct the tree $T$. Assume the notation $b_0$ for $C$.
End parallel.

5.5 For $i = 1$ to $1 + r$ do in parallel

5.6 For every child $B$ of $B_{i-1}$ do in parallel

5.7 If $B \cap B_i \neq \Phi$ then

5.7.1 If $B \cap B_{i-1} \subseteq C$ then

5.7.2 Remove edge $bb_{i-1}$ and create a new edge $cb$.

5.7.2 ELSE

5.7.3 Report that $T$ cannot be modified as desired undo the change done in steps 5.3 and 5.4 and return the original $T$ without any modification.

5.7.4 End if
End if

5.8   End parallel
5.9   End parallel
5.10   Return the modified tree T in success.

Now we are fully equipped to develop the procedure $ATTACH(ST, T_i)$, which has been used in step 7 of the procedure $PROCESS(i,j)$. Let $G_{ST}$ denote the graph induced by the union of cliques represented by the nodes of $ST$.

Let $G_{ST} \cap G_i$ be denoted by $W(ST)$. In $T_j$, one node of $ST$ was adjacent to one node of $T_j \backslash ST$. Let us assume the notation that the node $c'$ of $ST$ was adjacent to the node $c''$ of $T_j \backslash ST$. Hence we have $W(ST) \subseteq C'$ and $W(ST) \subseteq C''$. The node $C''$ is also a node in $T_i$. We can try to make $c'$ of $ST$ adjacent to the node $c''$ of $T_i$. However, if $c$ is a node of $T_i$ such that $W(ST) \subseteq C$ then we may try to make $c'$ adjacent to $c$ and attach $ST$ to $T_i$.

Let $N_{ST} = \{c \backslash c$ is a node in $T_i$ and $W(ST) \subseteq C\}$

$N_{ST}$ is the set of all possible neighbors for $ST$ in $T_i$. From the above discussion $c'' \in N_{ST}$ and, hence, $N_{ST}$ is nonempty for every subtree $ST$. $ST$ can be attached to a node $c$ of $T_i$ by creating a new edge $(c'c)$, if and only if $T_i$ is modified such that $c$ is an end node for the path corresponding to each vertex of $W(ST)$. We can verify this in parallel for every vertex of $W(ST)$. If it is not possible to modify $T_i$ for a vertex of $W(ST)$ then the node $c$ cannot be made adjacent to $c'$ of $ST$. For every node $c$ of $N_{ST}$ we try in parallel if $c$ can be made adjacent to $c'$. If it is possible for one node $c$ of $N_{ST}$ then we immediately join $ST$ to $T_i$ by creating the new edge $(cc')$. If it is impossible to make $c'$ adjacent to any of the elements of $N_{ST}$, we conclude that $ST$ cannot be attached to $T_i$ and, hence, $G_i \cup G_j$ is not a UV graph. The following is a formal procedure for attaching $ST$ to $T_i$.

**Procedure Attach ($ST$, $T_i$)**
1.   Let $G_{ST}$ be the graph induced by the union of cliques represented by the nodes of $ST$.
2.   $W(ST) = G_{ST} \cap G_i$.
3.   $N_{ST} = \Phi$
4.   For every node $c$ of $T_i$ do in parallel.
5.   If $W(S) \subseteq C$ then
     $N_{ST} = N_{ST} \cup \{c\}$
     End if
6.   End parallel
7.   For every $c \in N_{ST}$ do in parallel
8.   For every $v \in W(ST)$ do in parallel
9.   $MODIFY(G_i, T_i, c, v)$.
     If the procedure MODIFY returns with failure then exit.
10.   End parallel
11.   In loop of steps 8 to 10, if the MODIFY is in failure for any
      one of the vertex $v$ then remove $c$ from $N_{ST}$.
12.   End parallel.

13. End parallel.
14. If $N_{ST} \neq \Phi$ then choose any node $c$ from $N_{ST}$ and make $c'$ adjacent to $c$.
    Else
    Abort the algorithm because we cannot attach $ST$ to $T_i$ and
    Hence $G_i \cup G_j$ is not a UV graph.
15. End ATTACH.

The above procedure attaches one subtrees $ST$ to $T_i$. In the procedure $PROCESS(i,j)$, steps 6 to 8 calls for attaching each subtrees $ST$ of $R$. However, we cannot do this in parallel for all the elements of $R$. We intend to do the ATTACH operation in parallel for all the subtrees $ST$ which are mutually disjoint. By doing so, the FOR loop of steps 6 to 9 run at the most $[\log n]$ times.

### 7.4.4  Correctness and Complexity

In this section we show that our algorithm works correctly and analyze the time and processor complexity. We start with Theorem 7.22.

**THEOREM 7.22**  *If $G_{(2i-1)+2i}$ is not a UV graph in step 4.5 of Algorithm NC-UV(G), then G is not a UV graph.*

*Proof.* Since UV graphs are intersection graphs of paths of a tree, they are hereditary. That is, every induced subgraph of a UV graph is also a UV graph. By the definition of $G_{a+b}$, we have $G_{(2i-1)+2i}$ is an induced subgraph of $G$. So, if $G$ is a UV graph, $G_{(2i-1)+2i}$ is also a UV graph. Hence the proof is complete.

**THEOREM 7.23**  *If the FOR-NEXT loop of steps 4.1 to 4.7 of Algorithm NC-UV graph is executed $[\log n]$ times and successfully comes out to step 5 without getting aborted, G is a UV graph.*

*Proof.* Let $G_1, G_2, \ldots G_n$ denote the graphs $G_{a1}, G_{a2}, \ldots G_{an}$ as explained at the end of step 3 of algorithm in NC-UV $(G)$ where the vertex of $G$ is $\{a_1, a_2, \ldots a_n\}$. At the end of the first run, we will have $[n/2]$ induced subgraphs of $G$, each one being a UV graph. At the last iteration of the loop, $G_{1+2}$ is precisely the graph $G$ as per renaming of the graph $G_{(2i-1)+2i}$ in step 4.5 of the algorithm. Hence $G$ is a UV graph.

**THEOREM 7.24**  *If we are not able to join $ST$ to $T_i$ as given in step 7 of Procedure PROCESS(i, j), then G is not a UV graph.*

*Proof.* In the procedure ATTACH$(ST, T_i)$, $N_{ST}$ is the set of all possible neighbors for $ST$. We decide that $ST$ cannot be joined to $T_i$ only when $N_{ST} = \Phi$ in step 13 of Procedure ATTACH. This means that we are not able to modify $T_i$ and make $ST$ a child of any node $c$ where $W(ST) \subseteq C$. If $c_1$ is another node such that $W(ST) \subseteq C_1$, then there is atleast one vertex $u$ of $W(ST)$, which is not in $C_1$. In this case, if $ST$ is attached at $c_1$, then the path of $u$ cannot enter $T_i$ at all. So, we cannot attach $ST$ to any $c_1'$ for which $W(ST) \subseteq C_1$. Hence the proof is complete.

**THEOREM 7.25** *In step 2 of Procedure MODIFY, if we return $T$ with a message that $T$ cannot be modified, we cannot modify $T$ so that $c$ is an end node of the path of vertex $v$ and $T$ is still a clique tree of the UV graph $G$.*

*Proof.* Since $(C_i \cap C)\backslash C_j' \neq \Phi$ and $(C_j' \cap C)\backslash C_i \neq \Phi$, we have $c_i$ and $c_j$ antipodal to each other, with reference to the separating clique $C$. Hence $c$ lies in the path from $c_i$ to $c_j$. Hence we cannot modify $T$ such that $c$ is an end node of the path of vertex $v$ and $T$ is still a clique tree of the UV graph $G$.

**THEOREM 7.26** *The operation performed in step 3.5 and step 4.5 does not change $T$ so as to violate the clique tree property of the UV graph $G$.*

*Proof.* Steps 3.5 and 4.5 are the same except for the symbols. So, let us prove here for step 3.5 and it will hold for step 4.5 also. In step 3.5 we remove $c_1'$ from $c$ and make it adjacent to $c_l$. The vertices of $c_1'\backslash c$ do not get affected by this change. If $v \in C\backslash C_1'$ then the change does not violate the condition at all. So, it is sufficient to verify if the new tree satisfies the UV clique tree condition for the vertices of $C \cap C_1'$.

In step 3.4 we have removed all the children of $c_l$ having nonempty intersection with $C_1'$. So, $C_l$ is the endpoint for all the vertices of $C_1' \cap C$. So, by making $c_1'$ a child of $c_l$, the path property is satisfied for all the vertices of $C_1' \cap C$. This proves the theorem.

**THEOREM 7.27** *If we return $T$ in step 5.7.3 of Procedure MODIFY, $T$ cannot be modified so that $C$ is an end node of $v$ and still $T$ satisfies the path property for all the vertices of $G$.*

*Proof.* Since we have crossed steps 5.3 and 5.4 we have for any $i$ and $j$ $(1 \leq i \leq j \leq r)B_i \leq B_j$. In such a case we try to remove all the children of $B_{i-1}$ which are attached to $B_i$. Since we are not able to remove some child $B$ of $B_{i-1}$ we return $T$ at step 5.7.3. Suppose $v \in B \cap B_i$. Then $v \in B$, $B_i$ and $B_{i-1}$ and these three cannot be kept in a single path. Hence the proof is complete.

**THEOREM 7.28** *Algorithm NC-UV(G) correctly recognizes a UV graph $G$.*

*Proof.* If $G$ is not chordal, step 1 tells that $G$ is not a UV graph. Otherwise, if $G_a$ is not an interval graph for a vertex $a$ of $G$ then $G$ is not a UV graph. If $G_a$ is an interval graph for every vertex $a$ of $G$, then we try to construct the clique tree for $G$. If step 5 is reached, then $G$ is a UV graph (Theorem 7.23). If it fails to reach step 5, then it is aborted in step 4.5, in which case $G$ is not a

UV graph (Theorem 7.24). For any input graph $G$, either the algorithm reached step 5 or aborts in step 4.5. Hence the algorithm correctly recognizes the UV graph $G$.

**Time and Processor Complexity.** Now let us analyze the time and processor complexity of the algorithm. Theorem 7.29 gives a bound which is useful in the complexity analysis.

**THEOREM 7.29** *Let $G = (V, E)$ be a chordal graph and $n_v$ denote the number of cliques containing $v$, Then,*

$$\sum_{v \in V} n_v = \sum_{C \in C} |C| \leq m + n,$$

*where $m$ is the number of edges and $n$ the number of vertices in $G$.*

*Proof.* Define a matrix $A(v, C)$, where the first index $v$ varies over $V$ and the second index $C$ varies over $C$ as follows:

$$A(vC) = \begin{cases} 0 & \text{if } v \notin C \\ 1 & \text{if } v \in C. \end{cases}$$

For any clique $C$ of $G$, we have

$$|C| = \sum_{v \in V} A(v, C).$$

Similarly, for any vertex $v \in V$, we have

$$n_v = \sum_{C \in C} A(v, C).$$

So we have

$$\sum_{C \in C} |C| = \sum_{C \in C} \sum_{v \in V} A(v, c) = \sum_{v \in V} n_v.$$

$\sum_{c \in C} |C| \leq m + n$ is proved in [GO86].
Hence the proof is complete.

**THEOREM 7.30** *Procedure MODIFY can be implemented to run in O(log n) time using O(m + n) processors.*
*Proof.* Step 2 can be implemented in $O(1)$ time using $O(n)$ processors

because in chordal graphs there are at the most $n$ cliques. Step 3 and step 4 takes $O(1)$ time using $O(n)$ processors. In step 5, the ordering of $B_i s$ in step 5.2 can be done in $O(\log n)$ time, using $O(n \log n)$ processors. Steps 5.6 to 5.8 can be done in $O(1)$ time, using $O(n)$ processors. Steps 5.5 to 5.9 is a loop that fully contains the loop 5.6 to 5.8. The node $B_{i-1}$ mentioned in step 5.6 has at the most $|B_{i-1}|$ children. $1 + r$ mentioned in step 5.5 is bounded by the number of cliques. So, the number of processors needed to implement steps 5.5 to 5.9 is bounded by $\sum_{C \in C} |C| \leq m + n$ (by Theorem 7.29). So steps 5.5 to 5.9 can be run in $O(1)$ time, using $O(m + n)$ processors. Hence procedure MODIFY needs $O(\log n)$ time using $O(m + n)$ processors. Hence the proof is complete.

**THEOREM 7.31** *Procedure ATTACH(ST, T) can be implemented to work in* $O(\log n)$ *time using* $O(m2)$ *processors.*

*Proof.* Steps 1, 2, and 3 can be implemented in constant time. Step 4 to 6 can be run in $O(1)$ time, using $O(n)$ processors. Notice that $|N_{ST}| \leq |C|$ and $|W(ST)| \leq |V|$ and, hence, by Theorem 7.29, we need $O(m + n)$ processors, each working MODIFY in parallel. So, by Theorem 7.30, steps 7 to 13 can be implemented in $O(\log n)$ time using $O((m + n)^2)$ processors. That is, the complexity of the procedure ATTACH is $O(\log n)$ time, using $O((m + n)^2)$.

**THEOREM 7.32** *Procedure Process* $(i, j)$ *can be implemented to work in* $O(\log n)$ *time using* $O(m^2)$ *processors.*

*Proof.* Steps 1 to 4 takes only $O(1)$ time and $O(n)$ processors. We have already shown that $R$ contains at the most $[\log n]$ collections of subtrees, each having mutually disjoint members. Hence, by Theorem 7.31, PROCESS$(i, j)$ needs $O(\log^2 n)$ time and $O(m^2 n)$ processors.

**THEOREM 7.33** *The problem of recognizing a UV graph is NC.*

*Proof.* Step 1 of the algorithm NC-UV $(G)$ uses Klein's algorithm which is NC. Step 2 uses the interval graph recognition algorithm of Klein. Step 3 can be implemented in $O(\log n)$ time, using $O(n \log n)$ processors. In step 4, the steps 4.3 to 4.6 can be implemented in $O(\log^2 n)$ time, using $O(m^2 n^2)$ processors (Theorem 7.31, 7.32, and 7.36). Step 4.1 to 4.7 is a FOR loop that runs $[\log n]$ times. Hence the overall complexity of our algorithm is $O(\log^3 n)$ time, using $O(m^3)$ processors in CREW PRAM.

## BIBLIOGRAPHY

Chandrasekharan, N. (1985) New Characterizations and Algorithmic Studies On Chordal Graphs and $k$-Trees, (M.Sc.(Engg.) Thesis), School of Automation, Indian Institute of Sciences, Bangalore, India.

Chandrasekharan, N. and Iyengar, S. S. (1988) NC Algorithms for Recognizing Chordal Graphs and *k* Trees, *IEEE Transactions on Computers*, **37(10)**.

Chandrasekharan, R. and Tamir, A. (1982) Polynomially Bounded Algorithms for Locating *p*-Centres on a Tree, *Math. Programming*, **22**, 304–315.

Naor, J., Naor, M. and Scjaffer, A. (1987) Fast Parallel Algorithm for Chordal Graphs, in *Proc. Symp. Theory Comput.*, New York.

Proskurowski, (1980) *k*-trees: Representations and Distances, Tech. Rep., CIS-TR-80-5, University of Oregon.

Xavier, C., (1995) Sequential and Parallel Algorithms for Some Graph Theoretic Problems, Ph.D. Thesis, Madurai-Kamaraj University, Madurai, India.

# ARRAY MANIPULATION ALGORITHMS

## CHAPTER 8

# Searching and Merging

## 8.1 SEQUENTIAL SEARCHING

Let $A = (a_1, a_2, a_3, \ldots a_n)$ be an array of data such that $a_1 < a_2 < \ldots < a_n$. Given an element $x$, we are interested in finding out the index $k$, such that $a_k \leq x < a_{k+1}$. In sequential computing, we can either verify the value of $a_k$ and $a_{k+1}$ for every $k$ or we can use the binary search technique. They are first given below:

**Algorithm Sequential Search**
    **Input:**   1. Array of data $a_1 < a_2 < \ldots a_n$
                2. An element $x$.
    **Output:**  Index $k$ such that $a_k \leq x < a_{k+1}$
      1. Set $a_0 = -\infty$ and $a_{n+1} = +\infty$
      2. For $k = 0$ to $n$ do
      3. If $a_k \leq x$ and $x < a_{k+1}$ then return $(k)$.
          else continue
      4. Next $k$
      5. END

The above sequential search method verifies the data one after the other. Hence it works in $O(n)$ time sequentially. The following binary search method solves the search problem in $O(\log n)$ time.

**Algorithm Binary Search**
    **Input:**   1. Array of data $a_1 < a_2 < a_3 < \ldots < a_n$.
                2. An element $x$.
    **Output:**  Index $k$ such that $a_k \leq x < a_{k+1}$.
      1. $a_0 = \infty$, $a_{n+1} = +\infty$
         left = 1, right = $n$
      2. While left $\leq$ right repeat
         mid = [left + right]/2
    Case:
         $x < a_{\text{mid}}$ : right = mid $-1$
         $x = a_{\text{mid}}$ : return (mid)

$x > a_{\text{mid}}$ : left = mid +1
End case.
3. End While
4. return (right)
5. END

In order to illustrate binary search, consider the following array $A$ = (20, 24, 25, 29, 32, 35, 39, 85). Suppose $x$ = 22.

**Initially:**     left = 1, right = 8 and mid = 4.
We compare $x$ = 22 and $a_{\text{mid}}$ = 29
We have $x < a_{\text{mid}}$. So, we set right = mid − 1 = 3.

**Iteration 1:**     left = 1, right = 3 and mid = 2.
Now compare $x$ = 22 and $a_{\text{mid}}$ = 24
We have $x < a_{\text{mid}}$. So, we set right = mid − 1 = 1.

**Iteration 1:**     left = 1, right = 1 and mid = 1.
Here we have $x > a_{\text{mid}}$ and so left = mid + 1 = 2.
Now We have left = 2, right = 1.
The condition of the while loop left ≤ right is not
satisfied and so we exit the loop and return the
value of right = 1.

For the same array, the working of the algorithm is illustrated for two more values of $x$ in the following tables:

| x = 20 | | | |
|---|---|---|---|
| iteration | left | right | mid |
| 0 | 1 | 8 | 4 |
| 1 | 1 | 3 | 2 |
| 2 | 1 | 1 | 1 |
| return 1 | | | |

| x = 100 | | | |
|---|---|---|---|
| iteration | left | right | mid |
| 0 | 1 | 8 | 4 |
| 1 | 5 | 8 | 6 |
| 2 | 7 | 8 | 7 |
| 3 | 8 | 8 | 8 |
| 4 | 9 | 8 | |
| return 8 | | | |

## 8.2 PARALLEL SEARCH IN CREW PRAM

Consider a CREW PRAM. The data verification $a_k \leq x < a_{k+1}$ can be done for all the values of $k$ simultaneously. That is, processor $P_0$ can verify if $a_0 \leq$

$x < a_1$; processor $P_1$ can verify if $a_1 \leq x < a_2$; processor $P_2$ can verify if $a_1 \leq x < a_3$; and so on.

The processor $P_i$ which finds out that $a_i \leq x < a_{i+1}$, writes the value of $i$ in a global variable RESULT. The algorithm is formally presented here.

**Input:**   1. Array $A = (a_1\ a_2\ a_3\ \ldots\ a_n)$ where $a_1 < a_2 < a_3 < \ldots a_n$.
          2. A value $x$.
**Output:**   Result $= k$ where $a_k \leq x < a_{k+1}$
  Step 0: $a_0 = -\infty$, $a_{n+1} = +\infty$.
  Step 1: For $k = 0$ to $n$ do in parallel
  Step 2: If $a_k \leq x$ and $x < a_{k+1}$ then
          set RESULT $= k$
          endif
  Step 3: End Parallel
  Step 4: END

**Complexity Analysis.** In the above algorithm, the parallel loop shows that $n + 1$ processors work simultaneously. Step 2 works in $O(1)$ time. Hence the algorithm can be implemented in $O(1)$ time using $O(n)$ processors. As the input array $A$ satisfies the condition $a_1 < a_2 < a_3 < \ldots a_n$, only one processor succeeds in setting the value of RESULT in step 2. Hence an exclusive write is sufficient. However, a data $a_i$ is used by processor $P_i$ as well as processor $P_{i-1}$ and hence a concurrent write is essential. So, the CREW PRAM model is essential to implement this algorithm.

Suppose the input array $A = (a_1\ a_2\ a_3\ \ldots\ a_n)$ are not in sorted form and two values $a_i$ and $a_j$ may be equal for distinct values of $i$ and $j$. In this case, we can talk about the searching problem of finding the index $k$ such that $a_k = x$. This can be done in parallel using an algorithm which is very similar to the one shown above. But the reader can verify that a concurrent write PRAM may be necessary.

## 8.3 PARALLEL SEARCH WITH MORE DATA

When the length of the array is more than the number of processors the algorithm Search–CREW cannot be implemented in $O(1)$ time. Consider the array $A = (a_1\ a_2\ a_3\ \ldots\ a_n)$, such that $a_1 < a_2 < a_3 \ldots a_n$. Let $x$ be a given value. Let $p$ be the number of processors. We are going to extend the binary search method.

In binary search, the array is divided into two subarrays and the middle element is verified by the processor. Here we are going to divide the array into $p+1$ subarrays of almost equal size and verify each of the $p$ interior elements. For convenience let $n = (p+1)r$. So, when we divide the array into $p+1$ segments each segment will have $r$ entries.

| $a_1\ a_2 \ldots a_r$ | $a_{r+1}\ a_{r+2} \ldots a_{2r}$ | $\ldots$ | $a_{pr+1} \ldots a_n$ |
|:---:|:---:|:---:|:---:|
| **Segment 1** | **Segment 2** | | **($p+1$)th Segment** |

$$R_i = 0 \text{ if } x = a_{ir}$$
$$= -1 \text{ if } a_{ir} < x$$
$$= +1 \text{ if } x < a_{ir}$$

If $R_i = 0$, then the value $i^*r$ is returned. If $R_i \cdot 0$ for all $i$, then choose the segment $k$ where $R_{k-1} = -1$ and $R_k = +1$. The value $x$ falls in the segment $k$. So, repeat the process in segment $k$. The algorithm is formally presented below:

**Algorithm Parallel Search**
   **Output:**   index $k$ such that $a_k \le x < a_{k+1}$
   **Input:**   1. An array $A = (a_1\ a_2\ a_3 \ldots a_n)$
          2. A value $x$.

   1. $p$ is the number of processor variable. If $n < p$ then use the algorithm Search-CREW algorithm and solve $O(1)$ time.
   2. If $n > p$ then without loss of generality assume that $n = r(p + 1)$ for an integer value $r$.
   3. For $i = 1$ to $p$ do in parallel
      Case:

$$a_{ir} = x : R_i = 0$$
$$a_{ir} < x : R_i = -1$$
$$a_{ir} > x : R_i = +1$$

      End case.
   4. End parallel
   5. For $i = 1$ to $p$ do in parallel
      If $R_i = 0$ then
      return ($i * r$)
      End if.
   6. End Parallel.
   7. Set $R_0 = -1$ and $R_{p+1} = 1$.
   8. For $k = 1$ to $p + 1$ do in parallel
   9. If $R_k = +1$ and $R_{k-1} = -1$ then choose
      the $k$th segment ($a_{(k-1)r}, a_{(k-1)r+1} \ldots R_{kr}$) and do the
      search operation recursively on this segment.
      Endif.

10. End parallel
11. END

In the above algorithm, in each recursive step, the size of the problem reduces by a factor of $p + 1$.

## 8.4  SEARCHING IN UNSORTED ARRAY

Let $A = (a_1\ a_2\ a_3\ \ldots\ a_n)$ be an array of unsorted entries. Let $x$ be a given value. We want to find the index $k$ such that $a_k = x$. If no such $k$ exists, then the value returned is 0. The following is a sequential algorithm to do the work.

**Algorithm Unsorted Search**
   **Input:**   1. An array of numbers $A = (a_1\ a_2\ a_3\ \ldots\ a_n)$.
             2. A value $x$.
  **Output:**   The index $k$ where $a_k = x$. If no such index $k$ exists
             then return $n + 1$.
   1. $k = 0$
   2. For $k = 1$ to $n$ do
   3. If $a_k = x$ then exit for loop
   4. Next $k$
   5. return $(k)$
   6. END

This algorithm can be implemented in $O(n)$ time in a sequential computer. This can also be parallelized straightaway. The for-next loop in steps 2 to 4 can be converted into a parallel loop. Such a parallel algorithm will work in $O(1)$ time, using $O(n)$ processors.

## 8.5  MERGING BY RANKING

Let $A = (a_1\ a_2\ a_3\ \ldots\ a_m)$ and $B = (b_1\ b_2\ b_3\ \ldots\ b_n)$ be two sorted arrays, Merging $A$ and $B$ means forming a new sorted array with the $(m + n)$ elements of $A$ and $B$. For example, if $A = (2, 4, 11, 12, 14, 35, 95, 99)$ and $B = (6, 7, 9, 25, 26, 31, 42, 85, 87, 102, 105)$, then the array got by merging $A$ and $B$ is $C = (2, 4, 6, 7, 9, 11, 12, 14, 25, 26, 31, 35, 42, 85, 87, 95, 99, 102, 105)$.

The sequential algorithm for merging traverses the two arrays and sends elements to $C$. Initially we shall have a pointer $i$ pointing at the first element of $A$ and a pointer $j$ pointing at the first element $B$. That is, initially $i = 1$ and $j = 1$. The index of entry to be filled in $C$ is denoted by $k$. $a_i$ and $b_j$ are compared and the smaller is sent to $c_k$. The pointers are appropriately incremented. The sequential algorithms is formally presented below:

**Sequential Algorithm Merge**

**Input:**   Sorted arrays $A$ and $B$ of size $m$ and $n$, respectively.

**Output:**   Merged sorted array $C = (c_1\ c_2\ c_3\ \ldots\ c_{m+n})$.

1. Set $a_{m+1} = b_{n+1} = +\infty$
2. Set $i = 1, j = 1, k = 1$.
3. While $k \le m + n$ do
4. If $a_i < b_j$ then

    $c_k = a_i$ and $i = i + 1$

    else

    $c_k = b_j$ and $j = j + 1$

    endif
5. $k = k + 1$
6. End while
7. END

The above sequential algorithm works in $O(m + n)$ computing time. This algorithm is inherently sequential. In order to parallelize the merging we introduce certain notations. Let $A\ (a_1\ a_2\ a_3\ \ldots\ a_m)\ B = (b_1\ b_2\ b_3\ \ldots\ b_n)$ be two arrays. Let $x$ be a value. We define the rank$(x:A)$ as the number of entries in $A$ which are less than or equal to $x$. For example, suppose $A = (2, 4, 11, 12, 14, 35, 95, 99)$, $B = (6, 7, 9, 25, 26, 31, 42, 85, 87, 102, 105)$. Then rank$(6:A)$ $= 2$, rank$(7:A) = 2$, rank$(9:A) = 2$, rank$(25:A) = 5$.

We further define that rank $(B:A)$ is an array $(r_1\ r_2\ r_3\ \ldots\ r_m)$ where $r_i =$ rank $(b_i:A)$. For example, for the arrays $A$ and $B$ shown above

$$\text{rank}(B:A) = (2, 2, 2, 5, 5, 5, 6, 6, 6, 8, 8)$$
$$\text{rank}(B:B) = (1, 2, 3, 4, 5, 6, 7, 8, 9, 10, 11)$$
$$\text{rank}(A:B) = (0, 0, 3, 3, 3, 6, 9, 9)$$
$$\text{rank}(A:A) = (1, 2, 3, 4, 5, 6, 7, 8)$$

Consider an entry $x$. rank$(x:A \cup B)$ is the number of entries in $A \cup B$ which are less than or equal to $x$. Hence rank$(x:A \cup B) = \text{rank}(x:A) + \text{rank}(x:B)$, when $A$ and $B$ are disjoint.

$$\text{rank}(A:A \cup B) = (1, 2, 3, 4, 5, 6, 7, 8) + (0, 0, 3, 3, 3, 6, 9, 9)$$
$$= (1, 2, 6, 7, 8, 12, 16, 17)$$

$$\text{rank}(B:A \cup B) = \text{rank}(B:A) + \text{rank}(B:B)$$
$$= (2, 2, 2, 5, 5, 5, 6, 6, 6, 8, 8) + (1, 2, 3, 4, 5, 6, 7, 8, 9, 10, 11)$$
$$= (3, 4, 5, 9, 10, 11, 13, 14, 15, 18, 19)$$

We have

$$\text{rank}(A:AUB) = (1, 2, 6, 7, 8, 12, 16, 17)$$
$$\text{rank}(B:AUB) = (3, 4, 5, 9, 10, 11, 13, 14, 15, 18, 19).$$

From the above two arrays, we can find the final position of each entry in $C$. From rank$(A:AUB)$ we read that rank $(a_5:AUB) = 8$. This means that there are 8 elements in $AUB$ which are less than or equal to $a_5$. So, $a_5$ must be the eighth entry in the merged array $C$. Similarly, since rank$(a_6:AUB) = 12$, $a_6$ must be assigned to $C_{12}$. If we denote $RA = \text{rank}(A:AUB) = (1, 2, 6, 7, 8, 12, 16, 17)$, then assign $C(RA_i) = A_i$. In example,

$$C(1) = a_1 = 2, \qquad C(2) = a_2 = 4, \qquad C(6) = a_3 = 11,$$
$$C(7) = a_4 = 12, \qquad C(8) = a_5 = 14, \qquad C(12) = a_6 = 35,$$
$$C(16) = a_7 = 95, \qquad C(17) = a_8 = 99,$$

If we denote $RB = \text{rank}(B:AUB)$, then we assign $C(RB_i) = B_i$. $RB = \text{rank}(B:AUB) = (3, 4, 5, 9, 10, 11, 13, 14, 15, 18, 19)$. Hence we assign

$$C(3) = b_1 = 6, \qquad C(4) = b_2 = 7, \qquad C(5) = b_3 = 9,$$
$$C(9) = b_4 = 25, \qquad C(10) = b_5 = 26, \qquad C(11) = b_6 = 31,$$
$$C(13) = b_7 = 42, \qquad C(14) = b_8 = 85, \qquad C(15) = b_9 = 87,$$
$$C(18) = b_{10} = 102, \qquad C(14) = b_{11} = 105$$

We are now ready to formally present the algorithm.

### Algorithm Merging and Ranking
**Input:**   1. Array $A = (a_1\ a_2\ \ldots\ a_m)$, such that $a_1 < a_2 < a_3 < \ldots < a_m$.
  2. Array $B = (b_1, b_2, \ldots\ b_n)$, such that $b_1 < b_2 < b_3 < \ldots b_n$.
**Output:**   Merged array $C = (C(1), C(2), C(3), \ldots\ C(m+n))$, such
  that $C(1) < C(2) < C(3) \ldots < C(m+n)$.
  1. For $i \in \{1, 2, \ldots m\}$ and $j \in \{1, 2, \ldots n\}$ do in parallel
  2. Find rank $(a_i:A)$ and Find rank $(b_j:B)$
  3. Find rank $(a_i:B)$ and Find rank $(b_j:A)$
  4. End parallel.
  5. Denote rank $(A:B)$ and rank $(B:A)$ as explained
    earlier.
  6. $RA = \text{rank}(A:A) + \text{rank}(A:B)$
  7. $RB = \text{rank}(B:A) + \text{rank}(B:B)$
  8. For $i = 1$ to $m$ do in parallel
  9. $C(RA_i) = A_i$
  10. End parallel
  11. For $i = 1$ to $n$ do in parallel
  12. $C(RB_i) = B_i$
  13. End parallel
  14. END

*Complexity Analysis.* Since $A$ and $B$ are sorted arrays, rank $(x : A)$ can be found using binary search in $O(\log m)$ time with one processor. Similarly rank $(x : B)$ can be found in $O(\log n)$ time. So, steps 1 to 4 can be implemented in $O(\log n)$ time using $O(m + n)$ processors. (Assume that $n \geq m$ without loss of generality). Steps 6 to 7 can be implemented in $O(1)$ time using $O(n)$ processors. Similarly steps 8 to 10 and steps 11 to 13 can also be done in $O(1)$ time using $O(n)$ processors. So the algorithm can be implemented in $O(\log n)$ time using $O(m + n)$ time. The steps 2 and 3 involve concurrent read operation. However exclusive write is sufficient. So, the algorithm can be implemented in CREW PRAM model.

## 8.6 BITONIC MERGING

An array $A = (a_0, a_1, \ldots a_{n-1})$ is said to be a bitonic array or bitonic sequence if there are integers $j$ and $k$ such that $(a_{j+1}, a_{j+2}, \ldots a_k)$ and $(a_{k+1(modn)}, a_{k+2(modn)}, \ldots a_j)$ are two monotonic sequences, one is monotonically increasing and the other decreasing. For example, the sequence $A = (22, 27, 39, 48, 42, 40, 35, 34, 32, 25, 24, 18, 8, 5, 7, 14)$ is a bitonic sequence. This is written in a table for better understanding as follows:

| $i$ | 0 | 1 | 2 | 3 | 4 | 5 | 6 | 7 | 8 | 9 | 10 | 11 | 12 | 13 | 14 | 15 |
|------|----|----|----|----|----|----|----|----|----|----|----|----|----|----|----|----|
| $A(i)$ | 22 | 27 | 39 | 48 | 42 | 40 | 35 | 34 | 32 | 25 | 24 | 18 | 8 | 5 | 7 | 14 |

*(j ↓ above column 0, k ↓ above column 12)*

If we write these numbers along the circumference of a circle then the data can be divided into two parts: one part monotonically increasing and the other monotonically decreasing.

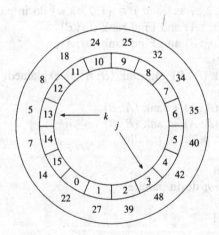

Let $A(0:2n-1)$ be a bitonic sequence. Let us define

$$L_i = \text{Min}\{a_i, a_{i+n}\} \qquad 0 \le i < n.$$
$$R_i = \text{Max}\{a_i, a_{i+n}\} \qquad 0 \le i < n.$$

We have the following results.

1. $L_o, L_1, L_2, \ldots L_{n-1}$ is a bitonic sequence.
2. $R_o, R_1, R_2, \ldots R_{n-1}$ is a bitonic sequence.
3. Each entry $L_i$ is less than or equal to each entry $R_j$.

In order to illustrate this, consider the array $A$ used in this section.

| $i$ | $a_i$ | $a_i$ | $i$ |
|---|---|---|---|
| 0 | 25 | 32 | 8 |
| 1 | 27 | 25 | 9 |
| 2 | 39 | 24 | 10 |
| 3 | 48 | 18 | 11 |
| 4 | 42 | 8 | 12 |
| 5 | 40 | 5 | 13 |
| 6 | 35 | 7 | 14 |
| 7 | 34 | 14 | 15 |

| $i$ | $L_i$ | $R_i$ | $i$ |
|---|---|---|---|
| 0 | 25 | 32 | 8 |
| 1 | 25 | 27 | 9 |
| 2 | 24 | 39 | 10 |
| 3 | 18 | 48 | 11 |
| 4 | 8 | 42 | 12 |
| 5 | 5 | 40 | 13 |
| 6 | 7 | 35 | 14 |
| 7 | 14 | 34 | 15 |

The above result is used to merge two sorted arrays. We proceed as follows:

1. Let $A(0:n-1)$ and $B(0:n-1)$ be two sorted arrays. Reverse the array $B$. That is, assign $(b_0, b_1, b_2, \ldots b_{n-1}) = (b_{n-1}, b_{n-2}, \ldots b_2, b_1, b_0)$. Now $A(o:n-1)$ is a monotonically increasing sequence and $B(0:n-1)$ is a monotonically decreasing sequence. Now extend the array $A$ with the

array $B$. That is assign $A(n:2n-1) = B(0:n-1)$. Now $A(0:2n-1)$ is a bitonic sequence.

2. For the values of $i = 0, 1, 2, \ldots (n-1)$ do the operation

$$a_i = \text{Min}\{a_i, a_{i+n}\}$$
$$a_{i+n} = \text{Max}\{a_i, a_{i+n}\}$$

This can be done by the following "if" statement.
If $a_i > a_{i+n}$ then interchange $a_i$ and $a_{i+n}$

By doing this we have,

$$(L_0, L_1, L_2, \ldots L_{n-1}) = (a_0, a_1, a_2, \ldots a_{n-1})$$
$$\text{and}$$
$$(R_0, R_1, R_2 \ldots R_{n-1}) = (a_n, a_{n+1}, a_{n+2} \ldots a_{2n-1})$$

Hence we have the following results:

1. $A(o:n-1)$ is a bitonic sequence
2. $A(n:2n-1)$ is a bitonic sequence
3. Every entry $a_i$ is less than or equal to every $a_j$ for $o \leq i < n$ and $n \leq j < n$. That is every entry of $A(o:n-1)$ is less than or equal to every entry of $A(n:2n-1)$.

Because of the above result, the subarrays $A(o:n-1)$ and $A(n:2n-1)$ can be handled separately. If $A(o:n-1)$ and $A(n:2n-1)$ are handled separately, $A(0:2n-1)$ will give the final merged array. We now present the algorithm formally.

**Algorithm Bitonic-Merge:**
  **Input:**   Sorted sequences $A(o:n-1)$ and $B(0:n-1)$.
  **Output:**   Merged sequence $A(0:2n-1)$
    1. Copy $A(n:2n-1) = B(0:n-1)$
    2. For $i = 0$ to $n-1$ do in parallel
    3. If $a_i > a_{i+n}$ then
          Interchange $a_i$ and $a_{i+n}$
        Endif
    4. End parallel.
    5. Do the above operations recursively on $A(o:n-1)$ and $A(n:2n-1)$ separately in parallel and make them sorted sequence.
    6. End.

***Complexity Analysis.*** In steps 2–4, $O(n)$ processors work in $O(1)$ time. In each iteration the size of the array is halved. So, there are only $O(\log n)$ recursive steps. Hence, this algorithm can be implemented in $O(\log n)$ time using $O(n)$ processors in EREW PRAM.

## BIBLIOGRAPHY

Cole, R., Parallel Merge Sort, *SIAM J. Computing*, **17(4)**:770–785, 1988.

Knuth, D., *Sorting and Searching*, Addison-Wesley, Reading, MA 1973.

Kruskal, C., Searching, Merging and Sorting in Parallel Computation, *IEEE Transactions on Computers*, **C-32(10)**:942–946, 1983.

Shiloach, Y., and U. Vishkin, Finding the maximum merging, and sorting in a Parallel Computation model, *Journal of Algorithms*, **2(1)**:85–102, 1981.

## CHAPTER 9

# Sorting Algorithms

Sorting refers to arranging things according to some order. Sorting a file with records $R_1, R_2, \ldots R_n$ is determining a permutation $\pi$ of symbols $1, 2, \ldots n$, such that $k_{\pi(i)} \leq k_{\pi(i+1)}$ for $i = 1, 2, \ldots n-1$, where $k_i$ is the key value of the record $R_i$. If $A$ is an array $A_{\pi(1)} \leq A_{\pi(2)} \ldots \leq A_{\pi(n)}$. Apart from the usual business applications, sorting has various application of which the following is a sample set:

- Suppose we have 10,000 random samples many of which have equal values. We want to rearrange these samples so that all equal occur in consecutive positions. This is called "togetherness" problem.
- Searching a particular entry is made easy only when the file is in a sorted form.
- Editing the files in computer usage.
- Computer manufacturers estimate that over 25 percent of the running time of computer is spent on sorting.

***Complexity of Sorting Algorithms.*** The complexity of a sorting algorithm measures the running time as a function of $n$, the number of records sorted. The following are the fundamental operations that take place during sorting

1. Comparison of two keys.
2. Interchange of records
3. Assignment of a record to a temporary location.

Normally, the complexity function measures only the number of comparisons, since the number of other operations is almost a constant factor of the number of comparisons. Before learning some parallel sorting algorithms, let us first review some sequential sorting methods.

## 9.1 SEQUENTIAL SORTING ALGORITHMS

Several sequential sorting algorithms have been designed by researchers from time to time. The most popular sorting method is bubble sort.

### 9.1.1 Bubble Sort

Bubble sort is commonly used sorting technique. In this method, if we want to sort the numbers $x_1, x_2, \ldots x_n$ then $x_i$ and $x_{i+1}$ are interchanged if $x_i > x_{i+1}$ for each $i = 1, 2 \ldots k$. Where $k$ varies as $n, n - 1, \ldots 2$. Here the number of comparison made is

$$1 + 2 + 3 + \ldots + (n - 1) = n(n - 1)/2 = O(n^2).$$

In this technique the number of comparison is irrespective of the data set, whether best or worst. Bubble sort is a very simple way of sorting. The bubble sort method can also be parallelized. Let us consider the sequential bubble sort with 8 numbers.

$$A_0 \quad A_1 \quad A_2 \quad A_3 \quad A_4 \quad A_5 \quad A_6 \quad A_7$$

In the bubble sort, the comparison starts from ($A_6$ and $A_7$). Then it proceeds as ($A_5$ and $A_6$), ($A_4$ and $A_5$), and so on. Let us employ four processors and assign the two numbers to each processor as follows:

| $P : A_0 \,\&\, A_1$ | $P_1 : A_2 \,\&\, A_3$ | $P_2 : A_4 \,\&\, A_5$ | $P_3 : A_6 \,\&\, A_7$ |
|---|---|---|---|

Each processor compares the two numbers and interchanges if necessary. That is, processor Pi does the following operation:

*Processor $P_i$* If $A_{2i} > A_{2i} + 1$, then interchange $A_{2i}$ and $A_{2i+1}$. For $i = 0$ to 3, the above work is done in parallel by the four processors (the above step is step 0).

In the next step (step 1), three processors are employed and the numbers assigned follow:

$$A_1 \,\&\, A_2 \quad A_3 \,\&\, A_4 \quad A_5 \,\&\, A_6$$
$$P_0 \qquad\quad P_1 \qquad\quad P_2$$

In this, each processor $P_i$ compares the two numbers $A_{2i+1}$ and $A_{2i+2}$ assigned to it and interchanges if $A_{2i+1} > A_{2i+2}$. In the next step (step 2), once again the processors are assigned as in step. In step 3 the work is done as in step 1.

This can be formally expressed in the following parallel algorithm:

**Algorithm Bubble-Sort**
   **Input:**   $A(0 : n - 1)$
   **Output:**   Sorted array $A(O : n - 1)$

   1. For $k = 0$ to $n - 2$

2. If $k$ is even then
    (a) for $i = 0$ to $(n/2) - 1$ do in parallel
    (b) If $A_{2i} > A_{2i+1}$ then interchange them
    (c) End parallel.
    Else
    (d) For $i = 0$ to $(n/2) - 2$ do in parallel
    (e) If $A_{2i+1} > A_{2i+2}$ then interchange them
    (f) End parallel.
    Endif
3. Next $k$

**Complexity Analysis.** Steps 1–3 is a loop that is repeated $n - 1$ times. So, the computing time is $O(n)$. In step 2, odd-numbered steps need $(n/2) - 2$ processors and even-numbered steps require $(n/2) - 1$ processors. So, this needs $O(n)$ processors. From the explanation of the process, it is very clear that EREW PRAM is sufficient for the implementation.

### 9.1.2 Insertion Sorting

If the first few records are already in a sorted form, an unsorted record can be inserted in the sorted set in its suitable place. This method is called *sorting by insertion*. Assume that given numbers, $A_1, A_2, \ldots A_n$ are such that

$$A_1 \leq A_2 \leq \ldots A_{j-1} \qquad \text{for some } 1 \leq j < n.$$

This method suggests inserting $A_j$ in the appropriate place between $A_1$ and $A_{j-1}$ so that we get $A_1 \leq A_2 \leq \ldots \leq A_j$. Since the above assumption is true for $j = 2$ in a given list of numbers, sorting is complete when the above procedure is repeated for $j = 2, 3, \ldots n$.

The following is the sequential algorithm for insertion sort.

**Algorithm Insertion Sort**

BEGIN
    1. For $j = 2, 3, 4, \ldots n$
    2. $i = j - 1, T = A_j$
    3. If $T > A_i$ go to step 6
    4. $A_{i+1} = A_i; i = i - 1$
    5. If $i > 0$ go to step $-3$.
    6. $A_{i+i} = T$
    7. Next $j$
END

The total computing times is $O(n^2)$ and, hence, this is not a good method.

***Improvements to the Straight Insertion Sort.*** Straight insertion involves two basic operations: (i) Scanning the ordered set of numbers $A_1, A_2, \ldots A_{j-1}$ to find the largest number less than or equal to $A_j$. (ii) Inserting $A_j$ at the specified place. The scanning is done by $j$ comparison in the worst case between $A_1$ and $A_j$. If the binary search technique is adopted, this reduces to $\log j$ comparison. But if we want to reduce the insertion time, the data structure of the given set has to be changed. If the linked list representation is used, the binary technique for scanning the sorted list cannot be used and, hence, this will not improve the total computing time.

### 9.1.3 Shell's Diminishing Increment Sort

If each pair of numbers are compared and sorted then total running time cannot be improved from $O(n^2)$. So it is essential to think of some other technique. Shell proposed a new technique in 1959 and it is called the *diminishing increment* method.

An integer $h$, called the *increment* $(0 \leq h \leq n)$ is considered and the given numbers are grouped into $h$ sets as

$$\text{Set } 1 = \{A_1, A_{h+1}, A_{2h+1} \ldots\}$$
$$\text{Set } 2 = \{A_2, A_{h+2}, A_{2h+2} \ldots\}$$
$$\ldots$$
$$\ldots$$
$$\text{Set } h = \{A_h, A_{2h}, A_{3h} \ldots\}$$

Each group is sorted using straight insertion. The increment $h$ is diminished and the process is repeated. Doing this for the diminishing increments $h_t, h_{t-1}, h_{t-2} \ldots h_3, h_2, h_1$, the sorting is complete. This means that $n \leq h_t \leq h_{t-1} \leq \ldots h_2 \leq h_1 = 1$. The algorithm is given below.

**Algorithm Shellsort**
 1. For $s = t, t - 1, \ldots, 3, 2, 1$ do
 2. $h = h_s$
 3. For $j = h + 1$ to $n$ do
 4. $i = j - h : T = A_j$
 5. If $A_j \leq T$ then go to step 8
 6. $A_{i+h} = A_i; i = i - h$
 7. If $i > 0$ go to step 5.
 8. $A_{i+h} = T$
 9. Next $j$
10. Next $s$

***Complexity Analysis.*** The following are the parameters of the algorithm:

1. $t$, the number of increments.
2. the increments $h_t, h_{t-1} \ldots h_3, h_2, h_1 = 1$.

The analysis on the computing time leads to some fascinating mathematical problems, not yet completely resolved; nobody has been able to determine the best possible sequence of increments for very large values of $N$.

Hunt has considered two increments alone and has shown that the computing time is $O(N^{5/3})$. This is a substantial improvement over straight insertion, from $O(N^2)$ to $O(N^{5/3})$. Since straight insertion sort is the best method for small values of $N$ such as 16, $h = N/16$ is chosen and Shell's algorithm run for various values of $N$. The computing time has been recorded and the graph analyzed.

If the increment $h_t h_{t-1} \ldots h_3, h_2, h_1$ are such that $h_{s-1}$ divides $h_s$ for $s = 2$, 3, $\ldots t$ we say that the increments satisfy the divisibility condition. The running time cannot be of less than $(N^{3/2})$. Papernov and Stasevich suggest that if the divisibility condition is not satisfied for every $s = 2$ to $t$, then Shell's method will be more efficient. The increments $h_s = 2^{s-1} = t, t - 1, \ldots 2, 1$ satisfies the divisibility condition, whereas $h_s = 2^s - 1, s = t, t - 1, \ldots 2, 1$ does not satisfy the same.

An interesting improvement to this was discovered in 1969 by Pratt. If the increments are chosen to be the set of all numbers of the form $2p3q$ which are less than $N$, the running time is of order $N(\log N)^2$. This will improve the general efficiency only when $N$ is very large.

Peterson and Rusell at Stanford University in 1971 conducted a large number of experiments choosing various increments for Shell's method. They also used a lot of empirical values of the increments. The empirical data by no means exhaust the possibilities and they have found no grounds for making strong assertions about what sequence of increments are best for Shell's method. It has been suggested that the following way of choosing the increments will make Shell's method reasonably efficient. Let $h_1 = 1$, $h_{s+1} = 3_h s + 1$ and stop with $h_t$ when $h_t + 2 \geq n$.

### 9.1.4 Heap Sort

In this section we study a way of structuring data which permits one to insert elements into a set and also to find the largest element efficiently. A data structure which provides for these two operations is called a *priority queue*. Many algorithms need to make use of priority queues and so an efficient way to implement these operations will be very useful. We might first consider using a queue, since inserting new elements would be very efficient. But finding the largest element would necessitate a scan of the entire queue. A second suggestion would be to use a sorted list which is stored sequentially. But an insertion could required moving all of the items in the list. What we want is a data structure that allows both operations to be done efficiently.

A *heap* is a complete binary tree with the property that the value at each node is at least its children (if they exist). This definition implies that a largest element is the root of the heap. If the elements are distinct, then the root contains the largest item.

The relation greater than or equal to may be reversed so that the parent node contains a value as small as its children. In this case, the root contains the smallest element. But clinging to historical tradition we will assume that the larger values are closer to the root. It is possible to take any binary tree containing values for which an ordering exists and move these values around so that the shape of the tree is preserved and the heap property is satisfied. However, it is more often the case that we are given $n$ items, say $n$ integers, and are free to choose whatever shape binary tree seems most desirable. In this case the complete binary tree is chosen and represented sequentially. This is why in the definition of heap we insist that a complete binary tree is used.

Now let us consider how to form a heap given $n$ integers stored in $A(1:n)$. One strategy is to determine how to insert one element at a time into an already existing heap. If we can do this, then we can apply the algorithm $n$ times, first inserting one element into an empty heap and continuing in that way until all $n$ elements have been inserted. The solution is simple, one adds a new item "at the bottom" of the heap and then compares it with its parent, grandparent, great grandparent, and so on, until it is less than or equal to one of these values. Procedures INSERT, describes this process in full detail.

**Procedure INSERT ((A, n))**
$j \leftarrow n$;
$i \leftarrow [n/2]$;
item $= A(n)$
while $i > 0$ and $A(i) <$ item do
$A(j) = A(i)//$ move the parent down
$j \leftarrow i$;
$i \leftarrow [i/2]//$ the parent of $A(i)$ is at $A([i/2])$
End While
$A(j) =$ item $//$ a place for $A(n)$ is found

It is very clear from the program that the time for INSERT can vary. In the best case, the new element is correctly positioned initially and no values need be rearranged. In the worst case the number of executions of the while loop is proportional to the number of levels in the heap. $n$ item in $A(1:n)$ may be set up as heap (which is also a complete binary tree) by the following program segment.

for $i \leftarrow 2$ to $n$ do
    Call INSERT $(A, i)$
End do

***Complexity Analysis.*** The data set that causes the heap creation method using INSERT to behave in the worst way is when elements are inserted in ascending order. Each new element will rise to become the new root.

There are at most $2^{i-1}$ nodes on level $i$ of a complete binary tree $1 \le i \le [\log(n+1)]$. For a node on level $i$, the distance to the root is $i - 1$. Thus the worst case time for heap creation using INSERT is $O(n \log n)$.

A surprising fact about INSERT is that its average behavior on $n$ random inputs is asymptotically faster than its worst case, $O(n)$ rather than $O(n \log n)$. This implies that on the average each new value only rises a constant number of levels in the tree. It is quite complicated to prove that INSERT does have this behavior, and so we will not present the proof here.

There is another algorithm for creating a heap which has a nice property—that its worst-case time is an order of magnitude faster than $n-1$ calls of INSERT. This reduction is achieved by an algorithm which regards $A(1:n)$ as a complete binary tree and works from the leaves up to the root, level by level. At each level, it will be the case that the left and right subtrees of any node may violate the heap property. Hence it is sufficient to devise a method which converts a binary tree in which only the root may violate the heap property into a heap. Procedure ADJUST does this for any binary true whose root is at location $i$. The algorithm assumes that this binary tree is a subtree of a binary tree represented sequentially as discussed earlier.

**Procedure ADJUST $((A,i,n))$**
/* The complete binary trees with roots $A(2*i)$ and $A(2*+1)$ are combined with $A(i)$ to form a single heap, $1 \le i \le n$. No node has a value greater than $n$ or less than $1*$/

```
    j = 2*i;
    item ← A(i)
    while j ≤ n do
    If j < n and A(j) ≤ A(j + 1) then
    j = j + 1
    endif
    If item ≥ A(j) then
    exit while
    else
    A([j/2]) = A(j)
    j = 2*j
    endif
    End while
    A([j/2]) ← item
END
```

Given $n$ elements in $A(1:n)$, we can create a heap by applying ADJUST. It is easy to see that leaf nodes are already heaps. So we may begin by calling

ADJUST for the parents of lead nodes and then work our way up, level by level, until the root is reached.

**Procedure HEAPIFY**
BEGIN
for $i = [n/2]$ to 1 by step $-1$ do
call ADJUST $(A, i, n)$
Next $i$
END

We have discussed a heap as a data structure with the property that the values in every node is atleast as large as the values in the children nodes. Now we present an algorithm for sorting using the heap structure.

**Procedure Heapsort$((A, n))$**
call HEAPIFY
for $i = n$ to 2 by step $-1$ do
$t = A(i)$;
$A(i) = A(1)$;
$A(1) = t$
call ADJUST $(A, i - 1)$
Next $i$

Though the call of HEAPIFY requires only $O(n)$ operations, ADJUST possibly requires $O(\log n)$ operations for each invocation. Thus the worst case time is $O(n \log n)$. Notice that the storage requirements, besides $A(1:n)$ are only for a few simple variables.

## 9.2 MERGE SORT

The merging can be effectively used for sorting. Consider the array $x(1:n)$. If you consider $x_1$ alone as an array it is sorted already. If you consider $x_2$ alone as an array it is sorted already. Now you can merge $x_1$ and $x_2$ to get the sorted array $x_1, x_2$. Similarly, when $x_1, x_2$ and $x_3, x_4$ are sorted arrays, we can merge them to get the sorted array $x_1 x_2 x_3 x_4$.

As an example consider the 16 given numbers:

| $x_1$ | $x_2$ | $x_3$ | $x_4$ | $x_5$ | $x_6$ | $x_7$ | $x_8$ | $x_9$ | $x_{10}$ | $x_{11}$ | $x_{12}$ | $x_{13}$ | $x_{14}$ | $x_{15}$ | $x_{16}$ |
|---|---|---|---|---|---|---|---|---|---|---|---|---|---|---|---|
| 71 | 81 | 83 | 85 | 23 | 19 | 64 | 19 | 36 | 53 | 87 | 48 | 8 | 96 | 10 | 0 |

Merging the pairs

$$x_1 \text{ and } x_2 \text{ to give } y_1, y_2$$
$$x_3 \text{ and } x_4 \text{ to give } y_3, y_4$$
$$\ldots$$
$$\ldots$$
$$x_{15} \text{ and } x_{16} \text{ to give } y_{15}y_{16}$$

results in following table:

| $y_1$ | $y_2$ | $y_3$ | $y_4$ | $y_5$ | $y_6$ | $y_7$ | $y_8$ | $y_9$ | $y_{10}$ | $y_{11}$ | $y_{12}$ | $y_{13}$ | $y_{14}$ | $y_{15}$ | $y_{16}$ |
|---|---|---|---|---|---|---|---|---|---|---|---|---|---|---|---|
| 71 | 81 | 83 | 85 | 23 | 19 | 64 | 19 | 36 | 53 | 87 | 48 | 8 | 96 | 10 | 0 |

Merging the pairs

$$y_1y_2 \text{ and } y_3y_4 \text{ to get } x_1x_2x_3x_4$$
$$\ldots$$
$$\ldots$$
$$y_{13}y_{14} \text{ and } y_{15}y_{16} \text{ to get } x_{13}x_{14}x_{15}x_{16};$$

we get the sequence 71, 81, 83, 19, 23, 64, 36, 48, 53, 87, 07, 08, 10, 96.

Continuing in this way we finally get a single sorted file. The pair marking method can be slightly modified to speed up the process and to open an avenue for further modifications in the technique. The modified pairs are $(x_1, x_n), (x_2, x_{n-1}) \ldots$ and the sorted elements are stored as $(y_1, y_2), (y_2, y_{n-1})$ $\ldots$, respectively. This is called the *straight merge sort* and the main feature of this method is that the number of records to be merged at any iteration is predetermined as 1, 2, $2^2$, $2^3$, $2^4$ $\ldots$ and so the total sorting requires $(\log n)$ merging iterations. When the merging operation is done in parallel, we can sort in $O(\log^2 n)$ time, using $O(n)$ processors in CREW PRAM model.

## 9.3  SORTING NETWORKS

Knuth tells that more than 25 percent of the CPU time is spent on sorting. Sorting has become such an important problem. So, it is high time to think of a special purpose hardware to sort a collection of data. In this section we assume two preliminary sorting hardwares which are capable of sorting two elements. They are shown in Fig. 9.1.

If four numbers $x_1$, $x_2$, $x_3$, and $x_4$ are to be sorted, we can design a sorting

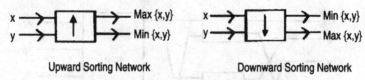

Upward Sorting Network          Downward Sorting Network

**Figure 9.1** Fundamental sorting networks.

network using the fundamental sorting networks. The sorting network is shown in Fig. 9.2.

In Fig. 9.2, $x_1$ and $x_2$ are sorted using a fundamental block $B_1$. Simultaneously $x_3$ and $x_4$ are sorted using another block $B_2$. The bigger output of $B_1$ and the bigger output of $B_2$ are sorted using $B_3$. The bigger output of $B_3$ is evidently the largest number. Hence it is called $x_4$. The smaller output of $B_1$ and the smaller output of $B_2$ are sorted using a block $B_4$. The smaller output of $B_4$ is evidently the smallest element of the array and hence it is called $x_1$. The smaller output of $B_3$ and the bigger output of $B_4$ are sorted using $B_5$ and named $x_2$ and $x_3$. Hence the output $(x_1, x_2, x_3, x_4)$ is a sorted array.

**Bitonic Sorting Networks.** If $A(o:n-1)$ is a bitonic sequence, then it can be sorted using the method similar to bitonic merging. When $A(o:n-1)$ is the given bitonic sequence, we can consider the two subsequences,

$$A\left(o:\frac{n}{2}-1\right) \text{ and}$$

$$A\left(\frac{n}{2}:n-1\right).$$

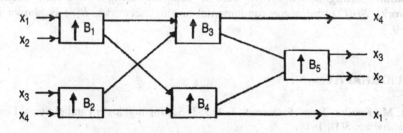

**Figure 9.2** Sorting network to sort four elements.

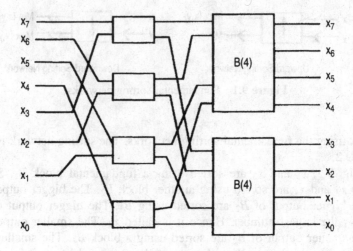

**Figure 9.3** Bitonic sorting network $B(8)$.

Let

$$L_i = \text{Min}\left\{a_i, a_i + \frac{n}{2}\right\} \qquad 0 \le i < \frac{n}{2};$$

$$R_i = \text{Max}\left\{a_i, a_i + \frac{n}{2}\right\} \qquad 0 \le i < \frac{n}{2}.$$

As we have already studied $L$ and $R$ form separate bitonic sequences and each element of $L$ is less than or equal to each element of $R$. Hence if $L$ and $R$ are sorted separately and output $R$ after $L$, we get the sorted sequence.

A network which will sort a bitonic sequence of $n$ elements is denoted by $B(n)$ and called a bitonic sorting network of size $n$. As explained above, a bitonic sorting network $B(n)$ can be designed using two bitonic sorting networks $B(n/2)$ and some fundamental sorting networks. $B(8)$ is shown in Fig. 9.3.

## BIBLIOGRAPHY

Ajtai, M., Komlos, J. and Szemeredi, E. (1983) Sorting in $c \log n$ Parallel Steps, *Combinatorica*, **3(1)**, 1–19.

Azar, Y. and Vishkum, U. (1987) Tight Comparison Bounds on the Complexity of Parallel Sorting, *SIAM Journal of Computing*, **16(3)**, 458–464.

Batcher, K. (1968) Sorting Networks and Their Applications, *AFIPS Spring JOINT Computing Conference*, Atlantic City, NJ, pp. 307–314.

Bilardi and Nicolau, A. (1989) Adaptive Bitonic Sorting, *SIAM J. Computing*, **18(2)**, 216–228.

Cole, R. (1988) Parallel Merge Sort, *SIAM J. Computing*, **17(4)**, 770–785.

Knuth, D. (1973) *Sorting and Searching*, Addison-Wesley, Reading, MA.

## EXERCISES

**9.1.** Prove that any bitonic sequence satisfies the unique crossover property.

**9.2.** Let $X$ be an array of elements. Develop a parallel algorithm to partition the array with $x_0$ such that after partition $x_0$ is position as $x_k$ and in the new array $x_0, x_1, x_2 \ldots x_n$, we have

$$x_i \leq x_k \text{ for all } i \leq k$$

and $x_k \leq x_j$ for all $j \geq k$.

**9.3.** Develop a nonrecursive version of the quick sort algorithm.

**9.4.** Draw the sorting network to sort an array of 64 entries.

**9.5.** Find the number of comparisons needed to find the horizontal cut with the unique crossover property in a bitonic sequence of length $2^k$.

# PART 4

# NUMERICAL ALGORITHMS

## CHAPTER 10

# ALGEBRAIC EQUATIONS AND MATRICES

## 10.1 ALGEBRAIC EQUATIONS

Consider an algebraic equation $f(x) = 0$. If $f(a)$ and $f(b)$ are of opposite sign, $f(x) = 0$ has a root between $a$ and $b$. For example, consider the equation $x^2 - 3x + 2 = 0$.

$$f(0) = 2 = \text{positive}$$
$$f(1.5) = -0.25 = \text{negative}$$

So, there is a real root for $x^2 - 3x0 + 2 = 0$ in between 0 and 1.5.

### 10.1.1 Geometrical Interpretation

Consider the equation $f(x) = 0$. In two-dimensional plane draw the curve $y = f(x)$. The point at which the curve intersects the $x$-axis is the root of the equation $f(x) = 0$. For example, consider the equation $x^2 - 3x + 2 = 0$. The curve $y = x^2 + 3x + 2$ is shown in Fig. 10.1.

The curve crosses the $x$-axis at two points; $x = 1$ and $x = 2$. So, these two values are the roots of the equation $x^2 - 3x + 2 = 0$.

In order to find a real root of an algebraic equation, several iterative methods have been developed. These methods start from an approximate value of a root $x_0$. An approximate iterative formula is developed to find a better root (that is a value which is closer to $x$ than $x_0$). Such a formula is called the *iterative formula* and it is of the form $x_{k+1} = f(x_k)$.

By substituting $k = 0, 1, 2, \ldots$ the approximate value of the root is improved and the process is terminated when the desired accuracy is reached. Some such methods are listed below:

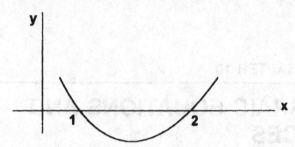

**Figure 10.1** The curve $y = x^2 - 3x + 2$.

### Iterative methods to solve $f(x) = 0$

| S. No | Method | Iterative Formula |
|---|---|---|
| 1 | Newton Raphson | $x_{k+1} = x_k - f(x_k)/f'(x_k)$ |
| 2 | Von Mises formula | $x_{k+1} = x_k - f(x_k)/f'(x_0)$ |
| 3 | Chord's method or Secant Method | $x_{k+1} = (x_k f(x_0) - x_0 f(x_k))/(f(x_0) - f(x_k))$ |
| 4 | Regula-Falsi or Method of False position | $x_{k+1} = (x_{k-1}f(x_k) - x_k f(x_{k-1}))/(f(x_k)) - f(x_{k-1}))$ |
| 5 | Successive approximation | If $f(x) = 0$ is the given equation rewrite it in the form $x = \Phi(x)$. Then the iterative formula is $x_{k+1} = \Phi(x_k)$ |

All the above five methods are inherently sequential. There is another method, called *bisection method*, in which some amount of inherent parallelism can be exploited.

### 10.1.2 Bisection Method

Consider the equation $f(x) = 0$. Let $a$ and $b$ be two points such that $f(a)$ and $f(b)$ are of opposite sign. Thus $f(x) = 0$ has a root between $a$ and $b$. Consider the midpoint of $a$ and $b$: $m = (a + b)/2$.

Already $f(a)$ and $f(b)$ are of opposite sign. Now, if $f(a)$ and $f(m)$ are also of opposite sign then $f(x) = 0$ has a root between $a$ and $m$. The interval $(a, m)$ is of half the length of $(a, b)$. If $f(a)$ and $f(m)$ are not of opposite sign, then $f(m)$ and $f(b)$ are of opposite sign and so the root lies between $m$ and $b$.

We have bisected the interval $(a, b)$ into two sub intervals $(a, m)$ and $(m, b)$ of equal length and we have located the root in one of these intervals. If we repeat this process further, the length of the interval containing the root will be halved in each iteration. When the length of the interval is very small, the value $m$ can be chosen as the root of the equation.

Let us consider the sequential algorithm for this problem. It is assumed that the initial values of $a$ and $b$ are known where $f(a)$ and $f(b)$ are of opposite sign (That is $f(a) * f(b) < 0$).

## Algorithm Bisection-SEQ

```
BEGIN
    1. While |a − b| > ε do
    2. m = (a + b)/2
    3. If f(a)f(m) < 0 then
         b = m
       else
         a = m
       Endif
    4. End While
    5. Return (a + b)/2
END
```

Here $\epsilon$ is the accuracy needed for the result. If $1/2^n \le \epsilon/b - 1 \le 1/2^{n-1}$, then the while loop of the algorithm BISECTION-SEQ is repeated $n$ times. Consider a model of a parallel machine which has a CREW PRAM. The following algorithm can determine the root in parallel.

Suppose we have only $p$ processors. Then the interval $(a, b)$ can be divided into $p$ subintervals and assigned to one processor each. The assigned processor verifies whether the root lies in the subinterval and designates that interval as $(a, b)$. This will improve the computing time $p$ times. The algorithm is given below:

## Algorithm Bisection-PARALLEL-1
**Input:** Given function $f(x)$, accuracy $\epsilon$
**Output:** root
```
    1. While |b − a| > ε do
    2. x₀ = a
    3. For i = 1 to p do in Parallel
    4. xᵢ = x₀ + i(b − a)/p
    5. If f(xᵢ₋₁)f(xᵢ) < 0 then
```

6. $a = x_{i-1}$
7. $b = x_i$
8. endif
9. End Parallel
10. End While
11. root $= (a + b)/2$
12. End

**Complexity Analysis.** In this algorithm more than one processor may assign simultaneously the values for $a$ and $b$ in steps 5 and 6. So, a concurrent write PRAM is needed for the implementation. The value $x_i$ is used by processor $i$ and also by processor $i + 1$ simultaneously. So, concurrent reading is also needed. Hence we need a CREW PRAM model for implementing this algorithm.

## 10.2 DETERMINANT OF A MATRIX

$$\text{Consider a matrix } A = \begin{bmatrix} a_{11} & a_{12} & a_{13} & \cdots & a_{1n} \\ a_{21} & a_{22} & a_{23} & \cdots & a_{2n} \\ \cdots & \cdots & \cdots & \cdots \\ \cdots & \cdots & \cdots & \cdots \\ a_{n1} & a_{n2} & a_{n3} & \cdots & a_{nn} \end{bmatrix}$$

The following are the elementary row operation.

*Operation 1.* Multiplying each element of a row by a constant. If the $i$th row is multiplied by a constant $k$ we write $R_i \leftarrow k.R_i$ and read it as $R_i$ becomes $k.R_i$.

*Operation 2.* Multiplying one row by a constant and subtracting it from another row. That is, $R_i$ can be replaced by $R_i - kR_j$. We write $R_i \leftarrow R_i - kR_j$.

*Operation 3.* Two rows can be exchanged. If $R_i$ and $R_j$ are exchanged, we write $R_i \leftarrow \rightarrow R_j$. When operation 1 is performed the determinant value is multiplied by $k$. If operation 2 is performed on a matrix, the determinant value is not affected. When operation 3 is performed, the sign of its determinant value changes.

| Operation | Effect on Determinant |
|---|---|
| 1 | Multiplied by $k$ |
| 2 | No effect |
| 3 | Sign reversed |

Consider a matrix in which all the lower diagonal entries of the first column are zeros:

$$|A| = \begin{bmatrix} a_{11}, & a_{12}, & a_{13}, & \cdots & a_{1n} \\ 0 & a_{22}, & a_{23}, & \cdots & a_{2n}, \\ 0 & a_{32}, & a_{33}, & \cdots & a_{3n}, \\ \cdots & \cdots & \cdots & \cdots & \cdots \\ \cdots & \cdots & \cdots & \cdots & \cdots \\ 0 & a_{n2}, & a_{n3}, & \cdots & a_{nn} \end{bmatrix}$$

$$= a_{11} \begin{bmatrix} a_{22}, & a_{23}, & a_{24}, & \cdots & a_{2n} \\ a_{32}, & a_{33}, & a_{34}, & \cdots & a_{3n} \\ \cdots & \cdots & \cdots & \cdots & \cdots \\ \cdots & \cdots & \cdots & \cdots & \cdots \\ a_{n2}, & a_{n3}, & a_{n4}, & \cdots & a_{nn} \end{bmatrix}$$

**Pivotal Condensation Method.** Consider a matrix:

$$|A| = \begin{bmatrix} a_{11}, & a_{12}, & a_{13}, & \cdots & a_{1n} \\ a_{21}, & a_{22}, & a_{23}, & \cdots & a_{2n}, \\ a_{31}, & a_{32}, & a_{33}, & \cdots & a_{3n}, \\ \cdots & \cdots & \cdots & \cdots & \cdots \\ \cdots & \cdots & \cdots & \cdots & \cdots \\ a_{n1}, & a_{n2}, & a_{n3}, & \cdots & a_{nn} \end{bmatrix}.$$

Consider the row operation

$$R_2 \leftarrow R_2 - \frac{a_{21}}{a_{11}} R_1.$$

If the above operation is performed in the matrix $A$, the $(2, 1)$ entry will become zero. Similarly do the operation

$$R_i \leftarrow R_i - \frac{a_{i1}}{a_{11}} R_1$$

for $i = 2, 3, \ldots, n$. Then the lower diagonal entries of the first column will become zero. Note that these operations will not affect the determinant value of $A$. In the above operation $a_{ij}$ would have now become $a_{ij} - (a_{i1}/a_{11})a_{1j}$. Let us denote these values by $a_{ij}$ once again. Therefore according to the new notation

$$|A| = \begin{bmatrix} a_{11}, & a_{12}, & a_{13}, & \cdots & a_{1n}, \\ 0 & a_{22}, & a_{23}, & \cdots & a_{2n}, \\ 0 & a_{32}, & a_{33}, & \cdots & a_{3n}, \\ \cdots & \cdots & \cdots & \cdots & \cdots \\ \cdots & \cdots & \cdots & \cdots & \cdots \\ 0 & a_{n2}, & a_{n3}, & \cdots & a_{nn} \end{bmatrix}$$

$$= a_{11} \begin{bmatrix} a_{22}, & a_{23}, & a_{24}, & \cdots & a_{2n} \\ a_{32}, & a_{33}, & a_{34}, & \cdots & a_{3n} \\ \cdots & \cdots & \cdots & \cdots & \cdots \\ \cdots & \cdots & \cdots & \cdots & \cdots \\ a_{n2}, & a_{n3}, & a_{n4}, & \cdots & a_{nn} \end{bmatrix}.$$

Now we can once again repeat the above procedure on the reduced matrix to get determinant

$$|A| = a_{11} a_{22} \begin{bmatrix} a_{33}, & a_{34}, & \cdots & a_{3n} \\ \cdots & \cdots & \cdots & \cdots \\ \cdots & \cdots & \cdots & \cdots \\ a_{n3}, & a_{n4}, & \cdots & a_{nn} \end{bmatrix}.$$

$A$ was a $n \times n$ matrix. In the first step we condensed it into a $(n - 1) \times (n - 1)$ matrix. Now it has been further condensed into $(n - 2) \times (n - 2)$ matrix.

Repeating the above procedure, we can condense the matrix into $1 \times 1$ matrix. So, determinant $|A| = a_{11} \, a_{22} \ldots a_{nn}$.

**Algorithm Development.** Let $A$ be the given matrix.

1. Do the row operation

$$R_i \leftarrow R_i - (a_{i1}/a_{11})R_1$$

for $i = 2, 3, 4, \ldots, n$. This makes all the lower diagonal entries of the first column zero.

2. Do the row operation

$$R_i \leftarrow R_i - (a_{i2}/a_{22})R_2$$

for $i = 3, 4, \ldots, n$. This makes all the lower diagonal entries of the second column zero.

3. Do the row operation

$$R_i \leftarrow R_i - (a_{i3}/a_{33})R_3$$

for $i = 4, 5, \ldots, n$. This makes all the lower diagonal entries of the third column zero.

In general, in order to make the lower diagonal entries of the $k$th column zero. Do the row operation

$$R_i \leftarrow R_i - \frac{a_{ik}}{a_{kk}} R_k \quad \text{for } i = k + 1, k + 2, \ldots n.$$

Doing the above operation for $k = 1, 2, 3, \ldots, (n - 1)$ makes all the lower diagonal entries of the matrix zero. Now the determinant is:

$$|A| = a_{11}\, a_{22}\, a_{33} \ldots a_{nn}.$$

Notice that the following segment will do the required row operation

ratio = $a_{ik}/a_{kk}$
For $j = 1$ to $n$
$a_{ij} = a_{ij} - \text{ratio} * a_{kj}$
next $j$.

This operation has to be repeated for $i = k + 1$ to $n$, in order to make the lower diagonal entries of the $k$th column zero. The complete algorithm is shown below:

**Algorithm Sequential Pivotal Condensation**
   **Input:**   Given Matrix $A(1 : n, 1 : n)$.
   **Output:**   Determinant.
   1. For $k = 1$ to $n - 1$
   2. For $i = k + 1$ to $n$
   3. *ratio* = $a_{ik}/a_{kk}$
   4. Do the row operation $R_i \leftarrow$ ration $* R_x$
   5. next $i$
   6. next $k$
   7. Determinant $a_{11} * a_{22} * \ldots * a_{nm}$
   8. END

In the above sequential algorithm the FOR-NEXT loop from steps 2 to 5 makes all the lower diagonal entries of the $k$ column zero. In this loop, any two iterations are independent to each other and so they can be done in parallel by different processors. All these processors will use the $k$th row entries and so concurrent read PRAM is needed for the implementation. In step 4 the row operation is sequentially done using a for next loop as follows:

4.1. For $j = 1$ to $n$
4.2. $a_{ij} \leftarrow a_{ij} - \text{ratio} * a_{kj}$
4.3. next $j$.

This can be done in parallel by $n$ different processors as follows:

4.1. For $j = 1$ to $n$ do in Parallel
4.2. $a_{ij} = a_{ij} - \text{ratio} * a_{kj}$
4.3. End Parallel

Step 7 can be evaluated in parallel using $O(n)$ processors in $O(\log n)$ time. The complete parallel algorithm is shown below:

**Algorithm Determinant**
**Input:** $A(1:n, 1:n)$.
**Output:** determinant of $A$ denoted by det.

BEGIN
  1. For $k = 1$ to $n - 1$
  2. For $i = k + 1$ to $n$ do in parallel
  3. ratio $= a_{ik}/a_{kk}$
  4. For $j = 1$ to $n$ do in parallel
  5. $a_{ij} = a_{ij} - \text{ratio} * a_{kj}$
  6. End parallel
  7. End parallel
  8. Next $k$
  9. det $= a_{11} * a_{22} * \ldots * a_{nm}$
END

The loop of step 1 to 8 is repeated $n - 1$ times. So, the computing time is $O(n)$. There are two nested loops of parallelism in steps 2 to 7 and steps 4 to 6. So we need $O(n^2)$ processors. Step 9 can be implemented in $O(\log n)$ time using $O(n)$ processors similar to the summation algorithm. So, the overall complexity of the above parallel algorithm is $O(n)$ time using $O(n^2)$ processors.

## 10.3 SYSTEM OF LINEAR EQUATIONS

Consider the following system of linear equations

$$a_{11}x_1 + a_{12}x_2 + \ldots + a_{1n}x_n = a_{1,n+1}$$
$$a_{21}x_1 + a_{22}x_2 + \ldots + a_{2n}x_n = a_{2,n+1}$$
$$\ldots \qquad \ldots \ldots \qquad \ldots \quad \ldots$$
$$\ldots \quad \ldots \quad \ldots \qquad \ldots \quad \ldots$$
$$a_{n1}x_1 + a_{n2}x_2 + + \cdots + a_{nn}x_n = a_{n,n+1}.$$

A solution to this system of equation is a set of values for $x_1, x_2, \ldots x_n$ which satisfies the above equations.

Consider the matrix:

$$\begin{bmatrix} a_{11}, & a_{12}, & a_{13}, & \cdots & a_{1n}, \\ a_{21}, & a_{22}, & a_{23}, & \cdots & a_{2n}, \\ a_{31}, & a_{32}, & a_{33}, & \cdots & a_{3n}, \\ \ldots & \ldots & \ldots & \ldots & \ldots \\ \ldots & \ldots & \ldots & \ldots & \ldots \\ a_{n1}, & a_{n2}, & a_{n3}, & \cdots & a_{nn} \end{bmatrix}$$

This is called the *coefficient matrix*. The vector

$$\begin{pmatrix} a_{1,n+1} \\ a_{2,n+1} \\ a_{3,n+1} \\ \ldots \\ \ldots \\ a_{n,n+1} \end{pmatrix}$$

is called the *right-hand-side vector*. In some special cases the solution can be obtained directly.

## Case 1

A square matrix is called a *diagonal matrix* if the diagonal entries alone are non zeros and all the nondiagonal entries are zeros. Suppose the coefficient matrix is a diagonal matrix.

That is, the coefficient matrix is of the form

$$\begin{bmatrix} a_{11}, & 0, & 0, & \cdots & 0 \\ 0, & a_{22}, & 0, & \cdots & 0 \\ \cdots & \cdots & \cdots & \cdots & \cdots \\ \cdots & \cdots & \cdots & \cdots & \cdots \\ \cdots & \cdots & \cdots & \cdots & \cdots \\ 0, & 0, & 0, & \cdots & a_{nn} \end{bmatrix}.$$

The equations will be of the following form

$$a_{11}x_1 = a_{1,n+1}$$
$$a_{22}x_2 = a_{2,n+1}$$
$$\cdots \quad \cdots \quad \cdots$$
$$\cdots \quad \cdots \quad \cdots$$
$$a_{nn}x_n = a_{n,n+1}$$

In this case the solution can be directly written as

$$x_1 = \frac{a_{1,n+1}}{a_{11}}, \qquad x_2 = \frac{a_{2,n+1}}{a_{22}}, \qquad \cdots, x_n = \frac{a_{n,n+1}}{a_{nn}}.$$

## Case 2

A matrix is said to be *lower triangular* if all its upper diagonal entries are zeros. Suppose the coefficient matrix is a lower diagonal matrix. That is, the coefficient matrix is of the following:

$$\begin{bmatrix} a_{11}, & 0, & 0, & \cdots & 0 \\ a_{21}, & a_{22}, & 0, & \cdots & 0 \\ \cdots & \cdots & \cdots & \cdots & \cdots \\ \cdots & \cdots & \cdots & \cdots & \cdots \\ a_{n1}, & a_{n2}, & a_{n3}, & \cdots & a_{nn} \end{bmatrix}.$$

The equations will be of the following form

$$a_{11}x_1 = a_{1n+1}$$
$$a_{21}x_1 + a_{22}x_2 = a_{2n+1}$$
$$\cdots \quad \cdots \quad \cdots \quad \cdots$$

$$a_{n1}x_1 + a_{n2}x_2 + \ldots + a_{nn}x_n = a_{nn+1}.$$

From the first equation, $x_1 = a_{1n+1}/a_{11}$. Since $x_1$ has now been found, we can find $x_2$ from the second equation as

$$x_2 = \frac{1}{a_{22}} (a_{2n+1} - a_{21}x_1).$$

After finding $x_2$ we can find $x.$ from the third equation as

$$x_3 = \frac{1}{a_{33}} (a_{3n+1} - a_{31}x_1 - a_{32}x_2).$$

Similarly, we can find $x_4, x_5, \ldots, x_n$. This is called *forward substitution method.*

## Case 3

Suppose the coefficient matrix is upper triangular. Then the equations will be of the following form:

$$a_{11}x_1 + a_{12}x_2 + \ldots + a_{1n}x_n = a_{1,n+1}$$
$$a_{22}x_2 + \ldots + a_{2n}x_n = a_{2,n+1}$$
$$\cdots \quad \cdots \quad \cdots \quad \cdots \quad \cdots$$
$$a_{nn}x_n = a_{n,n+1}.$$

We can start from the last equation. The last equation gives the value of $x_n$ as

$$x_n = \frac{a_{n,n+1}}{a_{nn}}.$$

The $(n-1)$th equation can now be used to evaluate $x_{n-1}$.

$$x_{n-1} = \frac{1}{a_{n-1,n-1}} (a_{n-1,n+1} - a_{n-1,n}x_n).$$

In general, after evaluating $x_n, x_{n-1}, \ldots x_{k+1}$, we evaluate $x_k$.

We can thus evaluate all the $x_i$ values. This is called the *backward substitution* method.

### 10.3.1  Gauss Elimination Method

Consider the equation

$$a_{11}x_1 + a_{12}x_2 + \ldots + a_{1n}x_n = a_{1n+1}$$
$$a_{21}x_1 + a_{22}x_2 + \ldots + a_{2n}x_n = a_{2n+1}$$
$$\cdots \quad \cdots \quad \cdots \quad \cdots \quad \cdots$$
$$\cdots \quad \cdots \quad \cdots \quad \cdots \quad \cdots$$
$$a_{n1}x_1 + a_{n2}x_2 + \ldots + a_{nn}x_n = a_{nn+1}$$

This can be represented in matrix form as follows:

$$
\begin{bmatrix}
a_{11}, & a_{12}, & a_{13}, & \cdots & a_{1n}, \\
a_{21}, & a_{22}, & a_{23}, & \cdots & a_{2n}, \\
a_{31}, & a_{32}, & a_{33}, & \cdots & a_{3n}, \\
\cdots & \cdots & \cdots & \cdots & \cdots \\
\cdots & \cdots & \cdots & \cdots & \cdots \\
a_{n1} & a_{n2} & a_{n3} & \cdots & a_{nn}
\end{bmatrix}
\begin{bmatrix}
x_1 \\ x_2 \\ x_3 \\ \cdots \\ \cdots \\ x_n
\end{bmatrix}
\begin{bmatrix}
a_{1,n+1} \\ a_{2,n+1} \\ a_{3,n+1} \\ \cdots \\ \cdots \\ a_{n,n+1}
\end{bmatrix}.
$$

Doing the row operations which were done for pivotal condensation method, the system reduces to

$$
\begin{bmatrix}
a_{11}, & a_{12}, & a_{13}, & \cdots & a_{1n}, \\
0, & a_{22}, & a_{23}, & \cdots & a_{2n}, \\
0, & 0, & a_{33}, & \cdots & a_{3n}, \\
\cdots & \cdots & \cdots & \cdots & \cdots \\
\cdots & \cdots & \cdots & \cdots & \cdots \\
0, & 0, & 0, & \cdots & a_{nn}
\end{bmatrix}.
$$

Now we can use backward substitution. The algorithms consist of the following three major stages.

1. Read the matrix $A$.
2. Reduce it to upper triangular form.
3. Use Backward substitution to get the solution.

Reduction of the matrix into upper triangular form has already been discussed in the Pivotal Condensation method. This can be done using a CREW PRAM in $O(n)$ time, using $O(n^2)$ processors. In the backward substitution, $x_k$ is calculated only after evaluation $x_{k+1}, x_{k+2}, \ldots x_n$.

So, the evaluation of $x_k$ values is inherently sequential. Each $x_k$ can be computed in $O(\log n)$ time using $O(n)$ processors. Hence the Gauss Elimination algorithm can be implemented in a CREW PRAM model in $O(n)$ time, using $O(n^2)$ processors.

**Partial Pivoting.** In gauss elimination method, the $k$th row is divided by the pivot element $a_{kk}$ and multiplied by $a_{ik}$ and the row operation performed. If $a_{kk}$ is zero or comparatively small in magnitude the process leads to computational errors such as truncation error, round off error, etc. In order to avoid this, we can select the diagonal and the lower diagonal entries of the $k$th column. If $a_{1k}$ is the largest, then we can interchange the $k$th row with the first row and then proceed the elimination procedure. This method is called *partial pivoting*. So, in the elimination procedure explained in the algorithm DETERMINANT, between steps 1 and 2, we must scan the diagonal and lower diagonal entries of the $k$th column and choose the largest magnitude entry $a_{1k}$. Then we must interchange the $k$th column with first column. Choosing the largest magnitude entry can be done in $\log(n - k + 1)$ time using $O(n)$ processors. So, if partial pivoting is introduced in Gauss elimination method, the solution can be implemented in a CREW PRAM model in $O(n \log n)$ time using $O(n^2)$ processors.

Sameh and Kuch presented a parallelization technique using the classical matrix factorization method called *Given's rotation*.

### 10.3.2 Given's Rotation

Consider a general dense square matrix $A$ of order $n$. Let $i, j, k$ be three integers $\leq n$. Let us assume that in the $i$th columns and in the $j$th row all the matrix entries of the first $(k-1)$ rows are zeros are the $k$th column entries are non-zeros. That is, the matrix is of the following form.

$$
\begin{bmatrix}
* & * & * & \cdots & \cdots & \cdots & \cdots & \cdots & * \\
\cdots & \cdots & \cdots & \cdots & \cdots & \cdots & \cdots & \cdots & \cdots \\
\cdots & \cdots & \cdots & \cdots & \cdots & \cdots & \cdots & \cdots & \cdots \\
0 & 0 & 0 & \cdots & 0 & * & * & \cdots & * \\
\cdots & \cdots & \cdots & \cdots & \cdots & \cdots & \cdots & \cdots & \cdots \\
\cdots & \cdots & \cdots & \cdots & \cdots & \cdots & \cdots & \cdots & \cdots \\
0 & 0 & 0 & \cdots & 0 & * & * & \cdots & * \\
\cdots & \cdots & \cdots & \cdots & \cdots & * & \cdots & \cdots & \cdots \\
\cdots & \cdots & \cdots & \cdots & \cdots & \textit{column } k & \cdots & \cdots & \cdots
\end{bmatrix}
$$

The $*$ in the above matrix represents nonzero entries. Given's rotation is a method which makes the entry at $(j, k)$ zero. So, using the Given's rotation we can make a lower diagonal entry zero. Now let us see how Given's rotation works. Consider the following matrix:

$$\begin{bmatrix} 1 & 0 & 0 & \cdots & \cdots & \cdots & \cdots & \cdots & 0 \\ 0 & 1 & 0 & \cdots & \cdots & \cdots & \cdots & \cdots & 0 \\ \cdots & \cdots & \cdots & & \cdots & & \cdots & & 0 \\ \cdots & \cdots & \cdots & & \cdots & & \cdots & & 0 \\ 0 & 0 & 0 & \cdots & 0c & \cdots & s & \cdots & 0 \\ \cdots & \cdots & \cdots & & \cdots & & \cdots & & \cdots \\ \cdots & \cdots & \cdots & & \cdots & & \cdots & & \cdots \\ 0 & 0 & 0 & \cdots & 0s & \cdots & c & \cdots & 0 \\ \cdots & \cdots & \cdots & & \cdots & & \cdots & & \cdots \\ \cdots & \cdots & \cdots & & \cdots & & \cdots & & \cdots \\ 0 & 0 & 0 & \cdots & column\ i & \cdots & column\ i & \cdots & 1 \end{bmatrix},$$

$$\text{where } c = \frac{a_{ik}}{\sqrt{a_{ik}^2 + a_{jk}^2}}$$

$$\text{and } s = \frac{a_{ik}}{\sqrt{a_{ik}^2 + a_{jk}^2}}.$$

The matrix $G$ is called the *Given's rotation matrix*. The following are some interesting properties of the product matrix $GA$.

## THEOREM 10.1

1. $G$ is an orthogonal matrix.

2. $GA(p,q) = a_{pq}$ for $p = i$ and for $p = j$.

3. $GA(i,q) = GA(j,q) = 0$ where $q < k$.

4. $GA(i,k) = 0$.

*Proof.* From the Euclidian norm it can be verified that $G$ is an orthogonal matrix. If $p = i$ and $p = j$, then the $p$th row of $G$ is the same as the $p$th row of the identity matrix. So, when the row is used in the product $GA$, it doesn't affect the entries of $A$. This is because of the fact that $a_{iq} = 0$ and $a_{jq} = 0$ for all $q \le k$.

$$GA(j,k) = \sum_{t=1}^{n} G(j,t)a_{tk}$$

$$= \sum_{t=i,j}^{n} G(j,t)a_{tk}$$

$$= sa_{ik} + ca_{tk}$$

$$= 0.$$

By choosing two rows of the matrix $A$ we can make a Given's rotation and make the $jk$th entry zero. It is very interesting to note that Given's rotation affects only the involved rows. So, by choosing pairs of distinct rows, Given's rotation can be applied in parallel and make the lower diagonal entries zero. If we want to vanish all the lower diagonal entries of the $k$th row, we can pair each of the rows $(k + 1)$, $(k + 2)$, ... , $n$ with another of the rows 1, 2, ... , $k$ and apply Given's rotation in parallel.

BEGIN
 For $j = k + 1$ to $n$ do in parallel
  ($i$ is a number from 1 to $k$ and distinct for each $j$.)
   Apply Given's rotation for $i$th and $j$th row.
  End parallel
END

The above algorithm segment makes the lower diagonal entries zero. Let us see the complexity of Given's rotation. The two matrices are

$$A = (a_{ij}) \qquad G = (g_{ij})$$

In the matrix product $GA$, only the $i$th and $j$th row of $A$ are altered and all other entries remain unaltered. We are going to evaluate $GA$ and store the entries in the same variables. So, the Given's rotation affects only the following entries of $A$.

$$a_{ik}\, a_{i,k+1} \ldots a_{in}$$
$$a_{jk}\, a_{j,k+1} \ldots a_{jn}.$$

So, we need not evaluate the matrix product $GA$. It is enough to evaluate only these entries of $GA$. But, the $i$th entry $GA$ is

$$(GA)_{it} = \sum_{q=i,j} g_{iq}a_{qt} \quad \text{where } t \geq k.$$

Similarly,

$$(GA)_{jt} = \sum_{q=i,j} g_{iq}a_{qt} \quad \text{where } t \geq k.$$

So, $(GA)_{it}$ and $(GA)_{jt}$ can be evaluated in constant time for each $t \geq k$.

The following program segment also implements the Given's rotation.

1. For $r = k$ to $n$ do in parallel
2. $a_{it} \leftarrow g_{ii} \, a_{it} + g_{ij} \, a_{jt}$
3. $a_{jt} \leftarrow g_{ji} \, a_{it} + g_{jj} \, a_{jt}$
4. End parallel

The Given's rotation for one pair of rows can hence be implemented in $O(1)$ time using $O(n)$ processors. All the lower diagonal entries of one row can be made zero by simultaneous Given's rotation of $[n/2]$ pairs of rows and therefore the complexity of converting all the lower diagonal-entries of one row to zero is $O(1)$ time using $O(n^2)$ processors. Hence the reduction of the given matrix into a lower diagonal matrix takes $O(n)$ time using $O(n^2)$ processors.

## 10.4  FOURIER TRANSFORMS

The square root of a negative number is not defined in the real field. However mathematicians have defined the imaginary number $i = \sqrt{-1}$ and developed a theory called *complex analysis*. It is surprising that these complex number theory is immensely useful in vital applications like digital image processing.

$(1)^{1/2}$ has two values $+1$ and $-1$. Similarly $1^{1/3}$ has three complex values. In general $1^{1/n}$ has $n$ roots. Let us denote them by $\omega, \omega^2, \omega^3, \ldots \omega^{n-1}, 1$. They are called the $n$th root of unity. $\omega$ is called the *primitive root of unity*. We can easily find that

$$\omega^k = \cos \frac{2k\pi}{n} + i \sin \frac{2k\pi}{n}.$$

Let us examine the case when $n = 3$:

$$\omega = \cos \frac{2.1.\pi}{3} + i \sin \frac{2.1.\pi}{3}$$

$$= \cos 120° + i \sin 120°$$

$$= \frac{-1}{2} + i \frac{\sqrt{3}}{2}$$

$$\omega^2 = \cos \frac{2.2.\pi}{n} + i \sin \frac{2.2.\pi}{n}$$

$$= \cos \frac{4\pi}{3} + i \sin \frac{4\pi}{3}$$

$$= \cos 240° + i \sin 240°$$

$$= \frac{-1}{2} - \frac{i\sqrt{3}}{2}$$

$$\omega^3 = \cos 2\pi + i \sin 2\pi$$

$$= 1$$

So, the cubic roots of unity are

$$\omega = \frac{-1}{2} + \frac{i\sqrt{3}}{2}$$

$$\omega^2 = \frac{-1}{2} - \frac{i\sqrt{3}}{2}$$

and

$$\omega^3 = 1$$

Similarly, the values of $(1)^{1/4}$ can be evaluated by using $n = 4$:

$$\omega = \cos \frac{2\pi}{4} + i \sin \frac{2\pi}{4} = \cos \frac{\pi}{2} + i \sin \frac{\pi}{2} = i$$

$$\omega^2 = \cos \pi + i \sin \pi = -1$$

$$\omega^3 = \cos \frac{3\pi}{2} + i \sin \frac{3\pi}{2} = -i$$

$$\omega^4 = \cos 2\pi + i \sin 2\pi = 1$$

So $i$, $-1$, $-i$ and $1$ are the fourth roots of unity. Let $W$ be a $n \times n$ matrix whose rows and columns are numbered from 0 to $(n-1)$, such that $W(i,j) = \omega^{ij}$, where $\omega$ is the primitive $n$th root of unity.

That is,

$$W(0,0) = \omega^o = 1$$
$$W(0,1) = \omega^o = 1$$
$$W(0,2) = \omega^o = 1.$$

More generally,

$$W(0,j) = 1 \text{ for } j = 0 \text{ to } n-1$$
$$W(i,o) = 1 \text{ for } i = 0 \text{ to } n-1$$
$$W(1,1) = \omega^1$$
$$W(1,2) = \omega^2$$
$$W(1,3) = \omega^3.$$

The $W$ matrix is shown below:

$$\begin{bmatrix} 1 & 1 & 1 & 1 & \cdots & 1 & \cdots & \cdots & 1 \\ 1 & \omega & \omega^2 & \omega^3 & \cdots & \omega^4 & \cdots & \cdots & \omega^{n-1} \\ 1 & \omega^2 & \omega^4 & \omega^6 & \cdots & \omega^8 & \cdots & \cdots & \omega^{2(n-1)} \\ \cdots & \cdots & \cdots & \cdots & \cdots & \cdots & \cdots & \cdots & \cdots \\ \cdots & \cdots & \cdots & \cdots & \cdots & \cdots & \cdots & \cdots & \cdots \\ 1 & \omega^{n-1} & \omega^{2(n-1)} & \cdots & \cdots & \cdots & \cdots & \cdots & \omega^{(n-1)(n-1)} \end{bmatrix}.$$

Using the fact that $\omega^n = 1$ we can get the $W$ matrix having the entries $\omega$, $\omega^2$, ..., $\omega^{n-1}$ and 1 only as follows:

$$\begin{bmatrix} 1 & 1 & 1 & 1 & \cdots & \cdots & \cdots & \cdots & 1 \\ 1 & \omega^1 & \omega^2 & \omega^3 & \cdots & \cdots & \cdots & \cdots & \omega^{n-1} \\ 1 & \omega^2 & \omega^4 & \omega^6 & \cdots & \cdots & \cdots & \cdots & \omega^{n-2} \\ \cdots & \cdots & \cdots & \cdots & \cdots & \cdots & \cdots & \cdots \\ \cdots & \cdots & \cdots & \cdots & \cdots & \cdots & \cdots & \cdots \end{bmatrix}.$$

Let

$$x = [x_0 x_1 \ldots x_{n-1}]$$

be a $n$ dimensional vector. The Discrete Fourier Transform of the vector $X$ is the vector $Y = WX$.

**Example**

Let $n = 3$, for which we have already evaluated $\omega = -1/2 + (\sqrt{3}/2)i$, $\omega^2 = -1/2 - (\sqrt{3}/2)i$, and $\omega^3 = 1$. The $W$ matrix will be

$$W = \begin{bmatrix} 1 & 1 & 1 \\ 1 & \omega & \omega^2 \\ 1 & \omega^2 & \omega \end{bmatrix}.$$

Let

$$x = \begin{bmatrix} x_0 \\ x_1 \\ x_2 \end{bmatrix}.$$

The Fourier Transform of $x$ is the vector

$$Y = WX = \begin{bmatrix} 1 & 1 & 1 \\ 1 & \omega & \omega^2 \\ 1 & \omega^2 & \omega \end{bmatrix} \begin{bmatrix} x_0 \\ x_1 \\ x_2 \end{bmatrix}.$$

That is,

$$Y_0 = x_0 + x_1 + x_2$$
$$Y_1 = x_0 + \omega x_1 + \omega^2 x_2$$
$$Y_2 = x_0 + \omega^2 x_1 + \omega x_2.$$

If

$$X = \begin{bmatrix} 1 \\ -1 \\ 0 \end{bmatrix},$$

then the Fourier Transform of $X$ is

$$Y = \begin{bmatrix} Y_0 \\ Y_1 \\ Y_2 \end{bmatrix},$$

where

$$Y_0 = x_0 + x_1 + x_2 = 1 - 1 + 0 = 0$$

$$Y_1 = x_0 + \omega x_1 + \omega^2 x_2$$

$$= 1 - \omega$$

$$= 1 + \frac{1}{2} - \frac{\sqrt{3}}{2} i = \frac{3}{2} - \frac{\sqrt{3}}{2} i$$

$$Y_2 = x_0 + \omega^2 x_1 + \omega x_2$$

$$= 1 - \omega^2$$

$$= 1 + \frac{1}{2} + \frac{\sqrt{3}}{2} i$$

$$= \frac{3}{2} + \frac{\sqrt{3}}{2} i.$$

The Fourier Transform of

$$X = \begin{bmatrix} 1 \\ -1 \\ 0 \end{bmatrix}$$

is the vector

$$Y = \begin{bmatrix} 0 \\ \dfrac{3}{2} - \dfrac{\sqrt{3}}{2} i \\ \dfrac{3}{2} + \dfrac{\sqrt{3}}{2} i \end{bmatrix}.$$

Let us now develop a parallel algorithm to find the Fourier Transform of a given vector $X$. Given the value of $n$, the value $\omega^k$ can be evaluated, using the formula

$$\omega^k = \cos \frac{2\pi k}{n} + i \sin \frac{2\pi k}{n}$$

for $k = 0$ to $n - 1$ in parallel using $n$ processors. Also the entries of the $W$ matrix can be evaluated by $n^2$ processors in parallel as

$$W(i,j) = \omega^{ij}, 0 \le i,j \le n - 1.$$

So, if $n^2$ processors are available, the $W$ matrix can be constructed in constant time. Fourier Transform is the product of the $n \times n$ matrix $W$ with the vector $X$. If we use the ordinary matrix multiplication, this work will be completed in $O(\log n)$ time using $O(n^2)$ processors. The parallel algorithm is shown below:

**Algorithm Fourier**
  **Input:**  $X(0:n-1)$
  **Output:**  $Y(0:n-1)$
    1. For $k = 0$ to $n - 1$ in parallel
    2. $\omega^k = \cos 2\pi k/n + i \sin 2\pi k/n$
    3. End parallel
    4. For $i = 0$ to $n - 1$ do in parallel
    5. For $j = 0$ to $n - 1$ do in parallel
    6. $W(i,j) = \omega^{ij}$
    7. End parallel
    8. End parallel
    9. For $i = 0$ to $n - 1$ do in parallel
   10. $Yi = \sum_{j=0}^{n-1} W(i,j) * x_j$
   11. End parallel

In the above algorithm step 10 is computed using the summation algorithm using $O(n)$ processors in $O(\log n)$ time. So, the overall time taken is $O(\log n)$ employing $O(n^2)$ processors.

***Efficient Parallel Algorithm for Fourier Transform.*** In this section we are going to develop a divide-and-conquer parallel algorithm which finds the Fourier Transform in the same time using fewer processors. That is, the algorithm developed here will work in $O(\log n)$ time, using only $O(n \log n)$ processors.

The structure of the $W$ matrix and the property $\omega^n = 1$ plays a major role in the development of the efficient parallel algorithm for Discrete Fourier Transforms. So, let us list the $W$ matrix for various values of $n$ first: When $n = 4$,

$$W = \begin{bmatrix} 1 & 1 & 1 & 1 \\ 1 & \omega & \omega^2 & \omega^3 \\ 1 & \omega^2 & 1 & \omega^2 \\ 1 & \omega^3 & \omega^3 & \omega \end{bmatrix}.$$

When $n = 8$,

$$W = \begin{bmatrix} 1 & 1 & 1 & 1 & 1 & 1 & 1 & 1 \\ 1 & \omega & \omega^2 & \omega^3 & \omega^4 & \omega^5 & \omega^6 & \omega^7 \\ 1 & \omega^2 & \omega^4 & \omega^6 & 1 & \omega^2 & \omega^4 & \omega^6 \\ 1 & \omega^3 & \omega^6 & \omega & \omega^4 & \omega^7 & \omega^2 & \omega^5 \\ 1 & \omega^4 & 1 & \omega^4 & 1 & \omega^4 & 1 & \omega^4 \\ 1 & \omega^5 & \omega^2 & \omega^7 & \omega^4 & \omega & \omega^6 & \omega^3 \\ 1 & \omega^6 & \omega^4 & \omega^2 & 1 & \omega^6 & \omega^4 & \omega^2 \\ 1 & \omega^7 & \omega^6 & \omega^5 & \omega^4 & \omega^3 & \omega^2 & \omega \end{bmatrix}.$$

Here using the value $w^4 = -1$ only in the odd rows we get,

$$\begin{bmatrix} 1 & 1 & 1 & 1 & 1 & 1 & 1 & 1 \\ 1 & \omega & \omega^2 & \omega^3 & -1 & -\omega & -\omega^2 & -\omega^3 \\ 1 & \omega^2 & \omega^4 & \omega^6 & 1 & \omega^2 & \omega^4 & \omega^6 \\ 1 & \omega^3 & -\omega^2 & \omega & -1 & -\omega^3 & \omega^2 & -\omega \\ 1 & -1 & 1 & -1 & 1 & -1 & 1 & -1 \\ 1 & -\omega & \omega^2 & -\omega^3 & -1 & \omega & -\omega^2 & \omega^3 \\ 1 & \omega^6 & \omega^4 & \omega^2 & 1 & \omega^6 & \omega^4 & \omega^2 \\ 1 & -\omega^3 & -\omega^2 & -\omega & -1 & \omega^3 & \omega^2 & \omega \end{bmatrix}.$$

We notice the following facts:

1. When $i$ is even and $0 \le i \le n-1$,
   $W(i,j) = W(i,2j)$ for $0 \le j \le n/2$.
2. When $i$ is odd and $0 \le i \le n-1$,
   $W(i,j) = -W(i,2j)$ for $0 \le j \le n/2$.

So, when $Y = WX$ is evaluated we have the following results:

1. When $i$ is even and $0 \le j \le n-1$,

$$y_i = \sum_{j=0}^{n/2-1} W(i,j)(x_j + x_{j+n/2}).$$

2. When $i$ is odd and $0 \le j \le n-1$,

$$y_i = \sum_{j=0}^{n/2-1} W(i,j)(x_j - x_{j+n/2}).$$

Also, we know that $\omega^2$ is the primitive $(n/2)$th root of unity. That is, the

$(n/2)$th roots of unity are $1, w^2, w^4, \ldots w^{n-2}$. Having this result in mind, let us assume that $i$ is a even integer such that $0 \le i \le n - 1$ and $i = 2t$, where $0 \le t \le n/2$.

$$y_i = \sum_{j=0}^{n/2-1} W(i,j) * (x_j + x_j + n/2)$$

$$= \sum_{j=0}^{n/2-1} \omega^{i,j} * (x_j + x_j + n/2)$$

$$y_{2t} = (\omega^2)^{tj} * (x_j + x_j + n/2)$$

$$y_{2t} = \sum_{j=0}^{n/2-1} (\omega^2)^{tj} * (x_i + x_j + n/2).$$

This show that

$$\begin{bmatrix} Y_0 \\ Y_2 \\ Y_4 \\ \vdots \\ Y_{n-2} \end{bmatrix}$$

is the Fourier transform of the vector

$$\begin{bmatrix} x_0 + x_{n/2} \\ x_1 + x_{n/2+1} \\ \cdots \\ \cdots \\ \cdots \\ x_j + x_{j+n/2} \\ x_{n/2-1} + x_{n-1} \end{bmatrix}.$$

Similarly, when $i$ is odd and $0 \le i \le n - 1$ such that $i = 2t + 1$ we can derive that

$$y_i = \sum_{j=0}^{n/2-1} (\omega^2)^{tj} * \omega^j (x_j + x_{j+n/2}).$$

This shows that

$$
\begin{bmatrix}
Y_1 \\
Y_3 \\
Y_5 \\
\vdots \\
Y_{n-1}
\end{bmatrix}
$$

is the Fourier Transform of

$$
\begin{pmatrix}
x_0 + x_{n/2} \\
\omega(x_1 - x_{n/2+1}) \\
\omega^2(x_2 - x_{n/2+2}) \\
\cdots\cdots\cdots\cdots \\
\cdots\cdots\cdots\cdots \\
\omega^{n/2-1}(x_{n/2-1}) + x_{n-1}
\end{pmatrix}.
$$

After evaluating the two Fourier transforms

$$
\begin{bmatrix}
Y_0 \\
Y \\
\vdots \\
Y_{n-2}
\end{bmatrix}
$$

and,

$$
\begin{bmatrix}
Y_1 \\
Y_3 \\
Y_5 \\
\vdots \\
Y_{n-1}
\end{bmatrix},
$$

we have evaluated the Fourier

$$
\begin{bmatrix}
y_0 \\
y_1 \\
\vdots \\
y_{n-1}
\end{bmatrix}
\text{ of }
\begin{pmatrix}
x_0 \\
x_1 \\
x_2 \\
\vdots \\
x_{n-1}
\end{pmatrix}.
$$

When $n = 2$, the process of evaluation of the Fourier transform of the vector

$$\begin{bmatrix} x_0 \\ x_1 \end{bmatrix}$$

is straight:

$$\begin{bmatrix} y_0 \\ y_1 \end{bmatrix} = \begin{bmatrix} x_0 + x_1 \\ x_0 - x_1 \end{bmatrix}.$$

Now we are fully equipped to write an efficient divide-and-conquer parallel algorithm to evaluate the Fourier transform of a given $n$ dimensional vector:

**Algorithm Efficient-FOURIER**
  **Input:** $x(0:1)$.
  **Output:** $Y(o:n-1)$.
   1. If $n = 2$ then

$$\begin{bmatrix} y_0 \\ y_1 \end{bmatrix} = \begin{bmatrix} x_0 + x_1 \\ x_0 - x_1 \end{bmatrix} \quad \text{and exit}$$

   2. Recursively evaluate the Fourier transform of the vector:

$$\begin{bmatrix} x_0 + x_{n/2} \\ x_1 + x_{n/2+1} \\ \cdots \\ \cdots \\ \cdots \\ x_j + x_{j+n/2} \\ x_{n/2-1} + x_{n-1} \end{bmatrix} \quad \text{and store as} \quad \begin{bmatrix} Y_0 \\ Y_2 \\ Y_4 \\ \vdots \\ Y_{n-2} \end{bmatrix}.$$

   3. Recursively evaluate the Fourier transform of the vector:

$$
\begin{bmatrix}
x_0 + x_{n/2} \\
\omega(x_1 - x_{n/2+1}x_{n/2} \\
\omega^2(x_1 - x_{n/2+1} \\
\cdots \\
\cdots \\
\cdots \\
x_j + x_{j+n/2} \\
\omega_{n/2-1}(x_{n/2-1} + x_{n-1})
\end{bmatrix}
\quad \text{and store as} \quad
\begin{bmatrix}
Y_1 \\
Y_3 \\
Y_5 \\
\vdots \\
Y_{n-1}
\end{bmatrix}.
$$

4. Output the vector $Y(o:n-1)$

**Complexity Analysis.** In the above algorithm steps 2 and 3 are independent of each other and so they can be done in parallel. The procedure divides the $n$-dimensional vector into two $(n/2)$-dimensional vectors and proceeds by recursion. So, the procedure takes $O(\log n)$ time and uses only $O(n \log n)$ processors. The EREW PRAM model can be used for the implementation.

Now let us see an interesting and frequently used application of Fourier transforms.

## 10.5 POLYNOMINAL MULTIPLICATION

Consider a polynominal $a(x)$ of degree $n$:

$$
a(x) = a_0 + a_1 x + a_2 x^2 + \ldots + a_n x^n.
$$

It is assumed that $a_n \neq 0$ (because the polynomial is of degree $n-1$ otherwise). This section deals with the problem of multiplying two polynomials of degree $n$ and $m$, respectively. Let

$$
a(x) = a_0 + a_1 x + a_2 x^2 + \ldots + a_n x^n.
$$
$$
b(x) = b_0 + b_1 x + b_2 x^2 + \ldots + b_m x^m.
$$

The product $a(x)b(x)$ is a $(m+n)$ degree polynomial defined by $a(x)b(x) = c(x) = c_0 + c_1 x + c_2 x^2 + \ldots + c_{m+n} x^{m+n}$, where

$$c_0 = a_0b_0$$
$$c_1 = a_0b_1 + a_1b_0$$
$$c_2 = a_0b_2 + a_1b_1 + a_2b_0$$
$$c_3 = a_0b_3 + a_1b_2 + a_2b_1 + a_3b_0$$
$$\cdots$$
$$\cdots$$

In general,

$$c_k = \sum_{j=0}^{k} a_j b_{k-1}.$$

Where $0 \leq k \leq m+n$ assuming that $a_i = 0$ for $i > n$, and $b_j = 0$ for $j > m$. If we try to solve the problem straight from the formula for $c_k$, each can be evaluated in parallel using $m + n$ groups of processors. In each group to calculate $c_k$, we need $k$ processors simultaneously to work for $O(\log k)$ time. So, the straight method takes $O(\log(m+n))$ time and $O(m+n)^2$ processors, because the maximum value for $k$ is $m + n$. Such an algorithm is stated below:

**Algorithm ST-POLY-MUL**
   **Input:**  $A(0:n)$ and $B(o:m)$
   **Output:**  $C(0:m+n)$

BEGIN
   1. Assign $A(n + 1 : n + m) = 0$
   2. Assign $B(m + 1 : n + m) = 0$
   3. For $k = 0$ to $m + n$ do in parallel
   4. Evaluate $c_k = \sum_{j=0}^{k} a_j b_{k-j}$.
   5. End parallel

The Fourier Transforms can be effectively used here to evaluate the product of two polynomials in $O(\log(m + n))$ time using only $O((m + n) \log (m + n))$ processors. The reader can easily verify that the implementation can be successfully done in an EREW PRAM model.

*Efficient Algorithm for Polynomial Multiplication.* The efficient Fourier transform algorithm that has already been discussed considers the vector of order $k$. Let $a(x)$ and $b(x)$ be two polynomial of degree $n$ and $m$, respectively. They are denoted by the arrays $a[o:n]$ and $b[o:m]$. Let $N$ be a integer such that $N$ is a power of 2 and $(n + m) < N \leq 2(n + m)$. Assign $a[n + 1 : N - 1] = b[m + 1 : n - 1] = 0$. Now compute the Fourier transform of the vectors $a$ and $b$, $Y = Wa$ and $Z = Wb$.
The following results are observed:

1. $y_i = (a(\omega)^i, \qquad 0 \leq i \leq N - 1$
2. $z_i = b(\omega^i), \qquad 0 \leq i \leq N - 1.$

Let us denote the vector $u = (u_0, u_1, \ldots u_{n-1})^T$ where $u_i = y_i z_i$. If $u = Wc$, where $c = [c_1, c_2, \ldots C_{n-1}]^T$ then $u(\omega_j) = a(\omega^i) b(\omega^j j)$. So we can verify that if $c$ is determined then $c$ is the product of the two polynomials $a$ and $b$. The first $m + n$ entries of the vector $c$ are taken as the coefficients of the product polynomial $c(x)$.

### Algorithm EFFICIENT-POLY-MUL
**Input:** $a[0:n]$, $b[0:m]$
**Output:** $c[0:m+n]$.
1. Let $N$ be the integer which is power of 2 such that $(m + n) < N \leq 2(m + n)$
2. Assign $a[n + 1 : N] = b[m + 1 : N] = 0$
3. Compute the Fourier transform of $a$, $Y = Wa$ using the efficient algorithm.
4. Compute the Fourier transform of $b$, $Z = Wb$ using the efficient algorithm.
5. For $i = 1$ to $N$ do in parallel.
6. $u_i = y_i z_i$
7. End parallel
8. Evaluate the inverse Fourier transform of $u$. i.e determine the vector $c$ such that $u = Wc$
9. $c[0:m+n]$ is the coefficient vector of the product polynomial $c(x)$

END

The efficient parallel algorithm to compute the Fourier transform takes $O(\log N)$ time using $O(N \log N)$ processors. The inverse Fourier transform can be evaluated similarly in $O(\log N)$ time using $O(N \log N)$ processors. Because of the choice of $N$ we have the following result:

If $a[x]$ and $b[x]$ are polynomial of degree $n$ and $m$, respectively, the product of the polynomial $c(x) = a(x)b(x)$ can be computed in parallel in $O(\log(m+n))$ using $O((m + n) \log(m + N))$ processors.

The reader can verify that the EREW PRAM model is sufficient to implement the algorithm.

If $a[o:n]$ and $b[o:m]$ are two vectors then the *convolution* of $a$ and $b$ is denoted by $a \times b$ and defined to be the vector $c = c[0:m+n+1]$, where $c[0:m+n]$ is the product of the polynomials represented by $a$ and $b$ and $c(m + n + 1) = 0$. The term *convolution* is used in several applications. The complexity of the evaluation of the convolution of two vectors is the same as that of the polynomial multiplication.

## 10.6  MATRIX INVERSION

Gauss Jordan elimination method can be used to find the inverse of a matrix.

$$A = \begin{bmatrix} a_{11}, & a_{12}, & a_{13}, & \ldots & a_{1n}, \\ a_{21}, & a_{22}, & a_{23}, & \ldots & a_{2n}, \\ a_{31}, & a_{32}, & a_{33}, & \ldots & a_{3n}, \\ \ldots & \ldots & \ldots & \ldots & \ldots \\ \ldots & \ldots & \ldots & \ldots & \ldots \\ a_{n1}, & a_{n2}, & a_{n3} & \ldots & a_{nn} \end{bmatrix}.$$

Consider the matrix:

$$A^{-1} A = \begin{bmatrix} 1, & 0, & 0, & \ldots & 0 \\ 0, & 1, & 0, & \ldots & 0 \\ 0, & 0, & 1, & \ldots & 0 \\ \ldots & \ldots & \ldots & \ldots & \ldots \\ \ldots & \ldots & \ldots & \ldots & \ldots \\ 0, & 0, & 0, & \ldots & 1 \end{bmatrix}.$$

Substituting value of $A$,

$$A^{-1} \begin{bmatrix} a_{11}, & a_{12}, & a_{13}, & \ldots & a_{1n}, \\ a_{21}, & a_{22}, & a_{23}, & \ldots & a_{2n}, \\ a_{31}, & a_{32}, & a_{33}, & \ldots & a_{3n}, \\ \ldots & \ldots & \ldots & \ldots & \ldots \\ \ldots & \ldots & \ldots & \ldots & \ldots \\ a_{n1}, & a_{n2}, & a_{n3}, & \ldots & a_{nn} \end{bmatrix} = \begin{bmatrix} 1, & 0, & 0, & \ldots & 0 \\ 0, & 1, & 0, & \ldots & 0 \\ 0, & 0, & 1, & \ldots & 0 \\ \ldots & \ldots & \ldots & \ldots & \ldots \\ \ldots & \ldots & \ldots & \ldots & \ldots \\ 0, & 0, & 0, & \ldots & 1 \end{bmatrix}.$$

Now using Gauss Jordan method, make the $A$ matrix of the left-hand side into an identity matrix. Do all the row operation to the right-hand side matrix also. We get:

$$A^{-1} \begin{bmatrix} 1, & 0, & 0, & \ldots & 0 \\ 0, & 1, & 0, & \ldots & 0 \\ 0, & 0, & 1, & \ldots & 0 \\ \ldots & \ldots & \ldots & \ldots & \ldots \\ \ldots & \ldots & \ldots & \ldots & \ldots \\ 0, & 0, & 0, & \ldots & 1 \end{bmatrix} = \begin{bmatrix} \ldots & \ldots & \ldots & \ldots & \ldots \\ \ldots & \ldots & \ldots & \ldots & \ldots \\ \ldots & \ldots & \ldots & \ldots & \ldots \\ \ldots & \ldots & \ldots & \ldots & \ldots \\ \ldots & \ldots & \ldots & \ldots & \ldots \\ \ldots & \ldots & \ldots & \ldots & \ldots \end{bmatrix}.$$

That is, the right-hand side matrix is $A^{-1}$. The algorithm consists of the following steps:

1. Read the matrix $A$
2. Let $B$ denote the matrix in the *RHS*. Initially assign $B$ = identity matrix.
3. Do the row operations for $A$ and continue the same for $B$ matrix also, so that finally $A$ reduces to the identity matrix.

The algorithm to reduce $A$ into an identify matrix row operations is similar to the Gauss Elimination method. The parallel algorithm is given below:

**Algorithm MATRIX-INVERSE**
**Input:** Matrix $A(1:n, 1:n)$
**Output:** Matrix $A^{-1}(1:n, 1:n)$

BEGIN
1. Assign $A^{-1}$ = identity matrix.
2. For $k = 1$ to $n$
3. For $i = 1$ to $n$ but $i \neq k$ do in parallel
4. do row operation for the matrices $A$ and $A^{-1}$
$R_i \leftarrow R_i - (a_{ik}/a_{kk})R_k$
5. End parallel
6. Next $k$.
END

In the above algorithm step 1 can be done in $O(1)$ time using $(n^2)$ processors. Step 4 is the row operation that needs $O(n)$ processor to complete in $O(1)$ time. So, steps 3 to 5 can be implemented by $O(n^2)$ processors in unit time. So the overall complexity of this algorithm is $O(n)$ time using $O(n^2)$ processors. This can be implemented in a CREW PRAM.

***Inverse of a Triangular Matrix.*** Consider a lower triangular square matrix, of order $n$ where $n$ is assumed to be a power of 2 for convenience.

$$\begin{bmatrix} a_{11} & 0 & 0 & \ldots & 0 \\ a_{21} & a_{22} & 0 & \ldots & 0 \\ a_{31} & a_{32} & a_{33} & \ldots & 0 \\ \ldots & \ldots & \ldots & \ldots & \ldots \\ \ldots & \ldots & \ldots & \ldots & \ldots \\ a_{n1} & a_{n2} & a_{n3} & \ldots & a_{nn} \end{bmatrix}.$$

Let us divide the matrix into four submatrices each of order $(n/2) \times (n/2)$.

$$A = \begin{bmatrix} A_1 & 0 \\ A_2 & A_3 \end{bmatrix}.$$

Since $A$ is nonsingular $A_1$ $A_3$ are also nonsingular. So, let us first evaluate $A_1^{-1}$ and $A_3^{-1}$:

$$\begin{bmatrix} A_1 & 0 \\ A_2 & A_3 \end{bmatrix} \begin{bmatrix} A_1^{-1} & 0 \\ -A_3^{-1} A_2 A_1^{-1} & A_3^{-1} \end{bmatrix} = \begin{bmatrix} I_{n/2} & 0 \\ 0 & I_{n/2} \end{bmatrix} = I_n.$$

So,

$$A^{-1} = \begin{bmatrix} A_1^{-1} & 0 \\ -A_3^{-1} A_2 A_1^{-1} & A_3^{-1} \end{bmatrix}.$$

So, the work of finding the inverse of $A$ can be split into the following steps:

1. Evaluate $A_{1-1}$ and $A_{3-1}$.
2. Evaluate $A_2 A_{1-1}$.
3. Evaluate $-A_{3-1A2} A^{-1}$.

In order to evaluate $A_{-1}^1$ and $A_{-1}^3$, we recursively use the same method. Since we are dividing the order of matrix by two during each recursive call, there are $\log n$ recursive steps. In each step we find the inverse of two smaller matrices and also evaluate the product of two smaller matrices in step 2 and also in step 3 shown above. The best known parallel algorithm to evaluate the product of two $n \times n$ matrices takes $O(\log n)$ time using $O(n^3)$ processor in CREW PRAM model.

If $T(n)$ denotes the computing time of the parallel algorithm to evaluate the inverse of a matrix of order $n$ the above discussion implies that:

$$T(n) = 2T(n/2) + 3O(\log n)$$
$$= 2\{2T(n/4) + 3)(\log n)\} + 3O(\log n).$$

This recursive equation can be solved to get $T(n) = O(\log^2 n)$. Hence the fast parallel algorithm described above works in $O(\log^2 n)$ time using $O(n^3)$ processors.

**Algorithm Triangular-Matrix-Inverse**
  **Input:**   Lower triangular matrix $A(1:n, 1:n)$.
  **Output:**   $A^{-1}(1:n, 1:n)$.
   1. Split $A$ as $A = \begin{bmatrix} A_1 & 0 \\ A_2 & A_3 \end{bmatrix}$

   2. Evaluate recursively $A^{-1}$ and $A_{3-1}$.
   3. Evaluate $A_2 A_1^{-1}$.
   4. Evaluate $-A_3^{-1} A_2 A_1^{-1}$.

5. $A^{-1} = \begin{bmatrix} A_1^{-1} & 0 \\ -A_3^{-1} & A_2 A_1^{-1} & A_3^{-1} \end{bmatrix}$

6. return $A^{-1}$

## 10.7  TOEPLITZ MATRIX

There is another interesting class of matrices which occur frequently in numerical problems of the signal processing applications. It is called *Toeplitz matrix*. Let us develop in this section a better algorithm to find the inverse of a triangular Topelitz matrix. Consider the following matrix:

$$\begin{bmatrix} a_{n-1}, & a_{n-2}, & a_{n-3}, & \ldots & a_1 & a_0 \\ a_n, & a_{n-1}, & a_{n-2}, & \ldots & a_2, & a_1, \\ a_{n+1}, & a_n, & a_{n-1}, & \ldots & a_3, & a_2, \\ \ldots & \ldots & \ldots & \ldots & \ldots & \ldots \\ \ldots & \ldots & \ldots & \ldots & \ldots & \ldots \\ a_{2n-2}, & a_{2n-3}, & a_{2n-4}, & \ldots & a_n, & a_{n-1} \end{bmatrix}.$$

The above matrix has only $(2n - 2)$ distinct entries. The matrix satisfies the following conditions:

$$A(i,j) = A(i+1, j+1) \qquad \text{for any } i,j = 1,2\ldots,n-1$$

All the diagonal entries are equal. Instead of representing a Toeplitz matrix by a $n \times n$ table, we can represent it by a vector of order $2n - 1$. That is,

$$A = [a_0, a_1, a_2, \ldots a_{2n-1}]^T$$

Example of a Toeplitz matrix:

| 29 | 13 | 8 | 9 | 5 |
|---|---|---|---|---|
| 15 | 29 | 13 | 8 | 9 |
| 1 | 15 | 29 | 13 | 8 |
| −1 | 1 | 15 | 29 | 13 |
| −11 | −1 | 1 | 15 | 29 |

That is a $5 \times 5$ Toeplitz. This can be represented by the vector [5, 9, 8, 13, 29, 15, 1, −1, 11]. The special structure of the Toeplitz matrix can be effectively exploited to design an efficient parallel algorithm. Consider a general matrix

$A(0:n-1, 0:n-1)$ and a vector $x = (x_0, x_1 \ldots x_{n-1})$. The straightforward matrix multiplication algorithm can be used to evaluate the product $Ax$ as follows:

**Algorithm Matrix-Vector-Product**
  **Input:**   $A(0:n-1, 0:n-1)$ and $x(0:n-1)$
  **Output:**   The product $Ax$ denoted by the vector $Y(0:n-1)$
    1. For $i = 0$ to $n-1$ do in parallel
    2. $y_i = \sum_{j=0}^{n-1} a_{ij}x_j$
    3. End parallel

In the above straightforward algorithm works in $O(\log n)$ time using $O(n^2)$ processors. The peculiar nature of the Toeplitz matrix can be exploited to decrease the number of processors needed. Let $A$ be a $n \times n$ square Toeplitz matrix. We have seen already that it can be represented by a vector. So let us denote the vector that represents the matrix $A$ by

$$a = [a_0, a_1 \ldots a_{2n-2}].$$

**THEOREM 10.7.1**  *Let $a = [a_0, a_1, \ldots a_{2n-2}]$ be the vector that represents a Toeplitz square matrix $A$ of order $n$. Let $x = (x_0, x_1, x_{n-1})$ be a vector. If the convolution of $a$ and $x$ is $y = ax$ then*

$$\begin{bmatrix} y_{n-1} \\ y_n \\ \vdots \\ y_{2n-2} \end{bmatrix} = Ax.$$

*Proof.* In the Toeplitz matrix $A$, the $k$th the row is $(a_{k+n-1} \ldots a_{k+1}\ a_k)$. So in the matrix product $C = Ax$ we get:

$$c_k = a_{k+n-1}x_0 + a_{k+n-2}x_1 + \ldots + a_k x_{n-1}.$$

By the definition of convolution, we have

$$y_{k+n-1} = a_{k+n-1}x_0 + a_{k+n-2}x_1 + \ldots + a_k x_k.$$

Hence the proof is complete.

Because of the above theorem Evaluation of the product of a Toeplitz matrix and a vector is equivalent to the evaluation of the convolution of two vectors and so we have the following theorem:

**THEOREM 10.7.2** *The product of $n \times n$ Toeplitz matrix and a vector of dimension $n$ can be computed in $O(\log n)$ time using $O(n \log n)$ processors.*

### 10.7.1 Lower Triangular Toeplitz Matrix

Consider a lower triangular Toeplitz matrix

$$\begin{bmatrix} a_0 & 0 & 0 & \dots & 0 \\ a_1 & a_0 & 0 & \dots & 0 \\ a_2 & a_1 & a_0 & \dots & 0 \\ \dots & \dots & \dots & \dots & \dots \\ \dots & \dots & \dots & \dots & \dots \\ a_{n-1} & a_{n-2} & a_{n-3}, & \dots & a_0 \end{bmatrix}.$$

The Toeplitz matrix is uniquely represented by its first column $[a_0, a_1, a_2, \dots, a_{n-1}]$. We are going to use the divide-and-conquer strategy to find the inverse of $A$. Let us partition $A$ into four blocks:

$$\begin{bmatrix} A_1 & 0 \\ A_2 & A_1 \end{bmatrix}.$$

The above partition is possible because of the Toeplitz nature of $A$. In the above partitioning $A_1$ is a lower Triangular Toeplitz matrix $A_2$ is a Toeplitz matrix.

Applying the result of inverse of a lower triangular matrix we have

$$A^{-1} = \begin{bmatrix} A_1^{-1} & 0 \\ -A_1^{-1} A_2 A_1^{-1} & A_1^{-1} \end{bmatrix}.$$

We must first recursively evaluate the inverse of $A_1$ (which is also a lower triangular Toeplitz matrix). As $A_1$ is a Toeplitz lower matrix it is efficient if we find the first column of $A_1^{-1}$. After evaluating $A_1^{-1}$, we have to evaluate the first column of $A_1^{-1} A_2 A_1^{-1}$. This can be in the following steps:

Let $e = [1, 0, 0, \dots 0]^T$. First compute $A_1^{-1}$. This will give the first column of $A_1^{-1}$. Then evaluate $A_2(A_1^{-1})$. This is also a product of a Toeplitz matrix and a vector. Then evaluate $A_1^{-1}(A_2(A_1^{-1}e))$. By associativity we have

$$A_1^{-1} A_2 A_1^{-1} e = A_1^{-1}(A_1(A_1 e)).$$

**Algorithm Tria-Toeplitz**
    **Input:** $A[0:n-1]$.
    **Output:** $A^{-1}[0:n-1]$.

1. Divide the matrix $A$ into the form $\begin{bmatrix} A_1 \& 0 \\ A_2 \& A_1 \end{bmatrix}$
2. Evaluate $A_{1-1}$ recursively
3. Let $e = [1, 0, 0, 0 \ldots]^T$
4. Evaluate $(A_1^{-1}e)$
5. Evaluate $A_1(A_1^{-1}e)$
6. Evaluate $A_1^{-1}(A_2^{-1}e))$
7. $A^{-1}[0:n/2-1] = (A_1^{-1}e)$
8. $A^{-1}[n/2:n-1] = A_1^{-1}(A_2(A_1^{-1}e)$.

END

In the above algorithm, the order of the matrix is halved each time of the recursive call and so there are $O(\log n)$ recursive call in the implementation. Steps 4, 5, and 6 are the evaluation of the product of a Toeplitz matrix and a vector and, hence, they can be done in $O(\log n)$ time using $O(n \log n)$ processors using EREW PRAM model. Since, there are $\log n$ recursive calls the inverse of the triangular Toeplitz matrix can be evaluated in EREW PRAM model in $O(\log^2 n)$ time using $O(n \log n)$ processors.

## 10.8  TRIDIAGONAL SYSTEMS

In several scientific experiments the final system of linear equations are of the following form:

$$a_{11}x_1 + a_{12}x_2 = b_1$$
$$a_{21}x_1 + a_{22}x_2 + a_{23}x_3 = b_2$$
$$a_{32}x_2 + a_{33}x_3 + a_{34}x_4 = b_3$$
$$a_{43}x_3 + a_{44}x_4 + a_{45}x_5 = b_4$$
$$\cdots\cdots\cdots\cdots\cdots\cdots\cdots\cdots\cdots\cdots\cdots\cdots$$
$$\cdots\cdots\cdots\cdots\cdots\cdots\cdots\cdots\cdots\cdots\cdots$$
$$a_{n-1,n-2}x_{n-2} + a_{n-1,n-1}x_{n-1} + a_{n-1,n}x_n = b_{n-1}$$
$$a_{n,n-1}x_{n-1} + a_{nn}x_n = b_n.$$

In general, the $i$th equation is of the form

$$a_{i,i-1}x_{i-1} + a_{i,i}x_i + a_{i,i+1}x_{i+1} = b_i,$$

where $1 < i < n$. When $i = 1$ or $i = n$, the equation contains only two terms. As an example, let us look at a system where $n = 6$.

$$3x_1 + 2x_2 = 1$$
$$x_1 + 2x_2 + 4x_3 = 3$$
$$12x_2 + 3x_3 + 2x_4 = 8$$
$$7x_3 - 3x_4 + 12x_5 = 2$$
$$2x_4 + 5x_5 + x_6 = 4$$
$$x_5 - x_6 = 12$$

Here, the system can be expressed in matrix form as follows:

$$
\begin{pmatrix}
3 & 2 & 0 & 0 & 0 & 0 \\
1 & 2 & 4 & 0 & 0 & 0 \\
0 & 12 & 3 & 2 & 0 & 0 \\
0 & 0 & 7 & -3 & 12 & 0 \\
0 & 0 & 0 & 2 & 5 & 1 \\
0 & 0 & 0 & 0 & 1 & -1
\end{pmatrix}
\begin{pmatrix}
x_1 \\ x_2 \\ x_3 \\ x_4 \\ x_5 \\ x_6
\end{pmatrix}
=
\begin{pmatrix}
1 \\ 3 \\ 8 \\ 2 \\ 4 \\ 12
\end{pmatrix}.
$$

Notice that the coefficient matrix has only the diagonal and it neighboring elements. This is called a *tridiagonal matrix*. This system of equations is called a *tridiagonal system*.

### 10.8.1 Gauss Elimination

If a tridiagonal system is to be solved, we can use the usual Gauss elimination strategy to eliminate the lower diagonal elements. In each column, only one lower diagonal element is present and it can be eliminated. Then we can apply the back substitution method to get the solution. The algorithm for solving the tridiagonal system using Gauss elimination method is formally shown below:

**Algorithm Tridiagonal—G**
  **Input:** $a(1:n, 1:n)$, $b(1:n)$.
  **Output:** $x(1:n)$.
  1. Use Gauss elimination method to reduce the matrix $a$ into an upper triangular matrix.
  2. Use Back substitution method now to solve the system.

***Complexity Analysis.*** For doing any row operation, we need $O(n)$ time. So, for step 1 of the algorithm $O(n^2)$ time is needed. The back substitution needs

$O(n^2)$ time. So, the time taken by Algorithm Tridiagonal-G is $O(n^2)$ in the sequential case. In a parallel model CREW PRAM, this can be implemented in $O(n)$ time using $O(n)$ processors.

Gauss elimination method is inherently sequential. This means that only after doing the row operation on column 1, we can do to column 2, and so on. There is no possibility of doing them simultaneously. So, this method does not suit for a parallel computer. Now let us discuss another method of solving a tridiagonal system of linear equations which is suitable for a parallel computer.

## 10.8.2 Odd–Even Reduction Method

The odd–even reduction, discussed in this section starts wtih a course of arithmetic manipulations on the coefficient matrix, which leads to the division of the system into two subsystems which could be solved in parallel separately. For example, suppose a tridiagonal system of 16 variables is given. Let the variables be $x_1, x_2 \ldots x_{16}$. There are 16 equations in these 16 variables. We will do some arithmetic manipulations on the coefficient matrix. When this arithmetic work is over, the system is divided into two subsystems as follows:

**Subsystem 1**

> *variables*: $x_1, x_3, x_5, x_7, x_9, x_{11}, x_{13}, x_{15}$
>
> *equations*: eight equations in these eight variables.

**Subsystem 2**

> *variables*: $x_2, x_4, x_6, x_8, x_{10}, x_{12}, x_{14}, x_{16}$
>
> *equations*: eight equations in these eight variables.

If these subsystems are solved separately, then we can get the solution of the original system; that is values of $x_1, x_2, \ldots x_{16}$.

In order to solve each of the above two subsystems, we can use the same strategy. That is, do some arithmetic manipulations so that the subsystem 1 divides into two smaller systems of 4 variables each. We can go on dividing the system, until we arrive at systems with only 2 variables, which can be solved in constant time.

Having seen the outline of the technique, let us go into the technical details of the calculations. Let the system be

$$b_1 x_1 + c_1 x_2 = r_1$$
$$a_2 x_1 + b_2 x_2 + c_2 x_3 = r_2$$
$$a_3 x_2 + b_3 x_3 + c_3 x_4 = r_3$$
$$a_4 x_3 + b_4 x_4 + c_4 x_5 = r_4$$
$$\cdots\cdots\cdots\cdots\cdots$$
$$\cdots\cdots\cdots\cdots\cdots$$
$$a_i x_{i-1} + b_i x_i + c_i x_{i+1} = r_i$$
$$\cdots\cdots\cdots\cdots\cdots$$
$$\cdots\cdots\cdots\cdots\cdots$$
$$\cdots\cdots\cdots\cdots\cdots$$
$$a_{n-1} x_{n-2} + b_{n-1} x_{n-1} + c_{n-1} x_n = r_{n-1}$$
$$a_n x_{n-1} + b_n x_n = r_n.$$

This can be expressed as,

$$b_1 x_1 + c_1 x_2 = r_1$$
$$a_i x_{i-1} + b_i x_i + c_i x_{i+1} = r_i$$
$$\text{(for } i = 2, 3, \ldots (n-1))$$
$$a_n x_{n-1} + b_n x_n = r_n.$$

If we permit dummy variables $x_0$ and $x_{n+1}$ with zero values, we have

$$a_i x_{i-1} + b_i x_i + c_i x_{i+1} = r_i,$$

where $1 \le i \le n$.

The $(i-1)$th equation, $i$th equation and the $(i+1)$th equation are,

$$a_{i-1} x_{i-2} + b_{i-1} x_{i-1} + c_{i-1} x_i = r_{i-1}$$
$$a_i x_{i-1} + b_i x_i + c_i x_{i+1} = r_i$$
$$a_{i+1} x_i + b_{i+1} x_{i+1} + c_{i+1} x_{i+2} = r_{i+1}.$$

Finding the value of $x_{i-1}$ from the $(i-1)$th equation

$$x_{i-1} = f(x_i, x_{i-2}),$$

where $f$ is a linear function of $x_i$ and $x_{i-2}$.

Similarly, the value of $x_{i+1}$ from the $(i+1)$th equation is

$$x_{i+1} = g(x_i, x_{i+2}),$$

where $g$ is a linear function of $x_i$ and $x_{i+2}$.

Substituting these values of $x_{i-1}$ and $x_{i+1}$ in the $i$th equation, we get an equation of $x_{i-2}$, $x_i$ and $x_{i+2}$.

Let us rename the coefficients of these equations as $a_i$, $b_i$, $c_i$ and the right-hand-side element $r_i$. Let us also introduce dummy variable $x_{-1}$ and $x_{n+2}$ with zero values.

We now get

$$a_i x_{i-2} + b_i x_i + c_i x_{i+2} = r_i \qquad o \le i \le n.$$

Let us now write these equations explicitly.

$$a_1 x_{-1} + b_1 x_1 + c_1 x_3 = r_1$$
$$a_2 x_0 + b_2 x_2 + c_2 x_4 = r_2$$
$$a_3 x_1 + b_3 x_3 + c_3 x_5 = r_3$$
$$a_4 x_2 + b_4 x_4 + c_4 x_6 = r_4$$
$$a_5 x_3 + b_5 x_5 + c_5 x_7 = r_5$$
$$a_6 x_4 + b_6 x_6 + c_6 x_8 = r_6$$
$$a_7 x_5 + b_7 x_7 + c_7 x_9 = r_7$$
$$a_8 x_6 + b_8 x_8 + c_8 x_{10} = r_8.$$

Now the above system of equations can be classified into two subsystems. Equations 1, 3, 5, ... form the equations with $x_1, x_3, x_5, x_7 \ldots$ and so they form subsystem 1. Subsystem 2 consists of equations 2, 4, 6, ... . They are shown below;

| *Subsystem 1* | *Subsystem2* |
|---|---|
| $a_1 x_{-1} + b_1 x_1 + c_1 x_3 = r_1$ | $a_2 x_0 + b_2 x_2 + c_2 x_4 = r_2$ |
| $a_3 x_1 + b_3 x_3 + c_3 x_5 = r_3$ | $a_4 x_2 + b_4 x_4 + c_4 x_6 = r_4$ |
| $a_5 x_3 + b_5 x_5 + c_5 x_7 = r_5$ | $a_6 x_4 + b_6 x_6 + c_6 x_8 = r_6$ |
| . . . . . . . . . . . . . | . . . . . . . . . . . . . |
| . . . . . . . . . . . . | . . . . . . . . . . . . |
| . . . . . . . . . . . | . . . . . . . . . . . . . |

Let us solve a problem using this method, so that the method becomes more clear.

**Solved Problem.** Solve the following system of simultaneous equations using odd–even reduction method.

$$4x_1 + x_2 = 2 \qquad \dots (i)$$
$$4x_1 + 11x_2 - 5x_3 = 7 \qquad \dots (ii)$$
$$2x_2 + 14x_3 - 6x_4 = 13 \qquad \dots (iii)$$
$$5x_3 + 18x_4 = 24 \qquad \dots (iv).$$

Here there are four equations and four variables. For equation (i), we must substitute the value of $x_2$ from equation (ii). Equation (ii) is

$$4x_1 + 11x_2 - 5x_3 = 7$$

$$x_2 = \frac{1}{11} \{7 - 4x_1 + 5x_3\}.$$

Substituting in equation (i) we get

$$4x_i + \frac{1}{11} \{7 - 4x_1 + 5x_3\} = 2.$$

That is,

$$\frac{40}{11} x_1 + \frac{5}{11} x_3 = \frac{15}{11}.$$

That is,

$$40x_1 + 5x_3 = 15.$$

This can also be written as

$$8x_1 + x_3 = 3 \dots (v).$$

This is the new form of the first equation.

Now we must reformulate equation (ii). In equation (ii) the value of $x_1$ must be substituted from equation (i) and the value of $x_3$ from equation (iii).

(i) implies, $x_1 = \frac{1}{4}\{2 - x_2\}$
(iii) implies, $x_3 = \frac{1}{14}\{13 - 2x_2 + 6x_4\}.$

Applying these two in equation (ii) we get

$$\{2 - x_2\} + 11x_2 - \frac{5}{14} \{13 - 2x_2 + 6x_4\} = 7$$

$$10x_2 - 2x_4 = 9 \dots (vi).$$

Now let us transform equation (iii). For this, we must substitute $x_2$ from equation (ii) and substitute $x_4$ from equation (iv). Thus we get

$$-24x_1 + 547x_3 = 651 \ldots (vii).$$

In equation (iv) we must replace $x_3$ using equation (iii). We get

$$-10x_2 + 282x_4 = 271 \ldots (viii).$$

Now equations (v) and (vii) form subsystem 1 and the subsystem 2 is the equations (vi) and (viii).

| *Subsystem 1* | *Subsystem2* |
|---|---|
| $8x_1 + x_3 = 3$ | $10x_2 - 2x_4 = 9$ |
| $-24x_1 + 547x_3 = 651$ | $-10x_2 + 282x_4 = 271.$ |

Each of the above subsystem is of two variables and two equations and so we can immediately solve to get the following solutions.

| *Subsystem 1* | *Subsystem 2* |
|---|---|
| $x_1 = \frac{9}{40}$ | $x_2 = \frac{11}{10}$ |
| $x_3 = \frac{6}{5}$ | $x_4 = 1.$ |

These two solutions together give the solution of the original system.

| $x_1 = \frac{9}{40}$ | $x_2 = \frac{11}{10}$ | $x_3 = \frac{6}{5}$ | $x_4 = 1$ |
|---|---|---|---|

The above method well suits parallel implementation. The calculations involved in the coefficient matrix for dividing into subsystems can be done in constant time using $O(n^2)$ processors in parallel. Successive division of subsystems lead to subsystems of 2 variables in $O(\log n)$ steps. So, the overall time complexity of the parallel implementation is $O(\log n)$. This can be implemented using $O(n^2)$ processors in CREW PRAM.

# BIBLIOGRAPHY

Ames, W. F. (1977) *Numerical Methods for Partial Differential Equations*, Academic Press, New York.

Bini, D. (1984) Parallel Solution of Certain Toeplitz Linear Systems, *SIAM J. of Comput*, **13(2)**, 268–276.

Borodin, A. and Munro, I. (1975) *The Computational Complexity of Algebraic and Numeric Problems*, Elsevier, New York.

Borodin, A. J. Von Zur Gathen and Hopercoft, J. H. (1975) *Fast Parallel Matrix and gcd Computation*, Elsevier, New York.

Chin-Wen, H. and Lee, R. D. T. (1990) A Parallel Algorithm for Solving Sparse Triangular Systems, *IEEE Trans. on Computers*, **39.**

Codenotti, B. and Favati, (1987) Iterative Methods for the Parallel Solution of Linear Systems. *Comput. Math. Applic.*, **13(7)**, 631–633.

Young, D. M. (1971) Iterative Solution of Large Linear Systems, Academic Press, New York and London.

Hellar, D. (1978) A Survey of Parallel Algorithms in Numerical Linear Algebra, *SIAM Review*, **20(4)**, 740–777.

Evans, D. J. (1982) Parallel Processing Systems an Advanced Course, Cambridge University Press, New York.

Fadeeva, V. N. (1959) *Computational Methods of Linear Algebra*, Dover Publications, New York.

Gallivan, K. A., Plemons, R. J., and Sameh, Parallel Algorithm for Dense Linear Algebra Computations, *SIAM Rev.*, **32**, 54–135.

Miranker, W. L. (1971) A Survey of Parallelism in Numerical Analysis", *SIAM Review*, **13(4)**, 524–547.

Sameh, A. H. and Kuck, D. J. (1977) A Parallel QR Algorithm for Symmetric Tridiagonal Matrices, *IEEE Trans. on Computers*, **C-26**, 147–153.

Stone, H. (1973) An Efficient Parallel Algorithm for the Solution of Tridiagonal Linear System of Equations, *J. ACM*, **20**, 27–38.

## EXERCISES

**10.1.** Consider the matrix recursive equations:

$$Y_1 = B_1;$$
$$Y_i = A_i Y_{i-1} + B_i (2 \leq i \leq n),$$

where $A_i$ and $B_i$ are the given $m \times m$ matrices. Develop an $O(\log n \log m)$ time parallel algorithm to compare all $Y_i$s.

**10.2.** Show that the product of two $n \times n$ lower triangular Toeplitz matrices is a lower triangular Toeplitz matrix.

**10.3.** Develop an $O(\log n)$ time algorithm to multiply two lower triangular Toeplitz matrices.

**10.4.** Is the product of two arbitrary Toeplitz matrices a Toeplitz matrix? Develop an algorithm to multiply two Toeplitz matrices.

## CHAPTER 11

# Differentiation and Integration

Computers were first constructed only for the purpose of numerical calculations. In almost all the branches of science and engineering, the numerical calculations are predominantly used. In this chapter, let us study some important numerical methods and design efficient parallel algorithms for them. To begin with, we start from the most elementary but very important topic, Differentiation.

## 11.1 DIFFERENTIATION

Consider a real-valued function $f(x)$ whose function values at the points $x_1, x_2, x_3, \ldots, x_n$ are given to be $f_0, f_1, f_2 \ldots f_n$

| $x$ values | $x_0$ | $x_1$ | $x_2$ | | $x_{n-1}$ | $x_n$ |
|---|---|---|---|---|---|---|
| $f$ values | $f_0$ | $f_1$ | $f_2.$ | | $f_{n-1}$ | $f_n$ |

Consider the Taylor's Series

$$f(x_i + h) = f(x_i) + \frac{h}{\lfloor 1} f'(x_i) + \frac{h^2}{\lfloor 2} f''(x_i) + \ldots$$

$$f_{i+1} = f(x_i) + \frac{h}{\lfloor 1} f'(x_i) + \frac{h^2}{\lfloor 2} f''(x_i) + \ldots$$

That is, when $h$ is very small $h^2 = o$ (approximately). So, we have

$$f_{i+1} = f_i + h f'_i,$$

where $f'_i$ denotes $f'(x_i)$. That is,

$$f'_i = \frac{f_{i+1} - f_i}{h}.$$

Using this formula $f'_0, f'_1, f'_2 \ldots, f'^{n-1}$ can be determined in parallel. The parallel algorithm is given below:

**Algorithm Differentiation**
  **Input:**   $x(0:n), f(0:n), h$
  **Output:**   $f'(0:n-1)$.
  BEGIN
    1. For $i = 0$ to $n - 1$ do in parallel
    2. $f'_i = (f_{i+1} - f_i)/h$
    3. End parallel
  END

**Complexity Analysis.** The above algorithm can be implemented in $O(1)$ time, using $O(n)$ processors in a CREW Parallel Random Access memory. The Concurrent Read is essential because

Processor $P_i$ which evaluates $f_i$.
Processor $P_{i-1}$ which evaluates $f'_{i-1}$ also uses $f_i$

For the first-order derivative, there are several other formulas. One such popular formula is:

$$f'_i = \frac{f_{i+1} - f_{i-1}}{2h}.$$

For the second-order and third-order derivatives of a function, there are several formulas given below:

$$f''_i = \frac{1}{h^2} \{f_{i-1} - 2f_i + f_{i+1}\}$$

$$f''_i = \frac{1}{12h^2} \{11f_{i-1} - 20f_i + 6f_{i+1} + 4f_{i+2} - f_{i+3}\}$$

$$f'''_i = \frac{1}{h^3} \{-f_{i-1} + 3f_i + 3f_{i+1} + f_{i+2}\}$$

$$f'''_i = \frac{1}{2h^3} \{-f_{i-2} + 2f_{i-1} - 2f_{i+1} + f_{i+2}\}$$

$$f''''_i = \frac{1}{h^4} \{f_{i-2} + 4f_{i-1} + 6f_i - 4f_{i+1} + f_{i+2}\}.$$

Using these, one can easily develop parallel algorithms to evaluate the higher-order derivatives.

## 11.2 PARTIAL DIFFERENTIATION

Let $U(x, y)$ be a function of $x$ and $y$. We shall use the following notations:

$U_x$: Partial derivative of $U$ with respect to $x$.

$U_y$: Partial derivative of $U$ with respect to $y$.

$U_{xx}$: Partial derivative of $Ux$ with respect to $x$.

$U_{yy}$: Partial derivative of $Uy$ with respect to $y$.

$U_{xy}$: Partial derivative of $Uy$ with respect to $x$.

$U_{yx}$: Partial derivative of $Ux$ with respect to $y$.

Similarly, we can define the symbols $U_{xyy}$, $U_{xxx}$ etc. The usual formula to find the derivative is

$$y'_i = \frac{y_{i+1} - y_i}{h}.$$

This formula can be used to find the value of $U_x$ and $U_y$.

$$U_x(x_i, y_i) = \frac{U(x_{i+1}, y_i) - U(x_i, y_i)}{h},$$

where $h = x_{i+1} - x_i$.

In the above formula, notice that $y_i$ does not change. The formula for $U_y$ is given below:

$$\frac{U(x_i, y_{i+1}) - U(x_i y_i)}{k},$$

where $k = y_{i+1} - y_i$.

We can use the three-point centered formula

$$y'_i = \frac{y_{i+1} - y_{i-1}}{2h}$$

and get the following formulas

$$U_x(x_i, y_i) = \frac{U(x_{i+1}, y_i) - U(x_{i-1}, y_i)}{2h}$$

$$U_y(x_i, y_i) = \frac{U(x_i, y_{i+1}) - U(x_i, y_{i-1})}{2k}.$$

For simplicity, we can write the above four formulas as follows:

$$U_{x,i,j} = \frac{U_{i+1,j} - U_{ij}}{h} \tag{11.1}$$

$$U_{y,i,j} = \frac{U_{i,j+1} - U_{ij}}{k} \tag{11.2}$$

$$U_{x,i,j} = \frac{U_{i+1,j} - U_{i-1,j}}{2h} \tag{11.3}$$

$$U_{y,i,j} = \frac{U_{i,j+1} - U_{i,j-1}}{2k}. \tag{11.4}$$

Before deriving the formula for higher-order partial derivatives, let us see more about the pivotal points in this two-dimensional case.

Consider the point $(x_i, y_i)$. Its neighboring points are shown in Fig. 11.1 and Fig. 11.2.

Now let us derive the formula for $U_{xy}$. As per definition,

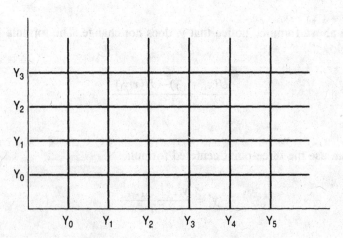

**Figure 11.1** Two-dimensional grid.

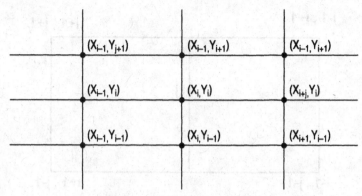

**Figure 11.2**  Points in a grid.

$U_{xy}$ = Partial Derivative of $U\dot{y}$ with respect to $x$.

$$U_{xyij} = \frac{U_{yi+1,j} - U_{yi-1,j}}{2h} \text{ (Using eq. 11.3)}.$$

Using eq. (11.4), we get:

$$U_{yi+1,j} = \frac{U_{i+1,j+1} - U_{i+1,j-1}}{2k}$$

$$U_{yi-1,j} = \frac{U_{i-1,j+1} - U_{i-1,j-1}}{2k}.$$

Applying these results in the above equation, we get

$$U_{xyij} = \frac{1}{4hk} (U_{i+1,j+1} + U_{i-1,j-1} - U_{i+1,j-1} - U_{i-1,j+1}).$$

This formula can be remembered by Fig. 11.3. In Fig. 11.3 we add the right-top and the left-bottom corners and subtract the other two and then divide by $4hk$. Similarly, we can also derive the following formula:

$$U_{xxij} = \frac{U_{i+1,j} - 2U_{ij} + U_{i-1,j}}{h^2}$$

$$U_{yyij} = \frac{U_{i,j+1} - 2U_{ij} + U_{i,j-1}}{k^2}.$$

The value $U_{xx} + U_{yy}$ is used for a number of problems. This is denoted by $\nabla^2 U$ and is called the *Laplacian of U*. $\nabla^2$ is called the *Laplacian operator*.

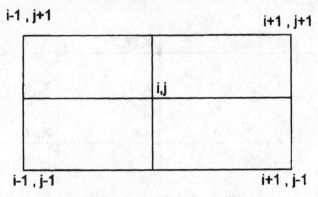

**Figure 11.3** Illustrating $U_{xyij}$ calculations.

$$\nabla^2 U = U_{xx} + U_{yy}.$$

Applying the values of $U_{xxij}$ and $U_{yyij}$, we get a formula for $U_{ij}$. Choosing $h = k$ we get

$$\nabla^2 U_{ij} = \frac{1}{h^2}(U_{i+1,j} + U_{i,j+1} + U_{i-1,j} + U_{i,j-1} - 4U_{ij}). \tag{7.5}$$

For the function given below, let us find the value of $\nabla^2 U$ at (1.5, 2.0):

| Y/X | 1.0 | 1.5 | 2.0 | 2.5 |
|-----|-----|-----|-----|-----|
| 1.0 | 12 | 15 | 15 | 16 |
| 1.5 | 13 | 14 | 16 | 19 |
| 2.0 | 21 | 23 | 27 | 35 |
| 2.5 | 31 | 34 | 37 | 38 |

The formula for $\nabla^2 U_{ij}$ can be illustrated using Fig. 11.4 in comparison with the table given in the problem.

$$\nabla^2 U_{ij} = \frac{1}{h^2}(U_{i+1,j} + U_{i,j+1} + U_{i-1,j} + U_{i,j-1} - 4U_{ij}).$$

That is, we must add the four sides and subtract four times the central value.

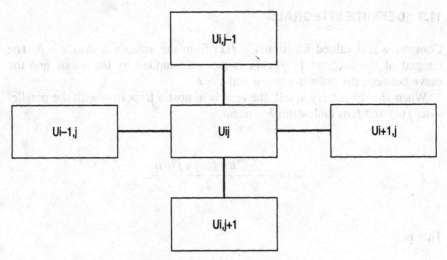

**Figure 11.4**    Laplacian operator.

$$\nabla^2 U_{22} = 15 + 23 + 13 + 16 + -4 * 14$$
$$= 11$$
$$\nabla^2 U_{32} = 15 + 27 + 14 + 19 - 4 * 16$$
$$= 11$$

Let us develop a parallel algorithm to evaluate $U_{ij}$ for $1 \le i \le m$ and $1 \le j < n$. From the formula, it is clear that this can be evaluated in parallel for all $i$ and for all $j$.

**Algorithm Laplace**
  **Input:**   $U[0:m, 0:n]$
  **Output:**   $\nabla^2 U[1:m-1, i:n-1]$
    1. For $i = 1$ to $m - 1$ do in parallel
    2. For $j = i$ to $n - 1$ do in parallel
    3. Calculate $\nabla^2 U_{ij}$, using the formula
    4. End parallel
    5. End parallel

The Algorithm LAPLACIAN can be implemented in $O(1)$ time using $O(nm)$ processors. From the formula, $U_{i+1,j}$ is used to evaluate $\Delta^2 U_{ij}$ as well as $\nabla^2 U_{i+2,j}$. So, a concurrent reading PRAM is needed. The model needed for the implementation is CREW PRAM.

## 11.3 DEFINITE INTEGRALS

Consider a real-valued function $y = f(x)$ from the value $x = a$ to $x = b$. The integral of the function $\int_a^b f(x)dx$ is the arc bounded by the $x$-axis and the curve between the ordinates $x = a$ and $x = b$.

When $(b - a)$ is very small, the area is almost a trapezoid with the parallel sides $f(a)$ and $f(b)$ and width $b - a$. So,

$$\text{area} = \frac{(b - a)(f(a) + f(b))}{2}.$$

That is,

$$\int_a^{a+h} f(x)dx = \frac{h}{2}(f(a) + f(a + h)).$$

when $h$ is very small. This formula is called *trapezoidal rule*. The trapezoidal rule will give a reasonable value only when $h$ is very small. This is shown in Fig. 11.6.

Suppose we want to find $\int_a^b f(x)dx$, where $b - a$ is not very small. In this case, the interval $[a\ b]$ can be divided into small equal subintervals as

$$a = x_0 \leq x_1 \leq x_2 \leq \ldots \leq x_n = b,$$

where $x_{i+1} - x_i = (b - a)/n = h$ (say) with $(0 \leq i \leq n)$ (see Fig. 11.5). The value of $n$ is chosen sufficiently large such that $h = (b - a)/n$ is very small.

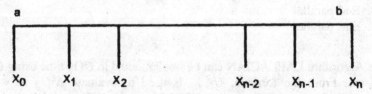

**Figure 11.5** Interval $[a, b]$ is divided into $n$ intervals.

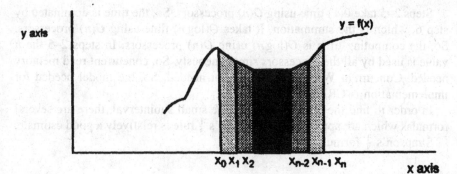

**Figure 11.6**  Trapezoidal rule.

$$\int_{x_i}^{x_{i+1}} f(x)dx = \frac{x_{i+1} - x_i}{2} \left( f(x_{i+1}) + f(x_i) \right)$$

$$= \frac{h}{2} \left( f(x_i) + f(x_i + h) \right)$$

$$\int_a^b f(x)dx = \int_{x_0}^{x_n} f(x)dx$$

$$= \int_{x_0}^{x_n} f(x)dx + \int_{x_1}^{x_2} \cdots \int_{x_{n-1}}^{x_n} f(x)dx$$

$$= \frac{h}{2} \{ f(x_0) + f(x_1) \} + \frac{h}{2} \{ f(x_1) + f(x_2) \} + \cdots$$

$$+ \frac{h}{2} \{ f(x_{n-1}) + f(x_n) \}.$$

This is shown in Fig. 11.6. The complete algorithm is now given.

**Algorithm Integral-Trapezoidal**
  **Input:**  Function $f(x)$, $a$, $b$, $n$.
  **Output:**  Integral $= f(x)dx$.
   1. $h = (b - a)/n$
   2. For $i = 0$ to $n - i$ do in parallel
   3. $x_i = a + ih$
   4. Integral $(i) = \frac{h}{2} \{ f(x_i) + f(x_i + h) \}$
   5. End parallel.
   6. Evaluate integral $= \sum_{i=0}^{n-1}$ integral $(i)$.

Steps 2–5 take 0(1) time using $O(n)$ processors. So, the time is dominated by step 6, which is the summation. It takes $O(\log n)$ time using $O(n)$ processors. So, the computing time is $O(\log n)$ using $O(n)$ processors. In steps 2–5 the $h$ value is used by all the processors simultaneously. So, concurrent read memory needed. Concurrent Write operation is not needed. So, the model needed for implementation is CREW PRAM.

In order to find the integral value of the small subinterval, there are several formulas which are approximate. Simpson's $\frac{1}{3}$ rule is relatively a good estimate. Simpson's $\frac{1}{3}$ formula is

$$\int_{x_1}^{x_1+2h} f(x)dx = \frac{h}{3}\left(f(xi) + 4f(xi+h) + f(xi+2h)\right)$$

This can be used to evaluate the integral. The interval $[a\ b]$ must be divided into $2n$ equal subintervals.

$$h = (b-a)/2n$$
$$x_i = a + ih.$$

The complete algorithm to evaluate the integral using Simpson's $\frac{1}{3}$ rule is given below:

**Algorithm Integral-Simpson**
  **Input:** Function $f(x)$, $a$, $b$, $n$ where $n$ is even.
  **Output:** Integral $\int_a^b f(x)\ dx$
    1. $h = (b-a)/2n$
    2. For each $i \in \{0, 2, 4, 6, 8 \ldots (n-2)\}$ do in parallel
    3. $x_i = a + ih$
    4. Integral $(i) = h/3\ \{f(x_i) + 4f(x_i + h) + f(x_i + h)\}$
    5. End parallel
    6. Evaluate Integral $= \sum$ Integral $(i)$,
       where sum is taken over all $i \in \{0, 2, 4, \ldots (n-2)\}$.

It is easy to verify that the ALGORITHM INTEGRAL-SIMPSON can be implemented to run in $O(\log n)$ time using $O(n)$ processors in a CREW PRAM model.

## 11.4 INTERPOLATION

Suppose $f(x)$ is a function whose value at certain points $x_0, x_1 \ldots x_n$. The values are $f(x_0), f(x_1), \ldots f(x_n)$. Consider a point $x$ different from $x_0, x_1, x_2, \ldots, x_n$. $f(x)$ is not known.

We can find to approximate value of $f(x)$ from the known values $f(x_0), f(x)$, ..., $f(x_n)$ the method of finding $f(x)$ from the values $f(x_0), f(x), \ldots f(x_n)$ is called interpolation. We say that we interpolate at various times are measured and tabulated.

| Time (sex c) | 0 | 10 | 32 | 128 |
|---|---|---|---|---|
| Temperature (°C) | 15 | 20 | 30 | 50 |

At the start, the temperature was 15°C. When the temperature reached 20°C, the time was 10 seconds. When the temperature reached 30°C the time was 32 seconds, and when it reached 50°C the time was 128 seconds. We may be interested in finding the temperature when time was 100 seconds. For this example $x = 100$.

| $x$ | $x_0$ | $x_1$ | $x_2$ | $x_3$ |
|---|---|---|---|---|
| (time) | 0 | 10 | 32 | 128 |
| $f(x)$ | 15 | 20 | 30 | 50 |
| (temperature) | $f_0$ | $f_1$ | $f_2$ | $f_3$ |

We want to interpolate $f(100)$.

### 11.4.1  Linear Interpolation

Let $x_0, x_1$, be two points and $f_0, f_1$ be the function values at $x_0$ and $x_1$, respectively. Let $x$ be a point between $x_0$ and $x_1$. We are interested in interpolating $f(x)$ from the values $f(x_0)$ and $f(x_1)$.

Consider the Taylor's Series

$$f(x_1) = f(x_0) + \frac{f'(x_0)}{\lfloor 1} (x_1 - x_0) + \ldots.$$

Considering only the first two terms we get

$$f_1 = f_0 + f'(x_0)(x_1 - x_0).$$

Therefore $f'(x_0) = (f_1 - f_0)/(x_1 - x_0) + \ldots$ The Taylor's series at $x$ gives

$$f(x) = f(x_0) + \frac{f'(x_0)}{\lfloor 1} (x_1 - x_0) + \ldots.$$

Considering only the first two terms we get

$$f(x) = f_0 + f'(x_0)(x - x_0) = f_0 + \frac{(f_1 - f_0)(x - x_0)}{(x_1 - x_0)}.$$

Denote $(x - x_0)/x_1 - x_0) = p$. We get

$$f(x) = f_0 + (f_1 - f_0)p$$

$$= (1 - p)f_0 + pf_1, \text{ where } p = \frac{x - x_0}{x_1 - x_0}.$$

This is called the *linear interpolation formula*. Since $x$ is point between $x_0$ and $x_1$, $p$ is a nonnegative fractional value. That is $0 \le p \le 1$.

**Computation.** $x_0, x_1, f_0, f_1$ will be given. $x$ is also given. $f(x)$ has to be found out. First find $p = (x - x_0)/(x_1 - x_0)$. Then find $f(x) = (1 - p)f_0 + pf_1$. For example consider the following functions.

| $x_i$ | 7 | 19 |
|-------|-----|-----|
| $f_i$ | 15 | 35 |

Let us interpolate $f(10)$

Here

$$x_0 = 7, \qquad x_1 = 19$$
$$f_0 = 15 \qquad f_1 = 35$$
$$x = 10.$$

Therefore,

$$p = (x - x_0)/(x_1 - x_0) = (10 - 7)/(19 - 7)3/12 = 0.25.$$
$$p = 0.25.$$

Therefore, $1 - p = 0.75$

$$f(10) = f(x) = (1 - p)f0 + pf1 = 20.$$

### 11.4.2 Quadratic Interpolation

Let $x_{i-1}, x_i, x_{i+1}$ be three point such that

$$x_i - x_{i-1} = x_{i+1} - x_i = h.$$

Let $f_{i-1}, f_i, f_{i+1}$ be the function values at $x_{i-1}, x_i, x_{i+1}$, respectively. Let $x$ be a point between $x_i$ and $x_{i+1}$.

By Taylor's Series,

$$f(x) = f(x_i) + \frac{f'(x_i)}{\lfloor 1} + \frac{f''(x_i)}{\lfloor 2} (x - x_i)^2 + \dots.$$

Considering only three terms and substituting

$$f'(x_i) = \frac{f_{i+1} - f_{i-1}}{2h}$$

$$f''(x_i) = \frac{1}{h^2} (f_{i-1} - 2f_{i+1}),$$

we get

$$f(x) = \frac{-p(1-p)}{2} f_{i-1} + (1-p)f_i + \frac{p(1+p)}{2} f_{i+1},$$

where $p = (x - x_i)/h$. This is called the *quadratic interpolation* formula.

### 11.4.3 Lagrange's Interpolation

Suppose $f(x)$ values at some points of $x$ are given (not necessary to be at equal intervals)

| X values | $x_0$ | $x_1$ | $x_2$ | $\dots$ | $x_n$ |
|----------|-------|-------|-------|---------|-------|
| $f(x)$ Values | $f_0$ | $f_1$ | $f_2$ | $\dots$ | $f_n$ |

The function values are known only at the points $x_0, x_1 \dots x_n$. We want to formulate the function $f(x)$ as a $n$th degree polynomial in $x$. The $n$th degree polynomial $f(x)$ must be formulated in such a way that $f(x_i) = f_i$ (given).

Consider the polynomial

$$P_k(x) = \frac{(x - x_0)(x - x_1)\ldots(x - x_{k-1})(x - x_{k+1})\ldots(x - x_n)}{(x_k - x_0)(x_k - x_1)\ldots(x_k - x_{k-1})(x_k - x_{k+1}(x_k - x_n)}.$$

Note that

$$P_k(x_i) = \begin{cases} 0 & \text{if } i \neq k \\ 1 & \text{if } i = k \end{cases}.$$

$P_k(x)$ can be formulated for $k = 0, 1, 2 \ldots, n$ from this function consider the polynomial

$$f(x) = f_o P_0(x) + f_1 P_1(x) + \ldots f_n P_n(x)$$
$$f(x_i) = f_i (0 \leq i \leq n).$$

This is called Lagrange's Interpolation Method.

**Algorithm Development.** Let us now design algorithm for Lagrange's interpolation. $n$ is the number of points at which the $f$ values are given.

$$x_1, x_2, \ldots x_n \text{ are the } x \text{ values.}$$
$$f_1, f_2, \ldots f_n \text{ are the } f \text{ values}$$

$y$ is the value at which the $f$ value is to be found. That is, $f(y)$ is to be determined. We denote $f(y)$ by $fu$ in the algorithm program. The following is an algorithm for the Lagrange's interpolation.

**Algorithm Lagrange**
  **Input:** $x(1:n)$ and $f(1:n)$ and $y$.
  **Output:** $f_y$
    1. For $k = 1$ to $n$
    2. $p_k = 1$.
    3. For $i = 1$ to $n$ do
    4. If $i = k$ go to step-6
    5. $P_k = P_k * (y - x_i)/(x_k - x_i)$
    6. next $i$
    7. next $k$
    8. $fy = 0$
    9. For $i = 1$ to $n$ do
    10. $fy = fy + P_i f_i$
    11. next $i$
    12. END

***Parallel Algorithm for Lagrange's Interpolation.*** Steps 1 to 7 in the above algorithm evaluates the values of $P_k$ ($1 \leq k \leq n$). The values of $P_k$ can be evaluated in parallel. The evaluation of each $P_k$ can be done in $O(\log n)$ time using the method similar to the addition of $n$ numbers using $O(n)$ processors using an EREW PRAM. Steps 9 to 11 evaluates the $fy$ values as a summation of $n$ tems. So that can also be implemented in $O(\log n)$ time using $O(n)$ processors. So, the overall time complexity of the parallel implementation of Lagrange's interpolation is $O(\log n)$ using $O(n^2)$ processors.

## BIBLIOGRAPHY

Actions, F. S. (1970) Numerical Methods That Work, Harper and Row, New York.

Andrew, L. (1985) Elementary Partial Differential Equations with Boundary Value Problems, Saunders College Publishing, Philadelphia.

Chandy, K. M., and Taylor, S. (1992) An Introduction to Parallel Programming, Jones and Bartlette, Boston.

Cooley, J. W., and Turkey, J. W. (1965) An Algorithm for the Machine Calculations of Complex Fourier Series, *Mathematics of Computations*, **19**, 297–301.

P. J. Davis, and Rabinowitz, P. (1967) *Numerical Integration*, Blaisdell, Waltham, MA.

Dongara, J., Duff, I., Sorensen, D., and Vander Vorst, H. (1991) *Solving Linear Systems on Vector and Shared Memory Computers*, SIAM, Philadelphia.

Forsythe, G. E. and Moler, C. B. (1967) *Computer Solutions of Linear Algebraic Systems*, Prentice-Hall, Englewood Cliffs, NJ.

D. Kahaner, Moler, C., and Nash, S. (1989) *Numerical Methods and Software*, Prentice-Hall, Englewood Cliffs, NJ.

Knuth, D. (1973) Sorting and Searching, Addison-Wesley, Reading, MA.

O'Neill, M. A. (1988) Faster than Fast Fourier, *Byte*, **13(4)**, 229–230.

Pinsky, M. A. (1991) Partial Differential Equations and Boundary Value Problems with Applications, McGraw-Hill, New York.

Wilkinson, J. H. (1963) Rounding Errors in Algebraic Process, Prentice-Hall, Englewood Cliffs, NJ.

Wilkinson, J. H. (1965) The Algebraic Eigenvalue Problem, Oxford University Press, London.

## EXERCISES

**11.1.** Develop an algorithm to find the integral of a function from $a$ to $b$, using the Monte Carlo Method.

**11.2.** Develop a method to find the differentiation of a function, using the method of differences.

**11.3.** What is Newton's Interpolation? Find its parallel complexity.

**11.4.** Develop a parallel procedure to find the integer of a function from $a$ to $b$, using a five-point centered formula by dividing $(a\ b)$ into $n$ intervals.

**11.5.** Develop a parallel procedure to find the third derivative of a function, using the method of differences.

## CHAPTER 12

# Differential Equations

## 12.1 EULER'S FORMULA

Consider the differential equation,

$$\frac{dy}{dx} = f(x, y),$$

with initial condition $y(x_0) = y_0$. Consider the points $x_0, x_1, x_2, \ldots, x_n$, where $x_{i+1} = x_i + h$. The value of $y$ at $x_i$ is denoted by $y_i$. As the initial value is given, this problem is called *Initial value problem*.

By Taylor's Series,

$$y_{i+1} = y_i + \frac{h}{\lfloor 1} y_i' + \frac{h^2}{\lfloor 2} y_i'' + \ldots$$

When $h$ is very small, $h^2$ is negligibly small and we get

$$y_{i+1} = y_i + h y_i'.$$

Given that $y' = f(x, y)$ and so we get

$$y_{i+1} = y_i + h f_i,$$

where $f_i$ denotes $f(x_i, y_i)$.

This is called *Euler's formula* for solving an initial value problem. Since $y_0$ is given, Euler's formula can be used to evaluate

$$y_1 = y_0 + h f_0.$$

After evaluating $y_1$, we can once again use Euler's formula to evaluate

$$y_2 = y_1 + h f_1.$$

Proceeding like this we can evaluate the values of $y_3$, $y_4$, $y_4$, ... $y_n$. From the above discussion it is clear that this method is inherently sequential. Parallelization of this method is impossible. Similarly there are some more inherently sequential method to solve the initial value problems. Now let us see partial differential equations.

## 12.2 PARTIAL DIFFERENTIAL EQUATIONS

An equation with two variables $x$ and $y$ and a function $u(x, y)$ and the partial derivatives of $u$ is called a *partial differential equation*. For example,

$$U_x + U_{xy} + x^2 \sin x U_y = e^{2x} \cos^2(xy)$$

is a partial differential equation. The order of the highest-order derivative present in the equation is called the order of the partial differential equation. The second-order partial differential equations are considered to be very important in the study because quite a number of physics and engineering calculations reduce to solving a second-order partial differential equations.

A general form of a second-order partial differential equation is

$$A U_{xx} + B U_{xy} + C U_{yy} = F,$$

where $F$ is a function of $x$, $y$, $U$, $U_x$ and $U_y$.

Depending upon the value of $A$, $B$, and $C$ these equations are classified into three classical types. If $B^2 - 4AC < 0$ the equation is called an *elliptic equation*; If $B^2 - 4AC = 0$ it is called a *parabolic equation*. The equation is said to be a *hyperbolic equation* if $B^2 - 4AC > 0$.

Some standard second-order differential equations are given below.

| 1 | Wave equation | $Uyy - a^2 Uxx = 0$ | $A = -a^2, B = 0, C = 0,$ $B^2 - 4AC = 4a^2 > 0,$ *Hyperbolic* |
|---|---|---|---|
| 2 | Heat flow equation | $kUxx = Uy$ | $A = k, B = 0, C = 0,$ $B^2 - 4AC = -4 < 0,$ *Elliptic* |
| 3 | Laplace equation | $Uyy + Uxx = 0$ | $A = 1, B = 0, C = 1,$ $B^2 - 4AC = -4 < 0,$ *Elliptic* |
| 4 | Poisson's equation | $Uyy + Uxx = F(x, y)$ | *Elliptic* |

In order to illustrate the classification, let us classify the following as parabolic, elliptic, or hyperbolic.

1. $2f_{xx} - 4f_{xy} + f_{yy} = (1 + x^2)(1 - y^2)$,
2. $(x^2/4)f_{xx} + \sqrt{1 - y^2}f_{xy} = (1 + x^2)f_x f_y$ given $x > 0$ and $0 < y < 1$.
3. $(1 - x^2)U_{xx} + 2yU_{xy} + U_{yy} = 0$.

First, let us consider the equation,

$$2f_{xx} - 4f_{xy} + f_{yy} = (1 + x^2)(1 - y^2).$$

Here $A = 2$, $B = -4$, $C = 1$ $B^2 - 4AC = 16 - 8 = 8 > 0$. So this is a hyperbolic equation.

Now consider the second equation,

$$(x^2/4)f_{xx} + \sqrt{1 - y^2}f_{xx} + f_{yy} = (1 + x^2)f_x f_y.$$

Here $A$ and $B$ are not constants. They are functions of $x$ and $y$. $A = x^2/4$, $B = \sqrt{1 - y^2}$, $C = 1$, $B^2 - 4AC = 1 - y^2 - x^2$. So, when $x^2 + y^2 > 1$, the equation is elliptic. When $x^2 + y^2 = 1$, the equation is parabolic. When $x^2 + y^2 < 1$, the equation is hyperbolic.

In order to have a better idea about the equation consider the unit circle in a two dimensional plane (see Fig. 12.1).

As it is given that $0 < y < 1$, the region under consideration is between the $y$ axis and vertical line $y = 1$. Inside the circle the value of $x^2 + y^2 < 1$ and so the equation is hyperbolic in the interior region of the circle. Outside the circle the equation is elliptic. It is parabolic on the circumference of the circle.

3. $(1 - x^2)U_{xx} + 2yU_{xy} + U_{yy} = 0$ where $A = (1 - x^2)$, $B = 2y$, $C = 1$ $B^2 - 4AC = 4(x^2 + y^2 - 1)$. So, the equation is elliptic if $x^2 + y^2 - 1 < 0$, parabolic if $x^2 + y^2 - 1 = 0$, hyperbolic if $x^2 + y^2 > 1$.

## 12.3 PARABOLIC EQUATIONS

The most popular parabolic equation is heat flow equation.

$$CU_{xx} = U_y.$$

We can try to solve this equation in rectangular region $[a_1, a_2] \times [b_1, b_2]$. $[a_1, a_2]$ can be subdivided into $m$ equal subintervals and $[b_1, b_2]$ into $n$ equal subintervals. Let

$$x_i = a_1 + ih \quad \text{and} \quad y_j = b_1 + jk,$$

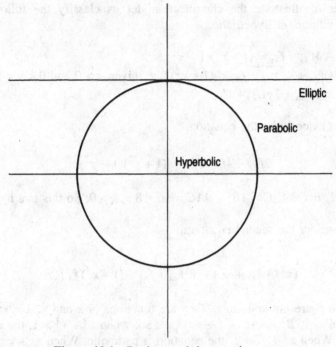

**Figure 12.1**  Regions and the equation types.

where

$$h = \frac{a_2 - a_1}{m} \quad \text{and} \quad k = \frac{b_2 - b_1}{n}.$$

This is shown in Fig. 12.2. For practical convenience, let us denote

$$U_{ij} = U(x_i, y_j).$$

Our aim is to find $U_{ij}$ for $1 \le i \le m$ and for $1 \le j \le n$.

### 12.3.1  Schmidt Method (To Solve a Parabolic Equation)

The given parabolic equation is

$$CU_{xx} = U_y.$$

That is,

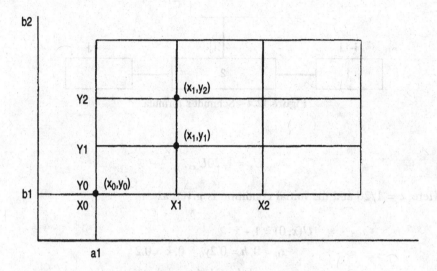

**Figure 12.2**  A two-dimensional grid.

$$C(U_{xx}) \text{ at } (x_i, y_j) = (U_y) \text{ at } (x_i y_j)$$

Using differentiation formulas, we get

$$U_{i,j+1} = (1 - 2r)U_{ij} + r(U_{i-1,j} + U_{i+1,j}),$$

where $r = ck/h^2$. This is called *Schmidt's formula* and illustrated by Fig. 12.3.

**Example**

Solve the parabolic equation $U_y = 1/20U_{xx}$ in the interior point of the mesh with $h = 0.2$, $k = 0.2$, $x = 0$ to 1, and $y = 0$ to 1.

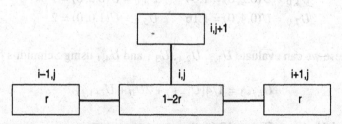

**Figure 12.3**  Schmidt Method.

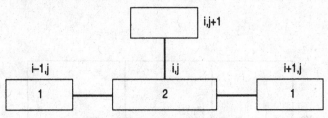

**Figure 12.4** Schmidt's formula.

$$U_y = 1/20 U_{xx}.$$

Here, $c = 1/20$ and the initial condition is given as

$$U(x,0) = 1 + x^2$$
$$x_0 = 0, h = 0.2 y_0 = 0, k = 0.2$$
$$r = ck/h^2 = 1/4.$$

Schmidt's formula is:

$$U_{i,j+1} = (1 - 2r)U_{ij} + r(U_{i-1,j} + U_{i+1,j})$$
$$= 1/2 U_{ij} + 1/4(U_{i-1,j} + U_{i+1,j}).$$

That is,

$$U_{i,j+1} = 1/4(2U_{ij} + U_{i-1,j} + U_{i+1,j}).$$

This is illustrated in Fig. 12.4. The pivotal points in the $x$ axis are $x = 0, 0.2,$ 0.4, 0.6, 0.8, 1.0. The pivotal points in the $y$ axis are $y = 0, 0.2, 0.4, 0.6, 0.8,$ 1.0. The mesh is shown in the Fig. 12.5.

Using the given initial condition that $u(x,0) = 1 + x^2$, we can evaluate the solution at all the points with $y = 0$. That is,

$$U_{0,0} = U(0,0) = 1 \qquad U_{3,0} = U(0.6,0) = 1.36$$
$$U_{1,0} = U(0.2,0) = 1.04 \qquad U_{4,0} = U(0.8,0) = 1.64$$
$$U_{2,0} = U(0.4,0) = 1.16 \qquad U_{5,0} = U(1.0,0) = 2.$$

Using these we can evaluate $U_{1,1}, U_{2,1}, U_{3,1}$ and $U_{4,1}$ using Schmidt's formula:

$$U_{i,j+1} = 1/4[U_{i-1,j} + 2U_{ij} + U_{i+1,j}\}.$$

To find $U_{1,1}$ (see Figure 12.6(a)),

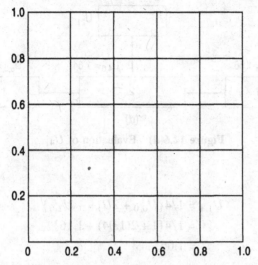

**Figure 12.5** Pivotal points and mesh.

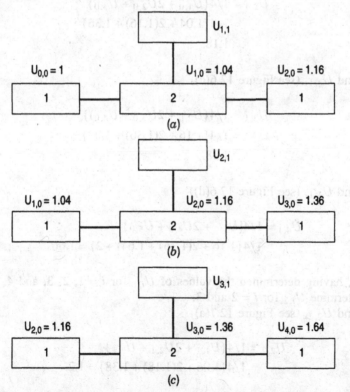

**Figure 12.6(a)** Evaluation of $U_{11}$. **(b)** Evaluation of $U_{21}$. **(c)** Evaluation of $U_{31}$.

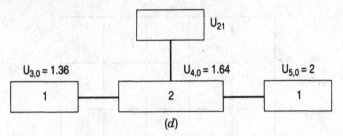

**Figure 12.6(d)**   Evaluation of $U_{41}$.

$$U_{1,1} = 1/4\{U_{0,0} + 2U_{1,0} + U_{2,0}\}$$
$$= 1/4\{1 + 2(1.04) + 1.16\}$$
$$= 1.06.$$

To find $U_{2,1}$, (see Figure 12.6(b))

$$U_{2,1} = 1/4\{U_{1,0} + 2U_{2,0} + U_{3,0}\}$$
$$= 1/4\{1.04 + 2(1.16) + 1.36\}$$
$$= 1.18.$$

To find $U_{3,1}$, (see Figure 12.6(c))

$$U_{3,1} = 1/4\{U_{2,0} + 2U_{3,0} + U_{4,0})\}$$
$$= 1/4\{1.16 + 2(1.36) + 1.64\}$$
$$= 1.38.$$

To find $U_{4,1}$, (see Figure 12.6(d))

$$U_{4,1} = 1/4[U_{3,0} + 2U_{4,0} + U_{5,0}\}$$
$$= 1/4\{1.16 + 2(1.36) + 1.64) + 2\} = 1.66.$$

Now, having determined the values of $U_{i,1}$ for $i = 1, 2, 3,$ and 4, we can now determine $U_{i,2}$ for $i = 2$ and 3.
To find $U_{2,2}$, (see Figure 12.7(a))

$$U_{2,2} = 1/4\{U_{1,1} + 2U_{2,1} + U_{3,1}\}$$
$$= 1/4\{1.06 + 2(1.18) + 1.38\} = 1.2.$$

To find $U_{3,2}$, (see Figure 12.7(b))

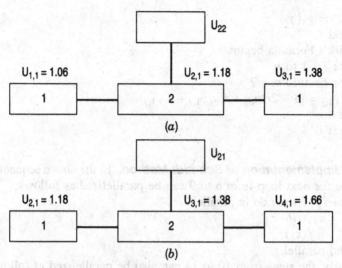

**Figure 12.7(a)** Evaluation of $U_{22}$. **(b)** Evaluation of $U_{32}$.

$$U_{3,2} = 1/4\{U_{2,1} + 2U_{3,1} + U_{4,i}\}$$
$$= 1/4\{1.18 + 2(1.38) + 1.66\} = 1.4.$$

The following is an algorithm to solve the heat flow equation:

$$cu_y = u_{xx}$$
$$y(x, b_1) = f(x)$$
$$u(a_1, b_1) = g_1(y)$$
$$u(a_2, y) = g_2(y).$$

**Algorithm Heat Flow**
1. Define $f(x)$, $g_1(y)$, $g_2(y)$.
2. Read $a_1$, $a_2$, $b_1$, $b_2$, $c$, $m$, $n$
3. $h = (a_2 - a_1)/m$,  $k = (b_2 - b_1)/n$
4. $r = ck/h^2$
5. $x_0 = a_1$, $y_0 = b_1$, $u_0 = f(x_0)$.
To find the initial values:
6. For $i = 1$ to $m$
7. $x_i = x_0 + ih$
8. $u_{i,o} = f(x_i)$
9. next $i$
10. For $j = 1$ to $n$
11. $y_i = y_0 + jk$
12. $u_{0,j} = g_1(y_j)$

13. $u_{m,j} = g_2(y_j)$
14. next $j$.
Schmidt's Formula begins
15. For $j = 1$ to $n$
16. For $i = 0$ to $m - 2$
17. $u_{i+1,j} = (1 - 2r)u_{i,j} + r(u_{i-1,j} + u_{i+1,j})$
18. next $i$
19. next $j$.

**Parallel Implementation of Schmidt Method.** In the above sequential algorithm, the for next loop from 6 to 9 can be parallelized as follows:
6. For $i = 1$ to $m$ do in parallel
7. $x_i = x_0 + ih$
8. $U_{i,0} = f(x_1)$
9. End parallel.
Similarly, the steps from 10 to 14 can also be parallelized as follows:
10. For $j = 1$ to $n$ do in parallel
11. $y_j = y_0 + jk$
12. $U_{0,j} = g_1(y_j)$
13. $U_{m,j} = g_2(y_j)$
14. End parallel.
END
Implementation of Schmidt's formula begins only as step 15. Step 17 can be evaluated in parallel for all values of $i$ in parallel. That is, Steps 16 to 18 can be written as follows:
16. For $i = 0$ to $m - 2$ in Parallel
17. $U_{i,j+1} = (1 - 2r)U_{i,j} + r(U_{i-1,j} + U_{i+1,j})$
18. End parallel

In Schmidt's method, the $U$ value at levels at level $j + 1$ is evaluated only using the $u$ values of level $j$. That is, the $U$ values are evaluated one after the other sequentially. So, the for loop of step 15 cannot be converted into a parallel loop.

From the above discussion, steps 6 to 9 and also steps 10 to 14 can be implemented in $O(1)$ time, using $O(m)$ and $O(n)$ processors respectively. Steps 15–20 can be implemented to work in $O(n)$ time using $O(m)$ processors.

### 12.3.2  Laasonen Method (to Solve a Parabolic Equation)

Laasonen Method uses the following formula for $U_y$:

$$u_{yi,j} = \frac{u_{i,j} - u_{i,j-1}}{k}.$$

Using this formula in the given parabolic equation (heat flow equation) we get

$$r\{u_{i-1,j} + u_{i+1,j}\} - (1 + 2r) = U_{ij} = -U_{i,j-1}$$
$$\text{where } r = \frac{ck}{h^2}.$$

This formula is called *Laasonen method*. If the $U_{i,j-1}$ values are known for all $i$, the above formula can be used to formulate a set of linear algebraic equations on $u_{1,j}, u_{2,j} \ldots$ By solving these equations, we get the values of $u_{1,j}, u_{2,j}, \ldots$

### Example
Solve the parabolic equation

$$20u_y = u_{xx} u(x, 0) = 1 + x^2, \qquad 0 \le x \le 0.6$$
$$u(0, y) = 1 \text{ for } y \ge 0 \qquad \text{and} \qquad u(0.6, y) = 1.36 \text{ for } y \ge 0.$$
$$h = 0.2 \qquad \text{and} \qquad k = 0.2.$$

The given equation is

$$u_y = \frac{1}{20} u_{xx},$$

where

$$c = \frac{1}{20}, \qquad k = 0.2, \qquad h = 0.2$$
$$r = \frac{ck}{h^2} = \frac{0.2}{20(0.04)} = \frac{1}{4}.$$

So, the Laasonen formula becomes

$$\tfrac{1}{4}(u_{i-1,j} + u_{i+1,j}) - \tfrac{3}{2} u_{ij} = -u_{i,j-1}.$$

That is,

$$u_{i-1,j} - 6u_{ij} + u_{i+1,j} = -4u_{i,j-1}.$$

Consider the mesh of points shown in Fig. 12.8. The values along $x = 0$ and $x = 1$ are all zeroes [given]. The values along the $x$-axis can be calculated by the function by the function $u(x, 0) = 1 + x^2$.

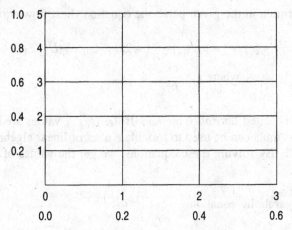

**Figure 12.8** A mesh of points.

$$u_{1,0} = u(0.2, 0) = 1.04$$
$$u_{2,0} = u(0.4, 0) = 1.16$$
$$u_{3,0} = u(0.6, 0) = 1.36.$$

Also given that $u_{0,j} = 1$ for $j = 0, 1, 2, \ldots$

$$u_{3,j} = 1.36 \text{ for } j = 0, 1, 2, \ldots$$

We have the solution value $u$ at the left side, right side and the lower boundary of the mesh. Put $i = 1, j = 1$ in the formula. We get (see Fig. 12.9.)

$$u_{0,1} - 6u_{1,1} + u_{2,1} = -4u_{1,0}.$$

Put $i = 2, j = 1$ in the formula. We get

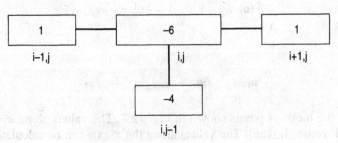

**Figure 12.9** Lassonen's formula.

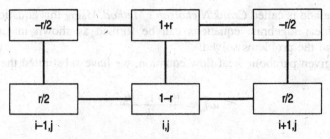

**Figure 12.10** Crank-Nicolson's Method.

$$u_{1,1} - 6u_{2,1} + u_{3,1} = -4u_{2,0}.$$

Using the value $u_{0,1} = 1$, $u_{3,1} = 1.36$, $u_{1,0} = 1.04$, $u_{2,0} = 1.16$, these two equations become:

$$-6u_{1,1} + u_{2,1} = 5.16$$
$$u_{1,1} - 6u_{2,1} = -6.$$

Solving these two equations, we get $u_{1,1} = -1.056$ and $u_{2,1} = 1.176$.

Similarly, by substituting $(i,j) = (1, 2)$ and then $(i,j) = (2, 2)$ we get two algebraic linear equations in $u_{1,2}$. By solving them we can find $u_{1,2}$ and $u_{2,2}$. We can repeat the same for finding any $u_{1,j}$ and $u_{2,j}$ for $j > 2$.

### 12.3.3 Crank Nickolson Method

In the derivation of Schmidt's method we have $r(u_{i+1,j} - 2U_{i,j} + u_{i-1,j}) = u_{i,j+1} - u_{i,j}$.

In the derivation of Laasonen's method, if we substitute with the point $(i,j+1)$ instead of $(i,j)$ we get

$$r(u_{i+1,j+1} - 2u_{i,j+1} + u_{i-1,j+1}) = u_{i,j+1} - u_{ij}.$$

Now equating the right-hand side with the average of the left-hand sides of the two equations, we get

$$\frac{r}{2}(u_{i+1,j} - 2u_{ij} + u_{i-1,j}) + \frac{r}{2}(u_{i+1,j} - 2u_{i,j} + u_{i-1,j+1}) = (u_{i,j+1} - u_{ij})$$

and

$$\frac{r}{2}(u_{i-1,j} + u_{i+1,j}) + (1-r)u_{i,j} = \frac{r}{2}(u_{i-1,j+1} + u_{i+1,j+1}) + (1+r)u_{i,j+1}.$$

This method is called *Crank Nickolson's Method*. Using this equation, simultaneous linear algebraic equations can be formed as shown in Laasonen's method and the problems solved.

In the given parabolic heat flow equation, we have substituted the formula

$$u_{yi,j} = \frac{u_{i,j+1} - u_{i,j}}{k}$$

and derived the Schmidt's method. By using the formula

$$u_{yi,j} = \frac{u_{ij} - u_{ij-1}}{k}$$

the Laasonen formula has been developed. Using the average technique, the Crank-Nicholson's method has been developed. We evaluate the value of $u_{i,j+1}$ from the values of $u_{i,j}$, $u_{i-1,j}$, $u_{i+1,j}$ etc. We say that $u_{ij}$ ($i = 0, 1, 2$) are in the $j$th level using these values at the $j$th level, the values for the $(j - 1)$ level are found so all these tree methods are said to be *two-level*, the values for methods of these *three*, the Schmidt's method explicitly tells the formula for $u_{i,j+1}$. The other two methods give implicit relationships among the $u$ values at the $(j+1)$th level. We use these relationships to form the linear algebraic equations and solve them to find the $u$ values at the $(j + 1)$th level. So, Schmidt's method is called an *explicit method* and Laasonen and the Crank-Nicholson's methods are said to be *implicit methods*.

### 12.3.4 Three-Level Difference Methods

Consider the three-point differentiation formula

$$u_{y,i,j} = \frac{u_{i,j+1} - u_{i,j-1}}{2k}.$$

Using this formula for the parabolic equation $cu_y = u_{xx}$, we get

$$\frac{2ck}{h^2} \{u_{i-1,j} - 2u_{ij} + u_{i+1,j}\} = u_{i,j+1} - u_{i,j-1}$$

This formula is called *Richardson's formula*. Notice that, in this formula, for calculating the value at a point at the $(j+1)$th level, we use the values at the $j$th the level, as well as the values at the $(j + 1)$th level. So, Richardson's formula is a three-level difference method.

Consider the Richardson's formula

$$u_{i,j+1} = u_{i,j-1} + 2r\{u_{i-1,j} - 2u_{ij} + u_{i+1,j}\}.$$

Let us substitute an approximation for the value $u_{ij}$ in the right-hand side as

$$u_{ij} = \frac{u_{i,j-1} + u_{i,j+1}}{2}.$$

We get

$$u_{i,j+1} = u_{i,j-1} + 2r\{u_{i-1,j} - u_{i,j-1} - u_{i,j+1} + u_{i+1,j}\};$$

$$(1+2)u_{i,j+1} = (1-2)u_{i,j} + 2r\{u_{i-1,j} + u_{i+1,j}\};$$

$$u_{i,j+1} = \frac{1-2r}{1+2r}\,u_{i,j-1} + \frac{2r}{1+2r}\,\{u_{i-1,j} + u_{i+1,j}\}.$$

This formula is called the *Dufort and Frankel's* method. Notice that both the Richardson's method and Dufort and Frankel's methods are explicit methods. Let us now develop an algorithm to solve the heat flow equation.

$$cU_y = u_{xx}$$

Using Dufort and Frankel's method. Assume that the initial conditions are given by

$$u(x, b_1) = f(x)$$
$$u(a_1, y) = g_1(y)$$
$$u(a_2, y) = g_2(y)$$

Since this is a three-level difference method, we need $u_{i,0}$ and $u_{i,1}$ (for all $i$) before we start Dufort Frankel method to evaluate $u_{i,2}$ ($i = 1, 2, \ldots$). We can use Schmidt's method to evaluate $u_{i,1}$. The algorithm is given below.

**Algorithm Dufort-Frankel**
  1. define $f(x)$
  2. define $g_1(x)$
  3. define $g_2(x)$
  4. read $a_1, a_2, b_1, b_2, m, n, c$.
  5. $h = (a_2 - a_1)/m$, $k = (b_2 - b_1)/n$
  6. $r = ck/h^2$
  7. $x_0 = a_1$; $y_0 = b_1$; $u_{m,o} = g_2(y_0)$; $u_{0,0} = f(x_0)$
/* To compute initial values of $u_{i-0}$ */
  8. For $i = 1$ to $m$
  9. $x_i = x_0 + ih$
  10. $u_{i,o} = f(x_i)$
  11. next $i$

*To compute $u_{0,j}$ and $um, j$ from given conditions /*.
    12. For $j = 1$ to $n$
    13. $y_i = y_0 + jk$
    14. $u_{0,j} = g_1(y_j)$
    15. $um, j = g_2(y_i)$
    16. next $i$
To compute $u_{i,1}$ using Schmidt method
    17. For $i = 1$ to $m - 1$
    18. $u_{i,1} = (1 - 2r)u_{i,0} + r(u_{i-1,0} + u_{i+1,0})$
    19. next $i$.
Now begins the Duefort Frankel's method
    20. For $j = 1$ to $n - 1$
    21. for $i = 1$ to $m - 1$
    22. $u_{i,j+1} = ((1 - 2r))u_{i,j-1} + (2r/(1 + 2r))\{u_{i-1,j} + u_{i+1,j}\}$
    23. Next $i$
    24. Next $j$
END

**Parallel Implementation for Dufort Frankel's Method.** In the sequential algorithm, steps 8 to 11 can be done is parallel for the values of $i = 1$ to $m$. Similarly, steps 12 to 16 can be done in parallel for $j = 1$ to $n$. That is, the steps 8 to 16 may be written as follows:

    8. For $j = 1$ to $n$ do in parallel
    9. $x_i = x_0 + ih$
    10. $u_{i,0} = f(x_i)$
    11. End parallel
    12. For $j = 1$ to $n$ do in parallel
    13. $y_i = y_0 + jk$
    14. $U_{0,j} = g_1(y_j)$
    15. $U_{m,j} = g_2(y_1)$
    16. End parallel.

Schmidt's method has been to evaluate $U_{i,j}$ in steps 17 to 19. This can be done in parallel for all $i = 1$ to $m - 1$, that is, the steps 17 to 19 rewritten as

    17. For $i = 1$ to $m - 1$ 1 do in parallel
    18. $U_{i,j+1} = (1 - 2r)U_{i,0} + r\{U_{i-1,0} + U_{i+1,0}\}$
    19. End parallel.

Dufort Frankel's method has been implemented to evaluate $U_{i,j+1}$, using the values of $U$ at level $j$ and level $j - 1$. This evaluation at step 22 can be done for $i = 1$ to $m - 1$ in parallel. However the FOR-statement in step 20 cannot be converted into a FOR Parallel statement. Steps 20 to 25 therefore be rewritten as follows:

20. For $j = 1$ to $n - 1$
21. For $i = 1$ 1 to $m - 1$ do in parallel
22. $U_{i,j+1} = ((1 - 2r)/(1 + 2r))U_{i,j-1} + (2r/(1 + 2r))\{u_{i-1,j} + U_{i+1,j}\}$
23. End parallel
24. Next $j$
25. Stop
END

In the parallel implementation steps 8 to 11, steps 12 to 16 and steps 17 to 19 can be done in $O(1)m$ time, using $O(m)$, $O(n)$ and $O(m)$ processors, respectively. Steps 20 to 26 can be done in $O(n)$ time using $o(m)$ processors. In step 22, $U_{i+i,j}$ is used to evaluate $U_{i,j+1}$. Also notice that $U_{i+2,j}$. Since step 22 is done in parallel for $i = 1$ to $m - 1$, this implementation needs a concurrent read parallel random access memory. So, this algorithm is implemented using CREW PRAM.

## BIBLIOGRAPHY

Action, F. S. (1970) *Numerical Methods That Work*, Harper and Row, New York.

Andrew, L. (1985) Elementary Partial Differential Equations with Boundary Value Problems, Saunders College Publishing, Philadelphia.

Chandy, K. M., and Taylor, S. (1992) *An Introduction to Parallel Programming*, Jones and Bartlette, Boston.

Cooley, J. W., and Turkey, J. W. (1965) An Algorithm for the Machine Calculations of Complex Fourier Series, *Mathematics of Computations*, **19**:297–301.

Davis, P. J. and Rabinowitz, P. (1967) *Numerical Integration*, Blaisdell, Waltham, MA.

Dongara, J., Duff, I. Sorensen, D. and Vander Vorst, H. (1991) *Solving Linear Systems on Vector and Shared Memory Computers*, SIAM, Philadelphia.

Forsythe, G. E. and Moler, C. B. (1967) *Computer Solutions of Linear Algebraic Systems*, Prentice-Hall, Englewood Cliffs, NJ.

Kahaner, D., Moler, C. and Nash, S. (1989) *Numerical Methods and Software*, Prentice-Hall, Englewood Cliffs, NJ.

Knuth, D. (1973) *Sorting and Searching*, Addison-Wesley, Reading, MA.

O'Neill, M. A. (1988) Faster than Fast Fourier, *Byte*, **13(4)**:292–230.

Pinsky, M. A. (1991) *Partial Differential Equations and Boundary Value Problems with Applications*, McGraw-Hill, New York.

Wilkinson, J. H. (1963) *Rounding Errors in Algebraic Process*, Prentice-Hall, Englewood Cliffs, NJ.

Wilkinson, J. H. (1965) The Algebraic EigenValue Problem, Oxford University Press, London.

## CHAPTER 1

## 1.6 RING NETWORK

If the two ends of the linear array network are connected together, we get a ring network as shown in Fig. A-1.

For a ring with $n$ nodes, the diameter is $n/2$. This is a regular graph with degree 2.

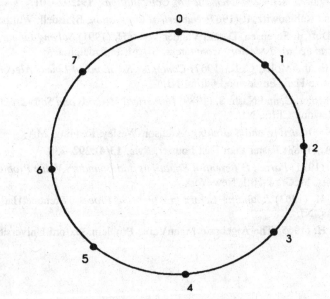

**Figure A-1** Ring network.

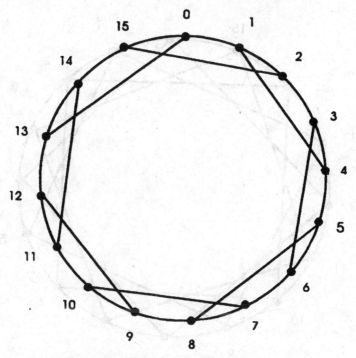

**Figure A-2** A chordal ring network of degree 3.

## 1.7 CHORD RING NETWORKS

Chordal ring networks are obtained from the ring by including additional connections and making the graph a regular graph of degree 3, 4, etc. For example, a chordal ring network of degree 3 is shown in Fig. A-2.

In this example, there are two nodes labeled as 0, 1, 2, 3, ... $(2^4 - 1)$. Every odd node $i$ is connected to an even node $j$, where

$$j = i + 3(\text{mod } 2^4).$$

For example,

1 is connected to 4
3 is connected to 6
5 is connected to 8
7 is connected to 10
9 is connected to 12
11 is connected to 0
14 is connected to 2.

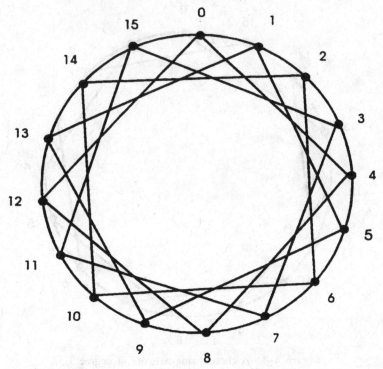

**Figure A-3** A chordal ring network of degree 4.

A chordal ring of degree 4 is shown in Fig. A-3. This is obtained from the ring by adding the following additional degree. For every node $i$ is connected to $i + 4 \pmod 4$.

## 1.8 BARREL SHIFTER NETWORK

A barrel shifter network is obtained from a ring network by including the following additional links:

Every node $i$ is connected to all the nodes $j$ whose distance from $i$ is a power of 2.

That is, $i$ is connected to all nodes that are at distance 2, 4, 8, 16 ... etc. For example, consider a ring network with 16 nodes labeled as 0, 1, 2, 3, ... 15. In this ring 0 is already connected to 1 and 15. The nodes 2 and 14 are at distance 2 from 0. So 0 must be connected to 2 and 14. The nodes 4 and 12 are at distance 4 from 0. So, 4 and 12 are linked with 0. 0 and 8 are connected with a link since tree distance between there is 8. So, in a barrel shifter network the nodes 1, 2, 4, 8, 12, 14 and 15 are connected to 0. Similarly, 1 is linked with 2, 3, 5, 9, 13, 15 and 0. This is shown in Fig. A-4.

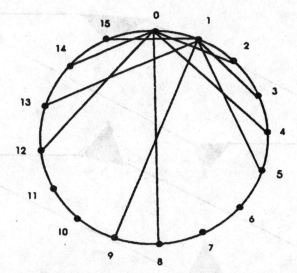

**Figure A-4** Barrel shifter network with 15 nodes. (Only the connection of 0 and 1 are shown).

## 1.11 CUBE-CONNECTED CYCLES

A $k$-cube connected cycle (k-CCC) is obtained from a $k$-cube by replacing every node of the $k$-cube with a $k$-cycle. For example, consider the 3-cube shown in Fig. A-5. A 3-CCC is obtained by replacing each node of the 3-cube by a 3-cycle. This is shown in Fig. A-6.

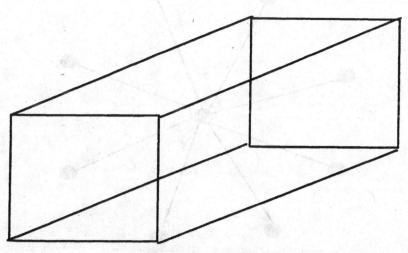

**Figure A-5** A 3-cube.

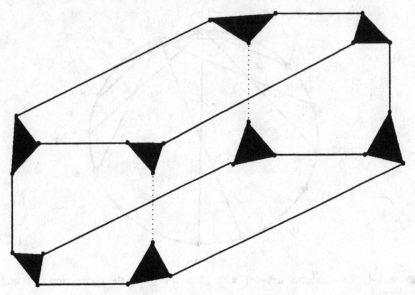

**Figure A-6** A 3-cube connected cycle.

## 1.12 STAR NETWORK

A star network with a nodes has one node as the central node and it is connected directly to all other nodes. It is shown in Fig. A-7. In a star network is 2, irrespective of the number of nodes.

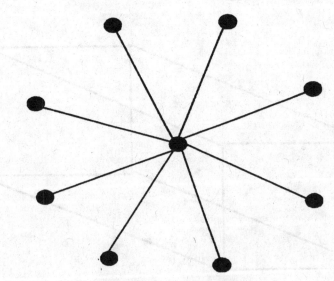

**Figure A-7** A star network.

## CHAPTER 3

**3.4(b)**   We assign one entry to each group of $n$ processors each. The group $i$ takes $A(i)$ and checks if $A(i)$ is true. If $A(i)$ is true then the group makes $A(j)$ = false for all $j > i$. Now the smallest index $A(i)$ such that $A(i)$ is true alone remains true.

**Algorithm Smallest Index_CRCW**
   **Input:**   $A(1:n)$, a boolean array
   **Output:**   Smallest index $k$ such that $A(k)$ is true.
   1. Copy $A(1:n)$ to $B(1:n)$
   2. For $i = 1$ to $n$ do in parallel
   3. if $B(i)$ = true then
      For $j = i + 1$ to $n$ in parallel
      $B(j)$ = false
      End parallel
   4. End parallel.
   5. For $i = 1$ to $k$
   6. if $a(i)$ = true
      return($k$)
   7. End Parallel
   8. END

**Complexity Analysis.**  Step 1 takes $O(1)$ time using $O(n)$ processors. Steps 2 to 4 needs $O(n^2)$ processors and works in $O(1)$ time. Steps 5 to 7 works in $O(1)$ time using $O(n)$ processors. The work $B(j)$ = false in step 3 needs a concurrent write operation. So the algorithm needs a CRCW PRAM. Hence $O(1)$ time using $O(n^2)$ processors in a CRCW PRAM model.
   **3.7**   When $n = 16$, the array $A(1:16)$ is divided into log $n$ groups.

Group 1    Group 2    Group 4    Group 5

$A(1:4)$    $A(5:8)$    $A(9:12)$    $A(13:16)$

In each group the minimum is found sequentially with one processor each. Then the parallel method is used. This is shown in the Fig. A-8.

## CHAPTER 4

**4.1**   Let count be an array count$(1:n)$ such that

$$\text{Count}(i) = 1 \text{ if } A(i) > X$$
$$= 0 \text{ otherwise}$$

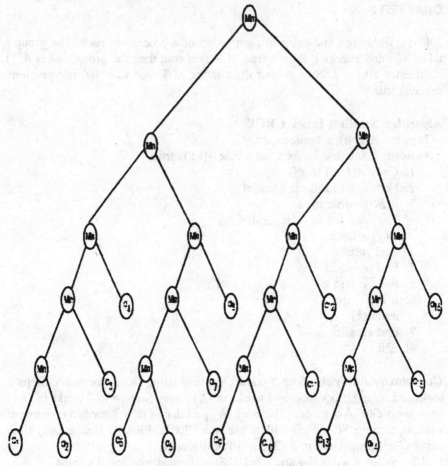

**Figure A-8** Minimum of an array.

Now find the sum of the entries of the count array this gives the number of elements in $A(1:n)$ which are greater than $X$. The algorithm is shown below:

**Algorithm Greater Count**
    **Input:** $A(1:n)$ and $X$.
    **Output:** $K$ = number of entries greater than $X$.
       1. For $i = 1$ to $n$ do in parallel
       2. if $A(i) > X$ then
          count$(i) = 1$
          else
          count$(i) = 0$
          endif

3. End parallel
4. Find the sum of the count $(1 : n)$ array and store the values in $k$.
5. return $k$.
6. END

**Complexity Analysis.** Steps 1–3 need $O(n)$ processors to work in $O(1)$ time. Step 4 is the summation algorithm and, hence, can be implemented in $O(\log n)$ time using $O(n^2)$ processors. So, the overall complexity is $O(\log n)$ using processors.

## 4.3  ALGORITHM SYMMETRIC MATRIX

**Input:** $A(1 : n, 1 : n)$
**Output:** Is $A$ a symmetric matrix?
1. For $i = 1$ to $n$ do in parallel
2. For $j = 1$ to $i$ do in parallel
3. If $A(i,j)$ and $A(j,i)$ are not equal then conclude that $A$ is not symmetric
   Abort the loop
   endif
4. End parallel
5. End parallel
6. Conclude that $A$ is Symmetric if the loop was not aborted in step-3.
7. END

**Complexity Analysis.** The algorithm works in $O(1)$ time, using $o(n^2)$ processors working in CRCW PRAM.